Studies in the History of Medieval Religion
VOLUME XLIII

KING JOHN AND RELIGION

Studies in the History of Medieval Religion

ISSN 0955–2480

Founding Editor
Christopher Harper-Bill

Series Editor
Frances Andrews

Previously published titles in the series
are listed at the back of this volume

KING JOHN AND RELIGION

Paul Webster

THE BOYDELL PRESS

© Paul Webster 2015

All Rights Reserved. Except as permitted under current legislation no part of this work may be photocopied, stored in a retrieval system, published, performed in public, adapted, broadcast, transmitted, recorded or reproduced in any form or by any means, without the prior permission of the copyright owner

The right of Paul Webster to be identified as the author of this work has been asserted in accordance with sections 77 and 78 of the Copyright, Designs and Patents Act 1988

First published 2015
The Boydell Press, Woodbridge
Paperback edition 2020

ISBN 978-1-78327-029-3 hardback
ISBN 978-1-78327-547-2 paperback

The Boydell Press is an imprint of Boydell & Brewer Ltd
PO Box 9, Woodbridge, Suffolk IP12 3DF, UK
and of Boydell & Brewer Inc.
668 Mount Hope Ave, Rochester, NY 14620-2731, USA
website: www.boydellandbrewer.com

A CIP catalogue record for this book is available
from the British Library

The publisher has no responsibility for the continued existence or accuracy of URLs for external or third-party internet websites referred to in this book, and does not guarantee that any content on such websites is, or will remain, accurate or appropriate

For My Parents

Contents

List of Illustrations		viii
Acknowledgements		ix
Abbreviations		x
Introduction		1
1	The Mass	19
2	The Saints	37
3	Powerhouses of Prayer	61
4	Family	85
5	Charity and Almsgiving	110
6	Religion, Politics, and Reputation: The Interdict and King John's Excommunication	131
7	Peace with the Pope: Diplomacy, Personal Religion, and Civil War	153
8	King John's Deathbed and Beyond	173
Conclusion		193
Bibliography		201
Index		233

Illustrations

Maps

1	Royal Chapels maintained by King John	25
2	Foundations associated with King John	72
3	Nunneries in receipt of alms 1212–13	121
4	Locations associated with posthumous provision for King John	182

Figure

1	The Angevin dynasty in the twelfth century	91

Tables

1	John's non-observance of fasts on Friday feast days, the eve of feast days, or the day following a feast day	116
2	Suggested religious calendar of King John's court	194

Acknowledgements

Any project of this nature creates a long list of thanks and debts of gratitude, which it is my pleasure to acknowledge here. Firstly, my thanks to what was then the Arts and Humanities Research Board, who provided financial assistance for the work on which my initial project was based. I owe a particular debt of gratitude to Carl Watkins, for his patient help and advice in steering my way through the mass of material accumulated in pursuit of the religious interests of King John. My thanks also to Nicholas Vincent for his detailed advice, and for sending copies of his forthcoming collection of the letters and charters of John as lord of Ireland and count of Mortain, and his unpublished paper on the career of Master Simon Langton. In the course of the research, and in developing it as a book, many people have offered encouragement and support, responded generously to my questions, shared their knowledge, commented on ideas, joined in the organisation of conference sessions, and sent copies of published or forthcoming articles and chapters, collections of source material or theses. Here, I thank Alison Alexander, Colette Bowie, Elma Brenner, Stephen Church, Julie Crockford (née Kanter), David Crouch, Kathryn Dutton, Judith Everard, Katherine Harvey, Leonie Hicks, Rosemary Horrox, Jitske Jasperse, Nicholas Karn, Nigel Ramsey, and Paolo Virtuani.

At Cardiff University, the Cardiff School of History, Archaeology and Religion provided financial support which enabled me to give some of my findings a trial run at conferences. The Arts and Social Studies Library in Cardiff obtained obscure sounding inter-library loans at critical moments. In the History Department, I am especially grateful to Helen Nicholson, who has provided a great deal of encouragement and advice that have helped this project to reach the finish line. Further support and advice, opportunities to present findings and discuss the reign of King John, and useful nuggets of information, have been provided by Peter Edbury, Dave Wyatt, James Jenkins, Chris Dennis, Rachel Reese, and Piero Tassinari. I thank you all. I am also grateful to the anonymous reader at Boydell and Brewer for his or her recommendation and helpful observations, and to Caroline Palmer and her team, for patiently and skilfully navigating me through the publishing process.

Away from the library and computer, numerous friends have provided hospitality and encouragement that have been of great benefit in seeing this project to its conclusion, knowing when to ask about progress, and when to seek the consoling comforts of the curry house. In Cardiff and its environs, thanks here to Peter Webber, Ian Harris, and David and Joanna Keir. Elsewhere, I thank Helen Bartlett and Tom Catchesides, Emma Beddoe and Gianluca Raccagni, the Dyer family, Rudi and Beth Eliott Lockhart, Simon Elliston Ball, and Paul Huggins.

I am above all grateful to my parents. Without their unstinting love, support, and interest in the Angevin world in which I am so often immersed, the completion of what follows would not have been possible. This book is for them.

Abbreviations

ANS	*Anglo-Norman Studies*
Barnwell	*Annals of Barnwell Priory*, ed. W. Stubbs, *Memoriale Walteri de Coventria. The Historical Collections of Walter of Coventry*, RS 58, 2 vols (London, 1872–73), vol. II, pp. 196–279
Carpenter, 'Burial'	D. A. Carpenter, 'The Burial of King Henry III, the Regalia and Royal Ideology', *The Reign of Henry III*, D. A. Carpenter (London and Rio Grande, OH, 1996), pp. 427–61
CCR	*Calendar of the Close Rolls Preserved in the Public Record Office*
CChR	*Calendar of the Charter Rolls Preserved in the Public Record Office*
CDF	*Calendar of Documents Preserved in France, Illustrative of the History of Great Britain and Ireland. Vol. I. 918–1206*, ed. J. H. Round, HMSO (London, 1899)
CDI	*Calendar of Documents Relating to Ireland Preserved in Her Majesty's Public Record Office, London*
Cheney, *Innocent*	C. R. Cheney, *Pope Innocent III and England* (Stuttgart, 1976)
Cheney, 'Papal Interdict'	C. R. Cheney, 'King John and the Papal Interdict', *Bulletin of the John Rylands Library*, 31 (1948), 295–317
Clarke	P. D. Clarke, *The Interdict in the Thirteenth Century: A Question of Collective Guilt* (Oxford, 2007)
CLR	*Calendar of the Liberate Rolls Preserved in the Public Record Office*
Coggeshall	*Radulphi de Coggeshall Chronicon Anglicanum*, ed. J. Stevenson, RS 66 (London, 1875)
CPR	*Calendar of the Patent Rolls Preserved in the Public Record Office*
CR	*Close Rolls of the Reign of Henry III Preserved in the Public Record Office*
Draper	P. Draper, 'King John and St Wulfstan', *JMH*, 10 (1984), 41–50

Dunstable	*Annales Prioratus de Dunstaplia (A.D. 1–1297)*, ed. H. R. Luard, *Annales Monastici*, RS 36, 5 vols (London, 1864–69), vol. III, pp. 1–420
EEA	*English Episcopal Acta*
EHR	*English Historical Review*
FR	*Fine Roll*
Gillingham, *Richard*	J. Gillingham, *Richard I* (New Haven, CT, and London, 1999)
GR	Gervase of Canterbury, *The Gesta Regum with its Continuation*, ed. W. Stubbs, *The Historical Works of Gervase of Canterbury*, RS 73, 2 vols (London, 1879–80), vol. II, pp. 1–106
HMSO	Her/His Majesty's Stationery Office
Hockey	F. Hockey, *Beaulieu: King John's Abbey. A History of Beaulieu Abbey Hampshire 1204–1258* (London, 1976)
Howden	*Chronica Magistri Rogeri de Houedene*, ed. W. Stubbs, RS 51, 4 vols (London, 1868–71)
'Itinerary'	T. D. Hardy, 'Itinerary of King John, &c.', *RLP*, unpaginated
JEH	*Journal of Ecclesiastical History*
JMH	*Journal of Medieval History*
Knowles and Hadcock	D. Knowles and R. N. Hadcock, *Medieval Religious Houses: England and Wales*, 2nd edn (London and New York, 1971)
LPI	*The Letters of Pope Innocent III (1198–1216) Concerning England and Wales. A Calendar with an Appendix of Texts*, ed. C. R. Cheney and M. G. Cheney (Oxford, 1967)
Magna Vita	*Magna Vita Sancti Hugonis. The Life of St Hugh of Lincoln*, ed. D. L. Douie and H. Farmer, NMT, 2 vols (London, 1961–62)
Mason, *St Wulfstan*	E. Mason, *St Wulfstan of Worcester c. 1008–1095* (Oxford, 1990)
Mason, 'Wulfstan's Staff'	E. Mason, 'St Wulfstan's Staff: A Legend and its Uses', *Medium Aevum*, 53 (1984), 158–79
Mortain	*The Letters and Charters of John Lord of Ireland and Count of Mortain*, ed. N. Vincent (forthcoming)

MR 1 John	*The Memoranda Roll for the Michaelmas Term of the First Year of the Reign of King John, Together with Fragments of the Originalia Roll of the Seventh Year of King Richard I (1195–6), the Liberate Roll of the Second Year of King John (1200–1), and the Norman Roll of the Fifth Year of King John (1203)*, with an introduction by H. G. Richardson, PRS, 59, ns 21 (London, 1943)
MR 10 John	*The Memoranda Roll of the Tenth Year of the Reign of King John (1207–8), Together with The Curia Regis Rolls of Hilary 7 Richard I (1196) and Easter 9 Richard I (1198) a Roll of Plate held by Hugh de Neville in 9 John (1207–8), and Fragments of the Close Rolls of 16 and 17 John (1215–16)*, ed. R. A. Brown, PRS, 69, ns 31 (London, 1957)
NMT	Nelson's Medieval Texts
ns	new series
ODNB	*Oxford Dictionary of National Biography*
OMT	Oxford Medieval Texts
PR 34 Henry II	*The Great Roll of the Pipe for the Thirty-Fourth Year of the Reign of King Henry the Second, A.D. 1187–1188*, PRS, 38 (London, 1925)
PR 7 Richard I	*The Great Roll of the Pipe for the Seventh Year of the Reign of King Richard the First, Michaelmas 1195 (Pipe Roll 41)*, ed. D. M. Stenton, PRS, 44, ns 6 (London, 1929)
PR 9 Richard I	*The Great Roll of the Pipe for the Ninth Year of the Reign of King Richard the First, Michaelmas 1197 (Pipe Roll 43)*, ed. D. M. Stenton, PRS, 46, ns 8 (London, 1931)
PR 10 Richard I	*The Great Roll of the Pipe for the Tenth Year of the Reign of King Richard the First, Michaelmas 1198 (Pipe Roll 44)*, ed. D. M. Stenton, PRS, 47, ns 9 (London, 1932)
PR 1 John	*The Great Roll of the Pipe for the First Year of the Reign of King John, Michaelmas 1199 (Pipe Roll 45)*, ed. D. M. Stenton, PRS, 48, ns 10 (London, 1933)
PR 2 John	*The Great Roll of the Pipe for the Second Year of the Reign of King John, Michaelmas 1200 (Pipe Roll 46)*, ed. D. M. Stenton, PRS, 50, ns 12 (London, 1934)
PR 3 John	*The Great Roll of the Pipe for the Third Year of the Reign of King John, Michaelmas 1201 (Pipe Roll 47)*, ed. D. M. Stenton, PRS, 50, ns 12 (London, 1934)

PR 4 John	*The Great Roll of the Pipe for the Fourth Year of the Reign of King John, Michaelmas 1202 (Pipe Roll 48)*, ed. D. M. Stenton, PRS, 53, ns 15 (London, 1937)
PR 5 John	*The Great Roll of the Pipe for the Fifth Year of the Reign of King John, Michaelmas 1203 (Pipe Roll 49)*, ed. D. M. Stenton, PRS, 54, ns 16 (London, 1938)
PR 6 John	*The Great Roll of the Pipe for the Sixth Year of the Reign of King John, Michaelmas 1204 (Pipe Roll 50)*, ed. D. M. Stenton, PRS, 56, ns 18 (London, 1940)
PR 7 John	*The Great Roll of the Pipe for the Seventh Year of the Reign of King John, Michaelmas 1205 (Pipe Roll 51)*, ed. S. Smith, PRS, 57, ns 19 (London, 1941)
PR 8 John	*The Great Roll of the Pipe for the Eighth Year of the Reign of King John, Michaelmas 1206 (Pipe Roll 52)*, ed. D. M. Stenton, PRS, 58, ns 20 (London, 1942)
PR 9 John	*The Great Roll of the Pipe for the Ninth Year of the Reign of King John, Michaelmas 1207 (Pipe Roll 53)*, ed. A. M. Kirkus, PRS, 60, ns 22 (London, 1946)
PR 10 John	*The Great Roll of the Pipe for the Tenth Year of the Reign of King John, Michaelmas 1208 (Pipe Roll 54)*, ed. D. M. Stenton, PRS, 61, ns 23 (London, 1947)
PR 11 John	*The Great Roll of the Pipe for the Eleventh Year of the Reign of King John, Michaelmas 1209 (Pipe Roll 55)*, ed. D. M. Stenton, PRS, 62, ns 24 (London, 1949)
PR 12 John	*The Great Roll of the Pipe for the Twelfth Year of the Reign of King John, Michaelmas 1210 (Pipe Roll 56)*, ed. C. F. Slade, PRS, 64, ns 26 (London, 1951)
PR 13 John	*The Great Roll of the Pipe for the Thirteenth Year of the Reign of King John, Michaelmas 1211 (Pipe Roll 57)*, ed. D. M. Stenton, PRS, 66, ns 28 (London, 1953)
PR 14 John	*The Great Roll of the Pipe for the Fourteenth Year of the Reign of King John, Michaelmas 1212 (Pipe Roll 58)*, ed. P. M. Barnes, PRS, 68, ns 30 (London, 1955)
PR 16 John	*The Great Roll of the Pipe for the Sixteenth Year of the Reign of King John, Michaelmas 1214 (Pipe Roll 60)*, ed. P. M. Barnes, PRS, 73, ns 35 (London, 1962)
PR 17 John	*Pipe Roll 17 John. Praestita Roll 14–18 John. Roll of Summonses 1214. Scutage Roll 16 John*, ed. R. A. Brown and J. C. Holt, PRS, 75, ns 37 (London, 1961)
PRS	Pipe Roll Society

RAC1	Reading Abbey Cartularies. British Library Manuscripts: Egerton 3031, Harley 1708 and Cotton Vespasian E xxv. 1. General Documents and those relating to English Counties other than Berkshire, ed. B. R. Kemp, Camden 4th ser., 31 (London, 1986)
RC	Rotuli Chartarum in Turri Londinensi asservati, Vol. I, Pt. 1, 1199–1216, ed. T. D. Hardy, RComm (London, 1837)
RComm	Record Commission
RL	Rotuli de Liberate ac de Misis et Praestitis regnante Johanne, ed. T. D. Hardy, RComm (London, 1844)
RLC 1204–24	Rotuli Litterarum Clausarum In Turri Londinensi asservati, Vol. I, 1204–1224, ed. T. D. Hardy, RComm (London, 1833)
RLC 1224–27	Rotuli Litterarum Clausarum in Turri Londinensi asservati, Vol. II, 1224–1227, ed. T. D. Hardy, RComm (London, 1834)
RLP	Rotuli Litterarum Patentium in Turri Londinensi asservati, Vol. I, Pt. 1, 1199–1216, ed. T. D. Hardy, RComm (London, 1835)
RM	'Rotulus Misae – Anni Regni Johannis Quarti Decimi', ed. H. Cole, Documents Illustrative of English History in the Thirteenth and Fourteenth Centuries, RComm (London, 1844), pp. 231–69
RN	Rotuli Normanniae in Turri Londinensi asservati: Johanne et Henrico Quinto, Angliae Regibus. Vol. I. 1200–1205, necnon de anno 1417, ed. T. D. Hardy, RComm (London, 1835)
ROF	Rotuli de Oblatis et Finibus In Turri Londinensi asservati, tempore regis Johannis, ed. T. D. Hardy, RComm (London, 1835)
RS	Rolls Series
SCH	Studies in Church History
SLI	Selected Letters of Pope Innocent III Concerning England (1198–1216), ed. and trans. C. R. Cheney and W. H. Semple, NMT (London, 1953)
St John Hope and Brakspear	W. H. St John Hope and H. Brakspear, 'The Cistercian Abbey of Beaulieu, in the County of Southampton', Archaeological Journal, 2nd ser. 13, vol. 63 (1906), 129–86

Stanley	*Annals of Stanley*, ed. R. Howlett, *Chronicles of the Reigns of Stephen, Henry II and Richard I*, RS 82, 4 vols (London, 1884-89), vol. II, pp. 501-83
TCE	*Thirteenth Century England*
Turner, Men	R. V. Turner, *Men Raised From the Dust: Administrative Service and Upward Mobility in Angevin England* (Philadelphia, PA, 1988)
VCH	*Victoria County History*
Vincent, 'Mary'	N. Vincent, 'King Henry III and the Blessed Virgin Mary', *The Church and Mary*, ed. R. N. Swanson, SCH, 39 (Woodbridge, 2004), pp. 126-46
Vincent, *Peter des Roches*	N. Vincent, *Peter des Roches: An Alien in English Politics, 1205-1238* (Cambridge, 1996)
Warren, *John*	W. L. Warren, *King John* (London, 1974, first published 1961)
Waverley	*Annales Monasterii de Waverleia (A.D. 1-1291)*, ed. H. R. Luard, *Annales Monastici*, RS 36, 5 vols (London, 1864-69), vol. II, pp. 127-411
Wendover	*Rogeri de Wendover liber qui dicitur Flores Historiarum ab anno domini MCLIV annoque Henrici Anglorum Regis Secundi Primo*, ed. H. G. Hewlett, RS 84, 3 vols (London, 1886-89)
Worcester	*Annales Prioratus de Wigornia (A.D. 1-1377)*, ed. H. R. Luard, *Annales Monastici*, RS 36, 5 vols (London, 1864-69), vol. IV, pp. 353-564
Worcester Cartulary	*The Cartulary of Worcester Cathedral Priory (Register I)*, ed. R. R. Darlington, PRS, 76, ns 38 (London, 1968 for 1962-63)

Note on biblical references
All biblical references are to the Vulgate version, cited here from the parallel Latin text and English translation available at: http://www.latinvulgate.com/

Note on money
All sums of money referred to in the text and footnotes are in pounds, shillings and pence sterling, unless otherwise stated.

Introduction

This is a study of the personal religion of one of England's most notorious kings: John. Its contribution lies within the developing study of the religious observance of England's medieval rulers. For various monarchs, in particular Henry III and Richard II, religion was central to their vision of kingship, whilst others – Henry I, Edward I, and Edward III – were generally successful kings who balanced personal religion as one of several aspects of rulership. An extended study of a king whose personal religion is rarely seen as important, indeed who has sometimes been condemned as irreligious, will illustrate the rich scope of the topic even for kings deemed to have failed as monarchs. This represents a further step towards an overall view of the theme for the post-Conquest kings of England, 'a study that richly deserves to be written, but that as yet has failed to attract an author'.[1]

It will be argued that despite King John's reputation, reflected by the chroniclers of his own day and developed by later writers within and since the medieval period, this was a king who recognised personal religion to be an important aspect of kingship. Throughout his active life on the political stage, John tried to engage with major elements of the religious observance of the elite of his day: attending religious services, maintaining chapels and chaplains, praying at the shrines of the saints, maintaining a collection of holy relics, endowing masses and prayers for himself and his kinsmen, founding and supporting religious houses, and feeding the poor. Were it not for his reputation for failure and misgovernment, he would rank alongside other medieval kings who recognised the importance of outwardly demonstrating their personal religion. This was a means of display. It emphasised the aura surrounding authority. Potentially – but ultimately harder to prove – it also provided for individual needs on a personal level.

In describing John's religious activity, the term 'personal religion' has generally been preferred to discussion of the king's 'piety'. The latter term can be problematic, although it was used by medieval kings, including John, in the phrase *divini pietatis intuitu*, which appears regularly in documents issued to religious institutions. Piety can be defined as 'reverence or obedience to God (or to the Gods); devotion to religious duties and observances; godliness, devoutness'. The origins of the term lie in medieval languages: Anglo-Norman and Middle French.[2] Much of the religious observance in which John was involved might be seen in someone

---

[1] N. Vincent, 'The Pilgrimages of the Angevin Kings of England 1154–1272', *Pilgrimage: The English Experience from Becket to Bunyan*, ed. C. Morris and P. Roberts (Cambridge, 2002), pp. 12–45 (p. 12).

[2] *Oxford English Dictionary Online* [http://www.dictionary.oed.com/, accessed 25 June 2014].

who fulfilled the requirements to be described as pious. However, as Nigel Saul has observed of Richard II's personal religion, 'the sources themselves highlight only the external manifestations of the king's devotions'.[3] Ultimately, we lack texts written by John explaining what he thought when he engaged in religious practices. We can suggest, and often prove, that he engaged in different types of religious activity, but we cannot know what he believed in so doing. Thus, it may be argued that he recognised the importance of spiritual observance as part of kingship, but we cannot be certain that this reflects genuine faith. In the late nineteenth century, John Richard Green observed that 'in his inner soul John was the worst outcome of the Angevins'.[4] It is precisely that inner soul into which it is now impossible to make a window, for the modern historian just as much as it was for Green.

Nevertheless, when historians address the theme of the personal religion of England's medieval kings, they often focus on whether or not these were pious men. The conclusion that a ruler was 'conventionally' religious has often been reached.[5] This description is applied to Henry I by Judith Green, early in her account of his piety, and whilst Edmund King acknowledges Stephen's reputation as 'the pious king', he also describes him as conventional. Lewis Warren describes Henry II's attitude to the clergy as 'in common with [that] of most men of conventional piety'. Similar phraseology appears in accounts of later kings. Sir Maurice Powicke described Edward I as 'a consistent and also a very conventional Christian', whilst Michael Prestwich states that 'there is no suggestion that he [Edward] was anything other than conventionally religious'. The pattern continues for Edward III, described as 'utterly conventional and predictable in his personal devotions'. Even Richard II has been described as 'entirely conventional', although his inner faith is acknowledged to have had greater depths.[6]

Until recent generations, historians have proved reluctant to describe King John as even conventionally devout. Taking their lead from the criticism of chronicles penned during the reign, and his castigation by the St Albans (and later) writers, observers from the eighteenth century onwards have seen lack of religious sensibility as one of the king's many failings. Thus, David Hume (1711-76) observed that the writers of John's day (by which he essentially means Matthew Paris, who wrote some decades after the king's death) 'threw great reproaches on this prince

---

[3] N. Saul, *Richard II* (New Haven, CT, and London, 1997), p. 304.

[4] J. R. Green, *A Short History of the English People* (London, 1874, reprinted 1992), p. 122.

[5] Reflecting a broader trend in study of medieval religion: M. Hicks, 'Four Studies in Conventional Piety', *Southern History*, 13 (1991), 1-21 (p. 2).

[6] J. A. Green, 'The Piety and Patronage of Henry I', *Haskins Society Journal*, 10 (2001), 1-16; E. King, *King Stephen* (New Haven, CT, and London, 2012), pp. 302-3; E. King, 'Stephen (c. 1092-1154)', *ODNB* (Oxford, 2004, online edn 2010) [http://www.oxforddnb.com/view/article/26365, accessed 27 June 2014]; W. L. Warren, *Henry II* (London, 1973), p. 552; M. Powicke, *The Thirteenth Century 1216-1307* (Oxford, 1953), p. 228; M. Prestwich, *Edward I* (New Haven, CT, and London, 1997), p. 112; M. Prestwich, 'The Piety of Edward I', *England in the Thirteenth Century: Proceedings of the 1984 Harlaxton Symposium*, ed. W. M. Ormrod (Grantham, 1985), pp. 120-8 (p. 120); W. M. Ormrod, 'The Personal Religion of Edward III', *Speculum*, 64 (1989), 849-77 (p. 853); Saul, *Richard II*, pp. 325-6.

for his impiety' which 'made him pass for them as an atheist'.[7] In the Victorian era, Bishop Stubbs memorably castigated John, concluding that 'of religion he has none, scarcely sense enough of it to found a monastery; he neither fears God nor cares for the souls of his people'.[8] Having grudgingly acknowledged the foundation of Beaulieu Abbey, Stubbs noted the perception that John was buried wearing a monastic habit. This, however, was as if 'he who had defied God by word and deed all his life, sought shelter from the terrors with which superstition, not conscience, had inspired him ... a posthumous tribute to religion, which he had believed only to outrage'.[9] This view proved enduring. In the 1920s, Powicke described John as 'a fool, in the Scriptural sense, who says in his heart that there is no God'. For Powicke, the king exceeded Henry II and Richard I, 'whose feelings of reverence were not highly developed, in his indifference to the claims of his Church upon his conscience'.[10] Similar views have held currency down to the twentieth century. David Carpenter observes that John 'was not a pious man'.[11]

Revisions to these conclusions have gradually evolved, perhaps influenced by V. H. Galbraith's view that 'a new approach to the problem of John's character' would reveal 'not the monster of tradition, but a very human and not uncommon medieval type'.[12] Nonetheless, such ideas were slow to gain ground. In 1949, Sidney Painter described the king as being 'as close to irreligious as it was possible for a man of his time to be', dismissing much of the evidence as 'superficial' and 'semi-political'. He maintained that 'one can find no evidence of any acts of piety on John's part. At the best his attitude towards the church and its clergy was coldly practical – at the worst it was almost insanely ferocious.'[13] Others, however, offered different conclusions. Austin Lane Poole, using much the same evidence, argued that John 'was not altogether out of sympathy with the church and religious life'.[14]

---

[7] D. Hume, *The History of England from the Invasion of Julius Caesar, to the Revolution of 1688*, 6 vols (Indianapolis, 1983, based on the 8-vol. edn published London, 1778), vol. I, p. 453. On historical analysis of the Angevin kings prior to the mid-nineteenth century: N. Vincent, 'Henry II and the Historians', *Henry II: New Interpretations*, ed. C. Harper-Bill and N. Vincent (Woodbridge, 2007), pp. 1–23 (pp. 2–6); J. Gillingham, *Richard I* (New Haven, CT, and London, 1999), pp. 7–13.

[8] *Memoriale Walteri de Coventria. The Historical Collections of Walter of Coventry*, ed. W. Stubbs, RS 58, 2 vols (London, 1872–73), vol. II, p. xi, and see also p. xv, where Stubbs repeated that John was 'without religion'.

[9] *Memoriale Walteri de Coventria*, vol. II, p. lxxx. The notion that John was buried in a monk's cowl is now thought unlikely: D. A. Carpenter, 'The Burial of King Henry III, the *Regalia* and Royal Ideology', *The Reign of Henry III*, D. A. Carpenter (London and Rio Grande, OH, 1996), pp. 426–61 (pp. 435–6).

[10] F. M. Powicke, 'England: Richard I and John', *The Cambridge Medieval History: Volume VI. Victory of the Papacy*, ed. J. R. Tanner, C. W. Previté-Orton and Z. N. Brooke (Cambridge, 1929), pp. 205–51 (p. 220). For the biblical allusion: Psalm 13:1.

[11] D. Carpenter, *The Struggle for Mastery: Britain 1066–1284* (London, 2003), p. 276.

[12] V. H. Galbraith, 'Good Kings and Bad Kings in Medieval English History', *History*, 30 (1945), 119–32 (p. 129).

[13] S. Painter, *The Reign of King John* (Baltimore, MD, 1949), pp. 152–3, 238.

[14] A. L. Poole, *From Domesday Book to Magna Carta 1087–1216*, 2nd edn (Oxford, 1955), p. 428.

In the 1960s, Warren saw his subject as 'at least conventionally devout', a man 'alive to religious proprieties'.[15]

Ralph Turner advanced similar views in the 1990s, concluding that 'although no model of piety, he [John] was conventionally pious'. Turner's assessment notes how earlier generations of historians, especially the Victorians, followed the monastic chroniclers, before 'applying standards based on traditional morality and Christian piety, but also adding Protestant family virtues as standards' for passing judgment. However, 'like his father [Henry II], his brother [Richard I], and most medieval nobles, John followed the forms of Christian practice without necessarily comprehending the substance of true Christianity. Chroniclers' reports of his blasphemy can be discounted.'[16] Christopher Cheney adds a further relevant point: in comparing Richard I and John: 'religious motives had no place in their dealings with pope and clergy'. Therefore, it 'would be rash to accuse these kings of atheism or of denying the tenets of the catholic faith'.[17]

Part of the problem here lies in the difficulty of reconstructing the personal character of the medieval kings of England. As C. Warren Hollister noted in 1961: 'Nearly every historian who touches on any aspect of John's reign feels compelled to offer his own judgement of John's puzzling character, his effectiveness, even his personal morality.'[18] In terms of the present theme, this again highlights the need to study the relationship between the king's personal religion and his rulership, as opposed to the thornier question of whether his faith went beyond the conventional to encompass genuine and sustained piety.[19] Thus, we may agree with John Gillingham that 'routine penitential acts reveal little about his [King John's] religious views', but we might add that they demonstrate the king's efforts to fulfil the expectations of the day.[20]

In one sense, royal religious responses were conventional, involving the royal family in similar activities to other members of the social elite. The implication could be that royal devotions were not especially important in the history of individual reigns. However, there was an acknowledged aura surrounding the monarch from coronation through to burial. Religious practice was an important way of developing and sustaining that aura. It could also set trends, rather than follow them. As Orderic Vitalis noted in the twelfth century: 'The barons of Normandy were inspired by the piety of their princes ... to undertake similar enterprises for the salvation of their souls.'[21]

Indeed, the aura of kingship was difficult, perhaps impossible, to discard.

---

[15] W. L. Warren, *King John* (London 1974, first published 1961), pp. 171–2.

[16] R. V. Turner, *King John* (London and New York, 1994), pp. 147–9, 258.

[17] C. R. Cheney, *Pope Innocent III and England* (Stuttgart, 1976), pp. 14–15.

[18] C. W. Hollister, 'King John and the Historians', *Journal of British Studies*, 1 (1961), 1–19 (p. 1).

[19] For similar views: Prestwich, 'Piety of Edward I', p. 120; Ormrod, 'Personal Religion', p. 853.

[20] J. Gillingham, 'John (1167–1216)', *ODNB* (Oxford, 2004, online edn 2010) [http://www.oxforddnb.com/view/article/14841, accessed 1 July 2014].

[21] Cited in D. Crouch, *The Image of Aristocracy in Britain, 1000–1300* (London and New York, 1992), p. 247.

Nicholas Vincent highlights this in discussing Henry II's penance at Canterbury in 1174, for his perceived culpability in the murder of Thomas Becket. Henry ordered the cathedral monks not to enact the usual ceremonial appropriate to a royal visit – a procession to escort the monarch to the church. 'To become a pilgrim ... Henry had first to command his subjects to respect his pilgrim status. A king who has to command the observation of his own humility cannot be said to be truly humbled.'[22] Rulers could not attend church unnoticed. Henry is known to have complained about this, noting the weight of sins threatening his chances of salvation. For the future of his soul, he argued, he needed to pay close attention to ceremonies such as the mass, but he was denied the opportunity because numerous petitioners saw his appearance in public as a chance to press for attention.[23] Thus, kings could not escape the expectations inherent in their royal status.

Nor, in terms of expressing the majesty of their power to their subjects, was it usually desirable for rulers to attempt to cast off its trappings. Richard I probably tried in his efforts to return from the Holy Land in 1192, abandoning his great ship in favour of hired galleys and cutting his entourage to a few knights. Richard may have disguised himself as a pilgrim, or as a Templar. His capture shows that he failed.[24] Such behaviour was clearly atypical. Returning to Henry II's pilgrimage to Canterbury in 1174, just as with his penance at Avranches in 1172, this was in part about making a statement to the ruler's subjects: the king needed publicity for his acknowledgement of complicity in the murder of the archbishop of Canterbury.

In linking personal religion and kingship, study of England's medieval rulers should also be set in European context. The use of devotional activity to emphasise the aura surrounding a king has long been associated with the Capetian monarchy in France.[25] The role of Abbot Suger of Saint-Denis, the cult of Christian kingship, and the image and legacy of Saint Louis, are standard material in the textbooks, with the kings concerned remembered as protectors, defenders, and benefactors of the church.[26] Even John's contemporary King Philip II is remembered for generous

---

[22] Vincent, 'Pilgrimages', pp. 15–16.

[23] '*Dialogus inter regem Henricum secundum et abbatem Bonnevallis*. Un écrit de Pierre de Blois réédité', ed. R. B. C. Huygens, *Revue Bénédictine*, 68 (1958), 87–112 (pp. 105, 111). For the jostling of the king when he appeared in public, see also *Walter Map's 'De Nugis Curialium'*, trans. M. R. James, with historical notes by J. E. Lloyd, ed. E. S. Hartland, Cymroddorion Record Series, 9 (London, 1923), p. 265. See also: Vincent, 'Pilgrimages', pp. 21, 23; J. C. Holt, 'The End of the Anglo-Norman Realm', *Magna Carta and Medieval Government*, J. C. Holt (London and Ronceverte, WV, 1985), pp. 23–65 (pp. 31–2).

[24] Gillingham, *Richard*, pp. 222, 230–3. For Richard's disguise: Howden, vol. III, pp. 185–6; *Chronique d'Ernoul et de Bernard le trésorier*, ed. L. de Mas Latrie, Société de l'histoire de France (Paris, 1871), pp. 296–8; H. J. Nicholson, *Love, War, and the Grail: Templars, Hospitallers, and Teutonic Knights in Medieval Epic and Romance 1150–1500* (Boston, MA, and Leiden, 2004), p. 98.

[25] For example: G. M. Spiegel, 'The Cult of St Denis and Capetian Kingship', *JMH*, 1 (1975), 43–69. See also G. Koziol, 'England, France, and the Problem of Sacrality in Twelfth-Century Ritual', *Cultures of Power: Lordship, Status, and Process in Twelfth-Century Europe*, ed. T. Bisson (Philadelphia, PA, 1995), pp. 124–48.

[26] M. Barber, *The Two Cities: Medieval Europe 1050–1320*, 2nd edn (London and New York,

provision for the commemoration of his soul. The attributes which qualified Louis IX for sanctity stand as a defining characteristic of his kingship: 'almost all modern assessments are coloured by it, and cloak Louis with a solemn and reverent aura'.[27]

By contrast, the Angevin dynasty that ascended the throne of England in 1154 is remembered in the claim that Henry II came from, and must surely return to, the devil, words attributed to Bernard of Clairvaux.[28] Henry also went down in history as having effectively sanctioned the murder of Thomas Becket. Meanwhile, historians of the Anglo-Norman and Angevin kings have tended to diminish the significance of religious activity as an aspect of power, favouring an approach that has taught us much about royal government as an administrative and political entity.[29] This is in part the result of the nature of the surviving sources. From the twelfth century, the king's administrators left an ever increasing parchment trail of letters, writs, charters, and enrolled documents recording the business of government, from *circa* 1200 on an almost daily basis. By the end of Henry III's reign the archive is positively overwhelming.[30] England's rulers are therefore seen as masters of administration and bureaucracy, or at least as its overseers. Such 'administrative kingship' could even function without the king being present, for long periods.[31] William the Conqueror, William Rufus, and Henry I spent periods of their reigns based in Normandy, as did Henry II and Richard I, who also had to attend to the Angevin lands in southern and western France. Thanks to his crusade, captivity, and campaigns in Normandy, Richard is especially notable, spending only six months in England during a ten year reign, whilst arguably losing little of his authority and ability to govern.[32]

Devotional expression can nonetheless be traced in the kingship of these monarchs. Various caveats need to be remembered, for instance Vincent's warning to be wary of seeing the Angevins as 'Ottonians with Pipe Rolls', and Carpenter's

---

2004), pp. 247-50, 252, 256, 265-6; E. M. Hallam and J. Everard, *Capetian France 987-1328*, 2nd edn (Harlow, 2001), pp. 239-45.

[27] Hallam and Everard, *Capetian France*, p. 263. On the development of the image of St Louis, with comparison with his sanctified English counterpart Edward the Confessor: M. Kaufmann, 'The Image of St Louis', *Kings and Kingship in Medieval Europe*, ed. A. J. Duggan (London, 1993), pp. 265-86.

[28] *Giraldi Cambrensis de Principis Instructione Liber*, ed. G. F. Warner, *Giraldi Cambrensis Opera*, RS 21, 8 vols (London, 1861-91), vol. VIII, p. 309.

[29] Although some works do consider the documents in terms of royal religion and conveying the image of kingship. For example: S. Marritt, 'Prayers for the King and Royal Titles in Anglo-Norman Charters', *ANS*, 32 (2010), 184-202.

[30] On the development of royal administration: M. T. Clanchy, *From Memory to Written Record: England 1066-1307*, 2nd edn (Oxford and Cambridge, MA, 1993), pp. 57-73, 162-71.

[31] C. W. Hollister and J. W. Baldwin, 'The Rise of Administrative Kingship: Henry I and Philip Augustus', *American Historical Review*, 83 (1978), 867-905. The subject also forms the basis of numerous studies of English kingship and government.

[32] On the impact of different approaches on Richard I's reputation: R. V. Turner and R. R. Heiser, *The Reign of Richard Lionheart: Ruler of the Angevin Empire, 1189-99* (London, 2000), pp. 1-16. For the fullest development of the argument that Richard I was an able and successful ruler: Gillingham, *Richard*.

reflection that although Henry II and his sons sought to enhance their status through ritual and display, increasing bureaucracy meant that 'the charisma of kingship was diminished by its routinization'.³³ Nor are we necessarily looking for religious activity on the scale practised by John's son, Henry III, or by Louis IX of France. Whilst these kings were renowned, respectively, for rebuilding the choir of Westminster Abbey to house the new shrine of St Edward the Confessor, and for the construction of the Sainte-Chapelle (to name but two of their religious projects), their piety was exceptional amongst medieval rulers. Neither should be seen as the norm.

In exploring the relationship between religious practice and kingship, various ways of expressing faith were adopted by successive monarchs, including John. Here, it is useful first to identify the characteristic religious responses of the laity of the period, although there is not always evidence to prove or disprove John's observance. Some can reasonably be expected in view of contemporary standards, for example baptism. In other cases, such as confirmation, it is clear that practice varied, so there may have been no expectation that they would take place. Meanwhile, for the Lord's Prayer and in particular the Creed, distinctions were drawn between implicit and explicit knowledge. Louis IX acknowledged the importance of implicit belief, in his reported exhortations to his courtiers. Clearer standards evolved only gradually. Lack of knowledge, even in literate laymen, could be tolerated, since it was not their profession to acquire it, and could be balanced by belief and through good works.³⁴

In many areas, however, the evidence to be discussed suggests that John observed expected religious requirements. He was thought on at least one occasion to have confessed his sins. He attended services where mass would have been celebrated and the Eucharist administered, and where, if it were received by laymen present, prior confession would have been expected. He marked Maundy Thursday, which David Crouch argues was recognised by the twelfth century as an annual opportunity to confess and receive penance.³⁵ In terms of penitential activity, John's foundation of Beaulieu Abbey can in part be interpreted as penance, as can his compensatory almsgiving. On at least one occasion he was absolved – albeit from the severest of ecclesiastical sanctions, excommunication. It seems reasonable to assume that his marriages were celebrated in the presence of the church, although equally John proved a serial adulterer to an extent no longer tolerable even in a king. He is also described as confessing and receiving the last rites on his deathbed.

Beyond this, further religious obligations have been identified which we might expect to see in lay practice.³⁶ Payment of tithes is evident from the Pipe Rolls

---

33 Vincent, 'Pilgrimages', p. 40; Carpenter, *Struggle*, pp. 294-5.
34 N. Tanner and S. Watson, 'Least of the Laity: The Minimum Requirements for a Medieval Christian', *JMH*, 32 (2006), 395-423. For Louis IX's exhortations: Jean de Joinville, 'The Life of Saint Louis', *Joinville and Villehardouin. Chronicles of the Crusades*, trans. M. R. B. Shaw (Harmondsworth, 1963), pp. 172-3.
35 D. Crouch, 'The Troubled Deathbeds of Henry I's Servants: Death, Confession, and Secular Conduct in the Twelfth Century', *Albion*, 34 (2002), 24-36 (pp. 25, 29-30).
36 Tanner and Watson, 'Least of the Laity', pp. 414-17.

(which record sums in *decimis constitutis*), and were consistently honoured by the crown, although this was an institutionalised feature of Angevin administration by John's reign, rather than presenting a picture of personal assiduity. Meanwhile, it seems unlikely that the king abstained from work – the business of kingship – on Sundays and feast days, but the evidence does suggest either awareness or observance of significant holy days. Finally, John's attitude to fasting and abstinence, as will be seen, is subject to some debate.

We can also look for ways in which high-status laymen sought to atone for sin and to better their chances of salvation at the Last Judgement.[37] This led some to crusade, although there is little evidence that John's crusading vow of 1215 was anything other than politically motivated. Others founded and supported religious houses. All this should be seen in the context of an emerging sense of Purgatory, and of ways of building up intercessory activity to ease the posthumous suffering of the soul. This might involve commissioning prayer, pilgrimage, offerings to the saints, and charity to hermits, the poor, and the sick. 'During the twelfth and early thirteenth centuries donations became more specific and there seems to be a greater awareness that particular liturgical acts have the capacity to extinguish measurable consequences of sin.'[38] Such penitential activity might take place all at once, on one's deathbed, or could be practised more consistently across a lifetime.[39] The extent to which this was the case for John will be investigated in the chapters that follow.

In exploring the personal religion of this particular king, characteristics identified in studies of other rulers of England should be noted, here focusing briefly on the period between the Norman Conquest (1066) and the Lancastrian revolution (1399). Foundation and benefaction of monasteries was an important aspect of Anglo-Norman religious activity. As Marjorie Chibnall notes, 'at all times the royal family helped to point the way'.[40] Leonie Hicks highlights how public (or political)

---

[37] Here, in relation to the Anglo-Norman world: C. Harper-Bill, 'The Piety of the Anglo-Norman Knightly Class', ANS, 2 (1979), 63–77, 173–6; H. M. Thomas, 'Lay Piety in England from 1066 to 1215', ANS, 29 (2007), 179–92; Crouch, *Image of Aristocracy*, pp. 237–54. For a reminder that worldly concerns were also involved: E. Mason, 'Timeo Barones et Donas Ferentes', *Religious Motivation: Biographical and Sociological Problems for the Church Historian*, ed. D. Baker, SCH, 15 (Oxford, 1978), pp. 61–75.

[38] C. S. Watkins, 'Sin, Penance and Purgatory in the Anglo-Norman Realm: The Evidence of Visions and Ghost Stories', *Past and Present*, 175 (2002), 3–33 (p. 21). For an earlier period (the eighth to eleventh centuries): M. McLaughlin, *Consorting with Saints: Prayer for the Dead in Early Medieval France* (Ithaca, NY, and London, 1994).

[39] Harper-Bill, 'Piety', pp. 69–71; Crouch, *Image of Aristocracy*, p. 240; D. Crouch, 'The Culture of Death in the Anglo-Norman World', *Anglo-Norman Political Culture and the Twelfth Century Renaissance*, ed. C. W. Hollister (Woodbridge, 1997), pp. 157–80 (pp. 172–8).

[40] M. Chibnall, 'Monastic Foundations in England and Normandy, 1066–1189', *England and Normandy in the Middle Ages*, ed. D. Bates and A. Curry (London and Rio Grande, OH, 1994), pp. 37–49 (p. 45). See also: C. N. L. Brooke, 'Princes and Kings as Patrons of Monasteries: Normandy and England', *Il monachismo e la riforma ecclesiastica (1049–1122)*, Miscellanea del centro di studi medioevali, 6 (Milan, 1971), 125–42; E. Mason, 'Pro statu et incolumnitate regni mei: Royal Monastic Patronage 1066–1154', *Religion and National Identity*, ed. S. Mews, SCH, 18 (Oxford, 1982), pp. 99–117.

and religious motives lay at the heart of the foundation of the abbeys of St-Etienne and of La Trinité in Caen by William the Conqueror and his wife Matilda, in the 1060s. This represented a combined statement of the founders' personal religion, of the reciprocal support of the ducal house and the church, and of the couple's association with the emerging urban centre at Caen.[41] Thus, piety *and* politics stood together in the activity of the Conqueror and his wife. Writing some twenty to thirty years after William I's death (1087), William of Malmesbury described him as 'a practising Christian in as far as a layman could be'.[42]

Henry I's personal religion, meanwhile, has provided the focus for Judith Green. Respect for the organised religious and the cult of saints, and the foundation of Reading Abbey, emerge as prominent features. Green highlights greater consistency in Henry's outlook than hitherto thought. Religion played its part across his reign rather than becoming prominent due to a spiritual crisis linked either to the White Ship disaster (1120) or to bleak prospects for the succession (c. 1130). In the later years of the reign, personal religion and dynastic politics combined through giving for the king's soul which reinforced the alliance brought about by the Empress Matilda's marriage to Geoffrey V of Anjou. Henry also followed family patterns of support for the Cluniacs, and established a reputation of his own as a patron of the Augustinian canons and founder of hospitals.[43] Similar trends are all to be found in the religious activity of King John.

Turning to the Angevin kings, Elizabeth Hallam and Marjorie Chibnall have highlighted Henry II's wide ranging role as a founder and benefactor of monasteries, whilst Emma Mason has shown how the king's pilgrimages served the interests of territorial politics as well as religion.[44] He supported the canonisation of Edward the Confessor, sought intercession through veneration of the hand of St James housed at Reading Abbey, and attempted to harness the cult of St Thomas Becket.[45] Nicholas Vincent has demonstrated the significance of pilgrimage for all

---

41 L. V. Hicks, *Religious Life in Normandy, 1050–1300: Space, Gender and Social Pressure* (Woodbridge, 2007), pp. 18, 26, 150.

42 William of Malmesbury, *Gesta Regum Anglorum*, ed. and trans. R. A. B. Mynors, R. M. Thomson and M. Winterbottom, OMT, 2 vols (Oxford, 1998–99), vol. I, pp. 492–3; B. Weiler, 'Bishops and Kings in England c. 1066–c. 1215', *Religion and Politics in the Middle Ages: Germany and England by Comparison*, ed. L. Körntgen and D. Wassenhoven (Berlin and Boston, MA, 2013), pp. 87–134 (p. 93). It seems possible that the quotation inspired Painter's observations about John, discussed above.

43 Green, 'Piety and Patronage', pp. 1–16.

44 E. M. Hallam, 'Henry II, Richard I and the Order of Grandmont', *JMH*, 1 (1975), 165–86; E. M. Hallam, 'Aspects of the Monastic Patronage of the English and French Royal Houses, c. 1130–1270' (unpublished PhD thesis, University of London, 1976); E. M. Hallam, 'Henry II as a Founder of Monasteries', *JEH*, 28 (1977), 113–32; M. Chibnall, 'The Changing Expectations of a Royal Benefactor: The Religious Patronage of Henry II', *Religious and Laity in Western Europe, 1000–1400: Interaction, Negotiation, and Power*, ed. E. M. Jamroziak and J. E. Burton (Turnhout, 2006), pp. 9–21; E. Mason, '"Rocamadour in Quercy above all other Churches": The Healing of Henry II', *The Church and Healing*, ed. W. J. Shiels, SCH, 19 (Oxford, 1982), pp. 39–54.

45 B. W. Scholz, 'The Canonisation of Edward the Confessor', *Speculum*, 36 (1961), 38–60; K. Leyser, 'Frederick Barbarossa, Henry II, and the Hand of St James', *EHR*, 90 (1975), pp.

four rulers from Henry II to Henry III, whilst Karl Leyser has shown the importance of living holy men – in the person of Bishop Hugh of Lincoln – to Henry II, Richard I, and John.[46] Meanwhile, whilst there is no published synthesis of the religious interests of King Henry III – arguably England's most pious medieval king – various aspects have been studied in depth. Wide ranging devotion to the saints, in particular St Edward the Confessor but also other significant cults, has been highlighted, along with the central significance of the king's programme of rebuilding work at Westminster, and Henry's extensive charity to the poor.[47]

For the later thirteenth century, Michael Prestwich highlights how study of records of the royal household, in this case the almoners' accounts of Edward I's reign, reveal a rich range of religious activity. Increasing numbers of paupers were fed, daily and on major holy days, with increasing prominence accorded to feasts of the Virgin Mary. Other saints were venerated, notably Becket. Edward gave alms when he failed to attend chapel, and for major family events. He made gifts to the organised religious, notably the friars, and founded Vale Royal Abbey (although here his investment ceased in 1290).[48] In various ways these practices were in

481–506; A. J. Duggan, 'Diplomacy, Status, and Conscience: Henry II's Penance for Becket's Murder', *Forschungen zur Reichs-, Papst- und Landesgeschichte: Peter Herde zum 65. Geburtstag von Freunden, Schülern und Kollegen dargebracht*, ed. K. Borchardt and E. Bünz, 2 vols (Stuttgart, 1998), vol. I, pp. 265–90; T. K. Keefe, 'Shrine Time: King Henry II's Visits to Thomas Becket's Tomb', *Haskins Society Journal*, 11 (1998), 115–22.

[46] Vincent, 'Pilgrimages'; K. J. Leyser, 'The Angevin Kings and the Holy Man', *St Hugh of Lincoln: Lectures Delivered at Oxford to Celebrate the Eighth Centenary of St Hugh's Consecration as Bishop of Lincoln*, ed. H. Mayr-Harting (Oxford, 1987), pp. 49–73.

[47] P. Binski, *The Painted Chamber at Westminster*, Society of Antiquaries Occasional Papers, ns, 9 (London, 1986); P. Binski, 'Reflections on *La estoire de Seint Aedward le rei*: Hagiography and Kingship in Thirteenth-Century England', *JMH*, 16 (1990), 333–50; P. Binski, 'Abbot Berkyng's Tapestries and Matthew Paris's Life of St Edward the Confessor', *Archaeologia*, 109 (1991), 85–100; P. Binski, *Westminster Abbey and the Plantagenets: Kingship and the Representation of Power 1200–1400* (New Haven, CT, and London, 1995); D. A. Carpenter, 'King Henry III and the Cosmati Work at Westminster Abbey', *The Reign of Henry III*, D. A. Carpenter (London and Rio Grande, OH, 1996), pp. 409–25; Carpenter, 'Burial'; D. A. Carpenter, 'King Henry III and St Edward the Confessor: The Origins of the Cult', *EHR*, 122 (2007), 865–91; S. Dixon-Smith, 'The Image and Reality of Alms-Giving in the Great Halls of Henry III', *Journal of the British Archaeological Association*, 152 (1999), 79–96; S. A. Dixon-Smith, 'Feeding the Poor to Commemorate the Dead: The *Pro Anima* Almsgiving of Henry III of England 1227–72' (unpublished PhD thesis, University of London, 2003); N. Vincent, *The Holy Blood: King Henry III and the Westminster Blood Relic* (Cambridge, 2001); N. Vincent, 'King Henry III and the Blessed Virgin Mary', *The Church and Mary*, ed. R. N. Swanson, SCH, 39 (Woodbridge, 2004), pp. 126–46; S. Badham, 'Edward the Confessor's Chapel, Westminster Abbey: The Origins of the Royal Mausoleum and its Cosmatesque Pavement', *Antiquaries Journal*, 87 (2007), 197–219. On Westminster prior to Henry III's reign: E. Mason, 'Westminster Abbey and the Monarchy between the Reigns of William I and John (1066–1216)', *JEH*, 41 (1990), 199–216; E. Mason, 'The Site of King Making and Consecration: Westminster Abbey and the Crown in the Eleventh and Twelfth Centuries', *The Church and Sovereignty c. 590–1918: Essays in Honour of Michael Wilks*, ed. D. Wood, SCH, Subsidia 9 (Oxford, 1991), pp. 57–76.

[48] Prestwich, 'The Piety of Edward I', pp. 120–8; A. J. Taylor, 'Edward I and the Shrine of St Thomas of Canterbury', *Journal of the British Archaeological Association*, 132 (1979), 22–8; J.

keeping with John's religious giving earlier in the century, although Edward's predecessor did not fulfil his crusading vow, nor did he touch sufferers from 'the king's evil' (scrofula).[49]

A similar pattern is evident for Edward II who, like John, is seen as a failed ruler. Here, household records highlight attendance at mass on major feasts, observance of holy days such as Maundy Thursday, and charity to the poor. Likewise, Edward venerated St Edward the Confessor, the Virgin Mary, and St Thomas Becket. He provided for the souls of deceased relatives, notably his mother, Eleanor of Castile, and supported the organised religious. The Dominicans were prime beneficiaries, and just as his father and eldest son apparently made monastic foundations when they felt their lives to be endangered, such was also said to explain Edward II's establishment of Kings Langley and his extension of the Carmelite house at Oxford. At the former, the king buried and commemorated his notorious favourite, Piers Gaveston.[50]

In keeping with a king lauded by the chroniclers, Edward III was described as liberally generous in his religious giving. Mark Ormrod's evaluation reveals a king who made religious provision (for instance endowing masses) for his soul, for direct relatives and for the wider *familia regis*. This family piety was emphasised through the decoration of royal chapels. Edward engaged extensively with the cult of the saints, maintained a substantial relic collection and went on pilgrimage. He showed great respect for the cult of the Virgin, but also for St Thomas Becket and the royal saints Edward the Confessor and Edmund, King and Martyr. Affection for St George was expressed in the foundation of the Order of the Garter in 1348. Here, Ormrod sees Edward III as 'more nationalistic in his devotions than any previous king'. Nonetheless, Edward emulated his predecessors. His almsgiving – in particular when he failed to fast – is comparable to that of King John. Like earlier kings he founded a Cistercian abbey, St Mary Graces beside the Tower of London. His pattern of benefaction was 'rooted ... in Plantagenet tradition'. It included previous royal foundations, like Cistercian Beaulieu, founded by John, and Augustinian Newstead, where John claimed to be co-founder along with Henry II.[51]

Ormrod notes the difficulty of reconstructing either the king's character or his personal wishes, and notes a clear distinction, based on the nature of the sources, between Edward's devotions and the politics of his relationship with the church.

H. Denton, 'From the Foundation of Vale Royal to the Statute of Carlisle: Edward I and Ecclesiastical Patronage', *TCE IV*, ed. P. R. Coss and S. D. Lloyd (Woodbridge, 1992), pp. 123-37.

[49] In addition to Prestwich's work, on Edward and the crusades, see: M. M. Reeve, 'The Painted Chamber at Westminster, Edward I and the Crusade', *Viator*, 37 (2006), 189-221. On the 'royal touch': M. Bloch, *The Royal Touch: Sacred Monarchy and Scrofula in England and France* (London, 1973); F. Barlow, 'The King's Evil', *EHR*, 95 (1980), 3-27; J. Huntington, 'Saintly Power as a Model for Royal Authority: The "Royal Touch" and Other Miracles in the Early Vitae of Edward the Confessor', *Aspects of Power and Authority in the Middle Ages*, ed. B. Bolton and C. E. Meek (Turnhout, 2007), pp. 327-43.

[50] S. Phillips, *Edward II* (New Haven, CT, and London, 2010), pp. 63-72.

[51] Ormrod, 'Personal Religion', pp. 849-77.

However, the evidence conveys a sense of the public image Edward III wished to project through displays of liturgical splendour, for instance at the coronation, but also at the baptism of royal children, their weddings, and those of their servants. This is in addition to the religious activity identified above, for instance (but not limited to) when Edward went on pilgrimage.[52] At the close of the fourteenth century, cultivation of such a religious aura is recognised as fundamental for Richard II, 'to an even greater degree than was common in men born to kingship in the middle ages'.[53] Here, historians focus again on the relationship between the crown and Westminster Abbey, on the king and the cult of saints, as demonstrated by artefacts such as the Wilton Diptych.[54]

A final dimension should also be noted: royal death and burial, the last opportunity to portray an image of kingship, but also indicative of personal wishes for provision for the soul. A variety of churches, often those founded by the kings themselves, received royal burials in the eleventh and twelfth centuries, with gradual development of royal *mausolea* or burial churches in the centuries that followed.[55] King John found himself in a difficult position due to repeated military setbacks: unable to be buried at Fontevraud because of territory lost on the continent, unable to be buried at Beaulieu due to civil war and French invasion, instead interred next to the shrine of St Wulfstan in Worcester Cathedral.

Where historians have identified aspects of the personal religion of John's predecessors and successors, some have explored these characteristics in relation to his reign itself. Peter Draper, Ute Engel, and Emma Mason have considered his enthusiasm for Worcester Cathedral and the cult of St Wulfstan.[56] Meanwhile,

---

[52] Ormrod, 'Personal Religion', esp. pp. 851-3, 865-7.

[53] Saul, *Richard II*, p. 325.

[54] Saul, *Richard II*, pp. 303-26; N. Saul, 'Richard II and Westminster Abbey', *The Cloister and the World: Essays on Medieval History in Honour of Barbara Harvey*, ed. J. Blair and B. Golding (Oxford, 1996), pp. 196-218; S. Mitchell, 'Richard II: Kingship and the Cult of Saints', *The Regal Image of Richard II and the Wilton Diptych*, ed. D. Gordon, L. Monnas and C. Elam (London, 1997), pp. 115-24; K. J. Lewis, 'Becoming a Virgin King: Richard II and Edward the Confessor', *Gender and Holiness: Men, Women, and Saints in Late Medieval Europe*, ed. S. J. E. Riches and S. Salih (London, 2002), pp. 86-100.

[55] S. D. Church, 'Aspects of the English Succession, 1066-1199: The Death of the King', ANS, 29 (2007), 17-34; E. M. Hallam, 'Royal Burial and the Cult of Kingship in England and France, 1060-1330', JMH, 8 (1982), 359-80; T. S. R. Boase, 'Fontevraud and the Plantagenets', *Journal of the British Archaeological Association*, 3rd ser., 34 (1971), 1-10; K. Nolan, 'The Queen's Choice: Eleanor of Aquitaine and the Tombs at Fontevraud', *Eleanor of Aquitaine: Lord and Lady*, ed. B. Wheeler and J. C. Parsons (New York and Basingstoke, 2002), pp. 377-405; C. T. Wood, 'Fontevraud, Dynasticism, and Eleanor of Aquitaine', *Eleanor of Aquitaine: Lord and Lady*, ed. B. Wheeler and J. C. Parsons (New York and Basingstoke, 2002), pp. 407-22; D. M. Palliser, 'Royal Mausolea in the Long Fourteenth Century (1272-1422)', *Fourteenth Century England III*, ed. W. M. Ormrod (Woodbridge, 2004), pp. 1-16; J. C. Parsons, '"Never was a Body Buried in England with such Solemnity and Honour": The Burials and Posthumous Commemorations of English Queens to 1500', *Queens and Queenship in Medieval Europe*, ed. A. J. Duggan (Woodbridge, 2002), pp. 317-37. See also the works on Westminster Abbey cited above.

[56] Draper; U. Engel, 'The Conversion of King John and its Consequences for Worcester Cathedral', *Christianizing Peoples and Converting Individuals*, ed. G. Armstrong and I. N. Wood

Brenda Bolton highlights the importance of John fulfilling the expectations of those with whom he conducted business. She notes that he shared a family respect for religion, and that in supporting papal foundations in Rome, the king 'fulfilled Innocent [III]'s injunction to busy himself with works of piety in a way which could only have greatly pleased the Pope'.[57] Christopher Cheney's extensive studies of the relationship between England, King John, and Pope Innocent III highlight a range of royal religious responses, noting that during the period of papal sanctions, 'whether or not he earned his reputation for impiety', John 'continued active in devotional works and promoted Christian piety amongst his subjects'.[58] These conclusions suggest that he fulfilled at least some royal obligations in the field of personal religion, despite the political dispute with the church that led to the severest penalties the medieval popes could impose.

Charity provides another area where historians have considered the king's religious responses. The centrality of almsgiving to medieval elites is highlighted by Hilda Johnstone, who sees John's giving as based 'almost entirely on the principle of a credit and debit account with Heaven'. Nonetheless, she suggests that re-consideration of the evidence would yield valuable results.[59] Charles Young concludes that John acted in accordance with contemporary expectations. Whilst 'charity had become so institutionalised that it was almost independent of the character of the monarch', nevertheless 'even a king with a reputation for impiety accepted the Christian obligations of his place in society'.[60] Meanwhile, Arnold Kellett has investigated the first known royal observance of Maundy Thursday, marked by King John at the royal castle of Knaresborough in 1210.[61]

Others have explored the impact of John's dispute with the church on the evolution of his posthumous reputation. Although Bradbury has observed that the writers of the reign itself 'are less damning that one might have expected' in judging the king's piety, a ruler who defied a general interdict on his kingdom and then personal excommunication could only incur the wrath of writers drawn wholly from the church.[62] This study will further chart this aspect of the evolution of the image of 'Bad' King John in the hands of medieval chroniclers. In

(Turnhout, 2000), pp. 321-30; E. Mason, 'St Wulfstan's Staff: A Legend and its Uses', *Medium Aevum*, 53 (1984), 158-79. Discussed below, Chapter 2.

[57] B. Bolton, 'Philip Augustus and John: Two Sons in Innocent III's Vineyard?', *The Church and Sovereignty c. 590-1918: Essays in Honour of Michael Wilks*, ed. D. Wood, SCH, Subsidia 9 (Oxford, 1991), reprinted in B. Bolton, *Innocent III: Studies on Papal Authority and Pastoral Care* (Aldershot, 1995), pp. 113-34 (pp. 126-8).

[58] C. R. Cheney, 'King John and the Papal Interdict', *Bulletin of the John Rylands Library*, 31 (1948), 295-317 (p. 307).

[59] H. Johnstone, 'Poor-Relief in the Royal Households of Thirteenth-Century England', *Speculum*, 4 (1929), 149-67.

[60] C. R. Young, 'King John and England: An Illustration of the Medieval Practice of Charity', *Church History*, 29 (1960), 264-74 (pp. 270, 272).

[61] A. Kellett, 'King John in Knaresborough: The First Known Royal Maundy', *Yorkshire Archaeological Journal*, 62 (1990), 69-90.

[62] J. Bradbury, 'Philip Augustus and King John: Personality and History', *King John: New Interpretations*, ed. S. D. Church (Woodbridge, 1999), pp. 347-61 (pp. 350-1); Warren, *John*, p. 9;

condemning him in light of his actions against the church, the narrative sources established a framework within which they were unlikely to regard other religious activities as indicative of genuine support for the church. Such views evolved into a coherent condemnation of the reign, and in the hands of Roger of Wendover and Matthew Paris, turned into a caricature of John that highlighted his many failings as king and deemed him an irreligious ruler.[63]

In analysing the narrative sources, it becomes increasingly clear that 'everyone disliked John'. Any sympathy during his early years as king did not endure.[64] Henry II's youngest son was a distinctly unpleasant character, yet this does not preclude him from engaging with religion in a manner appropriate for a king. The chroniclers provide glimpses of efforts to make religious responses, ones which they either failed, or determined not, to understand. As will be seen, in the *Life of St Hugh of Lincoln*, Adam of Eynsham portrayed John as a ruler who lacked faith. However, even in so doing, he revealed him capable of religious responses. In recounting John's meeting with Hugh at Fontevraud in 1199, Adam described the two men approaching the porch of the church, where sculpture depicted the Last Judgement. The bishop pointed out kings prominent amongst the damned. He instructed John to keep their perpetual suffering in mind: '"by frequently recalling their misfortunes you will learn the great risks those incur who for a short space of time are set over others as rulers, and who by not ruling themselves are eternally tortured by demons."' Yet Adam suggests that John had an alternative interpretation, leading Hugh to the other side of the porch, identifying sculpted figures of rulers 'conducted joyously by angels to the king of Heaven. "My lord bishop," he said, "you should have shown us these, whom we intend to imitate and whose company we desire to join".'[65]

Cheney, *Innocent*, pp. 14–15; C. Harper-Bill, 'John and the Church of Rome', *King John: New Interpretations*, ed. S. D. Church (Woodbridge, 1999), pp. 289–315 (p. 298).

63 For what remains an important framework for analysis of the narrative sources of John's reign: J. C. Holt, *King John*, Historical Association Pamphlets, 53 (London, 1963), pp. 16–25. For context and discussion of various writers of the period: A. Gransden, *Historical Writing in England, c. 550 to c. 1307* (Ithaca, NY, and London, 1974); A. Gransden, 'Prologues in the Historiography of Twelfth-Century England', *England in the Twelfth Century: Proceedings of the 1988 Harlaxton Symposium*, ed. D. Williams (Woodbridge, 1990), pp. 55–81; D. A. Carpenter, 'Abbot Ralph of Coggeshall's Account of the Last Years of King Richard and the First Years of King John', *EHR*, 113 (1998), 1210–30; J. Gillingham, 'Historians Without Hindsight: Coggeshall, Diceto and Howden on the Early Years of John's Reign', *King John: New Interpretations*, ed. S. D. Church (Woodbridge, 1999), pp. 1–26; J. T. Appleby, 'Richard of Devizes and the Annals of Winchester', *Bulletin of the Institute of Historical Research*, 36 (1963), 70–7; C. R. Cheney, 'Notes on the Making of the Dunstable Annals A.D. 33–1242', *Essays in Medieval History Presented to Bertie Wilkinson*, ed. T. A. Sandquist and M. M. Powicke (Toronto, 1969), pp. 79–98; R. Kay, 'Walter of Coventry and the Barnwell Chronicle', *Traditio*, 54 (1999), 141–67; V. H. Galbraith, *Roger of Wendover and Matthew Paris*, Glasgow University Publications, 61 (Glasgow, 1944, reprinted 1970).

64 Gillingham, 'Historians Without Hindsight', pp. 2, 25; Gillingham, 'John'.

65 *Magna Vita Sancti Hugonis. The Life of St Hugh of Lincoln*, ed. D. L. Douie and H. Farmer, NMT, 2 vols (London, 1961–62), vol. II, pp. 139–40. Fragments of a Last Judgement frieze can still be found at Fontevraud.

Further evidence for personal religion can be found in sources familiar to the historian of the political, military, and administrative affairs of John's reign, in particular surviving charters and royal letters, notably the centralised enrolments which begin to survive in abundance from 1199.[66] These can be supplemented by surviving records of the recipients of documents – usually religious houses – and by the collected *acta* of significant individuals within the period.[67] In terms of matters religious, these sources provide information ranging from John's dealings with the monastic orders to his charity. The documents reflect recipients' keenness to obtain confirmation of earlier grants, and show how the crown could confer lands, goods, churches, fairs, rights, and letters of protection on religious communities. In the case of the *Oblata* and Fine Rolls, the sources reveal how recipients sometimes paid for the privileges granted.

Letters and charters issued by the king, or in his name, can present various forms of wording potentially indicative of religious sentiments. Of particular interest are those which claim to have been made for the wellbeing of the king's soul, for his salvation, and for that of his relatives, with specific members of his family often mentioned. Other phrases add religious solemnity, including 'for God' (*pro Deo*), 'for the love of God' (*pro amore Dei*), and 'in the sight of God' or 'for the sake of God' (*intuitu Dei*). Similarly, grants were sometimes made 'for the sake of God's love' (*divini amoris intuitu*), 'for the sake of God's mercy' (*divini pietatis intuitu*), and 'for the sake of charity' (*intuitu caritatis*).[68] Many were gifts in perpetual alms. These phrases were sometimes accompanied by statements of devotion to the saints, for instance St Edmund the Martyr, St Thomas Becket, or the Virgin Mary.

How far do such sentiments reflect the king's outlook? For the Anglo-Norman period, Stephen Marritt argues that 'despite the frequency of the *pro anima* clauses, there seems no doubt that they were intended to be effective'.[69] Was this still true

---

[66] On the origins of enrolment: R. Bartlett, *England Under the Norman and Angevin Kings 1075–1225* (Oxford, 2000), pp. 199–200; N. Vincent, 'Why 1199? Bureaucracy and Enrolment under John and his Contemporaries', *English Government in the Thirteenth Century*, ed. A. Jobson (Woodbridge and London, 2004), pp. 17–48; D. Carpenter, '"In Testimonium Factorum Brevium": The Beginnings of the English Chancery Rolls', *Records, Administration and Aristocratic Society in the Anglo-Norman Realm: Papers Commemorating the 800th Anniversary of King John's Loss of Normandy*, ed. N. Vincent (Woodbridge, 2009), pp. 1–28. For a lively critique of Carpenter's argument, see Vincent's introduction to the latter volume, pp. xvi–xviii.

[67] I would particularly like to thank Nicholas Vincent for permission to consult his forthcoming edition of the letters and charters issued by John before he became king: *The Letters and Charters of John Lord of Ireland and Count of Mortain*, ed. N. Vincent (forthcoming). See also the volumes of *English Episcopal Acta*, listed in the bibliography below.

[68] On fluctuations in usage of such terms in lay charters of the period: M. Gervers and N. Hamonic, '*Pro Amore Dei*: Diplomatic Evidence of Social Conflict in the Reign of King John', *Law as Profession and Practice in Medieval Europe: Essays in Honour of James A. Brundage*, ed. K. Pennington and M. H. Eichbauer (Farnham, 2011), pp. 231–59 (pp. 255–8).

[69] Marritt, 'Prayers', p. 187. Similarly, invocation of ancestors is argued to carry meaning in the *acta* of the twelfth-century kings of Jerusalem: D. Gerish, 'Ancestors and Predecessors: Royal Continuity and Identity in the First Kingdom of Jerusalem', *ANS*, 20 (1998), 127–50 (pp. 135–6).

by the reign of King John? Sir James Holt notes that the tone of royal letters could vary according to the subject and audience. Thus, their 'expressive qualities' may derive not from the monarch 'but from his advisers, officers, and clerks'. Holt cites the period of John's overseas campaign in 1214, when the Close Roll records the governmental activity of Peter des Roches, Bishop of Winchester and justiciar: 'Chancery routine already determined the form of letters and the general arrangement of the roll, whatever the form of authority ... [and] the justiciar could adopt tones just as menacing as the king's.'[70] That said, it was desirable for letters issued in the king's name to convey an equivalent authority to the ruler's words if he was actually present. Thus, the religious sentiments used convey an element of the religious dimension to kingship. Their use added to the solemnity and authority of royal letters and charters. This can be seen in a document where we know that John proved almost instantly unwilling to abide by its content, but where it was vital to both parties that the terms set out should be couched in terms of binding authority: Magna Carta. Styled as a charter for the king's 'faithful subjects', the second sentence stated that it had been issued 'from reverence for God and for the salvation of our soul and those of all our ancestors and heirs, for the honour of God and the exaltation of Holy Church, and the reform of our realm'.[71] This does not preclude the possibility that sometimes such wording indicated the personal religious sentiment of the king, but clearly this was not always the case. It nonetheless shows how religious phraseology could be used to convey an image of authoritative royal rule.

The centralised enrolments also allow us to track extraordinary aspects of John's dealings with the church, such as the general seizure of church property that followed the imposition of the general interdict in 1208. After the dispute with Rome was settled in 1213–14, many letters dealt with electing new heads at houses where vacancies had occurred. Meanwhile, the Pipe Rolls present evidence of royal levies on the church and of the administration of seized property. In addition, these sources sometimes reveal ongoing payment of sums granted by the king or, more frequently, continuity in honouring gifts made by his predecessors. Again, this covers themes including royal involvement with the monastic orders, charity, and provision for the royal chapel.

Finally, surviving records of King John's household for the eleventh and fourteenth regnal years allow us to track royal behaviour such as maintenance of the royal chapel, gifts of food and wine to religious houses, and of materials to assist construction of religious buildings.[72] These records reveal the king's almsgiving, often provision of food for the poor, relating to particular feast days or over a defined period. The entries sometimes reveal the reasons for John's charitable distributions. It is unfortunate that more of these rolls do not survive, since they bring us closer to the king's personal religious interests that any other single

---

[70] Holt, *King John*, p. 9.
[71] J. C. Holt, *Magna Carta*, 2nd edn (Cambridge, 1992), pp. 448–9.
[72] 7 May 1209 to 26 May 1210, and 3 May 1212 to 22 May 1213. John's regnal years are unusual in their uneven length. The records began each administrative year on a moveable feast day, Ascension, on which the king had been crowned in 1199.

document, allowing a brief window into the daily life and religious responses of the court.

In exploring John's devotional activity, and its place in the history of his rule, the following chapters will consider his efforts to cultivate the image of a good Christian, beginning with his involvement with religious services and engagement with the cult of the saints. As befitted the wealthy, John founded and supported religious houses: holy men and women praying for the donors' souls in perpetuity. These will be the focus in Chapter 3. Filial piety will then be considered, institutions commissioned to pray not only for John, but for his relatives. The study will then consider the king's efforts to fulfil the obligation of the rich to give to the poor and sick. Two chapters then reassess the king's dispute with the church over Hubert Walter's successor as archbishop of Canterbury, considering John's attitude, and his reaction to the sanctions of general interdict and personal excommunication – the severest sanctions the medieval church could impose – pronounced against him by Pope Innocent III. This will reveal the surprising extent to which royal religious activity continued unabated during these years, but highlight how nonetheless, John's actions were responsible for creating a caricature of his kingship which has proved remarkably enduring, down to the present day. In the final chapter, focus will turn to the king's provision for his body and soul on his deathbed, examining his choice of burial at Worcester Cathedral, and the surprising extent to which provision for his soul continued to be made and honoured in the years, decades and generations that followed.

1

The Mass

John's attendance at religious services provides a starting point in the search for evidence of his personal religion. In particular, to what extent did he engage with the ritual of the mass? This rite was of central importance to medieval men and women, albeit that it attracted 'a broad spectrum of responses ... from the extravagant, intense and devout on one end, to the distracted, apathetic, dismissive or hostile on the other'.[1] The schoolmen of the day tied themselves in complex intellectual knots debating the transformation that took place in the consecrated host. Yet on the more practical level of the ordinary churchgoer it is often hard to determine how often they were in attendance. It was only if something out of the ordinary occurred that those present (or absent) attracted the attention of medieval commentators, themselves often men of religion for whom the mass was an accepted part of daily routine. This chapter considers the king's engagement with two different types of mass. Firstly, those for the living community of the faithful, which John is likely to have attended in person and, in the context of the royal household, for which he sometimes provided in terms of paraphernalia and personnel. Here, it should be noted at the outset that we are not necessarily looking for evidence of his having taken communion. The Fourth Lateran Council (1215) laid down that this should occur only three times a year, at Whitsun, Easter, and Christmas, with Easter as an acceptable minimum requirement. Rather, increasing focus on the wondrous nature of the Eucharist – the presence in the priest's hands of the body and blood of Christ – led to an emphasis on the value of *seeing* the ceremony take place.[2] Thus, it is valuable to seek evidence of occasions when John is known to have been present on an occasion when mass was celebrated, and to consider what steps he took to ensure that it could take place within his household. Secondly, discussion focuses on masses commissioned by John, to be performed on his behalf but in his absence, for his wellbeing whilst alive, and for his soul after his death. Here, he participated in trends associated with ideas of

---

[1] Tanner and Watson, 'Least of the Laity', p. 409.
[2] Bartlett, *England*, pp. 449–51; C. W. Bynum, *Holy Feast and Holy Fast: The Religious Significance of Food to Medieval Women* (Berkeley and Los Angeles, CA, and London, 1987), pp. 48–69; M. Kobialka, *This Is My Body: Representational Practices in the Early Middle Ages* (Ann Arbor, MI, 1999), pp. 148–60, 197–216; T. Thibodeau, 'Western Christendom', *The Oxford History of Christian Worship*, ed. G. Wainwright and K. B. Westerfield Tucker (Oxford, 2006), pp. 216–53 (p. 236).

easing the path of the soul through Purgatory, and which evolved in the twelfth and thirteenth centuries into the phenomenon of the chantry.³

In a memorable account of Easter Sunday, 1199, the *Life of St Hugh of Lincoln* records John's impatience as Bishop Hugh preached a lengthy sermon concerning the fates awaiting good and bad rulers. 'He sent someone to him three times to implore him earnestly to wind up his sermon and celebrate mass.' The author of the *Life*, Adam of Eynsham, wasted no time in adding to the charges against Richard I's successor: John did not receive communion either on Easter Sunday or on Ascension Day, when he was crowned king of England in Westminster Abbey. Even worse, the new king's followers declared that he had never done so since coming of age.⁴ Taken at face value, this is hardly a promising sign of his personal religion. Yet it contrasts with evidence that John attended mass and that he endowed monks and priests to perform masses and pray for his soul both during his lifetime and after his death.

Adam of Eynsham's account presents a mixture of information. John is shown making an offering at an appropriate moment during the service, albeit that this is contrasted with his reluctance to hand over the gold coins provided for the purpose. He is recorded as having observed the required fast.⁵ Alongside his desire to eat, a variety of reasons might explain his keenness for Hugh to cut down his sermon. As heir-apparent on the verge of coronation, he may have been heartily fed up with churchmen lecturing him about good and bad kingship. Like his son and heir, Henry III, he could have preferred to witness the sacrament of the mass rather than to listen to sermons. Henry reportedly told Louis IX of France that he favoured seeing the Saviour to hearing about him.⁶ Importantly, John was present at mass on Easter Sunday, the most important day on the religious calendar.

This raises the question of how seriously we should credit the allegation that in 1199, John had never voluntarily taken communion. Adam of Eynsham's account was written in 1213 or 1214, years when John was absolved from excommunication and the general interdict on England was lifted.⁷ The king's long-running dispute with the church had a knock-on effect on the author's attitude towards him. The suggestion that a king refused to take communion was exactly the sort of accusation a disgruntled writer might lay against him. A similar charge was rumoured to have been made against Richard I, who allegedly refused the sacrament for seven

---

3   E. Duffy, 'Religious Belief', *A Social History of Medieval England*, ed. R. Horrox and W. M. Ormrod (Cambridge, 2006), pp. 293–339 (p. 309); Thibodeau, 'Western Christendom', p. 220; A. Vauchez, 'The Church and the Laity', *The New Cambridge Medieval History: Vol. V. c. 1198–c. 1300*, ed. D. Abulafia (Cambridge, 1999), pp. 182–203 (pp. 194–7). Religious services commissioned by John for deceased members of his kin group will be considered in Chapter 4.

4   *Magna Vita*, vol. II, pp. 143–4.

5   *Magna Vita*, vol. II, pp. 142–3.

6   Hallam and Everard, *Capetian France*, p. 264. This echoes an argument by the Cluniac Abbot Peter the Venerable in the mid-twelfth century: Kobialka, *This Is My Body*, p. 152.

7   *Magna Vita*, vol. I, pp. xi–xii, vol. II, p. 74; Gransden, *Historical Writing*, pp. 312–13, 317.

years, due to his hatred of Philip II of France.[8] Adam was concerned to glorify Hugh as an exemplary churchman worthy of canonisation. It served his purpose to contrast the holy man with the unrepentant sinner.[9] If John was expected to take communion at his coronation, we might reasonably assume other writers, particularly those of the period either side of 1200, would have commented if he had failed to do so. One of the problems of analysing royal religion is that if a king did what was expected, his actions are unlikely to have been deemed noteworthy.[10] Furthermore, whilst evidence for John's attendance at mass, and reception of the sacrament, is fleeting, it does suggest his awareness of its importance.

The coronation ritual culminated in the mass, following the swearing of oaths to rule well, anointing, and the crowning of the new king. During the coronation mass, the ruler was led to the high altar to offer a gold mark there. John would have witnessed this at his brother's coronation in 1189, where he carried one of the three swords from the royal regalia.[11] His inauguration as duke of Normandy in 1199 followed the model of Richard's coronation as king. It took place in Rouen Cathedral on the Sunday after Easter: the week after John had allegedly refused communion in the presence of Bishop Hugh of Lincoln. Yet Roger of Howden, writing only shortly afterwards, made no mention of improper conduct. Walter of Coutances, archbishop of Rouen, invested the new duke with his sword of rule, and placed a gold circlet on his head. John swore oaths on relics of the saints and the evangelists. The *Life of St Hugh* noted that this was 'during the celebration of high mass', without repeating the allegation that John did not participate (although it does accuse the duke of undue levity).[12]

It seems likely that John's coronation as king of England, at Westminster Abbey on 27 May 1199, Ascension Day, followed a similar model. Howden noted simply that John was crowned and consecrated, giving no sense of anything unusual, such as refusal to take communion. Instead, he noted the presence of a host of archbishops, bishops, earls, and barons, suggesting that the ritual took its usual form and order.[13] According to the fourteenth-century *Liber Regalis*, the king would have worn, for a week, the coif placed on his head after his anointing. This was to protect the sacred oil. The coif would have been removed following mass on the eighth day.[14] Again, if John broke with convention here, nobody commented. Perhaps during this period, or soon afterwards, the new king fulfilled a vow to visit

---

8 Coggeshall, p. 96; firmly countered in Gillingham, *Richard*, pp. 258, 325 n. 15.

9 Hugh was officially canonised in 1220: D. H. Farmer, *The Oxford Dictionary of Saints*, 4th edn (Oxford, 1997), p. 245.

10 For a similar conclusion regarding Henry I: 'his attendance at divine service, unremarked, was unremarkable': Green, 'Piety and Patronage', p. 4.

11 Howden, vol. III, pp. 6-12.

12 Howden, vol. IV, pp. 87-8; *Magna Vita*, vol. II, pp. 142-4. See also: P. Webster, 'King John and Rouen: Royal Itineration, Kingship, and the Norman "Capital", c. 1199-c. 1204', *Society and Culture in Medieval Rouen, 911-1300*, ed. L. V. Hicks and E. Brenner (Turnhout, 2013), pp. 309-37 (pp. 328-9).

13 Howden, vol. IV, pp. 89-90.

14 Carpenter, 'Burial', p. 435.

Bury St Edmunds Abbey, presumably to pay his respects at the shrine of the saint. The abbey chronicler, Jocelin of Brakelond, criticised the king's failure to make a meaningful gift in return for the monks' hospitality, noting disapprovingly that 'he gave only a silk cloth which his servants had on loan from our sacrist – and still they have not paid for it'. This critique nevertheless reveals that before leaving Bury, the king attended mass, making a donation of thirteen shillings.[15]

On other occasions, John's presence at one of the principal churches of the realm is likely to have been accompanied by participation in the ritual of the mass. Before he ascended the throne, during King Richard's absence on crusade, it seems likely that the count of Mortain was present at mass in 'the great church' at Reading on Sunday 6 October 1191, when William de Longchamp, bishop of Ely and Chancellor, was excommunicated. On this occasion, it fell to John's ally, Hugh de Nonant, bishop of Coventry and Lichfield (1188-98), to explain the sentence to the assembled laymen.[16] Presumably the 'great church' was Reading Abbey, prominent in John's devotion to the cult of the saints, the foundation and burial place of his great-grandfather, Henry I. A further instance of John's likely attendance at mass comes from the second year of his reign as king, in 1200. On Sunday 8 October he brought his young queen, Isabella of Angoulême, to Westminster Abbey, where they were crowned by Archbishop Hubert Walter.[17] Religious solemnities on this occasion included performance, by clerks named Eustace and Ambrose, of the chant *Christus Vincit*, an anthem associated with glorification of kings.[18] It seems likely that mass was celebrated, although again it was not mentioned by the chroniclers.

Further evidence can be found in 1202, when Pope Innocent III noted in a letter to Hubert Walter that the archbishop had informed him that the king had confessed his sins – a necessary precursor for those who wished to receive communion.[19] Meanwhile, Gerald of Wales recounts an instance from the period of the disputed election to the bishopric of St David's in the early years of the reign, in which he came upon King John when he was in his chapel hearing mass.[20]

Three further examples add to this picture. During the interdict, the king

---

[15] Jocelin of Brakelond. *Chronicle of the Abbey of Bury St Edmunds*, trans. D. Greenway and J. Sayers (Oxford and New York, 1989), pp. 102-3.

[16] *Giraldus Cambrensis de vita Galfridi Archiepiscopi Eboracensis: sive certamina Galfridi Eboracensis Archiepiscopi*, ed. J. S. Brewer, *Giraldi Cambrensis Opera*, RS 21, 8 vols (London, 1861-91) vol. IV, pp. 401-2; *The Chronicle of the Reigns of Stephen, Henry II, and Richard I, by Gervase, the Monk of Canterbury*, ed. W. Stubbs, *The Historical Works of Gervase of Canterbury*, RS 73, 2 vols (London, 1879-80), vol. I, p. 507; *EEA 17. Coventry and Lichfield 1183-1208*, ed. M. J. Franklin (Oxford, 1998), pp. xli-xlii.

[17] Howden, vol. IV, p. 139; *Radulfi de Diceto Decani Lundoniensis Opera Historica. The Historical Works of Master Ralph de Diceto, Dean of London*, ed. W. Stubbs, RS 68, 2 vols (London, 1876), vol. II, p. 170; Coggeshall, p. 103.

[18] *RL*, p. 1.

[19] *SLI*, pp. 37-9 (no. 13); K. Harvey, 'The Piety of King John' (unpublished MA thesis, King's College London, 2008), pp. 37-8 and n. 152.

[20] *Giraldi Cambrensis de jure et statu Menevensis ecclesiae dialogus*, ed. J. S. Brewer, *Giraldi Cambrensis Opera*, RS 21, 8 vols (London, 1861-91) vol. III, pp. 301-2.

signified to John de Cella, abbot of St Albans, that he wished him to celebrate mass. The abbot refused, but the implication is that the king wished to take communion.[21] In July 1213, the king's absolution from excommunication took place at Winchester Cathedral. John was absolved 'under the customary discipline', taken into the church, and 'reconciled at the horn of the altar' (*cornu altaris*). The cathedral monks sang the *Te Deum laudamus*, and the archbishop of Canterbury, Stephen Langton, celebrated mass in John's presence. The king offered a gold mark on the high altar.[22] Pope Innocent III later expressed displeasure at Langton celebrating mass for John, presumably referring to this occasion.[23] In theory, it was the first time since 1208 that the king had been able to take communion, since the sentence of interdict barred priests from performing the sacrament of mass, whilst excommunication in 1209 effectively made John an outlaw from the church. Whether or not the sentences had been respected, however, is difficult to gauge. There remains the possibility, albeit unproven, that the king had found priests prepared to administer the sacrament.[24] A final piece of evidence comes from the last hours of the reign. Roger of Wendover noted that, on his deathbed, the severely ill king 'confessed himself and received the Eucharist' from the abbot of Croxton.[25]

Evidence for the king's attendance at mass, although fleeting, begins to demonstrate that he realised the importance of religious expression. We should be wary of accepting the allegations of the *Life of St Hugh*. John was present at mass on a number of occasions, often associated with crown-wearing, or the making or renewal of vows to rule well. Kings rarely attracted attention for attending mass. Medieval writers tended to take this for granted. We cannot reach firm conclusions about how often the king received the sacrament. The records are not as detailed as for the reign of Henry III, who apparently heard at least one mass a day.[26] Henry's piety, however, was exceptional. Nor should we assume that attendance

---

[21] *Gesta Abbatum Monasterii Sancti Albani, a Thoma Walsingham, regnante Ricardo Secundo, ejusdem ecclesiae praecentore, compilata*, ed. H. T. Riley, RS 28, 3 vols (London, 1867-69), vol. I, p. 235. On John's hostile response: M. Clasby, 'The Abbot, the Royal Will and Magna Carta: The Amercement of the Abbot of St Albans for Non-Attendance at the Common Summons of the Yorkshire Forest Eyre in 1212', *Henry III Fine Rolls Project. Fine of the Month September 2009* [http://www.finerollshenry3.org.uk/content/month/fm-09-2009.html, accessed 7 November 2012].

[22] Barnwell, p. 213; Dunstable, pp. 37-8; Waverley, p. 276; Wendover, vol. II, pp. 81-2. For John's offering: *RLC 1204-24*, p. 148b. For further discussion, see below, Chapter 7.

[23] *SLI*, p. 172 (no. 64); Cheney, *Innocent*, p. 351.

[24] A papal letter of March 1213 could suggest that John took communion during the interdict and his excommunication: *SLI*, pp. 139-40 (no. 47). However, Cheney revised his interpretation of this letter, arguing that it refers not to those who had given the sacrament to the king but to interaction 'with excommunicates for which the canons provided in certain cases': C. R. Cheney, 'A Recent View of the General Interdict on England, 1208-1214', *SCH*, 3 (1966), 159-68 (p. 167).

[25] Wendover, vol. II, p. 196.

[26] Carpenter, 'Burial', pp. 437-8, esp. n. 65. Henry was rumoured to hear up to four masses daily, although there is no recorded occasion of this.

at mass and reception of communion was something that John was expected to do particularly often. It is likely to have been deemed appropriate for the king to receive the Eucharist on the major feasts, Christmas, Easter, and Whitsunday, whilst the Fourth Lateran Council (1215) enjoined reception of communion at least annually.[27] Often, it may have been enough for the king to be present. The evidence suggests that he attended mass when it was expected, engaging in the appropriate formalities. On its own, this is not enough to demonstrate religious commitment. However, John also maintained an infrastructure that enabled performance of mass and other services in his presence, on a potentially much more regular basis.

King John's provision for chapels and their personnel reveals that he maintained the option of attending masses or services when he arrived, or during his stay, at various favoured locations on his itinerary. Chaplains and clerks were employed to serve the chapels of these residences, and received wages, for instance at Geddington (Northamptonshire), Horston Castle (Derbyshire), Winchester and Woodstock (Oxfordshire).[28] Wages of chaplains were accounted for in Ulster and Oriel, probably during John's expedition to Ireland in 1210.[29] Others were given money to repair their robes, as at Guildford in 1205.[30] Sometimes, such chaplains are named. Nicholas, the king's chaplain at Winchester, was given 8s 4d for 'towels and other ornaments for the altar' in 1205. An individual named William served the king's chapel at Oxford in the early years of the reign. The clerk James of Cirencester was given the royal chapel in Nottingham Castle.[31] Steps were taken to create chapels. At Winchester Castle, £10 19s 8d was paid for establishment of a chapel and granary. Meanwhile, at Ludgershall (Hampshire), repairs were made to an existing chapel at the king's residence.[32]

More significantly, items were acquired for the performance of religious services: altar cloths and ornaments, books, and vestments. A surplice was purchased for the king's chapel at Winchester Castle, and towels for the chapel of Clipstone (Nottinghamshire). Books, vestments, and lights were provided for the chapel of St Katherine at Guildford. The royal chapel at Bere (Dorset) received a beautiful crucifix in 1206, whilst a chalice, vestment, and altar ornament were provided for Kingshaugh (Nottinghamshire) in 1215. Similar provision was made at other chapels, for example those of St Stephen and St John at Westminster, and at

---

[27] Kobialka, *This Is My Body*, p. 157; *Disciplinary Decrees of the General Councils: Text, Translation and Commentary*, ed. H. J. Schroeder (St Louis, 1937), pp. 236-96, from *Internet Medieval Sourcebook* [http://www.fordham.edu/halsall/basis/lateran4.html, accessed 16 November 2010], canon 21; Thibodeau, 'Western Christendom', p. 236.

[28] *RLC 1204-24*, pp. 30b, 51a, 84a; *PR 2 John*, pp. 21, 190; *PR 9 John*, p. 114.

[29] 'The Irish Pipe Roll of 14 John, 1211-1212', ed. O. Davis and D. B. Quinn, *Ulster Journal of Archaeology*, 4, supplement (1941), 1-76 (pp. 56-61, 64-5).

[30] *RLC 1204-24*, p. 59b.

[31] *PR 1 John*, p. 219; *PR 2 John*, p. 190; *PR 3 John*, pp. 205, 206; *PR 4 John*, pp. 203, 204; *RLP*, p. 59b.

[32] *PR 6 John*, p. 121; *RLC 1204-24*, p. 40b.

Map 1 Royal Chapels maintained by King John

Silverstone (Northamptonshire).[33] King John made sure that his chaplains were appropriately dressed and equipped with the tools of their trade.

Provision of the raw materials for celebrating mass in the king's chapels was not regularly recorded in the records of royal government. Nonetheless, on one occasion, communion bread was provided for the altar at Winchester.[34] Two similar examples add to the picture of a king aware both of the importance of the mass,

---

[33] *PR 3 John*, pp. 89, 103; *PR 4 John*, p. 12; *PR 8 John*, p. 48; *PR 10 John*, p. 172; *RLC 1204–24*, pp. 72a, 96a, 192b.

[34] *PR 6 John*, p. 131.

and of being remembered by those performing it. In 1205, the Cistercian Abbot John of Forde was given a barrel of wine for religious services. In 1206, the custodians of the king's wine in Southampton were ordered to provide the monks of the king's foundation at Beaulieu with a cask of wine for use in the sacrament of the mass. This was repeated in 1215.[35] This may mark the beginning of what became an annual grant. In 1236, Henry III provided Beaulieu with a cask of wine for celebrating mass, to be given each year from the royal stocks at Southampton, between Christmas and the feast of the Purification of the Virgin Mary (2 February).[36] Wine was still being provided in the later years of Henry's reign, and in the fourteenth and fifteenth centuries.[37]

The locations where John maintained chapels and chaplains span the residences visited on his itinerary. They included traditional centres of government, such as Winchester; major castles, such as Nottingham; and locations that had originated as hunting lodges but were favoured by the Angevins for both business and pleasure, such as Ludgershall and Woodstock. In addition, a chapel travelled with John as part of his entourage, providing the possibility of masses and other services being performed at short notice in the course of his itineration. Royal arrangements for this travelling chapel included payments for new robes for its chaplains, and for the maintenance or replacement of vestments, cloths, and items such as silver phials, to be placed on the altar.[38] The king's investment extended to the chapel of his queen, Isabella of Angoulême, shortly after the birth of the couple's first child, the future Henry III, in October 1207 – a fleeting example of the care John sometimes showed for his wife.[39]

The itinerant royal chapel was prominent in an event of the last days of the reign, in October 1216, at the culmination of a period in which John had criss-crossed England seeking to counter the complete breakdown of his authority during the civil war and subsequent French invasion which followed Magna Carta. In early October, he attempted to travel from Norfolk into Lincolnshire. His route took him across the notorious quicksands of the Wash. Part of the royal baggage train became trapped, and was lost, including the itinerant chapel and the king's relic

---

[35] RLC 1204–24, pp. 18a, 62b, 225b.

[36] *The Beaulieu Cartulary*, ed. S. F. Hockey, with an introduction by P. D. A. Harvey and S. F. Hockey, Southampton Records Series, 17 (Southampton, 1974), pp. 5–7 (no. 2); CChR. Henry III. 1226–1257, HMSO (London, 1903), p. 217. For honouring of Henry III's grant: CLR 1226–1240, p. 330; CLR 1240–1245, pp. 91, 162, 198, 278; CLR 1245–1251, pp. 8, 103, 160, 269, 324; CLR 1251–1260, pp. 4, 58, 93, 150, 181, 256, 339, 417, 445, 493; CLR 1260–1267, pp. 14, 70, 131, 164, 197, 199, 266; CLR 1267–1272, pp. 6 (no. 49), 57 (no. 526), 127 (no. 1104), 152 (no. 1346), 175 (no. 1569); CR 1242–1247, p. 74; CR 1247–1251, p. 24; CR 1268–1272, pp. 382–3.

[37] *The Account-Book of Beaulieu Abbey*, ed. S. F. Hockey, Camden 4th ser., 16 (London, 1975), p. 228; CCR Edward III. 1360–1364, p. 46; CCR Edward IV. 1461–1468, p. 119.

[38] PR 1 John, p. 129; PR 6 John, p. 94; PR 8 John, p. 55; PR 9 John, p. 49; RLC 1204–24, pp. 49b, 68b, 81b, 99b, 103a, 104b.

[39] RLC 1204–24, p. 103a; PR 9 John, p. 31. On John's relationship with his queen: N. Vincent, 'Isabella of Angoulême: John's Jezebel', *King John: New Interpretations*, ed. S. D. Church (Woodbridge, 1999), pp. 165–219.

collection.⁴⁰ The travelling chapel's presence during the greatest crisis of his rule demonstrates how John kept the means of attending services and participating in devotional acts close at hand. This suggests that his chapel, and provision for masses and other services, had a role of daily importance.

It is difficult to believe that King John would have maintained chapels and chaplains, or kept a chapel at the core of his travelling entourage, if he had not believed in the importance of the role such provision fulfilled. In the absence of direct evidence of his attendance, however, it is difficult to be sure which religious rituals were performed in his presence. One aspect stands as an exception: the *Laudes Regiae*, the laudatory chant that began *Christus Vincit, Christus Regnat, Christus Imperat*.⁴¹ This linked the earthly and heavenly hierarchies by matching the ranks within both. The idea was that the heavenly forces interceded for the earthly. Anointed kings had a group of angels and archangels as their supporters. 'In sum the *Laudes* were a unique form of litany addressed solely and triumphantly to the victorious Christ in his divinity as the king of heaven and earth, and the prime example and guarantor of power and prosperity to all rulers who safeguarded the fabric of Christian society.'⁴²

John was not the first king of England to order the *Laudes Regiae* to be performed in his presence. This had been done for Henry II, for instance on Whitsunday 1188, and for Richard I, for example at the crown-wearing that followed his return from captivity in 1194.⁴³ So, in part, John acted in accordance with royal tradition in ordering the *Laudes* to be sung by his chapel clerks on major court occasions: Christmas, Easter, and Whitsunday.⁴⁴ It was also chanted at Queen Isabella's coronation in 1200.⁴⁵ The *Laudes* were part of royal ceremonial across John's reign, except during the interdict, when presumably it ceased, or at least was not documented. Either side of the period of sanctions, the records consistently note payments of twenty-five shillings to two or occasionally three clerks who performed the chant, described as *Christus Vincit*. Eight or nine clerks of the royal chapel were involved in the course of the reign: Ambrose, Master Henry of Cerne, Eustace, Master Henry of Hereford, Hugh of Hereford, Hugh Rigal' (possibly the same man as Hugh of Hereford), R. of Salisbury, James of the Temple, and Master Robert of Saintes. The king probably wore a crown on these occasions, and the ceremony

---

40 Coggeshall, pp. 183-4; J. C. Holt, 'King John's Disaster in the Wash', *Nottingham Medieval Studies*, 5 (1961), 75-86.
41 On this chant: E. H. Kantorowicz, *Laudes Regiae: A Study in Liturgical Acclamations and Mediaeval Ruler Worship* (Berkeley and Los Angeles, CA, 1958); I. D. Bent, 'The Early History of the English Chapel Royal, ca. 1066-1327', 2 vols (unpublished PhD thesis, University of Cambridge, 1969), vol. I, pp. 320-61, vol. II, pp. 244-86.
42 R. Strong, *Coronation: A History of Kingship and the British Monarchy* (London, 2005), p. 40.
43 PR 34 Henry II, p. 19; *Chronicle of the Reigns of Stephen, Henry II, and Richard I, by Gervase, the Monk of Canterbury*, pp. 524-7.
44 MR 1 John, p. 90; RL, pp. 14, 25, 93; RLC 1204-24, pp. 4a, 26b, 34b, 51b, 62b, 71a, 82a, 85b, 99a, 183b, 196b, 222a; RLP, p. 150a; Bent, 'Early History of the English Chapel Royal', vol. II, pp. 250-3.
45 RL, p. 1.

would have added to the religious aura surrounding him. This was also recognised by John's successor, Henry III, especially in the 1230s, when it was performed on a wide variety of festivals.[46] It is noteworthy that Henry, a king with an impeccable reputation for piety, inherited this aspect of royal religious practice from his father. Again, it provides evidence that King John was aware of the importance of attending and engaging with religious ceremonies as part of his kingship.

Personal attendance at masses and services was not the only way in which John acted to provide for the wellbeing of his soul. He also commissioned religious activity, to be performed on his behalf in churches and chapels across the Angevin lands. This involved personal initiative on his part, in that it was his decision to establish these prayers. The advantage, from John's point of view, was that they would take place daily or annually, whether or not he was present. They would also continue after his death, in theory until the last days of the world.

The establishment of chantry priests to celebrate in John's name was paramount amongst these commissioned devotions. Thus, he played a role as part of the generation in which a major shift in high-status religious activity occurred. The chantry 'was essentially an endowment for the performance of masses and other works of charity for the benefit of the souls of specified persons'.[47] Its emergence was part of a gradual move away from donors creating endowments in expectation that services would be performed, towards a system whereby gifts specified the spiritual return required. This 'was the practical outcome ... of the development of the doctrine of Purgatory'.[48] Those who could afford to sponsor a priest to celebrate on their behalf were keen to take advantage of a means of reducing the time their soul suffered cleansing punishment before being deemed fit for heaven.[49] Again, King John was no exception to the trend. He sponsored anniversary masses and chantries in numerous locations, including, in one instance, a chapel on the bridge at Lincoln.[50]

---

[46] Kantorowicz, *Laudes Regiae*, pp. 174-5; I. Bent, 'The English Chapel Royal before 1300', *Proceedings of the Royal Musical Association*, 90 (1963-64), 77-95 (pp. 88-9). Evidence for performance of the chant dies out in the 1240s.

[47] H. M. Colvin, 'The Origin of Chantries', *JMH*, 26 (2000), 163-73 (p. 164). Colvin sees the chantry as developing later than John's rule. David Crouch, however, shows that the office originated by the 1180s: D. Crouch, 'The Origin of Chantries: Some Further Anglo-Norman Evidence', *JMH*, 27 (2001), 159-80. See also Crouch, *Image of Aristocracy*, pp. 240-4; Crouch, 'Culture of Death', pp. 174-7.

[48] B. Thompson, 'From "Alms" to "Spiritual Services": The Function and Status of Monastic Property in Medieval England', *Monastic Studies: The Continuity of Tradition*, 2, ed. J. Loades (Bangor, 1991), pp. 227-61 (p. 251). On Anglo-Norman and Angevin evidence for the development of the doctrine of Purgatory: C. S. Watkins, *History and the Supernatural in Medieval England* (Cambridge, 2007), pp. 172-201.

[49] On Purgatory as a place where 'the sinful but repentant soul could, through purgatorial of cleansing punishment, complete the process of making satisfaction for sin and so be rendered fit for Heaven': R. Horrox, 'Purgatory, Prayer, and Plague: 1150-1380', *Death in England: An Illustrated History*, ed. P. C. Jupp and C. Gittings (Manchester, 1999), pp. 90-118 (p. 90, and see also p. 109).

[50] *RC*, p. 53b.

More commonly associated with the later Middle Ages, chantries were gradually becoming an aspect of religious activity by the time John came to the throne. Indeed his relatives played their part in this development. Following the death of John's brother, Henry the Young King, in 1183, his wife and brothers assiduously provided services for his salvation. Margaret of France, the Young King's widow, commissioned the Abbot of Clairvaux to administer a fund supporting chaplains at an altar provided by the dean of Rouen. Henry's (and John's) brother Geoffrey endowed a chaplaincy at Rouen Cathedral, where the Young King was buried. In 1189 John, in turn, granted £10 for the canons' participation in services on the anniversary of Young Henry's death.[51] This in part confirmed a gift originally made by Henry II to Walter of Coutances, before the latter became archbishop of Rouen in 1184, involving the collegiate chapel of Blyth (Nottinghamshire) with its appurtenant chapels and churches. John, however, added that part of the revenue the cathedral gained was to be used to fund anniversary masses for his own soul after his death.[52] This gift demonstrates that establishment of anniversary masses and chantry priests was an aspect of John's religious practice before he became king. Patronage of Rouen Cathedral continued. In 1200, he confirmed his earlier grants, as part of his response to the fire in the city that caused substantial damage to the cathedral.[53]

At Lichfield, John's largesse in the early 1190s shows clear characteristics of the chantry. In 1192, on the day after Easter, he endowed the cathedral with the church of Bakewell (Derbyshire). In return, a prebendary priest was to celebrate mass daily for John's health and safety during his lifetime, continuing after his death, in perpetuity, for the salvation of his soul. At Bakewell itself, three priests were to remain to serve the church. John renewed his grant of Bakewell in his first year as king.[54] His association with chantries at Lichfield continued. In 1206, Geoffrey Muschamp (bishop of Coventry and Lichfield 1198–1208) issued a letter referring to the continuing generosity of John and his predecessors to Lichfield. In consequence, the bishop granted that three chaplains would celebrate mass daily for the souls of Henry II, Henry the Young King, Richard I, Geoffrey of Brittany,

---

[51] Crouch, 'Origin of Chantries', p. 172.
[52] For Henry II's grant: *Recueil des actes de Henri II, roi d'Angleterre et duc de Normandie, concernant les provinces françaises et les affaires de France*, ed. L. Delisle and E. Berger, 3 vols (Paris, 1909-27), vol. II, pp. 11–12 (no. 462). The text of John's grant will appear in *Mortain*; summarised in CDF, p. 12 (no. 46). See also: N. Vincent, 'Jean, comte de Mortain: le futur roi et ses domaines en Normandie. 1183-1199', *1204: La Normandie entre Plantagenêts et Capétiens*, ed. A.-M. Flambard Héricher and V. Gazeau (Caen, 2007), pp. 37–59 (p. 43). According to later tradition, the chapel of Blyth was founded by John's mother, Eleanor of Aquitaine: R. V. Turner, *Eleanor of Aquitaine: Queen of France, Queen of England* (New Haven, CT, and London, 2009), pp. 129, 276. See also Chapter 4, below.
[53] RC, pp. 75b–76a. For John and Rouen Cathedral, see also Webster, 'King John and Rouen', pp. 328-32.
[54] Crouch, 'The Origin of Chantries', p. 177; *Mortain*; RC, pp. 34b–35a. For arrangements made by Bishop Hugh de Nonant following John's grant of 1192: *EEA 17*, pp. 36-7 (nos. 40, 41).

and in particular for John. Presumably these were priests at Lichfield Cathedral, where an annual obit for John was still recorded under Henry VIII.[55]

Lichfield's commitment to intercessory masses for the Angevins is worth exploring further. In the mid-1180s, Hugh de Nonant, bishop of Lichfield, had been sent to Rome by Henry II to seek papal permission for John to be crowned king of Ireland. By the early 1190s, Hugh was closely involved in John's efforts to establish himself as heir-apparent during Richard I's absence on crusade and in captivity. He was prominent in ousting William de Longchamp in 1191, and ended up in hiding in France in 1194, after his brother refused to act as a hostage for Richard's release. Hugh later received a substantial fine, and retreated to the political background for the remainder of his episcopate.[56] It is tempting to see the 1192 endowment as part of the political alliance between John and Hugh, one of the rewards that the bishop reaped from the association.

However, the extent to which John was buying the bishop's support is debateable. If the chantry linked to Bakewell was established out of political expediency, this does not explain why provision was later continued and confirmed. Clearly care was taken to ensure that masses were performed for the king and his relatives. These were not the only grants to demonstrate religious feeling on John's part. Bishop Hugh also received the church of Hope with the chapel of Tideswell (Derbyshire), in an alms grant made for John, and for the souls of his father, his mother, and his brother Richard.[57] The churches concerned all lay within the diocese of Lichfield, in lands in Derbyshire that John had been granted by Richard in 1189. They constituted easily accessible endowments from the recipient's point of view. All this suggests that John's chantry provision reflected more than political motives. Indeed, Bishop Hugh might well have encouraged John to promote this sort of foundation. Despite his later reputation, that no confessor would absolve him on his death, de Nonant was exactly the sort of bishop appointed by the Angevins.[58] He combined administrative and political nous with a religious awareness not uncommon amongst bishops of the time, but which often takes second place in analysis of their reputations. As such he fits into a line of royal servants under Richard I and John which included William de Longchamp, Hubert Walter, and Peter des Roches.[59] It is not unexpected that Hugh, described at least once as

---

[55] *EEA* 17, pp. 96–7 (no. 113); *Valor Ecclesiasticus temp. Henr. VIII auctoritate regia institutus*, ed. J. Caley and J. Hunter, RComm, 6 vols (London, 1810–34), vol. III, p. 136.

[56] M. J. Franklin, 'Nonant, Hugh de (d. 1198)', *ODNB* (Oxford, 2004) [http://www.oxforddnb.com/view/article/20245, accessed 14 December 2010]; *EEA* 17, pp. xli–xliii.

[57] Mortain. Funds from Hope were later assigned to Lichfield for provision of ale: *EEA* 17, pp. 95–6 (no. 112).

[58] Gillingham, *Richard*, p. 228; Franklin, 'Nonant, Hugh de'.

[59] For summaries noting the religious awareness of these bishops: R. V. Turner, 'Longchamp, William de (d. 1197)', *ODNB* (Oxford, 2004, online edn 2007) [http://www.oxforddnb.com/view/article/16980, accessed 14 December 2010]; R. C. Stacey, 'Walter, Hubert (d. 1205)', *ODNB* (Oxford, 2004, online edn 2008) [http://www.oxforddnb.com/view/article/28633, accessed 14 December 2010]; N. Vincent, 'Roches, Peter des (d. 1238)', *ODNB* (Oxford, 2004, online edn 2008) [http://www.oxforddnb.com/view/article/22014, accessed 14 December 2010].

the future king's friend, should have been involved in establishing John's chantry at Lichfield.⁶⁰

The examples from Rouen and Lichfield were not the only chantries endowed by John before he became king. In 1198, another was established at the Premonstratensian abbey of St Nicholas of Blanchelande, in the diocese of Coutances in Normandy. This house received the church of St Lawrence on Jersey. The endowment was to pay for intercession for John at the abbey during his life and for celebration of his anniversary after his death. On the day of his obit, the convent was to be supplied with victuals.⁶¹

John continued to commission anniversary masses and chantry priests after he came to the throne, with evidence from English cathedrals suggesting continuity in this aspect of his religious practice. When Salisbury Cathedral received confirmation of grants made by Henry I and Henry II, John added his own gift of the church of Melksham (Wiltshire), to provide for the solemn celebration of the anniversary of his father's death, and in time of his own.⁶² Two churches were given to St Paul's Cathedral in London with a similar statement of the expected return. The first, at Shoreditch, just outside the city of London, was one to which the right to present new incumbents had previously pertained to the king. In granting the church, John stipulated that it was to support a precentor in St Paul's Cathedral, to hold his office for the king's soul and those of his ancestors. In turn, Bishop William of London, who had petitioned for the grant, gave Shoreditch to the precentor Benedict of Sawston, who became bishop of Rochester in 1214.⁶³ The second church, Maldon (Essex) was given in return for annual commemoration of the anniversary of Henry II's death, special services for John during his lifetime, and anniversary celebration after his death. Part of the manor had originally been granted to the lepers of Le Bois-Halbout and the canons of Nôtre-Dame du Val (both in the Calvados region), and an exchange was duly made, probably in 1202 or 1203, so that Maldon could be used for the services specified. In 1223, Eustace

---

60 For Hugh described as John's friend: *EEA 17*, pp. 17-18 (no. 17).
61 G. Dupont, *Histoire du Cotentin et de ses iles*, 4 vols (Caen, 1870-85), vol. I, p. 489 (no. 42); *CDF*, p. 312 (no. 873); Vincent, 'Jean', p. 43; J. A. Everard and J. C. Holt, *Jersey 1204: The Forging of an Island Community* (London, 2004), p. 75.
62 *RC*, p. 67a. In the 1220s Richard Poor (Bishop of Salisbury 1217-28) granted Melksham to the common fund of the cathedral canons, making no mention of the anniversaries commissioned by John, but providing for pittances and almsgiving on the bishop's anniversary: *EEA 19. Salisbury 1217-1228*, ed. B. R. Kemp (Oxford, 2000), pp. 341-2 (no. 359). However, alms on the anniversary of Henry II's death was still associated with Melksham at the dissolution of the monasteries: *Valor Ecclesiasticus*, vol. II, p. 79.
63 *Early Charters of the Cathedral Church of St Paul, London*, ed. M. Gibbs, Camden 3rd ser., 58 (London, 1939), pp. 34-5 (no. 49), 41 (no. 57), 42 (no. 58); *RC*, p. 124a-b; *EEA 26. London 1189-1228*, ed. D. P. Johnson (Oxford, 2003), pp. 144-5 (nos. 162-3). On Benedict: J. Le Neve, *Fasti Ecclesiae Anglicanae 1066-1300. I. St Paul's, London*, rev. edn by D. E. Greenway (London, 1968), pp. 22, 23, 64; M. N. Blount, 'Sawston, Benedict of (d. 1226)', *ODNB* (Oxford, 2004) [http://www.oxforddnb.com/view/article/24660, accessed 19 December 2012].

de Fauconberg, bishop of London (1221-28), provided for the royal grant to be honoured and the obits performed.[64]

These examples suggest that John sought intercession from some of the major cathedral churches of the Anglo-Norman world. This desire also extended to other locations. Geographically, it included religious houses closely associated with the counts of Anjou and dukes of Aquitaine. At the nunnery of Fontevraud, John backed his mother's provision for her commemoration. He gave one hundred *livres Poitevin* and confirmed Eleanor of Aquitaine's gifts to God, the Virgin Mary, and the nuns. Services were to be celebrated on the anniversary of Eleanor's death, on those of the king's brothers and, in due course, on that of the king himself. John's charter was issued 'for the sake of charity', for the salvation of Henry II, Eleanor of Aquitaine, his brothers, and himself. After Eleanor's death (1204), he went further, associating himself with a chantry dedicated to St Lawrence, founded by his mother at Fontevraud.[65]

Further south, royal largesse in 1214, to the Benedictine monks of Saint-Maixent, provides a similar combination of quest for intercession and dynastic concerns. The monks were declared quit of a payment they were obliged to make to the Angevin rulers when the latter arrived at the abbey, and of monies due to the seneschal of Poitou. In return, they were to feed three paupers and celebrate two masses every day of John's life, for his soul and those of his ancestors and successors.[66] The timing of the grant is significant. The king's desire for intercession came ahead of his ambitious campaign to regain the lands lost to Philip II of France earlier in the reign. During this ultimately failed venture, he stayed at the Abbey of Saint-Maixent in July, August, and September 1214.[67] However, the king was not just seeking divine intercession in the hope of military success. The provision for the poor and the desired intercessory masses appear identical to those requested in a gift made by John's mother, Eleanor of Aquitaine, in 1200, granting the monks services previously rendered to her by her foresters.[68] Perhaps John sought acknowledgement or affirmation of his status as Eleanor's heir to Aquitaine, seeking to ensure that intercession for his mother was extended to almsgiving and masses on his behalf.

Chantry provision extended to the chapels of the king's castles. At Falaise in Normandy, the Premonstratensian canons of the Priory of St John were given two chapels in the ducal castle. They were to staff each with a priest, serving daily,

---

[64] *The Cartae Antiquae Rolls 1-10*, ed. L. Landon, PRS, 55, ns 17 (London, 1939), pp. 3-4 (no. 9); *Norman Charters from English Sources: Antiquaries, Archives and the Rediscovery of the Anglo-Norman Past*, ed. N. Vincent, PRS, 97, ns 59 (London, 2013), pp. 111-13 (no. 4); *EEA* 26, pp. 199-200 (no. 229). For masses at St Paul's for the souls of the kings of England, established under Richard I by Richard fitz Nigel (Bishop of London 1189-98), at the altars of St Thomas Becket and St Denis: *Early Charters of the Cathedral Church of St Paul*, pp. 145-6 (no. 186).

[65] *RL*, p. 92; *RC*, pp. 72a, 127b. Fontevraud will be considered further in Chapter 4.

[66] *RLP*, p. 115b.

[67] 'Itinerary'.

[68] Turner, *Eleanor*, p. 293.

performing masses and the other services of the monastic day for the benefit of the king's soul and those of his ancestors. Their wages were two shillings *Angevin* per day. Why John chose Falaise is not revealed, although he visited this important ducal castle each year prior to the loss of Normandy in 1204.[69] Conceivably, this represents the sort of commemoration that took place in royal chapels across the land, but for which evidence no longer survives. Whether or not this was the case, provision at Falaise was not unique. At Argentan in Normandy, similar services were commissioned from a royal clerk, Robert of St Christopher, who was granted the chaplaincy and ordered to perform services for the king's soul, that of Henry II, and John's ancestors and successors.[70]

Provision could also be established in chapels located in or near the hunting lodges frequented by John as he travelled. In 1205, it was ordered that forty shillings a year were to be paid to the hermit of Clipstone, who 'sings [*cantat*] in the chapel of St Edwin in the hay of Birchwood' (probably Edwinstowe, Nottinghamshire). The recipient was to celebrate for the king's soul and those of his ancestors, and the money was duly paid each year.[71] Also in 1205, Robert, hermit of St Werburg, was granted his hermitage, 'for the love of God' (*pro amore Dei*) and for the king's salvation. The hermit and his successors were also paid fifty shillings for serving the king's chapel of Brill (Buckinghamshire) in perpetuity. Here, a chaplain would celebrate mass daily for the king, his ancestors and heirs. This may reflect an earlier arrangement. In 1201–02, 'Robert chaplain of St Werburg' was paid ten shillings for celebrating mass in the chapel at Brill, presumably in the king's presence, and in 1202–03 and from 1208–09 onwards payments were made to the chaplain of Brill.[72] Finally, in one instance a chantry priest had insufficient means to fund his work. In 1214, the royal clerk Henry Abbot was to be provided with ten marks from a vacant benefice. John's letter noted that Henry 'vigilantly celebrates divine service for us', suggesting either that he performed masses in the king's presence or, perhaps more likely, on behalf of the king and for the wellbeing of his soul.[73]

Chantries would therefore appear to have been an important aspect of King John's religious provision. Others also gave orders for masses, services, and prayers to be performed in his name during his lifetime.[74] In 1203, Hubert Walter, archbishop of Canterbury, requested special prayers during the daily mass performed by clergymen across the land, accompanied by processions on Fridays. Alongside the Holy Land, the peace of the Church and the kingdom, good weather and good

---

[69] *RC*, p. 69a; *RN*, p. 15; 'Itinerary'.
[70] *RC*, p. 69a.
[71] *RLC*, p. 20a; *PR 7 John*, pp. 220–1; *PR 8 John*, p. 75; *PR 9 John*, p. 114; *PR 11 John*, p. 109; *PR 12 John*, p. 124; *PR 13 John*, p. 211; *PR 14 John*, p. 161; *PR 16 John*, p. 156.
[72] *RC*, p. 158b; *PR 3 John*, p. 163; *PR 4 John*, p. 30; *PR 10 John*, p. 128; *PR 11 John*, p. 178; *PR 12 John*, p. 11; *PR 13 John*, p. 139; *PR 14 John*, p. 124; *PR 16 John*, p. 14; *PR 17 John*, p. 23.
[73] *RLP*, p. 119a.
[74] On *pro anima* giving invoking the souls of earlier kings of England: Marritt, 'Prayers', pp. 194–201.

crops, this was in aid of the king, in the light of the tribulation he faced at the hands of his enemies.[75]

Hubert was not alone. Various courtiers made grants referencing the wellbeing of John's soul, as when Meiler fitz Henry, justiciar in Ireland, gave land in Kerry to the canons of Cirencester. Similarly, Fulk de Cantilupe gave two acres of meadow to the church of Bourne, for John's soul and his, for provision of lights day and night in front of the high altar.[76] In around 1204, John issued a charter to Simon of Wells, Bishop-elect of Chichester, giving the church of Bapchild (Kent). Simon assigned it to the cathedral's common fund, saving a vicarage which he retained, and specified that the king's anniversary (and his own) was to be kept annually, with services and lights as were provided on the more solemn feast days.[77]

In 1210, Geoffrey fitz Peter, Earl of Essex and justiciar, granted all that he held in Winchester from Thomas of St-Valéry to the city's cathedral community. Geoffrey specified that annual anniversary masses should be performed on behalf of the three kings he had served: Henry II, Richard I, and John. In addition, a monk was to perform mass for the faithful at the altar of St Katherine in the cathedral, where the justiciar's father, Peter of Ludgershall, was buried. This mass was for the souls Geoffrey had named previously (the three Angevin kings, his father, mother, and wives) and for all the faithful dead. The grant was made at the cathedral's high altar in 1210, on the vigil (23 June) of the feast of the Nativity of St John the Baptist, so at the height of the interdict and whilst King John was excommunicate.[78] It is interesting that the justiciar could make this commission at this time, given that communion was forbidden during the interdict and that some of these masses were for an excommunicate.[79] Perhaps it is significant that this was a grant

---

[75] C. R. Cheney, 'Levies on the English Clergy for the Poor and for the King, 1203', EHR, 96 (1981), 577-84 (pp. 579-80, 582-4).

[76] The Cartulary of Cirencester Abbey Gloucestershire, ed. C. R. Ross and M. Devine, 3 vols (Oxford, 1964-77), vol. II, pp. 537-8 (no. 634); The Chartulary of the High Church of Chichester, ed. W. D. Peckham, Sussex Record Society Publications, 46 (Lewes, 1946), p. 89 (no. 332).

[77] Chartulary of the High Church of Chichester, pp. 29 (no. 129), 369 (no. 1090); The Acta of the Bishops of Chichester 1075-1207, ed. H. Mayr-Harting, Canterbury and York Society, 56 (London, 1964), pp. 196-7 (no. 147); EEA 22. Chichester 1215-1253, ed. P. M. Hoskin (Oxford, 2001), p. 2 (no. 3); EEA III. Canterbury 1193-1205, ed. C. R. Cheney and E. John (Oxford, 1991), pp. 74-5 (no. 408). The documents state that John had promised this in honour of the dedication of Chichester Cathedral (12 September 1199). If so, he cannot have been present: 'Itinerary'.

[78] London, British Library, Additional Ms. 29436, ff. 31v-32r; R. V. Turner, Men Raised From the Dust: Administrative Service and Upward Mobility in Angevin England (Philadelphia, PA, 1988), pp. 62, 64; Cheney, Innocent, p. 312. It is intriguing that lands previously held by Thomas of St-Valéry, brother of Matilda de Briouze, were put to this use in the year in which John starved Matilda to death in his prison at Windsor or Corfe. For Thomas of St-Valéry's fluctuating allegiance: D. Power, The Norman Frontier in the Twelfth and Early Thirteenth Centuries (Cambridge, 2004), pp. 425-6, 454-5.

[79] On what was permitted and what was forbidden during the interdict: Cheney, 'Papal Interdict', pp. 297-300; Cheney, 'Recent View', pp. 161-2. On the impact of the sanctions, see Chapter 6.

to Winchester Cathedral, whose bishop – Peter des Roches (first amongst the charter's witnesses) – had not joined his colleagues in exile, and who trod a careful line between his role as a confidant of the king and his status as a senior churchman.[80] Further context is provided by the fact that at much the same time as this grant, John embarked on a campaign in Ireland, leaving Geoffrey, as justiciar, in charge of royal government in England.[81]

Such arrangements suggest that, contrary to his posthumous reputation, some of John's contemporaries, in particular those closely associated with his court, felt it worth the effort to make provision for the king's soul. Perhaps not all considered him irredeemable. Geoffrey fitz Peter's instructions were not unique, and the king was happy to sanction arrangements that offered masses and prayers on his behalf. Prior to his death in 1205, Archbishop Hubert Walter sought to establish such provision as part of his project to re-found the secular college of Wolverhampton as a Cistercian monastery. The college had long-standing royal associations, with the church originally granted to the monks of Worcester by William the Conqueror. It was also a royal free chapel, but by the early thirteenth century its dean, Peter of Blois, reported urgent need for reform and resigned his office to the archbishop.[82] Hubert's proposed re-foundation was supported by the king, whose grant of forest rights noted that the archbishop had promised that the religious at Wolverhampton would perform services in perpetuity for the king's soul, ancestors and heirs, during John's lifetime and after his death.[83] Prior to the archbishop's death, the project proceeded apace. The king gave land and building materials. Hubert secured papal exemption from episcopal jurisdiction, and called upon the abbot of Boxley to advise on conversion to the Cistercian order.[84] A royal charter was drawn up confirming Archbishop Hubert's gifts to God, the Blessed Virgin Mary, and the Cistercians, in free, pure and perpetual alms, for John's salvation and that of his ancestors and heirs. This document remained unsealed, appearing as cancelled on the Charter Roll.[85] Hubert Walter's death (13 July 1205) deprived the project of its principal patron. Wolverhampton remained a secular college, retaining its status as a royal free chapel (although in 1224 an agreement with Alexander of Stainsby, bishop of Coventry and Lichfield, recognised the latter's authority over aspects of

---

80 On des Roches and the interdict: Vincent, *Peter des Roches*, pp. 74–88. Vincent argues that the sentence is likely to have been respected in the diocese of Winchester.
81 F. J. West, 'Geoffrey fitz Peter, Fourth Earl of Essex (d. 1213)', *ODNB* (Oxford, 2004, online edn 2008) [http://www.oxforddnb.com/view/article/9626, accessed 7 December 2010].
82 For Wolverhampton's complex history and various royal grants: *EEA 14. Coventry and Lichfield 1072–1159*, ed. M. J. Franklin (Oxford, 1997), pp. 4–5 (no. 4); *EEA 18. Salisbury 1078–1217*, ed. B. R. Kemp (Oxford, 1999), pp. 16–17 (no. 21, a probable forgery); *EEA 33. Worcester 1062–1185*, ed. M. Cheney, D. Smith, C. Brooke, and P. M. Hoskin (Oxford, 2007), pp. xxxviii, 23–4 (no. 26); *The Cartulary of Worcester Cathedral Priory (Register I)*, ed. R. R. Darlington, PRS, 76, ns 38 (London, 1968 for 1962–63), pp. xlvii–xlvix, 138–41 (nos. 259–67, of which no. 266 is a probable forgery). On Peter of Blois' resignation: C. R. Cheney, *Hubert Walter* (London, 1967), p. 154 n. 4.
83 *RC*, p. 115a.
84 *RC*, pp. 135b, 152b, 153a; *RLC 1204–24*, pp. 8a, 20b, 25b, 56a; *Coggeshall*, p. 160.
85 *RC*, p. 154a.

the community's activities).[86] It seems likely that prayers for the king continued in their traditional form.

In the later years of the reign, there was further collaboration between a bishop and the king in the creation of a religious house offering prayers on John's behalf. In 1215, Peter des Roches, bishop of Winchester, established a Premonstratensian abbey at Halesowen (Worcestershire). John donated the manor of Hales, on which the house was to be founded, stating that this was to be used for Peter 'to found a religious house of what religious he wishes'.[87] The bishop's foundation charter stated that the canons were to pray for the souls of King John and his forebears. The house received continued royal support in the reign of Henry III.[88]

Taken as a whole, it can be seen that King John attended mass when he was expected to, and it is likely that he participated in ways that his contemporaries deemed appropriate. He also created an infrastructure that allowed masses and services to be performed in his presence across the land. John also established masses, prayers, and services to be performed for the benefit of his soul. Chantries were an important element of this strategy, created at churches and chapels across the land on the initiative of the king and by those most closely associated with his rule. The examples discussed have been drawn from the period of the king's lifetime. Further evidence of the establishment of anniversary masses and prayers for his soul can be found in the activity of his son and former courtiers after his death.[89] In considering John's personal religion whilst he was alive, however, we now turn to other ways in which he sought intercession for the wellbeing of his soul and of his kingdom, and for his salvation after his death.

---

[86] J. H. Denton, *English Royal Free Chapels, 1100–1300: A Constitutional Study* (Manchester, 1970), pp. 41–4.
[87] RC, pp. 201b–202a, 217a. See also RLC 1204–24, p. 174b.
[88] EEA IX. *Winchester 1205–1238*, ed. N. Vincent (Oxford, 1994), pp. 10–12 (no. 13). See also H. M. Colvin, *The White Canons in England* (Oxford, 1951), pp. 179–81, 350–1.
[89] Discussed below, Chapter 8.

2

The Saints

Seeking support from the saints, both in relation to everyday problems and for the future of the soul, was a fundamental aspect of medieval lay religion. For kings, the backing of the saints could be sought in the affairs of government and kingdom, and against opponents within and outside the realm. Such intercession could be sought as a potential buttress to authority, or for more day-to-day matters such as health and welfare. Despite this, John's interest in the cult of the saints stands first on Painter's list of 'the more superficial forms' of religious activity in which the king engaged.[1] This assessment undoubtedly belittles the importance of this aspect of John's personal religion. He sought intercession from saints native to the kingdom of England and from the major Christian cults, doing so at individual cult centres, or by visiting several shrines in succession as he travelled. He also maintained a private relic collection that he could call upon during his near constant itineration.

Pre-eminent amongst the cults of late twelfth- and early thirteenth-century England was that of Thomas Becket. Whether or not Henry II sanctioned the murder of the archbishop of Canterbury in his own cathedral, the Angevins were tarred by association. John (born on 24 December 1166) had just turned four when Becket was killed, and was only seven at the time of his father's dramatic penance at Canterbury Cathedral (12–13 July 1174).[2] He could not have initiated the royal response to the cult of St Thomas, but nonetheless inherited its legacy. After 1174, Henry II was a regular pilgrim to Becket's shrine, visiting each time he returned from the Continent (except in 1188, when the cathedral was under interdict).[3] Henry also advertised his devotion to the saint he had inadvertently created, joining high-status pilgrims to Canterbury, as the cult blossomed into one of Europe-wide significance. These visitors included Henry II's son, Henry the Young King, King Louis VII of France, Count Philip I Flanders (twice), William of Blois archbishop of Rheims (twice), and Count Theobald V of Blois.[4] The king of

---

[1] Painter, *Reign*, p. 152.
[2] On John's date of birth: A. W. Lewis, 'The Birth and Childhood of King John: Some Revisions', *Eleanor of Aquitaine: Lord and Lady*, ed. B. Wheeler and J. C. Parsons (New York and Basingstoke, 2002), pp. 159–75 (pp. 161–5).
[3] Duggan, 'Diplomacy', esp. pp. 272–84; A. J. Duggan, 'Henry II, the English Church and the Papacy, 1154–76', *Henry II: New Interpretations*, ed. C. Harper-Bill and N. Vincent (Woodbridge, 2007), pp. 154–83; Keefe, 'Shrine Time', pp. 115–22.
[4] D. Webb, *Pilgrimage in Medieval England* (London and New York, 2000), p. 50; Keefe, 'Shrine Time', p. 115.

Scots, William I – captured at Alnwick almost at the moment when Henry II prayed at Becket's tomb at Canterbury in 1174 – founded Arbroath Abbey in honour of St Thomas (in 1178) and made pilgrimages to the saint's shrine. In 1181, he travelled to Canterbury with Henry II, when the two kings returned from Normandy. William returned to Canterbury in 1189, to join Richard I, who quitclaimed the Treaty of Falaise, imposed on the Scottish king after his capture in 1174.[5] William 'surely gave thanks to the sainted archbishop' for Richard's concession.[6]

Although the Lionheart spent little time in England as king, he visited Canterbury in both 1189 and 1194, on the latter occasion allegedly prioritising the cathedral ahead of any other church in England.[7] In 1189, John was with his brother, and had good reason to remember what took place. He witnessed various charters, and was absolved by the papal legate, John of Anagni, from the interdict imposed on him by Archbishop Baldwin of Canterbury because of his consanguineous marriage to his second cousin, Isabella of Gloucester. In addition, Richard bestowed Cornwall, Devon, Dorset, and Somerset on his younger brother.[8]

As king, John visited Canterbury regularly, staying away only in 1200 and 1202, when his affairs largely confined him to the Continent, and between 1208 and 1212, when he resisted the appointment of Archbishop Langton.[9] It may be argued that the association between the ruling house and the Becket cult continued, but John did not pursue devotion to Becket alone. Nor did he approach other cults on the basis that each should be regarded in isolation. Rather, he combined his devotion to the saints, for example by visiting their shrines in close succession as he travelled.[10] In particular, this can be seen in his devotion to St Thomas Becket, St Edward the Confessor, and St Edmund, King and Martyr, in the early years of the reign.

In 1199, John came to Canterbury within his first month in England as king. His combined pilgrimage in this period seems ripe with potential significance. The opportunities for association with the saints began at his coronation, at Westminster Abbey. Taking place in front of the high altar, this event occurred in close

---

5   D. D. R. Owen, *William the Lion: Kingship and Culture* (East Linton, 1997), pp. 63, 78–80; M. Penman, 'The Bruce Dynasty, Becket and Scottish Pilgrimage to Canterbury, c. 1178–c. 1404', *JMH*, 32 (2006), 346–70 (pp. 348–52).

6   A. Jordan, 'The St Thomas Becket Windows at Angers and Coutances: Devotion, Subversion, and the Scottish Connection', *The Cult of St Thomas Becket in the Plantagenet World, c. 1170–c. 1250*, ed. P. Webster and M.-P. Gelin (Woodbridge, forthcoming).

7   L. Landon, *The Itinerary of King Richard I with Studies on Certain Matters of Interest Connected with his Reign*, PRS, 51, ns 13 (London, 1955), pp. 17–21, 85; *Chronicle of the Reigns of Stephen, Henry II, and Richard I, by Gervase, the monk of Canterbury*, p. 524.

8   Landon, *Itinerary*, pp. 19, 21. John's presence at Canterbury is also considered in: P. Webster, 'Crown, Cathedral, and Conflict: King John and Canterbury', *Cathedrals, Communities and Conflict in the Anglo-Norman World*, ed. P. Dalton, C. Insley, and L. J. Wilkinson (Woodbridge, 2011), pp. 203–19 (pp. 204–9).

9   'Itinerary'. In 1200 John spent seven months in his continental lands. He was overseas all year in 1202 and during the first eleven months of 1203. His itinerary in 1211 is largely unknown.

10 On the significance of royal itinerant pilgrimage: Vincent, 'Pilgrimages'.

proximity to the shrine of John's canonised royal kinsman, Edward the Confessor, as it was located prior to the translation of 1269. The Confessor is most closely associated with King Henry III, who commissioned a new shrine, and rebuilt the choir at Westminster in Edward's honour in the mid-thirteenth century.[11] However, the saint's canonisation in 1161 had been promoted by John's father, Henry II, in whose presence the relics were first translated in 1163. This suited Henry's policy of asserting continuity between his rule and that of his Anglo-Norman predecessors, who themselves had used their relationship with the Confessor to demonstrate continuity with the Anglo-Saxon past. Henry emphasised his kinship with the Confessor: 'Physical descent from his saintly stock is the particular boast of our King Henry.' Potentially, this conferred an aura of sanctity on his kingship and dynasty.[12] The Becket crisis probably prevented him from asserting this more strongly. However, the possibilities were not lost on Henry's successors.

Although surviving acts of Henry II, Richard I, and John do not resound with evidence of devotion to St Edward, even before the canonisation of 1161, it was acknowledged that the coronation took place in proximity to the Confessor's tomb.[13] By *circa* 1200, the *regalia* are thought to have included various items associated with the saint, notably a crown, two sceptres, a dove-topped staff, a cross St Edward was said to have rescued during the sea-crossing to return to England in 1041, a chalice and paten, an ivory comb, and possibly various vestments.[14] Some of these items, notably the dove-topped rod, can be identified in Howden's description of Richard I's coronation, although given that Henry III and Edward I were probably buried with similar rods, parts of the *regalia* may have been made anew at the start of each reign.[15] Meanwhile, a crown said to have been St Edward's was associated with Westminster Abbey from at least the time of Osbert of Clare's efforts to secure the Confessor's canonisation in the 1120s and 1130s. The first recorded use of this crown was at Henry III's second coronation in 1220. Whether such a crown was used by John is impossible to determine. Crowns were amongst the items commissioned either for his first coronation (1199), or his second (1200) when Queen Isabella was first crowned.[16] Nonetheless, it seems likely that items which, at the very least, invoked the memory of St Edward were available for use at the coronation of King John. Taken together, this suggests that the saint's presence was an important element of ritual accompanying the start of the reign, with which the new king can hardly fail to have been impressed.

In this context, there is added significance to John's pilgrimage after his coronation. His path took him to another royal shrine, at Bury St Edmunds, before he turned towards Canterbury. This was 'impelled by a vow and out of devotion' to St Edmund king and martyr, the ninth-century East Anglian king killed by Viking

---

[11] See, for example, Binski, *Westminster Abbey*; Carpenter, 'Henry III and St Edward'.
[12] *Life of St Edward the Confessor by St Aelred of Rievaulx*, trans. J. Bertram (Southampton, 1997), p. 16; Scholz, 'Canonisation', pp. 49–60.
[13] Carpenter, 'Henry III and St Edward', p. 866; Scholz, 'Canonisation', p. 46.
[14] Strong, *Coronation*, pp. 54–6.
[15] Howden, vol. III, pp. 9, 11; Carpenter, 'Burial', pp. 430–1, 440–3.
[16] Carpenter, 'Burial', pp. 446, 448–52.

invaders in 869.[17] Edmund's cult had made the abbey one of the richest and most privileged in the land. The kings of England had associated themselves with the martyr, including rulers from the eleventh century onwards: Cnut, Harold II, and in particular Edward the Confessor, who had exempted the lands of St Edmund from all royal taxes and impositions. After the Norman Conquest, William the Conqueror, Henry I, Henry II, and Richard I can be added to the list. John confirmed his predecessors' gifts.[18]

Again, John's pilgrimage may have been influenced by his immediate forebears. Gransden has argued that the 'Angevin kings had a reverence for St Edmund only exceeded by their reverence for St Thomas of Canterbury.' Henry II made at least two pilgrimages to St Edmund's shrine, shortly after Easter, 1177, and in 1188 within a month of assuming the cross of a crusader. Henry also gave a golden chalice to the abbey. His forces fought under the saint's banner in 1173, with victory attributed to Edmund's aid.[19] The royal pilgrimage of 1177 bears comparison with John's in 1201. Before Easter, Henry accompanied Count Philip of Flanders to Becket's shrine at Canterbury. After Easter, he made his own pilgrimage to Bury St Edmunds, then travelled to St Etheldreda's shrine at Ely.[20]

Richard I likewise expressed his devotions at Bury. As John would do in 1199, after his coronation (1189), Richard 'piously sought after St Edmund for the purpose of prayer'. He made gifts in honour of the saint, and was probably at Bury on Edmund's feast day, 20 November.[21] In 1190, the Lionheart placed his crusading fleet under St Edmund's protection, alongside St Thomas and St Nicholas, and the three saints were reported to have confirmed their backing in a vision experienced by one of the king's followers *en route*. Richard also presented the abbey with the banner captured from the Cypriot ruler Isaac Comnenus.[22] Just as he visited Canterbury almost as soon as he landed in England in 1194, Richard was recorded at Bury St Edmunds within a week of his return.[23]

John's post-coronation pilgrimage in June 1199 was therefore part of an Angevin tradition. It linked the beginning of his rule to two royal saints – Edward and Edmund – and to St Thomas, already the foremost cult in England. He may also have prayed at the tomb of St Alban, the third-century saint regarded as the first British martyr. This would have been wise in terms of securing favour at the abbey. Amongst John's predecessors, William Rufus was remembered at St Alban's

---

[17] GR, p. 92; *Radulfi de Diceto*, vol. II, p. 166; *Jocelin of Brakelond*, pp. 102–3. On St Edmund: Farmer, *Oxford Dictionary of Saints*, pp. 151–2.

[18] Webb, *Pilgrimage*, p. 25; A. Gransden, *A History of the Abbey of Bury St Edmunds 1182–1256: Samson of Tottington to Edmund of Walpole* (Woodbridge, 2007), p. 60; RC, p. 38a–b.

[19] Gransden, *History of the Abbey of Bury*, p. 63.

[20] Webb, *Pilgrimage*, p. 115. Webb describes 1177 as the 'annus mirabilis' of Henry II as a pilgrim: he planned to go to Compostela, and also paid his respects to relics of St Petroc. Etheldreda's shrine was not included in John's pilgrimage of 1201.

[21] Coggeshall, p. 97; Gransden, *History of the Abbey of Bury*, p. 63; Landon, *Itinerary*, p. 16.

[22] Gransden, *History of the Abbey of Bury*, p. 63; Gillingham, *Richard*, p. 147; Webb, *Pilgrimage*, p. 160.

[23] Landon, *Itinerary*, p. 85.

in the thirteenth century as a persecutor of the church who died as a result of the saint's intervention.²⁴ Roger of Wendover claims that John visited after the coronation. This is not referred to in other sources, but seems likely. The king's itinerary from Northampton (7 and 9 June 1199) to Westminster (11 June) probably took him past St Albans, providing context for the charter issued at Westminster on 11 June, confirming the abbey's possessions. This referred to the redemption of John's soul and of the souls of his parents.²⁵ The king then continued to Canterbury. Taken as a whole, his journey resonated with historical associations between crown and church. It is noteworthy that the king felt it necessary to undertake this spiritual journey at the outset of the reign, prioritised ahead of pressing territorial concerns. After completing the pilgrimage, John hastened to Normandy to secure his continental inheritance.

In making his combined pilgrimage, John was not simply going through the motions of appropriate behaviour for a newly crowned king. This is shown by its repetition on at least two occasions. In 1201, his route south from Northumberland and Yorkshire brought him to Bury St Edmunds on 19 March. Within a week he was at Canterbury. On Easter Day (25 March), he and his queen were crowned by Archbishop Hubert Walter, who went to 'great, not to say superfluous expense, in entertaining them'. Four days after leaving Canterbury, John was at Westminster. This was a pilgrimage made during the most important period in the religious calendar – the fortnight between Palm Sunday and the first Sunday after Easter. Again, John visited three of the most important shrine sites in England. Here, there is evidence of how royal religion and affairs of state were often intertwined. The king's presence at Canterbury provided the opportunity for reconciliation with Archbishop Hubert, who had angered John at Christmas with celebrations matching those of the king. The Easter crown-wearing perhaps represented mutual recognition of the status of both parties.²⁶

A similar pilgrimage occurred prior to Christmas 1203, following John's return from over eighteen months on the Continent. He arrived in England on the feast of St Nicholas (6 December), went to St Edmunds on 18 and 19 December, and then to St Thomas' shrine at Canterbury on Christmas Day.²⁷ The three saints days involved here were those invoked by Richard I to protect his journey to the Holy Land. In 1203, visits by John to Westminster or St Albans are not recorded, but both locations occur on the king's likely route.²⁸ Whilst at Bury St Edmunds,

---

24 S. J. Ridyard, 'Condigna Veneratio: Post-Conquest Attitudes to the Saints of the Anglo-Saxons', ANS, 9 (1987), 179–206 (p. 190); Gesta Abbatum, vol. I, p. 65.
25 Wendover, vol. I, p. 288; 'Itinerary'; Cartae Antiquae Rolls 1–10, pp. 18–20 (no. 37). On St Alban: Farmer, Oxford Dictionary of Saints, pp. 10–11.
26 Annales S. Edmundi a. 1–1212, ed. F. Liebermann, Ungedruckte Anglo-Normannische Geschichtsquellen (Strasbourg, 1879), p. 139; Wendover, vol. I, p. 311; Radulfi de Diceto, vol. II, p. 172; GR, p. 93; Howden, vol. IV, p. 160; 'Itinerary'.
27 Annales S. Edmundi, p. 143; Itinerary; Wendover, vol. I, p. 320.
28 Assuming either that his route from Newbury (Berkshire) to Ongar (Essex) took him through London, and therefore Westminster, or that travelling from Lilley (Hertfordshire) to Canterbury took him through Westminster and St Albans: 'Itinerary'.

he granted ten marks annually for the repair of the saint's shrine, money given in lieu of an offering of a ruby and sapphire in Edmund's honour. John had opted to retain these stones during his lifetime, but they were to be transferred to the abbey on his death.[29] It seems that the precious stones were given to the abbey when John died. In 1234, Henry III requested that the sapphire previously loaned to John should now be loaned to William (IV), earl of Warenne.[30]

These pilgrimages seem as significant as those made after John's coronation. His return to England in December 1203 created the impression that he had abandoned Normandy. However, in early 1204, John began preparations to lead an army to the duchy, only thwarted by the momentum of Philip II's successful advance.[31] John's pilgrimages perhaps sought combined saintly intercession to support his renewed campaign. His presence at Bury and at Canterbury suggests an appeal to two saints associated with Angevin military activity. Both St Edmund and St Thomas had apparently interceded for Henry II during the Great Rebellion of 1173–74. John faced a similarly serious situation, but with the right backing it was not irrevocable.

Thus John emulated his Anglo-Norman and Angevin predecessors and responded to the needs of the moment. His interest in these shrine-sites apparently continued across the reign. He visited Bury for three days in 1205, and again in 1214 and 1216. In 1214, this was clearly linked to the disputed election of Abbot Samson's successor, with the king entering the chapter house to negotiate with the monks. Here, John observed that he came to the meeting only 'after performing my pilgrimage'.[32] His grants to Bury also included renewal of Richard I's provision for lights to burn around St Edmund's shrine, a grant honoured annually under John.[33] Notably, following the royal seizure of church property after the imposition of the interdict (1208), John returned the possessions of Bury St Edmunds on account of his reverence for the saint.[34] Although this sounds like a formula, such wording is rare, if not unique, amongst property returns of this time. Three centuries later, under Henry VIII, both Richard I and John were remembered as donors to the abbey.[35]

For Westminster and the cult of the Confessor, the evidence is harder to interpret because the king's frequent presence was usually not linked to religious concerns. That said, John was at Westminster on the feast of St Edward's

---

[29] *RLP*, p. 37b; *RC*, p. 114b. The Close Rolls for 14, 15, and 16 John record payments suggesting fulfilment of this grant: *RLC 1204–24*, pp. 125b, 153b, 176a.

[30] *CPR Henry III. 1232–1247*, HMSO (London, 1906), p. 43.

[31] Webster, 'King John and Rouen', pp. 314–15.

[32] 'Itinerary'; *The Chronicle of the Election of Hugh Abbot of Bury St Edmunds and later Bishop of Ely*, ed. and trans. R. M. Thomson, OMT (Oxford, 1974), pp. 118–19.

[33] *RC*, p. 38a-b; *PR 1 John*, p. 262; *PR 2 John*, p. 129; *PR 3 John*, p. 127; *PR 4 John*, p. 103; *PR 5 John*, p. 235; *PR 6 John*, p. 233; *PR 7 John*, pp. 240, 241; *PR 8 John*, p. 21; *PR 9 John*, p. 166; *PR 10 John*, p. 1; *PR 11 John*, pp. 38, 39; *PR 12 John*, p. 42; *PR 13 John*, p. 13; *PR 14 John*, p. 170; *PR 16 John*, p. 167.

[34] *Annales S. Edmundi*, pp. 146–7.

[35] *Valor Ecclesiasticus*, vol. III, pp. 461–4.

translation (13 October) in 1204 and 1213. Within weeks of the 1204 visit, the king issued a charter confirming the abbey's possession of Islip (Oxfordshire), the manor where the saint was born. Islip had probably been granted by the Confessor himself, but had passed out of the abbey's control. Opportunity for the monks to reclaim it came in 1203, when the then landholder Robert de Courcy defected from John's camp to that of Philip II of France.[36] John's grant was appropriate both given his presence at Westminster, and as a king seeking intercession for recovery of lost lands. However, if he was inspired by devotion to the Confessor, this did not prevent the levying of two hundred marks for the concession.[37] A more positive conclusion seems possible for John's visit in 1213. On 11 October, two days prior to the feast of the Confessor, the papal legate, Cardinal-Bishop Nicholas of Tusculum, issued a twenty-day indulgence to all who visited the abbey on the feasts of St Peter, St Edward, and the holy relics.[38] John was well placed to take advantage of this remission of penance.

Further tentative evidence of a bond between the king and the Westminster monks is suggested by John's renewal of various exemptions made by Richard I for the souls of their parents. In the civil war which followed Magna Carta, the abbey remained loyal to the king. In October 1215, John ordered his soldiers not to enter the abbey precincts, church, or cemetery – in contrast to what they got away with elsewhere.[39] When Louis of France occupied London in 1216, Westminster was one of only five churches in (or near) the city to uphold John's claims. By contrast, Louis was received at St Paul's Cathedral by a procession of the clergy and people.[40]

The prominence of St Edmund and St Edward in the pilgrimages of John's early years as king suggests his awareness of the significance of association with saintly predecessors and kinsmen, perhaps emphasising the sort of rule he hoped to practice. Both saints were seen as exemplary figures in eleventh- and twelfth-century courtly literature.[41] Did John hope also to foster a cult of sanctified kingship?

---

36 'Itinerary'; RC, 139b; *Westminster Abbey Charters 1066–c.1214*, ed. E. Mason, London Record Society Publications, 25 (London, 1988), p. 78 (no. 149). On treatment of Robert de Courcy's lands: *The 'Lands of the Normans' in England (1204–1244)* [http://www.hrionline.ac.uk/normans/appearances.jsp?person=187, accessed 20 December 2012].

37 Carpenter, 'Henry III and St Edward', p. 866. Although the Confessor's grant was probably genuine, Westminster Abbey possessed forged charters of Edward and of William I relating to Islip, perhaps produced when petitioning John: *Westminster Abbey Charters*, pp. 26 (no. 3), 78 (no. 149). See also E. Mason, *Westminster Abbey and its People c. 1050–c. 1216* (Woodbridge, 1996), pp. 73–4, 160–1.

38 *Westminster Abbey Charters*, pp. 92–3 (no. 193).

39 *Westminster Abbey Charters*, pp. 76 (no. 142), 79 (no. 151); RLP, pp. 157b–158a. John's order of 1215 was issued whilst besieging Rochester, where his army was said to have camped in the cathedral: Coggeshall, p. 176.

40 Stanley, pp. 522–3; *Histoire des ducs de Normandie et des rois d'Angleterre*, ed. F. Michel (Paris, 1840), pp. 171–2. The latter lists the other four churches as Holy Trinity (Aldgate, founded by Henry I's queen Matilda), St Martin-le-Viel (*sic*), possibly St Martin-le-Grand, a royal free chapel, and the churches of the Temple and the Hospital. For the rewards of Westminster's loyalty: EEA 26, pp. lvii, 175–8 (nos 205–6).

41 S. Waugh, 'Histoire, hagiographie et le souverain idéal à la cour des Plantagenêt', *Plantagenêts*

Alongside his pilgrimages to royal shrines, the Canterbury crown-wearing of 1201 might seem to support this argument, suggesting emphasis on royal status and the deference to be shown to a king. However, it is not clear that John prioritised royal saints. Instead, he saw them as equally important as saints such as Becket. His pilgrimages to Canterbury came at important times in the religious calendar, including solemnities most closely associated with the life, death, and resurrection of Christ. In 1199, John is recorded in the city on 12 June, the eve of Trinity Sunday, a feast observed in England in this period, and promoted by Becket himself.[42] His visits coincided with Easter Day in 1201 and Christmas Day in 1203. On each, John spent an important religious day at Canterbury, rather than at the sites of the royal shrines at Bury St Edmunds or Westminster.

John's grants to Canterbury Cathedral further suggest his reverence for the saints buried there. Two confirmation charters were issued out of reverence for the Blessed Thomas and all the saints whose relics were buried there – further indication of John seeking the combined, rather than individual, intercession of the saints.[43] As with St Edmund, support was not confined to confirmations issued during his first months as king. In October 1201, John confirmed quittance of customs granted by Henry II (and also confirmed by Richard I) on one hundred measures of wine given to the Canterbury monks by King Louis VII of France when he came to Canterbury on pilgrimage in 1179. John's predecessors' letters were issued for the love of God and of St Thomas. Here, and in 1204, John's charters spoke of his reverence for the saint.[44] This is hardly religious giving on the scale of Henry III, but as evidence for John's religious activity it suggests veneration of St Thomas in the early years of his reign, and stands up to comparison with John's largesse to Bury St Edmunds and Westminster Abbey.

It seems, therefore, that Canterbury, and the shrine of St Thomas, stood *alongside* the royal cults in John's efforts to secure saintly intercession, that the king attached as much importance to cults of major canonised churchmen as he did to those of important royal saints. Canterbury, site of the premier cathedral church and foremost shrine in England, was an appropriate place for a king to express his devotion and to mark major religious occasions. Perhaps this helps to explain John's strategy in his early years as king. He did not intend to support one saint or group of saints to the exclusion of all others. Thus there was nothing contradictory in venerating St Edmund, St Edward, *and* St Thomas, and in coming to Canterbury for major feast days.

This conclusion contradicts the suggestion that John sought to foster the cult

---

et Capétiens: confrontations et héritages , ed. M. Aurell and N.-Y. Tonnerre (Turnhout, 2006), pp. 429-46 (pp. 430-1, 435-9).

[42] 'Itinerary'. For Becket's promotion of Trinity Sunday: B. Golding, *Gilbert of Sempringham and the Gilbertine Order, c. 1130–c. 1300* (Oxford, 1995), pp. 223-4. Jocelin of Brakelond refers to the 'office' observed on Trinity Sunday. The Stanley annalist noted the feast as the day of Langton's consecration as Archbishop in 1207: *Jocelin of Brakelond*, p. 23; Stanley, p. 509.

[43] RC, pp. 22b, 23a.

[44] *Norman Charters from English Sources*, pp. 217-20 (nos 91-3); RC, p. 138a.

of sanctified kingship.⁴⁵ That this comes as a surprise is due to the longstanding currency of J. C. Russell's theory, first put forward in 1929, that St Thomas was the first and foremost of a 'noteworthy series of contemporary anti-royal leaders who were honoured, partially at least, as saints', in whom 'resistance to the king had been canonised'. Russell argued that as 'saints ranked higher than kings in the Middle Ages', the crown might counteract this 'by weighting the balance of saint-hood on their own side'.⁴⁶ Certainly, rebels against the crown might invoke the aid of St Thomas. Furthermore, Henry II sought the benefits of a canonised ancestor when he supported the campaign to make Edward the Confessor a saint, and association between the royal saint and the crown is clear in Henry III's rebuilding at Westminster. It is tempting to see John's actions in a similar way. However, we should be wary of imposing unity on these activities: there was no long-term plan to marginalise the Canterbury saints, as the devotions of Henry II, Richard I, and John demonstrate. Even Henry III's commitment to the Confessor was not to the exclusion of Becket. The compatibility of the cults had been demonstrated to Henry in 1220. Between mid-May and early July Archbishop Langton master-minded the king's re-coronation at Westminster, followed by the translation of the relics of St Thomas to their new shrine at Canterbury.⁴⁷ The possibilities for parallel devotion to the two saints were not lost on Henry in later years. In addition to lavish patronage of Westminster, he emulated his predecessors in coming to Canterbury and making offerings there. He celebrated his marriage to Eleanor of Provence at Canterbury in 1236.⁴⁸

John's early pilgrimages as king demonstrate similar awareness of the potential for combined intercession of the saints. The dispute over Hubert Walter's successor at Canterbury, and the ensuing interdict, would have provided the perfect excuse to promote sanctified royalty. There is no evidence that John tried to do so. Indeed, for much of the reign, a bishop, St Wulfstan of Worcester, beside whose tomb the king chose to be buried, ranked highly amongst his preferred saints.

John's interest in Wulfstan became prominent after the loss of Normandy. This has been seen to reflect realisation that the future of Angevin kingship lay in the crown's English possessions.⁴⁹ Yet this assumes that John accepted what others may have been quicker to recognise. The campaigns he launched, or attempted to launch, to recover his continental lands do not suggest a willingness to acknowledge

---

45 For a similar view: R. Eales, 'The Political Setting of the Becket Translation of 1220', *Martyrs and Martyrologies*, ed. D. Wood, SCH 30 (1993), pp. 127-39 (esp. pp. 138-9).

46 J. C. Russell, 'The Canonization of Opposition to the King in Angevin England', *Twelfth Century Studies*, J. C. Russell (New York, 1978), pp. 248-60 (pp. 249, 250, 256).

47 Eales, 'Political Setting', pp. 127-39.

48 A. J. Duggan, 'The Cult of St Thomas Becket in the Thirteenth Century', *St Thomas Cantilupe Bishop of Hereford: Essays in his Honour*, ed. M. Jancey (Leominster, 1982), pp. 21-44 (p. 31); Binski, *Westminster Abbey*, p. 4. For some of Henry's gifts in honour of Becket: CLR 1226-1240, pp. 356, 404, 488; CLR 1240-1245, p. 17; CR 1237-1242, HMSO (London, 1911), pp. 175, 181, 208, 227.

49 Draper, p. 48.

that Philip II's conquests were permanent. Recognition of the Capetian achievement did not come until well into the reign of Henry III. Similarly, although John's decision to be buried next to Wulfstan's shrine is widely seen to demonstrate his attachment to the cult, in many ways this choice was dictated by the territorial situation in the final days of the reign, perhaps determined as much by the bishops surrounding John on his deathbed as by the king.[50] Once again, this aspect of royal religious activity needs setting in its wider context.

Wulfstan, bishop of Worcester 1062-95, was the last Anglo-Saxon bishop. Although the Worcester monks cultivated local devotion from the time of his death, and a failed canonisation attempt was made in 1147, the cult did not receive publicity from the bishops of Worcester until the episcopate of Roger of Gloucester (1163-79), cousin of Henry II.[51] Roger's career illustrates the diplomatic challenges facing a bishop with loyalties to both crown and church during the Becket dispute, and his promotion of Wulfstan should probably be seen in the context of the exponential growth of the Becket phenomenon after 1170. Archbishop Thomas had himself created an association in 1163, claiming, as fee for participating in the translation of the Confessor, the relic of the tombstone in which Wulfstan had wedged his staff during a supposed encounter with William the Conqueror.[52] In 1198, reported visions persuaded John de Coutances (bishop of Worcester 1196-98) to carry out a nocturnal translation of the saint's bones and the vestments in which he was buried.[53] Bishop John died a few weeks later, but after new miracles, and the fire which swept the cathedral in 1202, Mauger (bishop of Worcester, 1200-1212), petitioned for Wulfstan's official canonisation. He was declared a saint by Pope Innocent III on 21 April 1203.[54]

John can hardly have been unaware of the developing cult, particularly as moves to secure Wulfstan's canonisation gathered pace. His first recorded visit as king came in April 1200, when relics of the bishop may have been on display on the cathedral's high altar.[55] The king was overseas at the time of the canonisation. His first opportunities to pay his respects to the new saint would have been his visits to the city in March and August 1204, when his court dealt with business

---

[50] Discussed further below, Chapter 8.
[51] E. Mason, *St Wulfstan of Worcester c. 1008-1095* (Oxford, 1990), pp. 277-80; Mason, 'Wulfstan's Staff', p. 158.
[52] Mason, *St Wulfstan*, p. 284; M. G. Cheney, 'Roger (c. 1134-1179)', *ODNB* (Oxford, 2004) [http://www.oxforddnb.com/view/article/23960, accessed 14 March 2011]; Mason, 'Wulfstan's Staff', pp. 158-79.
[53] P. Hoskin, 'Coutances, John de (d. 1198)', *ODNB* (Oxford, 2008) [http://www.oxforddnb.com/view/article/95187, accessed 8 March 2011]; Mason, *St Wulfstan*, p. 278. A nocturnal shrine-opening also occurred at Bury St Edmunds in 1198: *Jocelin of Brakelond*, pp. 98-102.
[54] Mason, *St Wulfstan*, pp. 278-80; *LPI*, pp. 77-8 (no. 472).
[55] 'Itinerary'; Draper, p. 45. Bishop John had placed the relics on the high altar, provoking widespread criticism. In 1201, prior to petitioning for canonisation, Bishop Mauger returned the bones to their tomb: Mason, *St Wulfstan*, pp. 278-9; J. Crook, 'The Physical Setting of the Cult of St Wulfstan', *St Wulfstan and his World*, ed. J. S. Barrow and N. P. Brooks (Aldershot, 2005), pp. 189-217 (p. 208).

involving the prior and monks.⁵⁶ His subsequent devotion to Wulfstan is best demonstrated in his visit to Worcester in 1207. Upon arrival at the cathedral, John was received by a solemn procession, before apparently being allowed an interlude in which 'he prayed a while at the tomb of the blessed Wulfstan' – a glimpse not only of the personal devotions of a king, but also of a ruler fulfilling expectations of how he should behave when visiting a Benedictine church.⁵⁷ Perhaps in return for being given time and space to pray, John responded favourably when Prior Ralph requested privileges in the manors of Lindridge, Wolverley, Stoke Prior, and Cleeve Prior. The king also pardoned one hundred marks which should have been paid in return for these rights, with the money to be put towards refurbishment of the cloister at Worcester.⁵⁸ Presumably this was a contribution to the repair and rebuilding programme that followed the 1202 fire.

Wulfstan was a saint equipped with royal associations, evident before and after the Norman Conquest. At his consecration (1062), he received his episcopal ring and staff from Edward the Confessor. He was clearly respected in elite circles, acting as confessor and spiritual adviser to Harold II before and during the latter's brief reign. As earl of Wessex, Harold had perhaps helped secure Wulfstan's election as bishop.⁵⁹ Wulfstan promoted prayers for the ruling dynasty during William the Conqueror's reign, establishing a monastic confraternity league whose values corresponded closely to those of the tenth-century *Regularis Concordia*, which attached great importance to prayers for the king and queen. Indeed, the bishop's monastic schooling in the principles of the latter document may help explain his adaptability to the changing fortunes of the English throne.⁶⁰

Association between Wulfstan and the crown is also seen in the legend which developed around his cult. An appointee of the Anglo-Saxon kings, he was said to have been confronted in Westminster Abbey by William the Conqueror and Archbishop Lanfranc, who demanded his resignation. Wulfstan retorted that he would only do so to the person who had made him bishop, plunging his staff into Edward the Confessor's tomb. He then proved to be the only person capable of removing it, and was allowed to retain his bishopric.⁶¹ The origins of the story lay in the writing of Osbert of Clare, the Westminster monk who first attempted to secure King Edward's canonisation in 1139. Osbert, in typical fashion, conflated various accounts to suit his purpose. He used legends associated with a different Wulfstan, archbishop of York and bishop of Worcester (in plurality) in the early

---

56 'Itinerary'; *Worcester Cartulary*, pp. 114-15 (no. 216).

57 Worcester, p. 395. On reception of guests: *The Monastic Constitutions of Lanfranc*, ed. and trans. D. Knowles, rev. edn C. N. L. Brooke, OMT (Oxford, 2002), pp. 105-9.

58 RC, p. 168b; *Worcester Cartulary*, pp. 171-2 (no. 326); RLC 1204-24, p. 96a; PR 9 John, p. 200; ROF, pp. 397-8.

59 Mason, *St Wulfstan*, pp. 66, 84; Mason, 'Wulfstan's Staff', p. 176 n. 108.

60 E. Mason, 'St Oswald and St Wulfstan', *St Oswald of Worcester: Life and Influence*, ed. N. Brooks and C. Cubitt (London and New York, 1996), pp. 269-84 (pp. 274-5); Mason, *St Wulfstan*, pp. 92, 197-201; Kobialka, *This Is My Body*, pp. 58-9, 95.

61 'La Vie de S. Edouard le Confesseur par Osbert de Clare', ed. M. Bloch, *Analecta Bollandiana*, 41 (1923), 5-131 (pp. 116-20); Mason, 'Wulfstan's Staff', pp. 157-71; Draper, p. 84.

eleventh century.⁶² These were combined with knowledge of a dispute between the later Bishop Wulfstan and Archbishop Thomas of York which culminated in favour of the former at the royal court in 1072.⁶³ By John's reign, the legend of Wulfstan's staff was an established part of the *miraculae* of St Edward, and one of the most popular miracles associated with Wulfstan.⁶⁴

One chronicle suggests that John knew of the example, one highly relevant to the issue of authority in the disputed election to the archbishopric of Canterbury that led to the interdict.⁶⁵ John surely saw the legend as illustrative of Wulfstan's belief that only a king could appoint a bishop. Mason suggests that this then explains the king's insistence on burial next to Wulfstan's tomb.⁶⁶ This is possible. John's association with the saint made Worcester an appropriate location for him to be interred. However, the choice was equally dictated by the territorial situation in 1216.⁶⁷ Nor does the saint's appeal to John during the Canterbury crisis explain his devotions at Worcester before he fell out with the church. Mason also proposes that the king's attachment to Wulfstan prompted his son's interest in the Anglo-Saxon saints.⁶⁸ However, such devotion, for instance to St Edward and St Edmund, was an aspect of royal religion which John inherited from his predecessors. Kingly devotion to Wulfstan was a new trend, but Henry III's religious activity should be seen in its longer-term context.

As with Becket and the royal cults, we should be wary of thinking St Wulfstan was adopted by the king to the exclusion of others, or of seeing John as latching on to cults on an issue by issue basis. The Worcester evidence demonstrates royal desire for intercession from a plurality of saints. Although John visited Worcester regularly, he was never there on the feast days of its two Anglo-Saxon saints: Wulfstan and Oswald (bishop of Worcester, 961–92, and archbishop of York 971–92). Instead, he often coincided with feast days of saints such as Mary and Peter, both associated with Worcester Cathedral. Observance of feasts of the Virgin had been introduced to the cathedral during Wulfstan's episcopate.⁶⁹ King John was in Worcester on the feast of the Assumption (15 August) in 1204, the Nativity of the Virgin (8 September) in 1207, the Visitation (2 July) in 1208, and, in 1209, the Purification (2 February). In 1212, he was present in the city on the feast of St Peter in Chains (1 August). John was there again at Christmas in 1214.⁷⁰

Unfortunately, no evidence survives for royal offerings or alms payments on

---

⁶² P. Wormald, 'Wulfstan (d. 1023)', *ODNB* (Oxford, 2004) [http://www.oxforddnb.com/view/article/30098, accessed 15 January 2013].

⁶³ Mason, 'Wulfstan's Staff', pp. 163–5.

⁶⁴ *Life of St Edward*, pp. 103–7; Mason, 'Wulfstan's Staff', p. 162.

⁶⁵ *Annales de Burton (A.D. 1004–1263)*, ed. H. R. Luard, *Annales Monastici*, RS 36, 5 vols (London, 1864–69), vol. I, p. 211; discussed further below, Chapter 7.

⁶⁶ E. Mason, 'Wulfstan [St Wulfstan] (c. 1008–1095)', *ODNB* (Oxford, 2004), [http://www.oxforddnb.com/view/article/30099, accessed 23 February 2011].

⁶⁷ Discussed further below, Chapter 8.

⁶⁸ Mason, *St Wulfstan*, p. 283; Mason, 'Wulfstan's Staff', p. 171.

⁶⁹ Knowles and Hadcock, p. 81; Worcester, p. 409; Mason, *St Wulfstan*, pp. 19–20, 130, 283.

⁷⁰ 'Itinerary'. For 1207: Worcester, p. 395.

these occasions. With the exception of the king's prayers at Wulfstan's shrine in 1207 and the grants that followed, it is unclear whether John was present in Worcester Cathedral. However, the coincidence of Marian feast days, in particular, seems striking. Royal offerings were made on other occasions, for instance in March 1204, when John gave a pall to the cathedral. This was perhaps impromptu. The item was leant to the king by the sacristan of Worcester. Two marks were paid a few days later to cover the transaction.[71] Perhaps the king had learnt of the fall of Château-Gaillard (Normandy) to Philip II of France, and sought intercession for the reversal of his increasingly desperate overseas fortunes.[72] Whether or not this was the case, the example adds to the sense that John's visits to Worcester were accompanied by appropriate devotional responses: observance of feast days, offerings, prayers at the shrines of the saints.

The potential link between the king's presence at Worcester and feast days of the Virgin Mary raises the wider question of the extent to which he sought intercession of the principal Christian saints. Devotion to Christ's mother was a feature of religious expression in England in the eleventh and early twelfth centuries.[73] Amongst kings, Henry I is said to have prayed to Mary and to have insisted that the feast of the Conception (8 December) be observed at his foundation, Reading Abbey. Henry II travelled to the Marian shrine at Rocamadour in 1170, whilst his reign contained several royal actions which took place on feast days of the saint. Richard I actively promoted fundraising by the canons of Chartres, who took their relics of the Virgin on tour following the cathedral fire of 1194.[74] Henry III expressed sustained and deep devotion to Mary throughout his life.[75] It would be surprising, therefore, if devotion to the Virgin did not play some part in John's religious activity.

An association can be suggested as early as 1187, when John allegedly claimed a relic of a miracle working statue of the Virgin at Déols (near Châteauroux). Mercenaries billed in Déols by John's brother Richard had pillaged the town and were ordered to burn it, along with the abbey there, one of the richest in Aquitaine. The local population, barred from the abbey church, gathered at its doors, where a stone statue of the Virgin Mary provided the focus for their prayers and lamentations. They were interrupted by the soldiers, one of whom grabbed a stone and hurled it against the sculpture, severing the Christ Child's arm. Blood sprang from the statue and the mercenary responsible was immediately struck dead. The next morning the stone arm was recovered, still warm and red with blood. An 'illustrious person', said to be John, claimed the relic. Whilst this is unproven,

---

71 RL, p. 84; PR 6 John, p. 89.
72 Harvey, 'Piety', p. 29. Château-Gaillard fell on 6 March. John was at Worcester on 16 March. If the Worcester offering was linked to this news, messengers covered 300 miles in 10 days, including a channel crossing, to reach the king.
73 Vincent, 'Mary', p. 128. See also E. Bishop, 'On the Origins of the Feast of the Conception of the Blessed Virgin Mary', *Liturgica Historica: Papers on the Liturgy and Religious Life of the Western Church*, E. Bishop (Oxford, 1918), pp. 238-59.
74 Vincent, 'Mary', pp. 128-31; Mason, 'Rocamadour', pp. 39-54.
75 Vincent, 'Mary', pp. 133-46.

it is noteworthy that near-contemporary writers associated the future king with devotion to the Virgin. The statue also reputedly moved and bared its breast, with Richard threatening to use his sword to prove the authenticity of the miracles to doubters. Henry II and his sons were amongst the first to visit the monastery as the furore continued, and a truce between the kings of England and France quickly followed.[76]

In terms of further possible evidence, John's decision to found a Cistercian abbey, early in his reign, automatically meant a community dedicated to the Virgin.[77] In addition, an open letter was issued by the king in 1205, supporting rebuilding work at Lincoln Cathedral. Here, John thanked the diocese for its contributions, but urged that more was needed to complete construction. Recipients were to respond 'for the sake of God and for the honour of the glorious Virgin' (*divino intuitu et pro honore gloriose Virginis*). The letter concluded that giving to a project in honour of such an excellent patron would surely be rewarded with a place in heaven.[78]

We have seen that John was frequently at Worcester on Marian feast days. This may reflect a wider pattern, in which he was present at the location of major churches, or those dedicated to the Virgin, on at least one of the saint's feast days each year.[79] Before 1204, John was regularly at Rouen on Marian feast days. He was there on the feast of the Annunciation (25 March) 1190, and the feast of her Nativity (8 September) in 1196.[80] As king, he was in Rouen on the eve of the Visitation in 1199 and 1202, and on the feast day itself (2 July) in 1203. In 1201, he was there on 9 December, the day following the feast of the Conception. Thus, Rouen seems a focal location for John's devotion to Mary. He was also in the city on the feasts of St Peter in Chains (1 August) 1199, Trinity Sunday (9 June) 1202, and St Peter and St Paul (29 June) 1203.

In 1199 and 1202, John was in Rouen on the feast of the city's patron, St Ouen (24 August).[81] This cult had associations with the rulers of Normandy believed to date to the period of the foundation of the duchy. This heritage might have

---

[76] J. Hubert, 'Le miracle de Déols et la trêve conclue en 1187 entre les rois de France et d'Angleterre', *Bibliothèque de l'Ecole des Chartes*, 96 (1935), pp. 285-300 (pp. 291-6, 298-300). For the claim that John took the relic: *Oeuvres de Rigord et de Guillaume le Breton, historiens de Philippe-Auguste*, ed. H. F. Delaborde, 2 vols (Paris, 1882-85), vol. I, pp. 79-80. Not all writers agreed: Hubert notes Gervase of Canterbury's opinion that it was taken by Adhémar V, Count of Limoges.

[77] Vincent, 'Mary', pp. 132-3. On Beaulieu Abbey, see below, Chapter 3.

[78] *RLP*, p. 57a.

[79] Based on analysis of 'Itinerary'. The conclusion applies to years for which the itinerary is sufficiently documented. The exceptions are 1211, 1215 (when John's presence at Rochester on the feast of the Presentation coincided with the royal siege of the castle), and 1216, although in the latter year the king was in Worcester the day after the feast of the Assumption. Further analysis will appear in: P. Webster, 'Making Space for King John to Pray: The Evidence of the Royal Itinerary', *Journeying Along Medieval Routes*, ed. A. L. Gascoigne, L. V. Hicks, and M. O'Doherty (Turnhout, forthcoming).

[80] Drawn from the itinerary compiled in: *Mortain*.

[81] 'Itinerary'.

been important to John as the successor of the early dukes. It could, however, have evoked mixed feelings amongst the monks of the Abbey of St Ouen, since William the Bastard had translated the saint's relics to Caen in 1047, as he sought to cement his authority in central and western Normandy.[82] Whilst this might have increased the saint's appeal to John as he fought to maintain control over the duchy, the community at St Ouen apparently sensed that Angevin fortunes were on the wane. In 1202, and therefore prior to the 'loss' of Normandy, they leased their lands in England to William de Ste-Mère-Eglise, bishop of London. This arrangement was renegotiated and extended in 1205, and confirmed by King John himself in 1206.[83]

Nonetheless, prior to the losses of 1204, Rouen, as ducal capital and archiepiscopal seat, with houses dedicated to the saints concerned, was an appropriate place for the king to spend major feast days. John knew the importance of the city's cathedral. A charter of 1200 noted: 'we ought to venerate the church of Rouen above all other churches of Normandy, and to love and keep it as the mother of all the churches of Normandy and as the one from which we and our predecessors received the honour of our dukedom'.[84] As at Worcester, there is no evidence for offerings or alms payments on these occasions, but the coincidence of the king's presence with major feast days again seems striking.

Further examples suggest that John favoured the cults of major saints. In 1204, he was at Westminster on the feast of the Annunciation (25 March). The abbey possessed various relics of Our Lady, including a piece of her girdle, supposedly given by Edward the Confessor, and relics allegedly given by Thomas Becket.[85] So royal devotion to a combination of saints again seems possible. A second example comes from the feast of the Conception of the Virgin (8 December) 1214, when John was at Reading Abbey, a royal foundation which by this time claimed relics of Mary including her hair, bed and belt.[86] Later that year, John was at Charroux in Poitou on the feast of the Assumption (15 August), perhaps visiting the Abbey of Saint-Sauveur, which housed numerous relics, including a piece of the True Cross.[87] Again, this suggests potential for combined devotion to the saints. In

---

[82] L. Trân-Duc, 'Les princes normands et les reliques (X^e-XIe siècles). Contribution du culte des saints à la formation territoriale et identitaire d'une principauté', *Reliques et sainteté dans l'espace médiéval*, ed. J.-L. Deuffic, PECIA, Ressources en médiévistique, vol. 8-11 (Saint-Denis, 2006), pp. 525-61 (pp. 526-7, 532-3, 550-1, 557-8).

[83] *EEA 26*, pp. 168-73 (nos 199-202); *RC*, p. 151b; Power, *Norman Frontier*, p. 327; Webster, 'King John and Rouen', p. 328.

[84] *RN*, pp. 2-3, trans. in Power, *Norman Frontier*, p. 62. On John and the churches of Rouen: Webster, 'King John and Rouen', pp. 326-32.

[85] Vincent, 'Mary', pp. 140-1.

[86] Vincent, 'Mary', p. 129 and n. 15; D. Bethell, 'The Making of a Twelfth-Century Relic Collection', *Popular Belief and Practice*, ed. G. J. Cuming and D. Baker, SCH 8 (Cambridge, 1972), pp. 61-72 (p. 67).

[87] 'Itinerary'; G. Augry, 'Reliques et pouvoir ducal en Aquitaine (fin X^{e}s.-1030)', *Reliques et sainteté dans l'espace médiéval*, ed. J.-L. Deuffic, PECIA, Ressources en médiévistique, vol. 8-11 (Saint-Denis, 2006), pp. 261-80 (p. 272).

1214, with his continental ambitions increasingly in tatters, John's fortunes stood in need of saintly intercession.

Surviving household rolls also suggest the place of feast days of the Virgin in the religious cycle observed at the royal court. Feasts noted in 1209–10 included those of the Assumption (15 August), Nativity (8 September), Conception (8 December), Purification (2 February), and Annunciation (25 March). The roll for 1212–13 included the Assumption, Nativity, and Purification. This was during the interdict and the period of John's excommunication. The rolls do not record royal religious activity on these dates, although on the feast of the Purification in 1213, John paid his gambling debts. This could be seen in two ways. As Vincent notes, it might suggest 'less than assiduous religious observance'. Yet the king was making recompense, and it will be seen that he diligently made reparation for his transgressions on feast days.[88]

Various examples provide further potential indication of royal devotion to the major Christian saints. In 1199 and 1202, John was at Caen, where the Conqueror's monastic foundation was dedicated to St Stephen, on the saint's feast day (26 December).[89] In 1206, William de Ste-Mère-Eglise, bishop of London, was granted the advocacy of St Osyth Abbey (Essex). The king's charter conferred the rights out of reverence for St Paul. This house had longstanding association with London's bishops. William ultimately took the habit at St Osyth's, where he died and was buried in 1224.[90] King John also offered a silk cloth at St Paul's Cathedral, on Wednesday (29 October) before the feast of All Saints in 1214.[91] This might tentatively be linked to his devotion to the saints. Additionally, in 1200, the king offered a gold chalice at the altar of St John the Baptist, at the time of Bishop Hugh's funeral in Lincoln Cathedral. Later, in 1206, John was at St Jean d'Angely on the feast of the birth of the saint (24 June). The abbey boasted a rich tradition of Aquitainian ducal patronage, closely linked to its prized relic of the Baptist's head.[92]

Meanwhile, clear evidence links John to the relics preserved at Reading Abbey. Here, we might expect him to have sought intercession from the religious and the saints. The abbey was the foundation and burial-house of his great-grandfather, Henry I.[93] Eleanor of Aquitaine had received rights of confraternity. Her father, William X of Aquitaine, had given a much prized statue of the Christ Child. John's

---

[88] Vincent, 'Mary', pp. 131–2 and n. 27; *RL*, pp. 127, 130, 141, 148, 158; *RM*, pp. 238, 240, 252–3. John's almsgiving following feast day transgressions is discussed further below, Chapter 5.

[89] 'Itinerary'.

[90] *RC*, p. 162a-b; F. A. Cazel Jr, 'Ste Mère-Église, William de (d. 1224)', *ODNB* (Oxford, 2004, online edn 2008) [http://www.oxforddnb.com/view/article/29474, accessed 21 March 2011]. See also Turner, *Men*, p. 33; D. Bethell, 'Richard of Belmeis and the Foundation of St Osyth's', *Transactions of the Essex Archaeological Society*, 3rd ser. 2, part 3 (1970), 299–328. Osyth was herself a seventh-century royal saint.

[91] *RLC 1204–24*, p. 175a.

[92] Howden, vol. IV, p. 141; 'Itinerary'; Augry, 'Reliques', pp. 265–70.

[93] *RAC1*, pp. 13–19.

eldest brother, William, was buried there, at the feet of Henry I, in 1156.[94] John supported Reading both before and after becoming king. He confirmed grants and privileges issued by the founder, by the Empress Matilda, and by Henry II – including the latter's gifts when he attended the abbey's dedication by Archbishop Becket in 1164.[95] This was despite Reading's backing for Richard I's supporters against the Count of Mortain's attempted seizure of the throne in 1194.[96] John's largesse, and that of his father, no doubt explains why both were remembered in a thirteenth-century calendar from Reading: further evidence that religious communities were prepared to honour the soul of King John.[97]

John is likely to have shown particular reverence to the abbey's prized relic, the hand of St James the Great, brought to England by the Empress Matilda on her return from Germany in 1126. Her father Henry I gave the hand to Reading, perhaps in 1133. It was removed by Henry of Blois, bishop of Winchester, King Stephen's brother, at around the time of Henry I's burial in 1136, but restored soon after Henry II's accession.[98] John's father proved a committed devotee, ordering the relic to be brought to his presence. On one of these occasions, he requested 'that he might worship it in votive devotion and be fortified by the protection and blessing of the apostle's hand before he went upon the sea'. Henry the Young King, John's brother, was also said to have refused to invest Drincourt (modern-day Neufchâtel-en-Bray) on St James's feast day in 1173.[99]

John may have known of the relic's healing powers. It was reported that when he set out for Ireland in 1185, a broken arm suffered by one of his men was healed through St James's intercession. When cured, the follower ungratefully failed to perform the pilgrimage he had promised, suffering a further break in retribution. This healed only when the penitent presented a wax image of the limb before the relics at Reading.[100] Whether or not John heard about the miracle, by the

[94] G. Constable, 'An Unpublished Letter by Abbot Hugh II of Reading Concerning Archbishop Hubert Walter', *Essays in Medieval History Presented to Bertie Wilkinson*, ed. T. A. Sandquist and M. R. Powicke (Toronto, 1969), pp. 17-31 (pp. 21-2); C. R. Cheney, 'A Monastic Letter of Confraternity to Eleanor of Aquitaine', *EHR*, 51 (1936), 488-93; Bethell, 'Twelfth-Century Relic Collection', p. 63; Leyser, 'Frederick Barbarossa', p. 497. John could not have known his brother. William died ten years before John's birth.

[95] *RAC1*, pp. 34-67 (nos 1-39, charters of John's predecessors), pp. 67-9, 412, 482 (nos 40-4, 546, 656, documents of John as Count of Mortain), 69-77, 322-5 (nos 45-50, 400-1, charters of John as king); *RC*, pp. 51a, 141b, 175a.

[96] Constable, 'Unpublished Letter', p. 23; *RAC1*, p. 161 (no. 206).

[97] Cheney, 'Monastic Letter', p. 492.

[98] *RAC1*, pp. 39-40 (no. 5); Leyser, 'Frederick Barbarossa', pp. 481-506. See also 'The Miracles of the Hand of St James', trans. B. R. Kemp, *Berkshire Archaeological Journal*, 65 (1970), 1-19; *Matthaei Parisiensis, Monachi Sancti Albani, Chronica Majora*, ed. H. R. Luard, RS 57, 7 vols (London, 1872-83), vol. II, pp. 159, 164, 210.

[99] 'Miracles of the Hand of St James', pp. 5, 11, 17, 18. In one instance, the relic generously performed miracles on its way back to Reading. At other times, relics of St Petroc housed at Reading were taken to the courts of Henry I and Henry II: Bethell, 'Twelfth-Century Relic Collection', p. 66.

[100] 'Miracles of the Hand of St James', p. 16.

early 1190s he was issuing documents to Reading that referred to the house as the 'church of St James'.[101] In one instance, he intervened when Abbot Hugh II fell into dispute with the chaplain, Bartholomew, of the abbey's church at Bucklebury. The latter resigned the church, which was restored to him at John's request.[102] His involvement might seem insignificant, but an association between the church, the relic of St James, and royal devotions already existed. Whilst returning to Reading, having taken the relic to King Henry II, presumably for the king to venerate, Abbot Roger stopped at Bucklebury. Here, the hand eradicated a plague besetting men and livestock. A memorial cross was then erected, which was promoted as a focus of pilgrimage.[103]

It is less clear that Richard I supported the cult. In 1189, the reliquary was removed to raise revenue for the crusade. A charter issued by John in 1200 referred to his brother denuding the hand of St James.[104] Thus, Reading was keen to secure grants for maintenance of its relics, as shown by the grant by Roger Bigod, earl of Norfolk (1189-1221), for repairing of shrines and reliquaries and other requirements of the high altar.[105] In 1192, John engaged in a devotional act specifically in aid of the reliquary of St James, providing revenues to fund crafting of a new cover for the relic.[106] He also provided a gold cup in 1191.[107]

Meanwhile, a gold mark was provided annually from John's exchequer as count of Mortain, a gift inaugurated in 1192 for John's wellbeing, for Henry II's soul, and at the inspiration of the hand of St James. This was confirmed after John became king.[108] Later evidence indicates the purpose. In 1290, Reading petitioned Edward I, arguing that John's donation was made to maintain lights placed around the high altar.[109] The abbey made assiduous efforts to ensure that John's successors honoured his commitment. Henry III's regency government at first paid the sum

---

[101] *RAC1*, p. 412 (no. 546).

[102] *Reading Abbey Cartularies. British Library Manuscripts: Egerton 3031, Harley 1708 and Cotton Vespasian E xxv. 2. Berkshire Documents, Scottish Charters and Miscellaneous Documents*, ed. B. R. Kemp, Camden 4th ser., 33 (London, 1987), pp. 31-2 (no. 694).

[103] 'Miracles of the Hand of St James', pp. 11-13; *Reading Abbey Cartularies 2*, pp. 30-1 (nos 692-3).

[104] *RAC1*, pp. 71-2 (no. 46); *RC*, p. 37b. An alternative theory is that the relic was stripped to settle the abbey's debts to Richard: B. Nilson, *Cathedral Shrines of Medieval England* (Woodbridge, 1998), pp. 140-1.

[105] *RAC1*, p. 221 (no. 263). Roger specified that the community celebrate his anniversary after his death.

[106] *Earldom of Gloucester Charters. The Charters and Scribes of the Earls and Countesses of Gloucester to A.D. 1217*, ed. R. B. Patterson (Oxford, 1973), p. 151 (no. 165); *RAC1*, p. 69 (nos 43-4); *PR 2 John*, p. 128.

[107] 'Annales Radingenses Posteriores, 1135-1264', ed. C. W. Previté-Orton, *EHR*, 37 (1922), 400-3 (p. 401).

[108] *RAC1*, pp. 68-9 (no. 42), 71-2 (no. 46); 'Annales Radingenses Posteriores', p. 401; *RC*, p. 37b.

[109] *The Parliament Rolls of Medieval England 1275-1504. I. Edward I 1275-1294*, ed. P. Brand, (Woodbridge and London, 2005), pp. 388 (text), 435 (translation) (Roll 02, appendix, no. 218).

in gold, but commuted the grant to one of silver in 1219. Further payments and confirmations followed in the ensuing years.[110] However, the crown clearly fell into arrears. Henry III ordered that the debt be paid in 1250, stating that John's original grant was for a great candle, to be placed in the abbey church at Easter.[111] However, a balance-sheet of 1270 indicated a full seventeen years in which the sum had not been paid, although orders of 1272 suggest royal efforts to honour the payment in the final part of the reign. Edward I attempted to pay off the backlog in 1286, before Reading finally accepted a £100 pay-off, surrendering the relevant charters of John and Henry III in 1292.[112]

There is further evidence that Reading provided a focal point for John's interest in the cult of relics. By the 1190s, the abbey played host to a panoply of holy remains, ranging from artefacts linked to Christ and the Virgin to patriarchs, prophets, apostles, martyrs, confessors, and virgins. The crown had been at the heart of their acquisition. Henry I sent envoys to Constantinople in 1118 specifically to acquire relics. Their haul included at least one of the abbey's pieces of the True Cross. The range of relics at Reading suggests that, in considering royal devotions there, we are again looking at an opportunity for the king to seek intercession from the saints in combination. Whilst St James, the Virgin Mary, and, as will be shown, St Philip, were all prominent, this also included royal saints, notably Edward the Martyr. The main focus of this cult was the saint's burial place at Shaftesbury. However, Reading inherited important remains from its precursor community at Leominster. Relics associated with saints that John venerated elsewhere were also to be found at Reading, including the Virgin Mary, Thomas Becket, cloths from the shrines of St Edmund and St Alban, and a piece of the tomb of Edward the Confessor.[113]

In addition, John was remembered at Reading as the donor of a major relic: part of the Apostle St Philip's head, brought to England following the sack of Constantinople in April 1204. Devotion to St Philip may have occurred at Reading before the relic was donated. Godfrey de Lucy, bishop of Winchester (1189–1204), was one of a number of bishops who granted an indulgence for those visiting Reading on the saint's feast day (1 May, jointly with St James the Less). Godfrey's indulgence was granted in or before 1201, before the relic was looted from Constantinople in 1204.[114] The sources suggest that the king's donation was made with

---

[110] RLC 1204-24, pp. 381b, 390a, 456a, 577b; RLC 1224-27, pp. 26b, 67a, 143b; CLR 1226–1240, pp. 109, 149; CPR 1225-1232, HMSO (London, 1903), p. 333; RAC1, pp. 81-2 (nos 58-9).

[111] CR 1247-1251, p. 389.

[112] RAC1, pp. 89-90 (no. 74), 92 (no. 79), 97 (no. 94); *Issues of the Exchequer, Being a Collection of Payments made out of His Majesty's Revenue from King Henry III to King Henry VI Inclusive*, ed. F. Devon (London, 1837), p. 104; *The Antient Kalendars and Inventories of the Treasury of His Majesty's Exchequer Together with other Documents Illustrating the History of that Repository*, ed. F. Palgrave, RComm, 3 vols (London, 1836), vol. I, pp. 49-50.

[113] Bethell, 'Twelfth-Century Relic Collection', pp. 65-9.

[114] Bethell, 'Twelfth-Century Relic Collection', p. 64; Leyser, 'Frederick Barbarossa', p. 498 n. 3; RAC1, pp. 174-5 (no. 217); EEA VIII. Winchester 1070-1204, ed. M. J. Franklin (Oxford, 1993), p. 180 (no. 233). On Godfrey, who died in September 1204: E. Venables, 'Lucy,

due pomp and ceremony, when he came to Reading on 1 May 1205, the feast of St Philip and St James. Numerous bishops attended, and John granted the abbey a four-day fair beginning on the vigil of the feast.[115] He also gave a gold reliquary, decorated with precious stones, to house the head of St Philip. This was used as a pledge in 1279, for repayment of sums raised in aid of the Holy Land that were deposited at Reading.[116] In addition, John made offerings in honour of the relics when he visited the abbey, giving seven bezants on Sunday (4 November) after the feast of All Saints in 1212. A further payment covered the offering of a knight who made his gift alongside the king 'when he saw the relics' on the following day.[117]

King John's interaction with Reading Abbey shows royal devotion to the cult of relics at individual religious houses. He also kept a private collection, which accompanied him as he travelled. The royal relic collection was one of the items said to have been lost in the so-called 'disaster in the Wash' in early October 1216, when John's baggage train was trapped by quicksands in his haste to move into Lincolnshire from East Anglia.[118] Earlier evidence reveals that a horse and coffers were provided to carry the relics from place to place.[119] In 1212, a royal servant named Hugh the Sumpterer was paid 8½d, having stayed at Odiham (Hampshire) on 8 and 9 May with a 'sumpter of relics'. This could either have been a horse and the relics it carried, or a saddle-bag of relics. John, meanwhile, undertook a two-day round trip that took him to Freemantle and Winchester.[120] Unfortunately, we do not know why the relics were left behind, although this took place during the octave of Ascension Day, the feast which fell on the anniversary of the beginning of John's reign. Perhaps the fact that the payment was recorded only once hints that it was unusual for the king to travel without his relic collection.

The potential use of these relics can be seen through a further example from early August 1212. John paid for three pounds of wax for candles to stand above the coffers of relics for three nights at Bridgnorth (Shropshire), corresponding with his characteristically short stay there. Candles were also placed before the relics at Winchester, where he had been a few days previously.[121] John was about to mount a major military expedition into Wales, on the scale of Edward I's campaigns later in the thirteenth century. This was abandoned when it became apparent to the king

---

Godfrey de (d. 1204)', rev. R. V. Turner, *ODNB* (Oxford, 2004, online edn 2006) [http://www.oxforddnb.com/view/article/17148, accessed 30 March 2011].

[115] *A Descriptive Catalogue of the Manuscripts in the Library of Lambeth Palace*, ed. M. R. James and C. Jenkins, 5 vols (Cambridge, 1930–32), vol. IV, p. 503 (no. 371); *RAC1*, pp. 75–6 (no. 49).

[116] *RAC1*, pp. 188–90 (no. 230).

[117] *RM*, pp. 246, 249.

[118] Coggeshall, pp. 183–4. See also Holt, 'King John's Disaster', pp. 75–86.

[119] *RM*, p. 233; *PR 14 John*, p. 44.

[120] *RM*, p. 231; 'Itinerary'.

[121] *RM*, p. 237; 'Itinerary'. On the medieval practice of burning candles next to relics: D. R. Dendy, *The Use of Lights in Christian Worship*, Alcuin Club Collections, 41 (London, 1959), pp. 108–19.

that his own side was conspiring against him.¹²² This treachery does not account for his apparent need for intercession: his presence at Winchester and Bridgnorth came a few days before the expedition was cancelled. Rather, John's desire for candles to burn before the relics should probably be attributed to desire for saintly support for the forthcoming campaign. That he did this at Winchester and then at Bridgnorth suggests that religious priorities had to be combined with his itinerary.

There is no evidence showing which saints' relics were carried with the king, but there is enough to suggest that he both owned relics and was a donor of holy remains to religious communities. In addition to his gift of the head of St Philip to Reading, he was remembered as a donor of relics purchased by Richard I to the Augustinian priory of Waltham Holy Cross (itself re-founded as part of Henry II's penance for complicity in the murder of Becket).¹²³ There is also some indication of the reliquaries John owned. In the immediate aftermath of Magna Carta he appears to have taken stock of his most valuable possessions, probably in order to gauge his remaining means of raising revenue, normal systems having broken down.¹²⁴ His valuable possessions were listed, including parts of his relic collection and the objects that housed it, presumably in anticipation of their potential use as a means of raising cash. In June and July 1215 John received, from the custody of the abbot of Reading, a silver shrine, embellished with onyxes and other stones, that contained relics, a small ivory shrine with relics, a ruby shrine with jewels, and a gold vase with pearls that had been sent by the pope. In July, he took delivery of a cross base, a gold cross, a shrine with precious stones which had belonged to the bishop of Chester, three gold 'phylacteries' (containers for relics), and two gold crosses with gold chains. These had been in the care of the abbot of Forde.¹²⁵ It therefore seems that alongside the collection carried with the household John possessed further relics, kept at favoured religious houses. It should not necessarily be assumed that all these treasures were sold off. Some may have remained in the king's possession when he died. The executors of William Marshal's testament rendered account of a large number of cloths, including four baldachins (canopies for altars, shrines, or thrones) from the late king's treasury at Corfe, suggesting that care was taken in presenting the relics owned by King John.¹²⁶

Finally, John sought to associate himself with a host of saints when presented with the opportunity to do so. Often, this is reflected in a few words inserted in confirmation charters. The Augustinian canons of Hartland (Devon), located in the lands John was granted before King Richard's departure on crusade, received a

---

122 Warren, *John*, pp. 199–200; Painter, *Reign*, pp. 266–7; J. C. Holt, *The Northerners: A Study in the Reign of King John* (Oxford, 1961), pp. 79–88; Wendover, vol. II, pp. 61–2.

123 *The Early Charters of the Augustinian Canons of Waltham Abbey, Essex 1062–1230*, ed. R. Ransford (Woodbridge, 1989), p. 435 (no. 637).

124 J. E. A. Jolliffe, 'The Chamber and the Castle Treasuries under John', *Studies in Medieval History Presented to Frederick Maurice Powicke*, ed. R. W. Hunt, W. A. Pantin and R. W. Southern (Oxford, 1948), pp. 117–42 (pp. 135–8).

125 *RLP*, pp. 145a, 147a–b.

126 *Roll of Divers Accounts for the Early Years of the Reign of Henry III*, ed. F. A. Cazel Jr, PRS, 82, ns 44 (London, 1982), p. 35.

confirmation in 1199. This referred to an earlier charter issued by John 'for the love of God and the blessed martyr Nectan' and for the salvation of Henry II. Nectan was a sixth-century hermit martyred by robbers he was attempting to convert. In 1160 the community of secular canons founded in his name was reformed as a body of canons regular. This was done with Henry II's blessing, and John's confirmation presumably reflects continuing royal approval, providing an opportunity to associate himself with the cult.[127]

Likewise at Peterborough Abbey, which housed an arm relic of St Oswald, the sixth-century king of Northumbria, there is fleeting evidence that Angevin devotion was continued by John when presented with the opportunity. Here, his confirmation of 1200 was issued out of love for God and St Peter, and reverence for St Oswald king and martyr.[128] Devotion to the latter was shown by John's sister Matilda and her husband Henry the Lion, duke of Saxony. Imagery of Oswald appeared on a reliquary commissioned at the time of the couple's marriage in 1168, and in a head reliquary of the saint commissioned in the late 1180s. Association between the Angevins and a lineage leading back to the saints was an important aspect of the outlook of the ruling family, which Matilda took with her to Germany, bolstering her husband's imperial ambitions.[129] Reciprocal gifts were made when the couple were in exile in England in the 1180s. A piece of the True Cross, previously held in Henry the Lion's chapel, was given to Reading.[130] Indeed, such activity may have been recognised as an important part of a royal marriage. In 1235, John's daughter Isabella was betrothed to the Emperor Frederick II. Henry III presented his sister with a crown decorated with images of 'the four martyr and confessor kings of England, to whom the king had especially assigned the care of his sister's soul'. He accompanied Isabella to Canterbury ahead of her departure, where they paid their respects at the shrine of St Thomas.[131] Once again, we can see royal association with a combination of cults, in which King John's offspring engaged in similar religious expression to that of their father.

John also supported new saints, as has been shown in the case of Wulfstan. Promotion of nascent cults can also be seen through his dealings with the Gilbertine order, and efforts to secure the canonisation of their founder, Gilbert of Sempringham. Again, John built on a heritage of royal involvement with an order for which the crown has been described as the 'paramount patron'. Gilbert 'an Angevin saint *par excellence*', enjoyed the favour of Henry II, who established Newstead Priory (Lincolnshire), probably in 1171 and no later than 1173. Here

---

[127] *Cartae Antiquae Rolls 1–10*, pp. 122–4 (no. 246); Farmer, *Oxford Dictionary of Saints*, p. 361; Knowles and Hadcock, pp. 140, 158.

[128] RC, p. 82b.

[129] E. Bozoky, 'Prolégomènes à une étude des offrandes de reliquaires par les princes', *Reliques et sainteté dans l'espace médiéval*, ed. J.-L. Deuffic, PECIA. Ressources en médiévistique, vols 5–8 (Saint-Denis, 2006), pp. 91–116 (pp. 105–6).

[130] Bethell, 'Twelfth-Century Relic Collection', p. 64.

[131] Wendover, vol. III, pp. 109–10. See also B. Wild, 'The Empress's New Clothes: A *rotulus pannorum* of Isabella, Sister of King Henry III, Bride of Emperor Frederick II', *Medieval Clothing and Textiles*, VII (2011), 1–31.

there is a link with the memory of Thomas Becket. This was the only Gilbertine house dedicated to the Holy Trinity, a feast promoted by the martyred archbishop.[132] John augmented his father's grants to Newstead, giving land in Howsham (Lincolnshire) worth sixty-six shillings a year. This was done for the king's salvation, and that of his ancestors and heirs, in pure and perpetual alms.[133] John also confirmed Henry II's gifts to Gilbertine Watton (Yorkshire), and his father's protection of the order as a whole.[134]

King John was also linked to efforts to have Gilbert of Sempringham declared a saint. Gilbert died in 1189. Attempts to secure his canonisation began in 1200. The king visited Sempringham in January 1201, attending the first inquiry into Gilbert's miracles, suggesting a close interest in the process. His grant to Newstead resulted in his being seen as co-founder. It showed respect for the house where Gilbert had received extreme unction shortly before his death. John also wrote to Pope Innocent III supporting the canonisation. Gilbert was declared a saint in January 1202, and translated to a new shrine in October of the same year, but there is little to suggest further devotion on the king's part.[135] Attendance at the translation may not have been possible because John was overseas. His interest in Gilbert seems driven by a desire to honour the commitments of his predecessors, and by the chance to associate with the cult in the early years of the reign. This is borne out by a confirmation of May 1204 in favour Gilbertine Marmont (Cambridgeshire), newly founded by Ralph de Hauvill and his wife Matilda. John's grant was issued a little over a month after the death of his mother, Eleanor of Aquitaine. The king took the opportunity to stipulate that a commemorative daily mass should be celebrated for her soul at Marmont.[136]

Overall, it is John's effort to secure the combined intercession of the saints that should be stressed. Canonised Anglo-Saxons were certainly prominent: Edward the Confessor, Edmund, King and Martyr, and Wulfstan. It was sensible practice for kings to associate themselves with canonised predecessors. They could claim kinship with many of them. This was doubly the case for rulers whose origins lay overseas, a useful means of integration and assertion of their credentials as kings of England. John's devotions also stood within a long-standing tradition of cultivation of 'English' cults by the Anglo-Norman and Anglo-Angevin ruling class, dating to the generation that arrived in England following the Norman Conquest.

---

[132] Golding, *Gilbert*, pp. 223-4, 312.

[133] *RC*, p. 84b.

[134] *RC*, pp. 18, 42a; *Cartae Antiquae Rolls 1-10*, pp. 31-3. In 1204, John also confirmed Alan de Wilton's gift for foundation of a Gilbertine priory, probably intended to be at Owton (County Durham). This never materialised: *RC*, pp. 127a-b; Golding, *Gilbert*, pp. 251-2.

[135] *The Book of St Gilbert*, ed. R. Foreville and G. Keir, OMT (Oxford, 1987), pp. 170, 171, 214, 215; Golding, *Gilbert*, p. 313; B. Golding, 'Gilbert of Sempringham [St Gilbert of Sempringham] (1083-1189)', *ODNB* (Oxford, 2004) [http://www.oxforddnb.com/view/article/10677, accessed 6 April 2011]; R. Graham, *S. Gilbert of Sempringham and the Gilbertines: A History of the only English Monastic Order* (London, 1901), pp. 23-4. On John as co-founder of Newstead, see below, Chapter 3.

[136] *RC*, p. 129a.

Many Anglo-Saxon cults experienced a renaissance as their custodians responded to the impact of the cult of St Thomas Becket from the 1170s onwards.[137] It was also entirely usual for incomers from outside England to cultivate local saints. Bishop Peter des Roches at Winchester was 'a Frenchman who did more than most Englishmen to foster the cult of the Anglo-Saxon saints'.[138] John's devotion to cults native to England should not necessarily be viewed as forced upon him due to his continental losses.

Whilst the king's efforts to seek saintly intercession had parallels in the actions of his predecessors, there are also parallels in the reigns that followed. Henry III, who only reluctantly abandoned his claims to the overseas lands, continued the tradition of which his father had been part. He attracted attention for reciting the names of the holy kings of England: Aethelbert, Edward the Martyr, Kenelm, Oswald, Oswin, Neithan, Wistan, Fromund, Edwuld, Edmund, and Edward the Confessor.[139] Nonetheless, royal devotion to the saints was not limited to those with whom the Angevins claimed kinship. Their attachment to Anglo-Saxon saints was part of a more nuanced policy. Kings realised that they could venerate saints in combination. John was no exception to this trend. Thus, St Thomas Becket was equally important in the royal quest for intercession as the cults of canonised kings. Likewise, major Christian saints, such as the Virgin Mary, St James the Great, St Philip, and St Peter, could be the focus of royal prayers. As a body, John could hope that the saints would intervene on his behalf to help to ensure (or regain) stability of rule and successful kingship. His visits to shrines, and to the homes of relics, and the evidence that he travelled with relics to protect him, provide compelling evidence that the saints were an element central to the personal religion of King John.

---

[137] Draper, pp. 47–8; Webb, *Pilgrimage*, pp. 114–15. See also Ridyard, 'Condigna Veneratio', pp. 179–206.

[138] Vincent, *Peter des Roches*, pp. 244–7, 478.

[139] *Matthaei Parisiensis*, vol. V, p. 617. Henry also listed 250 English baronies.

3

Powerhouses of Prayer

Establishment of religious communities to pray for the founder's soul lay at the heart of elite strategies for securing salvation, creating powerhouses of prayer for themselves and their families. King John was part of this trend, but this is not how he is remembered. Historians view his principal foundation, Beaulieu Abbey (Hampshire), with scepticism. Bishop Stubbs argued that the king had scarcely enough sense of religion to found it. Others see Beaulieu neither as John's idea nor as well-endowed by its founder. Painter describes it as 'the result of a semi-political bargain'. Harper-Bill argues that 'it is clear that the idea was Archbishop Hubert Walter's, and the investment was little enough for a monarch of John's resources'.[1] Yet the evidence for the king's investment demonstrates that founding monasteries was part of John's religious activity. The project probably began as a penitential act. Hubert Walter, patron and *confrater* of the Cistercians, certainly played a role in its early stages, mediating when John fell into dispute with the white monks early in the reign.[2] However, the archbishop died in 1205, whilst John showed commitment to Beaulieu across his reign. It represented a significant element of royal desire for intercessory prayer, fitting a family and regnal tradition of establishing houses of ascetic orders. Most significantly, it was a personal religious initiative. John may even have intended to be buried at Beaulieu.

The king's decision to establish a Cistercian house can be seen as an act of atonement for repressive treatment of the order following dispute over taxation. As he sought to secure his continental lands, John reached an agreement with Philip II of France in January 1200, formally confirmed in the Treaty of Le Goulet in May. Under its terms, the English king was obliged to pay twenty thousand marks to his French counterpart.[3] To raise the money, John levied a carucage of three shillings per plough. He demanded this from the Cistercians at York in late March, but the abbots refused, arguing they were exempt unless special permission was granted by the General Chapter. They were presumably also keen to avoid establishing a precedent.[4]

---

[1] *Memoriale Walteri de Coventria*, vol. II, p. xv; Painter, *Reign*, p. 153; Harper-Bill, 'John and the Church of Rome', p. 300.
[2] Cheney, *Hubert Walter*, pp. 82-4.
[3] Gillingham, 'John'; *Diplomatic Documents Preserved in the Public Record Office. Volume I. 1101-1272*, ed. P. Chaplais, HMSO (London, 1964), pp. 20-3 (no. 9).
[4] Painter, *Reign*, pp. 155-6; Hockey, pp. 11-12. The meeting at York presumably took place 25-8 March: Hardy, 'Itinerary'. The Cistercian strategy may have become standard practice. In 1256, they refused Henry III's financial demands on similar grounds: Gransden, *Historical Writing*, p. 415.

The ensuing dispute is portrayed by the Cistercian chronicler Ralph of Coggeshall, whose account shows how John's peace with France led, through the resultant demands for money, to royal dispute with the Cistercians.[5] The dispute took place before the king had confirmed the gifts and privileges granted to the order by his predecessors. Thus, he withheld approval. Ralph emphasised the reputation of the white monks for 'the value of their life and the rigour of their religion'. This was an order which 'the kings and princes of this country have always up to now held in such great veneration that they gave them lands and great possessions and protected everything of theirs with the shield of defence'. Meanwhile, Archbishop Hubert was portrayed as the order's champion. He 'upbraided the king, with unrestrained voice, over such great harshness, proclaiming him to be the persecutor of the holy church'. When John refused to relent, Hubert offered one thousand silver marks for confirmation of charters and liberties granted by Richard I, but 'this offering ... he [John] utterly spurned as if tiny'. The king set sail for Normandy 'full of threats and slaughter against the disciples of Christ'.[6]

The ostracising of the Cistercians was not quite so complete as Coggeshall suggests. Some houses had received confirmations or grants of royal protection. These included Fountains Abbey (September 1199), which received confirmation of a charter of Henry II.[7] Furness, founded by John's predecessor (both as king and count of Mortain) Stephen, received confirmation of charters of Henry II and Richard I in late March and early April 1200, although the abbot paid £100 for the privilege.[8] Also in April, a charter of Henry II to Strata Florida was confirmed.[9] Yet from late April, when John sailed for Normandy, until November, documents in favour of the white monks are conspicuous by their absence from the rolls. It is clear that they were in dispute: after the king's return, on the day of Isabella of Angoulême's coronation as queen at Westminster Abbey (8 October 1200), John ordered the Cistercians to remove their livestock from his forests. Any animals remaining were to be captured and sold to the profit of the crown.[10]

The king's proposed foundation was part of the ensuing settlement, brokered by Archbishop Hubert, who summoned the Cistercian abbots to negotiate with John at Lincoln in November 1200, 'so that united they might more easily incline

---

[5] Gillingham, 'Historians Without Hindsight', p. 6.
[6] Coggeshall, pp. 102–3.
[7] RC, p. 18b.
[8] RC, pp. 41a–b, 52b; ROF, p. 55. Before John sailed for Normandy he confirmed his grant of quittance from tolls and other customs in Ireland, issued to Furness before he became king: RC, pp. 53a, 53b.
[9] RC, p. 44b. Further charters (July 1199 and April 1200) confirmed documents issued by John as count of Mortain for Bindon (Dorset) and Crokeden (Valle St Mary) in Ireland: *The Cartae Antiquae Rolls 11–20*, ed. J. C. Davies, PRS, 71, ns 33 (London, 1960), pp. 117–18; RC, p. 61b. Strata Marcella also received confirmations in April 1200, linked to the king's desire to placate its patron, Gwenwynwyn: RC, p. 44b; J. H. Jenkins, 'King John and the Cistercians in Wales', *Monastic Research Bulletin*, 17 (2011), 16–18 (p. 17).
[10] 'Itinerary'; Coggeshall, pp. 103–4.

the wild mind of the king ... to pity and the grace of reconciliation'.[11] The chroniclers agree on the penitential nature of John's climb-down. He prostrated himself before the abbots, in tears according to Coggeshall, who added that John requested fraternity with the order and that its monks should pray for him. He promised to be the defender and patron of the Cistercians, and issued letters receiving them back into his protection. The king then instructed the abbots to look for a suitable location for the foundation of a new abbey. He promised to build this for the wellbeing of his soul and the souls of his kinsmen, for the stability of his realm, and as his future burial place.[12]

Elsewhere, John's actions are described as the outcome of a vision. A fifteenth-century description recounts the dispute, suggesting that he ordered his servants to trample the Cistercian abbots under their horses. This they refused to do. On the following night the king dreamt that he was led before a judge, who ordered him to be beaten by the assembled abbots. When John, who was said to have felt the effects of his scourging the next morning, explained his dream to 'a certain ecclesiastical personage of his court', he was persuaded to seek pardon.[13] This reads like a later invention, but Coggeshall's account provides a sense in which the king's *volte-face* could have been seen as the work of God. Other chroniclers echoed the idea that the decision was made with 'divine inspiration'.[14]

Whatever inspired it, the king's peace with the Cistercians and promise to found an abbey took place at the funeral of Bishop Hugh of Lincoln in November 1200. John participated, helping to carry the coffin during the funeral procession. The bishop's biographer noted the religious importance of this: 'It was no small matter of congratulation for anyone to be granted the privilege of carrying the body of one whose merits could save from destruction the souls and bodies of those who rendered him this service and secure their admission into the kingdom of Heaven.' Hugh was noted for his piety and for his influence on successive Angevin kings: another possible context for a major religious act on John's part. The account noted that over fifty Cistercian abbots were present. Its final sentence records the king's promise to found an abbey of their order.[15]

---

[11] Coggeshall, p. 104.

[12] Coggeshall, pp. 105-10, esp. 108-9; Howden, vol. IV, p. 145; *Annales de Margan (A.D. 1066-1232)*, ed. H. R. Luard, Annales Monastici, RS 36, 5 vols (London, 1864-69), vol. I, p. 25; Gillingham, 'Historians Without Hindsight', p. 12.

[13] St John Hope and Brakspear, pp. 129-30, 135. The account is drawn from: London, British Library, Cotton Ms. Domitian A. xii, f. 87 verso. See also *English Monastic Archives*, database 2 (http://www.monasticarchives.org.uk/databrowse/monarc/archive/objects/3391/, accessed 18 July 2013); W. Dugdale, *Monasticon Anglicanum: A History of the Abbies and other Monasteries, Hospitals, Frieries, and Cathedral and Collegiate Churches, with their Dependencies, in England and Wales*, ed. J. Caley, H. Ellis and B. Bandinel, 6 vols (London, 1817-30), vol. V, p. 682.

[14] Waverley, pp. 254, 256.

[15] *Magna Vita*, vol. II, pp. 225, 332. King William I of Scotland was also present, but was reportedly too upset to assist. John resumed issuing documents in favour of Cistercian abbeys. On 24 November Swineshead received confirmation of protection granted when he was count of Mortain: *RC*, p. 80b.

The king's climb-down at Lincoln, and the announcement of his proposed foundation at a major religious occasion, where most of the leading Cistercians in England were assembled, suggests awareness of the value of religious publicity. Henry Mayr-Harting highlights the political value of John's behaviour. As an international order, the white monks were well placed to promote or to castigate his treatment of the church. 'Thus it suited him to find a way of giving in while saving his face.'[16] Nonetheless, if his foundation was part of the solution to an immediate crisis, John had sufficient sense to promote the project for the remainder of his life.

Further evidence sustains the view that the abbey eventually sited at Beaulieu was in part created as an act of penance. In a letter of 1202, Pope Innocent III noted that Archbishop Hubert had informed him that the king had confessed the sins of his adult life and promised to make reparation to God. Hubert had advised John to found a Cistercian monastery. The pope noted that the fulfilment of this instruction would be sufficient for the remission of the king's sins. Innocent exhorted John to 'henceforth give yourself wholly to works of piety, and make amends for past sins in such a way that you carefully guard against them in the future'. Benefits would follow: 'your kingdom will prosper and your royal honour even in this life will be enhanced'.[17]

The archbishop was in fact prompting the king to continue a project already in hand. In February 1201, around three months after the funeral of Hugh of Lincoln, John sent Abbot William of Rievaulx to the Cistercian abbots of Yorkshire to present information and request their advice concerning the new foundation.[18] In the months that followed a site was identified and, in 1202 or 1203, the Cistercian abbot of La Ferté-sur-Grosne took possession of the manor of Faringdon (Oxfordshire).[19] They were there by July 1203, when John ordered inquiries into how much they had spent sowing seed and in other expenses, and into the quantity of timber needed for sheep-folds and other necessities. The wood was to be provided from the royal forest.[20] La Ferté was located some sixty-five kilometres from Cîteaux, whose abbot had dispatched the founding community. It was to the latter that John formally granted Faringdon in November 1203, for the wellbeing of his soul, and for the souls of his ancestors and heirs, in pure and perpetual alms.[21] At the same time, the king ordered that the community was to receive

---

[16] H. Mayr-Harting, *Religion, Politics and Society in Britain 1066–1272* (Harlow, 2011), p. 163.

[17] SLI, pp. 37–9 (no. 13). Hubert also suggested that John provide 100 knights for the Holy Land.

[18] RC, p. 101a. For the identification of 'Abbot W.': D. Knowles, C. N. L. Brooke and V. C. M. London (eds), *The Heads of Religious Houses: England and Wales 940–1216* (Cambridge, 1972), p. 140.

[19] Waverley, p. 254; *Annales de Margan*, p. 26; Hockey, p. 14; J. H. Jenkins, 'The King's Beaulieu' (unpublished MA thesis, Cardiff University, 2009), p. 25. Due to modern boundary changes, Faringdon is now in Oxfordshire. It was formerly in Berkshire.

[20] RL, p. 47.

[21] RC, p. 114b; Hockey, p. 14. The charter is recorded in the Faringdon Cartulary: London, British Library, Cotton Ms. Nero A. xii.

sufficient timber to build their monastery. Presumably this was for construction of initial accommodation. The quantity of wood was to be determined by the number of monks living there. The Pipe Roll for 1203–04 noted that no account had been rendered concerning Faringdon, since the monks had been given what the king should receive there. It also noted a fifty mark contribution towards the purchase of one hundred oxen.[22]

However, the new community, numbering some thirty monks, soon relocated. Faringdon became a grange of the new abbey, sited at Beaulieu Regis, a royal hunting lodge in the New Forest. It is possible that John was at work on this lodge before giving it to the Cistercians. The Norman Exchequer Roll for 1203 notes the payment of £40 for one hundred flat stones for roofing 'for the work of the king's houses of the New Forest'.[23] The switch had been made by July 1204. In August, John wrote to all Cistercian abbots, urgently asking for an aid for the new abbey of *Bellus Locus*, begun in the New Forest. The abbots were instructed to write back to tell him what they were able to do.[24]

John's foundation charter, of January 1205, emphasised that this was an act of family piety. He referred to the wellbeing of his own soul, and to the souls of his father Henry II, his mother Eleanor of Aquitaine, his brothers Henry the Young King and Richard, and all his ancestors and heirs. The charter refers to John as a *confrater* of the white monks, echoing the chroniclers' view of the wishes expressed at Lincoln in 1200.[25] This meant that he had a bond of association with the order. They undertook to pray for his soul in all Cistercian monasteries. Given the list of kinsmen noted in the foundation charter, it might reasonably be expected that the king's abbey would dedicate its activity to prayers for its founder and the relatives he had named.

All this occurred before the death of Archbishop Hubert Walter in July 1205. There remains the possibility that he exerted an important influence, especially as only one further charter from John survives for his new foundation. Issued in 1215, this gave the service, lands, and holdings of Roger de Kyvilly, citizen of Bristol, and his heirs, along with eight shillings annual dues. It was granted 'for the sake of God' (*intuitu Dei*), in free, pure and perpetual alms, for the king's salvation and that of his ancestors and heirs.[26] Nonetheless, as will be seen, John's gifts spanned the reign. If the project was Hubert's initiative, the king must have been

---

[22] RL, p. 70; PR 5 John, pp. 46, 59; Hockey, p. 14.

[23] *Magni rotuli scaccarii Normanniae sub regibus Angliae*, ed. T. Stapleton, 2 vols (London, 1840–44), vol. II, p. 510.

[24] RLC 1204–24, pp. 2b, 3b, 32b.

[25] *Cartae Antiquae Rolls 1–10*, pp. 109–11 (no. 222); *Beaulieu Cartulary*, pp. 3–5 (no. 1).

[26] London and Oslo, The Schøyen Collection, Ms. 610 [http://www.schoyencollection.com/palaeography-collection-introduction/latin-documentary-scripts/gothic-court-secretary/court-scripts/ms-610, accessed 28 February 2015]; *Beaulieu Cartulary*, pp. 10 (no. 6), 30–1 (no. 29); RC, p. 204b; Hockey, p. 21. Under Henry III, efforts were made to secure payment of arrears due to the abbey from Roger's heir Jordan: *FR 5 Henry III*, Henry III Fine Rolls Project [http://www.finerollshenry3.org.uk/content/calendar/roll_015.html, accessed 30 July 2013], no. 325; *CR 1237–1242*, p. 92.

more than a passive follower, seeing the Beaulieu project as to his advantage. Other schemes begun by the archbishop, such as the planned Cistercian re-foundation of the secular college of Wolverhampton, were simply abandoned after his death, despite his efforts to involve John.[27] Kings were not afraid to pull the plug on religious projects if other financial demands were more pressing. Edward I abandoned sponsorship of Vale Royal in 1290 to focus instead on the north Welsh castles and his work at Westminster.[28]

Even Cistercian chroniclers are often terse in describing the new abbey. Coggeshall noted its name and location, *Bellus Locus* in the New Forest, adding that John installed thirty monks there, before a similarly short acknowledgement that William de Briouze founded a house in Wales.[29] The Stanley annalist observed that Cîteaux was the mother-house and that the king endowed his foundation with 'great lands'.[30] This suggests the ambition of the project. It appears that Beaulieu was intended to be substantial. The scale of the buildings, although unfinished during John's lifetime, indicates that it was intended to be the largest Cistercian abbey in England, reflecting its royal patronage. The ground plan of the church has been compared to the great Cistercian abbeys of Clairvaux and Pontigny, whilst the sizeable lay brothers' accommodation also signifies the intention for Beaulieu to be large and prosperous.[31]

The abbey remained unfinished at John's death (1216), making it easy to think that he lacked commitment. However, it was not unusual for many years to pass between foundation and dedication, even when a king was principal benefactor. Henry I founded Reading Abbey in 1121. The abbey church was dedicated over forty years later (1164).[32] The timescale at Beaulieu was similar. Founded in the early thirteenth century, it was dedicated in 1246.[33] Perhaps this is no coincidence. Both projects were interrupted by civil war and the political consequences of uncertain royal succession.

There is further evidence that King John's abbey was neither small nor poorly endowed. In 1236, a papal letter relating to a disputed church noted that Beaulieu boasted £1000 of annual rents. Gregory IX had perhaps accepted the word of the abbey's opponents, who had clearly created the impression of a rich community,

---

[27] See above, Chapter 1.

[28] R. A. Brown and H. M. Colvin, 'The King's Works 1272–1485', *The History of the King's Works: Vol. I. The Middle Ages*, ed. R. A. Brown, H. M. Colvin and A. J. Taylor, HMSO (London, 1963), pp. 161–292 (p. 252); Jenkins, 'The King's Beaulieu', pp. 49–50.

[29] Coggeshall, p. 147. Briouze's proposed foundation perhaps became a grange of Abbey Dore: D. H. Williams, *The Welsh Cistercians* (Leominster, 2001), p. 4.

[30] Stanley, p. 507.

[31] St John Hope and Brakspear, pp. 148, 165; R. A. Brown and H. M. Colvin, 'The Angevin Kings 1154–1216', *The History of the King's Works: Vol. I. The Middle Ages*, ed. R. A. Brown, H. M. Colvin and A. J. Taylor, HMSO (London, 1963), pp. 51–91 (p. 91). For comparative ground-plans: Brown and Colvin, 'The King's Works 1272–1485', p. 255 fig. 28.

[32] J. A. Green, *Henry I: King of England and Duke of Normandy* (Cambridge, 2009), pp. 170–2; A. Duggan, *Thomas Becket* (London, 2004), p. 61.

[33] Hockey, p. 29. On progress after John's reign, see also Chapter 8.

'revelling' in its possessions, wealthy enough to support 'many more monks'.[34] At around this time, Beaulieu provided monks for three daughter houses: Netley, Hailes, and Newenham.[35] The founding community of Netley was sent in 1239. Henry III ordered provision of food and drink for their first day. At Hailes, established in the year of Beaulieu's dedication, the founder, John's younger son Richard of Cornwall, secured twenty monks and ten lay brothers from the mother house. In 1247, Newenham also received monks from John's foundation.[36] It would therefore appear that a sizeable community had been recruited in Beaulieu's first forty years.

John's investment provided principally for the early stages of building work. He did not stint. Provision for construction included one hundred marks given in 1204, followed by 250 marks the following year, provided from the testament of Godfrey de Lucy, bishop of Winchester (d. 1204). In 1207–08, five hundred marks were given 'for building the church'. A further nine hundred marks were given in 1213. Two sums of £100 followed in 1214, one paid to the Prior, Anestasius. The second was issued at Beaulieu itself, by the justiciar Peter des Roches, bishop of Winchester, to Brother Aszoni, whilst the king was campaigning overseas. According to the Pipe Rolls, £236 18s 2d was given in 1211–12, and £354 2s 7d in 1212–13. In 1215, John granted everything ordered for the works of the abbey. In the same year, fifty marks were given, along with £15 for 'repair' of the church.[37] The king's known outlay on construction work was in the region of £2,000.[38] Comparative figures suggest that this sum was roughly equivalent to Henry II's expenditure in erecting new buildings at his re-foundations of Waltham and Amesbury, as part of his penance for his perceived role in the murder of Thomas Becket.[39]

---

34 *Calendar of Entries in the Papal Registers Relating to Great Britain and Ireland. Papal Letters. Vol. I. A.D. 1198–1304*, ed. W. H. Bliss, HMSO (London, 1893), p. 155.

35 St John Hope and Brakspear, pp. 185–6. Each had royal connections. At Netley, established through the testament of Peter des Roches, bishop of Winchester (d. 1238), Henry III stepped in as joint-founder: C. A. F. Meekings (ed. R. F. Hunnisett), 'The Early Years of Netley Abbey', *Studies in 13th Century Justice and Administration* (London, 1981), pp. 1–37; CLR 1240–1245, p. 221; and, for further references, H. M Colvin, 'Henry III 1216–1272', *The History of the King's Works: Vol. I. The Middle Ages*, ed. R. A. Brown, H. M. Colvin and A. J. Taylor, HMSO (London, 1963), pp. 93–159 (p. 158 n. 2). Newenham also recognised Henry as co-founder: Dugdale, *Monasticon*, vol. V, p. 692. Hailes was founded by John's younger son, Richard, earl of Cornwall: see below. A later daughter house, St Mary Graces, was founded by Edward III in 1350, although only with six monks: Knowles and Hadcock, pp. 120, 121. See also: C. Holdsworth, 'Royal Cistercians: Beaulieu, her Daughters and Rewley', *TCE IV*, ed. P. R. Coss and S. D. Lloyd (Woodbridge, 1992), pp. 139–50.

36 H. A. Doubleday and W. Page (eds), VCH *Hampshire and the Isle of Wight*, 5 vols (London, 1900–12), vol. II, p. 142; CLR 1226–1240, p. 390, and see also pp. 446, 455–6; Waverley, p. 337; Knowles and Hadcock, p. 123.

37 RLC 1204–24, pp. 12b, 26a, 101a, 144a, 175b, 185b, 194a, 211b; MR 10 John, p. 132; PR 7 John, p. 12; PR 13 John, p. 178; PR 14 John, p. 91; St John Hope and Brakspear, pp. 132–4.

38 Brown and Colvin, 'The Angevin Kings', p. 90. To reach this figure, in addition to the sums discussed above, see: RLC 1204–24, p. 8b; PR 6 John, pp. 218, 219; PR 14 John, p. 67; RM, p. 257.

39 Brown and Colvin, 'The Angevin Kings', pp. 88–90. The authors calculate that Henry spent £2,454 8s 5d on Waltham and Amesbury, and a further £466 on Witham.

Royal support for Beaulieu extended beyond money for building work. John gave additional lands, and grain, either for the monks' food or to ensure that the community had well stocked barns.[40] Some of this was taken from lands in the king's hand following the deaths of leading churchmen. In August 1205, a month after the death of Archbishop Hubert Walter, wheat was to be provided by the custodians of the vacant archbishopric. Similar arrangements were made in 1207 from lands of the bishop of Exeter.[41] The latter included the price of plough oxen, so that Beaulieu's lands could be cultivated. Royal grants, including 120 cows and twelve bulls, allowed the monks to begin to develop its herd of livestock. In 1208, the king issued letters of protection for brothers buying sheep and other stock.[42]

King John also provided materials for religious services. This may have been the purpose of a gold cup entrusted to the abbot's care in 1204.[43] It was certainly the purpose of a cask of wine given in 1206 and 1215. The king's letters specifically stated that this was for celebration of mass.[44] This implies that John expected the regular pattern of services to be carried out amidst the construction work. Perhaps to help summon the monks to their devotions, John provided fourteen marks for a bell. Cistercian statutes forbade large bell towers, so we might speculate that this was not particularly large.[45]

The royal itinerary shows three visits to Beaulieu, in May 1206, December 1212, and March 1213. On the third of these, John gave the abbot money whilst he was there.[46] This infrequency of the royal presence does not mean that the king made an initial endowment and then lost interest. The chronology of documents issued in favour of the abbey, abbot and monks, shows that the king consistently supported his foundation. Consideration of the locations at which grants were issued, and the royal itinerary leading up to such gifts, suggests that Beaulieu was regularly in the king's thoughts when he was in the south of England.[47]

Nonetheless, members of such a foundation could expect demands to be made of them. Abbot Hugh of Beaulieu, noted for his eloquence, was a regular royal envoy, 'something of a public relations officer for the king'. As a member of an international religious order this was something which he was well placed to do.[48] Hugh was paid 107½ marks for going to the Cistercian General Chapter in 1205,

---

[40] *RLC 1204–24*, p. 2b.
[41] *RLC 1204–24*, pp. 47b, 93b, 95b, 97a. Henry Marshal, bishop of Exeter, died in October 1206. Due to John's dispute with the church, Simon of Apulia was not elected until 1214: F. Barlow, 'Marshal, Henry (d. 1206)', *ODNB* (Oxford, 2007) [http://www.oxforddnb.com/view/article/94379, accessed 19 July 2013]; F. Barlow, 'Apulia, Simon of (d. 1223)', *ODNB* (Oxford, 2007) [http://www.oxforddnb.com/view/article/94380, accessed 19 July 2013].
[42] *RLC 1204–24*, pp. 15b, 18a; *RLP*, p. 78a.
[43] *RLC 1204–24*, p. 3b.
[44] *RLC 1204–24*, pp. 62b, 225b; Hockey, p. 22; and see above, Chapter 1.
[45] *PR 8 John*, p. 48; Hockey, p. 22.
[46] 'Itinerary'; *RM*, p. 257.
[47] Based on comparison of the date and location of issue of grants discussed above with the preceding royal itinerary.
[48] Waverley, p. 298; Mayr-Harting, *Religion*, p. 164.

with a further fifty marks promised for the abbot and his house.⁴⁹ Thereafter, he was regularly sent on diplomatic missions during the disputed election to the archbishopric of Canterbury which followed Hubert Walter's death (1205). In March and August 1206, and February 1207, provision was made for Hugh's journeys to the papal court. This included sums of money, orders for provisions, and letters of introduction. In 1208, Hugh delivered the conditions on which John was prepared to admit Stephen Langton into England as archbishop.⁵⁰

The abbot continued to act as an envoy during the ensuing interdict and the period of royal excommunication. When the executors of the interdict, the bishops of London, Ely and Worcester, sought clarification of its terms, Hugh carried the pope's reply. In 1209, he met papal negotiators sent to England to attempt to stave off John's excommunication.⁵¹ There were benefits. Beaulieu, like Margam, was exempted from the king's heavy taxation of the Cistercians in 1210. However, immunity was not always available. In 1210, even Abbot Hugh was forbidden to travel to the Cistercian General Chapter.⁵²

During the negotiation of a settlement, Hugh engaged in a medieval equivalent of shuttle diplomacy between England and Rome. He made the journey in 1212 and in the winter of 1213–14, when only three of the six envoys arrived at the curia, the remainder taken captive in transit.⁵³ After the king's stand-off with the church was resolved, Hugh served as an envoy during the political crises of John's later years. He represented the king at abbatial and episcopal elections, for Bury St Edmunds, Evesham, and Worcester.⁵⁴ In 1214, he was amongst the envoys charged to take the queen, Isabella of Angoulême, and two of the royal children, Richard and Joan, to join John in south-western France.⁵⁵ He returned to Rome, during the Fourth Lateran Council (1215), to present the king's case that Archbishop Langton had incited baronial rebellion.⁵⁶ Here, he argued in support of John's erstwhile ally, Count Raymond VI of Toulouse, on trial for supporting the Albigensian heretics. Hugh presented an unsuccessful case that even if the father was condemned, his son, also Raymond, had a right to the inheritance of his mother

---

⁴⁹ RLC 1204–24, p. 47b; St John Hope and Brakspear, p. 133.
⁵⁰ RLC 1204–24, p. 66a; RLP, pp. 67a, 69a; LPI, pp. 120 (no. 725), 131 (no. 793); Hockey, p. 24; H. Summerson, 'Hugh (d. 1223)', ODNB (Oxford, 2008) [http://www.oxforddnb.com/view/article/95122, accessed 19 July 2013].
⁵¹ LPI, p. 132 (nos 799, 800); Hockey, p. 24; Summerson, 'Hugh'.
⁵² Annales de Margan, p. 30; GR, p. 105; Hockey, Beaulieu, p. 23.
⁵³ RM, p. 264; Hockey, p. 24; Summerson, 'Hugh'. In 1213–14, the other envoys to arrive were the Templar Alan Martel and the Hospitaller William of St Ouen: SLI, pp. 130–1 (no. 45); P. Webster, 'The Military Orders at the Court of King John', The Military Orders: Volume 5. Politics and Power, ed. P. W. Edbury (Farnham, 2012), pp. 209–18 (p. 211). See also LPI, pp. 149–50 (no. 905), 155 (no. 940); RLP, p. 123b; RLC 1204–24, p. 126a.
⁵⁴ Hockey, p. 24; Chronicle of the Election, pp. 30–3, 54–5; RLP, p. 107a.
⁵⁵ RLP, p. 117a; Jenkins, 'The King's Beaulieu', p. 56.
⁵⁶ Wendover, vol. II, p. 159.

Joanna, John's sister.[57] During the civil war of the final months of the reign, the prior of Beaulieu gathered revenues on behalf of John's constant supporter, Peter des Roches, bishop of Winchester, during the invasion of England by Louis of France.[58]

Abbot Hugh's involvement in royal diplomacy, and closeness to King John, ultimately brought him into conflict with the annual Cistercian General Chapter. His relationship with this assembly was changeable. He was sometimes instructed to fulfil the Chapter's wishes in England, although he did not always do so. In 1214, he was ordered to perform three days' penance, one on bread and water, for not assisting William Marshal's efforts to found a Cistercian house.[59] However, he was commended for upholding the order's privileges at the outset of the interdict in 1208. At this time, and in the following years, complaints were made about Hugh's conduct. In 1213-16 he was in dispute with the abbot of Stanley.[60] Matters came to a head in 1215. He was accused of extravagant living: dining with earls and companies of knights, having lay servants who served on bended knee, using silver dishes at his table, keeping a dog with a silver chain at the foot of his bed, 'and concerning whom much else is said'. In 1216, the General Chapter ordered the abbot of Cîteaux to take action. Hugh was deposed, probably by 1218.[61] We can reasonably infer that this was the result of the accusations. Here, he reaped the benefits of his years of royal service. He had been elected, but never installed, as bishop of Coventry in 1213, but he was successfully nominated and consecrated at Carlisle in 1218-19. The appointment owed much to the influence of the papal legate, Guala. A letter sent to Pope Honorius III in the name of King Henry III, referred to the former abbot as 'careful in his doings, illustrious in letters and morals, devoted to the Roman church, and faithful to the king'. Hugh held the bishopric until his death in 1223.[62]

King John's involvement with Beaulieu was sustained and significant, providing

---

[57] N. Vincent, 'England and the Albigensian Crusade', *England and Europe in the Reign of Henry III (1216-1272)*, ed. B. K. U. Weiler with I. W. Rowlands (Aldershot, 2002), pp. 67-97 (pp. 77-8).

[58] Vincent, *Peter des Roches*, p. 129.

[59] *Statuta Capitulorum Generalium Ordinis Cisterciensis ab anno 1116 ad annum 1786. Tomus I. Ab anno 1116 ad annum 1220*, ed. J.-M. Canivez, Bibliothèque de la revue d'histoire ecclésiastique, 9 (Louvain, 1933), pp. 318 (no. 55), 414 (no. 51), 416 (no. 62), 420 (no. 10).

[60] *Statuta Capitulorum Generalium*, pp. 351 (no. 28), 354 (no. 41), 355 (no. 46), 377 (no. 42), 416-17 (no. 64), 425 (no. 40), 443 (no. 41), 460 (no. 53). In 1214 orders required settlement notwithstanding any secular interference. For discussion: Summerson, 'Hugh'; Hockey, p. 24; D. Knowles, *The Monastic Order in England: A History of its Development from the Times of St Dunstan to the Fourth Lateran Council, 943-1216* (Cambridge, 1949), p. 658.

[61] *Statuta Capitulorum Generalium*, pp. 445 (no. 48), 460 (no. 54); Waverley, p. 291; Hockey, p. 25; Knowles, *Monastic Order*, p. 659; Summerson, 'Hugh'.

[62] Summerson, 'Hugh'; *The Letters and Charters of Cardinal Guala Bicchieri Papal Legate in England 1216-1218*, ed. N. Vincent, Canterbury and York Society, 83 (Woodbridge, 1996), pp. lii, liii, 11 (no. 12); *CPR 1216-1225*, p. 164; *Calendar of Documents Relating to Scotland Preserved in Her Majesty's Public Record Office, London. Vol. I. 1108-1272*, ed. J. Bain (Edinburgh, 1881), p. 126; *RLC 1204-24*, p. 405a; Jenkins, 'The King's Beaulieu', p. 62; Hockey, p. 25.

a wealth of evidence for religion as an aspect of his kingship. He participated at the funeral of a noted holy man, Hugh of Lincoln. He saw the value of expressing contrition to the assembled Cistercian abbots, and confessed his sins to a leading churchman, Archbishop Hubert Walter. In creating an abbey of ascetic Cistercian monks, he showed the classic pre-occupation of founders of religious houses: desire to provide for the wellbeing of his soul and for the souls of members of his family through the act of foundation and the ensuing prayers of the monks. He is said to have expressed a desire to be buried at the religious community he created. His decision to give up one of his own hunting lodges for the new monastery should not be underestimated, given the Angevin addiction to the sport. In entering into confraternity with an international religious order, he became 'the object of prayers in every Cistercian house in the world'.[63]

Beaulieu should also be set in long-term context. Aristocratic society in the second half of the twelfth century has been described as 'the last generation which took it for granted that the foundation of religious houses was amongst its spiritual obligations'.[64] Yet the royal family continued this practice for much of the remainder of the Middle Ages. The houses established were usually Cistercian. John's foundation can be seen as part of family tradition. His paternal grandmother, the Empress Matilda, backed five new houses of the order in England and Normandy. These were supported by her son Henry II, who also granted a sizeable quantity of lead for construction of a new church at Clairvaux. Richard I, in turn, became a *confrater* of the order in 1185 and supported the abbey of Le Pin near Poitiers, whose abbot was appointed royal almoner and confessor. Richard also founded Bonport Abbey in Normandy. A further sense that this was an appropriate order for the patronage of kings comes from the links the Cistercians had established with other ruling houses, notably the Capetian kings of France. The white monks' place on the international stage made them 'the most powerful factory of prayer' in medieval Europe.[65]

Besides Cistercian Beaulieu, John has also been linked with various smaller foundations (see Map 2): the Benedictine nunnery of Broomhall (Berkshire); the Black Monk priory at Otterton (Devon) and cells at Waterford and Cork (Ireland); Gilbertine Marlborough (Wiltshire), perhaps founded by John or his brother Richard; and houses of Augustinian canons at Newstead (Nottinghamshire), where the king claimed to be co-founder with his father, Henry II, and at Waterford, dedicated to St Katherine. It also included several possible hospital foundations: St Lawrence, Bristol; St Leonard, Chesterfield; St Leonard, Lancaster; and St Nicholas, Carlisle. In Ireland, John was said to have founded the hospital of St Stephen at Waterford. Several of these communities can be linked to the period before John became king.

---

[63] Holdsworth, 'Royal Cistercians', p. 140.
[64] Colvin, *White Canons*, p. 30.
[65] Holdsworth, 'Royal Cistercians', pp. 142–4. On Henry II and Clairvaux: F. Madeline, 'Le don de plomb dans le patronage monastique d'Henri II Plantagenêt: usages et conditions de la production du plomb anglais dans la seconde moitié du XIIe siècle', *Archéologie Médiévale*, 39 (2009), 31–51 (pp. 39–41).

Map 2 Foundations associated with King John

Links to these foundations might suggest that establishing new houses was an important aspect of John's religious activity. The evidence is worthy of review here, as in several cases it is patchy. It is sometimes suggested that John founded the nunnery of St Margaret, Broomhall.[66] He was certainly a benefactor, granting the church of nearby Sunninghill in 1200, in pure and perpetual alms, 'for the sake of God's love' (*divini amoris intuitu*), for his wellbeing and for the souls of his ancestors. In 1204, he pardoned, in perpetuity, payment of forty pence a year owed for a virgate of land in Windsor. A further gift, forty shillings, followed in 1213.[67]

Later kings followed suit, notably Henry III, but with no indication that his forebears founded the nunnery.[68] Under Edward I, letters granting licence to enclose an area within the forest of Windsor referred to the welfare of the souls of the king

[66] Knowles and Hadcock, p. 256; Hallam, 'Aspects', pp. 148–50.
[67] RC, pp. 48b, 136a; London, National Archives, C52/26, membrane 4; RM, p. 258. For possible evidence of honouring the pardon: PR 6 John, pp. 56, 57; PR 8 John, p. 226. See also: P. D. Ditchfield and W. Page (eds), VCH Berkshire, 4 vols (London, 1906-24), vol. II, p. 80.
[68] CChR 1226–1257, pp. 70, 242, 290; CChR. Henry III–Edward I. 1257–1300, HMSO (London, 1906), p. 43; CPR 1225–1232, p. 470; CPR 1232–1247, p. 479; CPR. Henry III. 1258–1266, HMSO (London, 1910), p. 462; FR 27 Henry III, Henry III Fine Rolls Project [http://www.finerollshenry3.org.uk/content/calendar/roll_040a.html, accessed 16 July 2013], no. 815; FR 33 Henry III, Henry III Fine Rolls Project [http://www.finerollshenry3.org.uk/content/calendar/roll_046.html, accessed 16 July 2013], no. 65.

and his ancestors, whilst elsewhere Queen Eleanor was described as patron.[69] In the fourteenth century, Edward III and Philippa of Hainault licensed provision to support a chaplain celebrating daily for the king's wellbeing, for his soul after death, and for the souls of his predecessors and of the queen's kinsmen.[70] At least part of the archive compiled by the nuns was lost to fire in 1462, although surviving thirteenth- and fourteenth-century charters suggest that the destruction cannot have been all-encompassing.[71] Finally, when the house was dissolved (1521), the inquest noted its foundation by Henry VIII's 'progenitors'.[72] Even so, John cannot have been founder. A Benedictine nunnery existed at Broomhall as early as 1157-58.[73] Nor do his gifts suggest sufficient largesse to support an argument that he sought to be treated as a founder or co-founder. The principal evidence indicates that royal association came later in the thirteenth century.

Nor was John the founder of Otterton, although he perhaps increased an existing endowment. The manor and further revenues were granted by William the Conqueror to the Norman abbey of Mont-St-Michel. John's role, according to later evidence, conceivably amounted to a re-foundation.[74] Inquiries in 1332 suggested that he had founded the priory after 1199, for the souls of his forebears. Four monks would celebrate masses there, with bread provided for the poor to the value of sixteen shillings per week, in perpetuity. To support this, the king had apparently given manors at Otterton, Sidmouth, and Budleigh, worth £100 a year.[75] A question mark remains: John appears to have been credited with grants made by William I and Henry I.[76]

The records of John's reign include few references to Otterton. In 1205, Prior Nicholas fined ten marks for custody of lands of the abbot of Mont-St-Michel, an

---

[69] CPR. Edward I. 1281-1292, HMSO (London, 1893), p. 58; Cambridge, St John's College, Ms. D 14.163.1, noted by English Monastic Archives, database 2: [http://www.monasticarchives.org.uk/databrowse/monarc/archive/objects/3211/, accessed 16 July 2013].

[70] CPR. Edward III. 1350-1354, HMSO (London, 1907), pp. 193, 319.

[71] Ditchfield and Page, VCH Berkshire, vol. II, pp. 80-1, vol. III, p. 88; F. Turner, 'The Benedictine Priory of Broomhall, Berks: Some New Facts Relating to its History and Suppression', The Berks, Bucks & Oxon Archaeological Journal, 27 (1922-23), 90-5, 183-9 (p. 90).

[72] Letters and Papers, Foreign and Domestic, Henry VIII, Volume III: 1519-1523, ed. J. S. Brewer, 2 vols (London, 1867), vol. II, p. 895 (no. 2080); Ditchfield and Page, VCH Berkshire, vol. II, p. 81.

[73] S. Thompson, Women Religious: The Founding of English Nunneries after the Norman Conquest (Oxford, 1991), pp. 8 n. 10, 164; EEA 18, p. xxxii.

[74] Knowles and Hadcock, pp. 84, 90-1; Hallam, 'Aspects', pp. 148-50. For William I's grant: Domesday Book. A Complete Translation, ed. A. Williams and G. H. Martin (London, 2002), p. 291b; D. J. A. Matthew, The Norman Monasteries and their English Possessions (Oxford, 1962), p. 31.

[75] Dugdale, Monasticon, vol. VI, pt 2, p. 1034; Monasticon Diocesis Exoniensis, ed. G. Oliver (Exeter and London, 1846), pp. 249-50; calendared in translation in CCR. Edward III. 1330-1333, HMSO (London, 1898), p. 480.

[76] Matthew, Norman Monasteries, pp. 42-3; Monasticon Diocesis Exoniensis, pp. 248a, 257b. In endowing Reading, Henry I had taken churches from Mont-St-Michel in exchange for revenues at Budleigh: RAC1, pp. 17 n. 1, 39 (no. 3), 144 (no. 175); Reading Abbey Cartularies 2, pp. 72-3 (no. 771).

arrangement reflecting the knock-on effects of the loss of Normandy. Nicholas promised not to send money to the mother house, and to respond to the king for his temporalities.[77] It seems the interdict caused Mont-St-Michel's estates in Devon and Cornwall to be taken into royal hands again. Their restoration was ordered in November 1212. We might presume that this included Otterton.[78] None of this suggests that John regarded this house with affection. If a connection was established by the fourteenth-century inquiry, evidence no longer survives. However, that investigators working over a century after his death deemed John capable of such a foundation is noteworthy, given his posthumous reputation.

The Gilbertine house of St Margaret at Marlborough may well have been a royal foundation. It was being claimed as such in 1399.[79] Evidence from Henry III's reign suggests that the house could have been founded under Henry II. However, it does not feature on a list of Gilbertine priories of c. 1195, leading Golding to suggest that the priory was established between 1195 and 1199.[80] This raises the possibility that the priory, located close to the royal castle, was founded by John or Richard I. Marlborough was a location favoured by John, both before and after he became king.[81] The antiquary Thomas Tanner believed that the house dated to the beginning of John's reign, but stopped short of naming the king as the founder, unlike Rose Graham.[82] The priory was specifically mentioned when John took the Gilbertine order under his protection in 1199. However, this renewed arrangements made by the king's father, and many (although not all) of the houses mentioned had been established during Henry II's reign.[83] Evidence from 1236 suggests a tentative link. Here, land at Marlborough once given by John, as count of Mortain, to one William Crossbowman, was given to the Gilbertine house to hold in perpetual alms. This was done for the soul of Henry III, his ancestors and heirs, with the assent of William's heir, Thomas. However, overall there is little to link John to this house. It appears that it was Henry III who was the principal royal benefactor.[84]

There is stronger evidence linking John to a second Gilbertine house, Newstead-on-Ancholme (Lincolnshire). Henry II created this house in the early 1170s. His

---

77 *ROF*, p. 328; 'Chartes d'Otterton, Prieuré dépendant de l'abbaye de Mont-Saint-Michel', ed. L. Guilloreau, *Revue Mabillon*, 5 (1909) 169–206 (pp. 171, 177); Matthew, *Norman Monasteries*, p. 73.

78 *RLC 1204–24*, p. 127b.

79 Dugdale, *Monasticon*, vol. VI, p. 981; *CPR. Richard II. 1396–1399*, HMSO (London, 1927), p. 560. See also R. B. Pugh and E. Crittal (eds), *VCH Wiltshire*, vol. III (London, 1956), pp. 316–19.

80 *CR 1227–1231*, HMSO (London, 1902), p. 190; Golding, *Gilbert*, pp. 225–7, 448.

81 Vincent, 'Jean', p. 42; 'Itinerary'; Golding, *Gilbert*, p. 226.

82 *Notitia Monastica: Or, an Account of all the Abbies, Priories, and Houses of Friers, heretofore in England and Wales; And also of all the Colleges and Hospitals founded before A.D. MDXL*, ed. T. Tanner (London, 1744), p. 604; Graham, *S. Gilbert of Sempringham*, list of errata.

83 *RC*, p. 18a-b; *Cartae Antiquae Rolls 1–10*, pp. 31–3 (no. 57).

84 *CChR 1226–1257*, p. 219; *Fine Roll 20 Henry III*, Henry III Fine Rolls Project [http://www.finerollshenry3.org.uk/content/calendar/roll_035.html, accessed 14 March 2011], no. 199; Pugh and Crittal, *VCH Wiltshire*, vol. III, pp. 316–17; Golding, *Gilbert*, pp. 226–7.

foundation charter made clear that this was for his soul, those of Queen Eleanor his wife, his father Geoffrey of Anjou, his grandfather Henry I, and of the kings who should succeed him. His son's gifts were sufficient for him to be remembered as co-founder.[85] In 1201, for the wellbeing of his soul, and for his ancestors and successors, in pure and perpetual alms, John granted the canons land in Howsham (Lincolnshire) for which sixty-six shillings was previously paid at the Exchequer.[86] This appears largely unremarkable, but Newstead was not heavily endowed, so perhaps the king's gift was sufficient to accord him the status of co-founder. In addition, this was the house where Gilbert of Sempringham, who established the order, received the last rites in 1188. John's grant came at around the time when he attended the first inquiry into Gilbert's miracles and wrote in support of his canonisation.[87] Perhaps this explains his grant, and why he was remembered as co-founder. At the dissolution of the monasteries, it was noted that on the anniversary of the deaths of the founders, Henry II and John, benefit was sought for their souls through distribution of alms to the poor.[88]

Confusingly, further evidence links John to another Newstead, the priory of Augustinian canons in Nottinghamshire. Here, he made a grant to the abbey as count of Mortain, stating that he had founded the priory with his father, Henry II. The grant, made for his wellbeing and for the souls of his ancestors, gave £7 6d of land in pure and perpetual alms, and confirmed his father's gifts.[89] Under Edward II, it was said that John's endowment included lands to the value of £15.[90]

Newstead's location, in a county given to John by Richard I in 1189, may explain the association.[91] As king, John confirmed his earlier grant, in 1205, this time for his soul and those of his ancestors and heirs. The revenues assigned to the abbey were paid annually.[92] His provision extended to the priory's buildings. In summer 1207, the canons were allowed to acquire marl and timber, provided this did not damage the royal forest, with more timber given in 1215. The prior received the prebend of Oxton (Nottinghamshire) at farm, custody of neighbouring Thurgarton when the priorate there fell vacant in 1205, and crops from a donor's lands seized

---

[85] Hallam, 'Henry II as a Founder', p. 120; Dugdale, *Monasticon*, vol. VI, pt 2, p. 966; Graham, *S. Gilbert of Sempringham*, p. 39.

[86] RC, p. 84b. The revenues were allocated across the reign: PR 3 *John*, p. 1; PR 4 *John*, p. 218; PR 5 *John*, p. 105; PR 6 *John*, p. 63; PR 7 *John*, pp. 197, 198; PR 8 *John*, p. 87; PR 9 *John*, p. 15; PR 10 *John*, pp. 76, 77; PR 11 *John*, p. 66; PR 12 *John*, p. 17; PR 13 *John*, p. 69; PR 14 *John*, p. 102; PR 16 *John*, p. 145.

[87] Graham, *S. Gilbert of Sempringham*, pp. 23-4. See also above, Chapter 2.

[88] *Valor Ecclesiasticus*, vol. IV, p. 72; Graham, *S. Gilbert of Sempringham*, p. 168.

[89] Mortain; drawn from London, College of Arms, Ms. Arundel 60 (Newstead Cartulary). Henry II made his foundation for his soul and those of Henry I and Geoffrey of Anjou: Dugdale, *Monasticon*, vol. VI, part 1, p. 474.

[90] EEA 27. *York 1189–1212*, ed. M. Lovatt (Oxford, 2004), pp. 54-5 (no. 46 n.).

[91] For the lands Richard conferred on John: Gillingham, *Richard*, pp. 119-20; Turner and Heiser, *Reign of Richard Lionheart*, pp. 75-7.

[92] RC, p. 145a-b; PR 2 *John*, pp. 7, 8; PR 3 *John*, p. 88; PR 4 *John*, p. 186; PR 5 *John*, p. 164; PR 6 *John*, p. 161; PR 7 *John*, p. 220; PR 8 *John*, p. 75; PR 9 *John*, p. 113; PR 11 *John*, p. 109; PR 12 *John*, p. 124; PR 13 *John*, p. 211; PR 14 *John*, p. 160; PR 16 *John*, p. 156.

into the king's hand in 1212. A further indication of royal favour followed the imposition of the interdict and seizure of church property. The prior was allowed his lands, dues, and possessions, for so long as it pleased the king.[93]

If Newstead was founded by Henry II in the 1160s, then his youngest son, aged only four at the end of the decade, is unlikely initially to have been co-founder.[94] In all likelihood he was not involved until the 1190s. Arrangements concerning Henry's grants to Newstead, made in 1191 by John's close associate, Bishop Hugh de Nonant, made no reference to the count of Mortain.[95] If John's activity post-dated 1191, it may well have emulated his father in claiming to be co-founder of already established religious communities. Henry II followed Henry I, Stephen, and the Capetian kings of France in acting in this way.[96]

Another of Henry II's sons supported this house. John's half-brother, the old king's illegitimate son Geoffrey, who became archbishop of York in 1189, issued charters in favour of Newstead in the 1190s. He gave revenues in the church of Misterton (Nottinghamshire), for Henry II's soul and his own. Monies from this church also formed part of the grant made by John. Geoffrey also confirmed several of Henry II's grants, making no mention of John's. It may be that this pattern continued. When Henry VIII broke with Rome, the *Valor Ecclesiasticus* (1535) noted Easter provision for the soul of Henry II, recorded as the priory's founder, with no reference to John.[97]

As Lord of Ireland, John is associated with two, perhaps three, foundations in Waterford. This was probably the first town he visited in Ireland in 1185, site of the infamous beard-pulling incident recounted by Gerald of Wales, but also the would-be 'king' of Ireland's centre of operations during his unsuccessful expedition.[98] John landed there again in 1210, and the town's place at the heart of royal affairs suggests why he might have felt it appropriate to found religious establishments there.[99] If so, he would have emulated his father, who granted land to the Templars at the point where he made landfall in 1171.[100] John's first foundation

---

[93] *RLC 1204–24*, pp. 87a, 90a, 112b, 123a, 192b; *RLP*, pp. 50b, 51b.
[94] Various dates are suggested. For c. 1163: Knowles and Hadcock, p. 167. For c. September 1165×66: *EEA 16. Coventry and Lichfield 1160–1182*, ed. M. J. Franklin (Oxford, 1998), pp. 72–3 (no. 79 n.). For c.1170: W. Page (ed), *VCH Nottingham*, vol. II (London, 1910), p. 112.
[95] *EEA 17*, pp. 39–40 (no. 44).
[96] Hallam, 'Henry II as a Founder', pp. 129–30, and see also p. 126.
[97] *EEA 27*, pp. 54–6 (nos 46–7); *Valor Ecclesiasticus*, vol. V, p. 154.
[98] S. Duffy, 'John and Ireland: The Origins of England's Irish Problem', *King John: New Interpretations*, ed. S. D. Church (Woodbridge, 1999), pp. 221–45 (pp. 229–31); F. X. Martin, 'Overlord Becomes Feudal Lord, 1172–85', *A New History of Ireland: II. Medieval Ireland 1169–1185*, ed. A. Cosgrove, second impression (Oxford, 1993), pp. 122–3, and see also p. 128.
[99] S. Duffy, 'King John's Expedition to Ireland, 1210: The Evidence Reconsidered', *Irish Historical Studies*, 30 (1996), 1–24 (p. 2); 'Itinerary'.
[100] C. L. Falkiner, 'The Hospital of St John of Jerusalem in Ireland', *Proceedings of the Royal Irish Academy. Section C: Archaeology, Celtic Studies, History, Linguistics, Literature*, 26 (1906/07), 275–317 (p. 287); *CDI, 1171–1251*, ed. H. S. Sweetman (London, 1875), p. 225 (no. 1488); *CDI 1285–1292*, ed. H. S. Sweetman (London, 1879), p. 329 (no. 666).

at Waterford was a Benedictine hospital and alms-house, dedicated to St John the Evangelist, in around 1191.[101] In the early 1190s the brothers and their men were taken into his peace and protection, receiving trading rights across his lands. John described the community as his alms-house.[102] Two further grants were issued for the soul of the count of Mortain's father, and for his brothers.[103] As king, John confirmed his earlier arrangements, and in 1204 approved an agreement whereby the house, of four brothers and three sisters, was attached to the English Benedictine Priory of St Peter and St Paul at Bath, who paid five marks for the confirmation.[104] Linked to this foundation in Waterford was a cell or hospital in Cork, again dedicated to St John the Evangelist and described by the lord of Ireland as his alms-house. John granted various lands in Cork and the surrounding area, burgage plots in Dungarvan, and a mill, for the souls of Henry II and for John's brothers. As at Waterford, the community linked up with Bath in 1204.[105]

The second Waterford community, the leper hospital of St Stephen, was begun after 1185 and confirmed by John to the town's poor.[106] It was traditionally believed that the foundation came about when either the king or his sons suffered some sort of skin complaint – which might have been perceived as leprosy – after overindulging on salmon and cider whilst at Lismore.[107] A third house, the Augustinian priory of St Katherine, was later linked with John. It received the king's protection in 1207, the earliest recorded reference to its existence. In 1290, Edward I noted that the community had been established, 'as is said', by his grandfather. The note

[101] A. Gwynn and R. N. Hadcock, *Medieval Religious Houses Ireland* (Dublin, 1970), pp. 108, 356; P. Power, 'The Priory, Church and Hospital of St John the Evangelist, Waterford', *Journal of the South East of Ireland Archaeological Society*, 2 (1896), 81-97; A. O'Neill, 'Waterford Diocese, 1096-1363: Part Five. Religious Foundations in the Diocese of Waterford', *Decies. Journal of the Old Waterford Society*, 47 (1993), 42-51 (pp. 45-7); Harvey, 'Piety', p. 15.

[102] *Chartae, Privilegia et Immunitates, Transcripts of Charters and Privileges to Cities, Towns, Abbeys, and Other Bodies Corporate. 18 Henry II to 18 Richard II (1171 to 1395)*, Irish Record Commission (Dublin, London and Edinburgh, 1829-30), p. 9; CChR. *Edward I, Edward II. 1300-1326*, HMSO (London, 1908), p. 282; *Mortain*.

[103] *Chartae, Privilegia et Immunitates*, p. 10; Oxford, Bodleian Library, Ms. Rawlinson B 479 fo. 55r-v. Both will be printed in: *Mortain*.

[104] RLP, p. 24a; CDI 1171-1251, p. 27 (no. 173) and see also pp. 33-4 (nos 219, 220), 38 (no. 250); RC, p. 136b; ROF, p. 212; PR 6 John, p. 185; Gwynn and Hadcock, *Medieval Religious Houses Ireland*, pp. 108, 356.

[105] Oxford, Bodleian Library, Ms. Rawlinson B 479 fo. 56r-57r; calendared in C. McNeill, 'Rawlinson Manuscripts (Class B)', *Analecta Hibernica*, 1 (1930), 118-78 (p. 123). A printed edition will appear in: *Mortain*. See also: RLC 1224-27, p. 133b; CDI 1171-1251, p. 217 (no. 1437); Gwynn and Hadcock, *Medieval Religious Houses Ireland*, p. 105.

[106] Harvey, 'Piety', p. 15; Gwynn and Hadcock, *Medieval Religious Houses Ireland*, pp. 356-7; 'Inquisition of 1601 Regarding the Lazar or Leper House, Waterford', *Journal of the Waterford and South East Ireland Archaeological Society*, 1 (1895), 115-18 (p. 115).

[107] G. A. Lee, *Leper Hospitals in Medieval Ireland with a Short Account of the Military and Hospitaller Order of St Lazarus of Jerusalem* (Blackrock Co. Dublin, 1996), pp. 42-3.

of caution is striking. It appears that buildings that perhaps had little connection with John were associated with him as early as the thirteenth century itself.[108]

Hospitals provide similar difficulties in determining whether or not John was founder and in gauging the extent of his investment. Working from south to north, that of St Bartholomew, Newbury, was remembered into the twentieth century as 'King John's alms-houses'. Amongst the surviving buildings, the clock tower, erected in 1698, bears an inscription claiming him as founder.[109] Medieval evidence comes from the grant of the right to hold a fair, issued in 1215 within weeks of Magna Carta. The fair was to last two days, starting on the feast of St Bartholomew (24 August). John's charter was issued 'for God', for the souls of the king, his ancestors and successors. The implication is that the hospital already existed, so the king was an important benefactor rather than founder.[110] It was established by c. 1210, as it is recorded in the *Mappa Mundi* of Gervase of Canterbury, who probably died in or shortly after that year.[111] No mention of John as founder was made when the hospital came to royal attention under Henry III. Whoever established this community is as unknown to us as it was to Edward VI's commissioners in the sixteenth century.[112]

More convincing evidence concerns the leper house of St Laurence, Bristol. In 1208, John confirmed letters patent he had issued as count of Mortain. Here, the lepers were given a croft outside Laffard's (or Lawford's) gate on the road to Bath. This they were permitted to enclose and inhabit. They received John's protection and land which had belonged to one William Balle.[113] The site is likely to have been carefully chosen. It conformed to expectations that lepers would live outside the urban community, but was 'within a few paces of the market', with all the benefits that could bring.[114] Royal protection was maintained across John's reign.

---

[108] *RLP*, p. 76b; Gwynn and Hadcock, *Medieval Religious Houses Ireland*, p. 197; *CDI 1285–1292*, p. 326 (no. 656); O'Neill, 'Waterford Diocese', p. 43. On buildings bearing John's name, see the comment in: Duffy, 'King John's Expedition to Ireland, 1210', p. 1.

[109] R. M. Clay, *The Mediaeval Hospitals of England* (London, 1909), p. 72; Dugdale, *Monasticon*, vol. VI, pt. 2, p. 754; S. T. Cope, 'St Bartholomew's Hospital, Newbury', *Berkshire Archaeological Journal*, 39 (1935), 35–57 (p. 35); 'St Bartholomew's Hospital Newbury', British Listed Buildings [http://www.britishlistedbuildings.co.uk/en-393611-st-bartholomews-hospital-newbury-, accessed 9 November 2013].

[110] *RC*, p. 212a; *RLC 1204–24*, p. 219b; Cope, 'St Bartholomew's Hospital', p. 49; Clay, *Mediaeval Hospitals*, p. 183; Knowles and Hadcock, p. 378.

[111] Gervase of Canterbury, *Mappa Mundi*, ed. W. Stubbs, *The Historical Works of Gervase of Canterbury*, RS 73, 2 vols (London, 1879–80), vol. II, p. 421; G. H. Martin, 'Canterbury, Gervase of (b. c. 1145, d. in or after 1210)', *ODNB* (Oxford, 2004) [http://www.oxforddnb.com/view/article/10570, accessed 21 August 2013]; Cope, 'St Bartholomew's Hospital', pp. 35–6.

[112] *FR 20 Henry III*, no. 94; Cope, 'St Bartholomew's Hospital', p. 36.

[113] *RC*, p. 175b. *Monasticon Anglicanum* prints this as a charter to the hospital of St John the Baptist, Bristol, but it is generally thought to have been for St Laurence: Dugdale, *Monasticon*, vol. VI, pt 2, p. 670; Knowles and Hadcock, p. 347; Harvey, 'Piety', p. 15; Hallam, 'Aspects', p. 151. The leper house of St John of Bristol received royal protection in 1200: *RC*, pp. 77b.

[114] C. Rawcliffe, *Leprosy in Medieval England* (Woodbridge, 2006), p. 311.

In 1215 the king ordered the constable of Bristol, Philip d'Aubigny to restore land taken from the lepers on the orders of the feared royal agent Girard d'Athée.[115]

On the outskirts of Northampton, the hospital of St David, or Holy Trinity, at Kingsthorpe, also claimed John as founder, according to sixteenth-century evidence. The *Valor Ecclesiasticus* recorded that two pauper brothers, Thomas Abroughe and John Young, prayed daily for the late king, the hospital's founder, receiving sixty-five shillings a year.[116] This house is thought to have been established in around 1200, from the Cluniac priory of St Andrew at Northampton.[117] Beyond this, lack of surviving evidence makes it impossible to confirm an association.

Another leper hospital, that of St Leonard, Chesterfield, is thought to have been founded or re-founded by John in around 1195. At around this time, the community began to receive an annual grant of £6, an endowment made along with other privileges, which Hallam argues constituted a re-foundation.[118] The community existed by 1195, when it is recorded holding a fair at Chesterfield.[119] It was granted royal letters of protection in 1199-1200.[120] In 1207, a royal charter was issued for John's wellbeing, for the souls of his ancestors and heirs, to God, the blessed Leonard, and the sick of Chesterfield. This confirmed an exchange made before John became king, when tolls given in the town's market and fair were replaced with payment of £6 per year in pure and perpetual alms. This sum was accounted to the lepers from the beginning of the reign onwards.[121] The grant may have predated 1195, with the count of Mortain's involvement explained by Chesterfield's location within the lands he was allocated by his brother. Whether John's commitment was sustained is debateable. The community paid twenty marks for the privilege confirmed in 1207.[122] There is no further evidence of benefaction,

---

[115] *RLC 1204-24*, p. 227a. D'Athée was dead by June 1215, when his relatives were proscribed in Magna Carta: N. Vincent, 'Athée, Girard d' (fl. 1198-c. 1210)', *ODNB* (Oxford, 2004, online edn 2008) [http://www.oxforddnb.com/view/article/39497, accessed 6 November 2013]; Holt, *Magna Carta*, pp. 264-5. D'Aubigny succeeded him as constable of Bristol in July 1215: N. Vincent, 'Aubigny, Philip d' (d. 1236)', *ODNB* (Oxford, 2004, online edn 2006) [http://www.oxforddnb.com/view/article/47227, accessed 6 November 2013].

[116] *Valor Ecclesiasticus*, vol. IV, p. 322. They also prayed for John's progenitors and successors as king.

[117] Knowles and Hadcock, p. 367; R. M. Serjeantson and W. R. D. Atkins (eds), *VCH Northampton*, vol. II (London, 1906), pp. 154-6.

[118] Hallam, 'Aspects', pp. 150-1; Knowles and Hadcock, p. 351; Harvey, 'Piety' p. 15.

[119] *PR 7 Richard I*, p. 16; *The Chancellor's Roll for the Eighth Year of the Reign of King Richard the First, Michaelmas 1196 (Pipe Roll 42)*, ed. D. M. Stenton, PRS, 45, ns 7 (London, 1930), p. 266; *PR 9 Richard I*, p. 144; *PR 10 Richard I*, p. 111; S. Letters, *Gazetteer of Markets and Fairs in England and Wales to 1516* [http://www.history.ac.uk/cmh/gaz/gazweb2.html, accessed 28 October 2013] (Derbyshire); Rawcliffe, *Leprosy*, pp. 314-15 n. 48.

[120] *RC*, p. 60b.

[121] *RC*, p. 167a; *PR 1 John*, pp. 199-200; *PR 2 John*, pp. 7, 8; *PR 3 John*, p. 88; *PR 4 John*, p. 186; *PR 5 John*, p. 164; *PR 6 John*, p. 161; *PR 7 John*, p. 222; *PR 8 John*, pp. 76-7; *PR 9 John*, pp. 115, 189; *PR 10 John*, p. 75; *PR 11 John*, pp. 92, 111; *PR 12 John*, p. 167; *PR 13 John*, p. 255; *PR 14 John*, p. 71; *PR 16 John*, p. 141; *PR 17 John*, p. 64. In the middle years of the reign, the lepers also received sums of 5 marks: *PR 10 John*, p. 7; *PR 11 John*, p. 44.

[122] *ROF*, p. 379; *PR 9 John*, p. 124.

although in 1225 it was noted that the alms given by John had been for a time withheld by William Brewer. Orders were issued for the payment to resume, as the king did not wish his alms to be lost. Brewer's descendants may not have obliged. The house claimed it was being impeded in receipt of its alms in 1234, when the annual payment of £6 was again confirmed.[123]

A second hospital dedicated to St Leonard, this time at Lancaster, was also said to have been founded by John.[124] The community appears to have existed by the early 1190s. Forest pleas of Edward I's reign preserve a charter of John, as count of Mortain, referring to the hospital when describing the boundary of lands given to Lancaster Priory in the reign of William Rufus.[125] Evidence from Henry III's reign suggests that his father probably granted rights to the hospital. In 1220, it was claiming to have lost its charters during the civil war that followed Magna Carta, but 'have given us to understand ... [that] they were established and founded in our alms'.[126] This did not persuade Henry to great acts of largesse, but the community received royal protection in 1225, and confirmation of forest rights held under John in 1229.[127] An inquisition of Edward II's reign claimed John as founder. The investigators concluded that he had established the hospital, giving land, a water-mill, and pasture. The endowment was sufficient for a master, chaplain, and nine paupers, three of whom were to be lepers. This is now thought unlikely to reflect the original arrangements.[128] Again, this is evidence that, over a century after his death, John could be remembered as founder of a religious community. However, this cannot be proved from the evidence of his lifetime itself.

Further north, Hallam suggests that in around 1199 Henry II's youngest son was either founder or a generous benefactor of the hospital of St Nicholas, Carlisle, although Clay suggests that this house received lay benefaction as early as 1180.[129] Others see the hospital as a royal foundation, but before John's reign,

---

[123] *FR 9 Henry III*, Henry III Fine Rolls Project [http://www.finerollshenry3.org.uk/content/calendar/roll_022.html, accessed 30 July 2013], no. 88; *CChR 1226–1257*, p. 177; *CR 1231–1234*, HMSO (London, 1905), pp. 215, 452; *CPR 1232–1247*, p. 57. For later royal grants: W. Page (ed.), *VCH Derby*, vol. II (London, 1907), pp. 81–2.

[124] Knowles and Hadcock, p. 368; Hallam, 'Aspects', p. 150; W. Farrer and J. Brownbill (eds), *VCH Lancaster*, vol. II (London, 1908), p. 165; Clay, *Mediaeval Hospitals*, p. 300.

[125] *The Lancashire Pipe Rolls of 31 Henry I, A.D. 1130, and of the Reigns of Henry II, A.D. 1155–1189; Richard I, A.D. 1188–1199; and King John, A.D. 1199–1216. The Latin text extended and notes added. Also Early Lancashire Charters of the period from the Reign of William Rufus to that of King John*, ed. W. Farrer (Liverpool, 1902), pp. 298–300, and see also pp. 289–90.

[126] RLC 1204–24, p. 414b; translated in *Lancashire Inquests, Extents, and Feudal Aids. A.D. 1205–A.D. 1307*, ed. W. Farrer, The Record Society for the Publication of Original Documents relating to Lancashire and Cheshire, 48 (Liverpool, 1903), p. 88.

[127] *CPR 1216–1225*, p. 525; *CR 1227–1231*, pp. 182, 195.

[128] *Calendar of Inquisitions Miscellaneous (Chancery) Preserved in the Public Record Office. Vol. II, Edward II–22 Edward III*, HMSO (London, 1916), p. 167 (no. 672); Rawcliffe, *Leprosy*, p. 320 n. 73. See also London, National Archives, SC8/123/6135; Farrer and Brownbill, *VCH Lancaster*, p. 165; E. Baines, *History of the County Palatine and Duchy of Lancaster*, 4 vols (London, Paris and New York, 1836), vol. IV, p. 517.

[129] Hallam, 'Aspects', p. 151; Clay, *Mediaeval Hospitals*, p. 130. Clay's unreferenced suggestion is probably based on: Dugdale, *Monasticon*, vol. VI, p. 757. This includes a grant of tithe

whilst excavations have found pottery dating to the late twelfth or early thirteenth century.[130] Possessions appear to have been granted either side of 1200, including a gift by Hugh de Morville, lord of nearby Burgh-by-Sands, who died in 1202.[131] Hugh's grant was made for himself, his wife, ancestors and heirs, including his father and mother, and for the soul of a prominent courtier of Henry II's reign, Hugh de Cressy, who died in 1189.[132] De Morville's donation was probably made during Richard I's reign, although possibly under John. It was certainly made by 1201.[133]

In the mid-1330s, a writ of Edward III referred to the hospital as a royal foundation.[134] During a visitation recorded in 1341, the community reported that records of their foundation had long since been burned. However, constitutions had been established in 1292-93 by Hugh of Cressingham, senior eyre justice in northern England, who was granted mastership of the hospital for life by Edward I. These stipulated that the inmates begin their day by entering the church or chapel 'to pray for the faithful departed, all benefactors of the hospital, and especially for the king, the queen and their children'. This, however, referred to the family of Edward I. The 1341 jurors swore that the hospital had been founded 'long before time of memory, by some king of England, whose name they know not', for a master, thirteen leprous men and women, and a chaplain performing mass daily for the benefactors. The anonymous royal founder had given: 'great possessions of lands for the perpetual support of the said alms, appointed for them a chapter,

---

revenues from Little Bampton (Cumbria) dated to 1180. Wiseman, however, notes reference to Bishop Bernard of Carlisle, suggesting the document dates c. 1200-14: W. G. Wiseman, 'The Hospital of St Nicholas, Carlisle and its Masters; Part 1 - The Period up to 1333', *Transactions of the Cumberland & Westmorland Antiquarian and Archaeological Society*, 95 (1995), 93-109 (p. 95 and n. 24); H. Summerson, 'Bernard (d. 1214)', *ODNB* (Oxford, 2008, online edn 2009) [http://www.oxforddnb.com/view/article/95121, accessed 7 November 2013].

[130] Knowles and Hadcock, p. 350; J. Wilson (ed.), *VCH Cumberland*, vol. II (London, 1905), p. 199; C. Howard-Davis and M. Leah, 'Excavations at St Nicholas Yard, Carlisle, 1996-7', *Transactions of the Cumberland & Westmorland Antiquarian and Archaeological Society*, 99 (1999), 89-115 (pp. 95-6, 102-4).

[131] *CPR. Edward III. 1340-1343*, HMSO (London, 1900), p. 121; Rawcliffe, *Leprosy*, p. 295; Wiseman, 'Hospital of St Nicholas, Carlisle and its Masters; Part 1', pp. 94-5. The donor is not to be confused with the Hugh de Morville involved in the murder of Thomas Becket: R. M. Franklin, 'Morville, Hugh de (d. 1173/4)', *ODNB* (Oxford, 2004) [http://www.oxforddnb.com/view/article/19379, accessed 29 October 2013]; N. Vincent, 'The Murderers of Thomas Becket', *Bischofsmord im Mittelalter*, ed. N. Fryde and D. Reitz (Göttingen, 2003), pp. 211-72 (p. 225).

[132] *The Register of John Kirkby. Bishop of Carlisle 1332-1352 and the Register of John Ross Bishop of Carlisle, 1325-32*, ed. R. L. Storey, 2 vols, Canterbury and York Society, 79 and 81 (Woodbridge, 1992 and 1995), vol. I, p. 38 (no. 226); vol. II, pp. 27-8 (no. 226); T. K. Keefe, 'Cressy, Hugh de (d. 1189)', *ODNB* (Oxford, 2004) [http://www.oxforddnb.com/view/article/57614, accessed 1 November 2013].

[133] Wiseman, 'Hospital of St Nicholas, Carlisle and its Masters; Part 1', p. 95 and n. 22.

[134] *Register of John Kirkby*, vol. I, pp. 56 (no. 296), 167 (no. 809); W. G. Wiseman, 'The Hospital of St Nicholas, Carlisle and its Masters; Part 2 - The Period from 1333', *Transactions of the Cumberland & Westmorland Antiquarian and Archaeological Society*, 96 (1996), 51-69 (p. 52).

and a common seal ... and ordained that the lepers should always be clad in cloths of russet'.¹³⁵

Can this foundation be linked to King John? Some historians have suggested that the royal founder was William Rufus, although the archaeological evidence suggests this is unlikely. In c. 1300 it was claimed that Aethelwold, the first bishop of Carlisle, was granted oversight of the hospital by Henry II in return for the appointment of a chaplain who would perform services for the king, his ancestors, and successors.¹³⁶ In the early fourteenth century, the prior and canons of Carlisle complained that a chaplain drawn from their ranks, who prayed for the souls of the kings of England, had been ousted during the episcopacy of Hugh of Beaulieu in favour of one of the bishop's clerks.¹³⁷ The association with Henry II might suggest why the lepers of St Nicholas sought John's protection in 1201, when he visited the city. This does not appear to have been a community that he established himself.¹³⁸ He may, however, have exercised the right to nominate its master, as Edward I's representatives argued in a dispute of 1292 with Bishop John Halton. King John was said to have conferred the hospital on his clerk, Robert fitz Ralph.¹³⁹ The hospital successfully petitioned the king for support in 1305, on the grounds that the advowson belonged to the king and that their buildings had been destroyed by Scottish raids.¹⁴⁰ In 1477, the hospital became the property of the prior and canons of Carlisle, but its longstanding royal links were acknowledged in the promise that a priest, known as the king's chaplain, would pray for Edward IV and his family.¹⁴¹

Overall, the various small houses to which John is linked as founder or principal benefactor were not houses envisaged as large or significant. In many ways, we should be wary of overstating their importance. There was no dynastic statement

---

¹³⁵ *CPR. 1340–1343*, pp. 119–23 (pp. 120–1); H. Summerson, 'Cressingham, Hugh of (d. 1297)', *ODNB* (Oxford, 2004, online edn 2008) [http://www.oxforddnb.com/view/article/6671, accessed 29 October 2013]; Wiseman, 'Hospital of St Nicholas, Carlisle and its Masters; Part 1', pp. 97–9.

¹³⁶ Wiseman, 'Hospital of St Nicholas, Carlisle and its Masters; Part 1', p. 94; H. Todd, *Notitia Ecclesiae Cathedralis Carliolensis et Notitia Prioratus de Wedderhal*, Cumberland and Westmorland Antiquarian and Archaeological Society, Tract Series 6 (Kendal, 1892), p. 35; Howard-Davis and Leah, 'Excavations', p. 112. For reference to Henry II's grant: London, National Archives, SC8/322/E517; *Northern Petitions Illustrative of Life in Berwick, Cumbria and Durham in the Fourteenth Century*, ed. C. M. Fraser, Surtees Society, 194 (Gateshead, 1981) pp. 110–11 (no. 76).

¹³⁷ London, National Archives, SC8/319/E372.

¹³⁸ *RC*, p. 101b; 'Itinerary'; Wiseman, 'Hospital of St Nicholas, Carlisle and its Masters; Part 1', p. 96.

¹³⁹ Wiseman, 'Hospital of St Nicholas, Carlisle and its Masters; Part 1', pp. 96–7; *Placita de quo warranto temporibus Edw. I. II. & III. in curia receptae scaccarii Westm. Asservata*, ed. W. Illingworth, RComm (London, 1818), p. 122a–b.

¹⁴⁰ London, National Archives, SC8/100/4954; *CCR. Edward I. 1302–1307*, HMSO (London, 1908), p. 256.

¹⁴¹ Wiseman, 'Hospital of St Nicholas, Carlisle and its Masters; Part 2', pp. 63–4; *CPR. Edward IV, Edward V, Richard III. 1478–1485*, HMSO (London, 1901), p. 35.

here, nor did John provide substantial backing compared to his resources, either as count of Mortain or as king. However, we should also be wary of criticising the size of the endowments he made. For the hospitals in particular, his grants may well have constituted a substantial part of their overall endowment, revenues appropriate to the scale of the community concerned. Alternatively, grants of fairs and trading privileges may not have directly endowed a community, but nonetheless provided primary sources of income. We should not always expect religious foundations to be large houses which required the lavishing of substantial sums of money.

Further important conclusions can be drawn. Most of the smaller foundations discussed appear to have been established before John became king.[142] There seems to be a territorial dimension. Many of the houses discussed were located within lands given to John by his brother Richard in 1189. Thus, in south-western England, he was an important benefactor, perhaps re-founder, of Otterton Priory, and founder – or at least the donor of the site – of the leper hospital of St Laurence at Bristol. In the Midlands, he sought to be remembered as co-founder of Augustinian Newstead and supported the leper hospital of St Leonard, Chesterfield. In the north-west, he seems to have given rights to the hospital of St Leonard at Lancaster, whilst in Ireland he is linked to foundations at Waterford and Cork. All this suggests a desire to establish links with the religious, as part of efforts to build and cement authority in his new lands. That said, there is no sense that John founded a religious house in the county of Mortain.

That no single foundation defined John's relationship with the organised religious when he became king adds weight to the significance of Beaulieu. The establishment of a major monastery could be used to emphasise or restate his God-given status as king. John's claim to the throne was not undisputed. The demise of Arthur of Brittany and the loss of Normandy and other lands cannot have increased his prestige. Perhaps this explains Hubert Walter's advice to make a major religious foundation, establishing a dynastic church of his own. It may also account for the initiation of the project at a time when John sought to assert his authority and defend his lands on the Continent. It could also explain his ongoing commitment to Beaulieu, and the plan that this should be the largest Cistercian abbey in England.

It is also significant that several houses were remembered in later centuries as the foundation of King John, whether or not they actually were. His posthumous reputation hardly suggests promise as a founder and benefactor of religious houses. Yet in the thirteenth, fourteenth, and later centuries it was thought that he had founded Otterton, Marlborough, various houses in Waterford, and the hospital of St Leonard at Lancaster. In the sixteenth century he was remembered as co-founder of Newstead-on-Ancholme, though his efforts to be seen similarly at Newstead in Nottinghamshire were apparently forgotten. In some cases, as at the hospital of St Bartholomew, Newbury, the association continued very nearly to the present day.

---

[142] The exception is Newstead-on-Ancholme.

In some cases, as at Broomhall, John was one benefactor amongst many. Here, the community appears to have been an earlier foundation, but was also a house which developed and maintained links with the ruling family across the Middle Ages, as can also be seen in the case of the hospital of St Nicholas, Carlisle. John, like his successors, may well have responded to a link between a religious house and his royal ancestors. This, the family dimension to his personal religion, will provide the focus in the next chapter.

4

Family

A sense of family obligations or unity is not always associated with Henry II and his sons. Henry the Young King, Richard, and Geoffrey of Brittany all rebelled against their father, more than once, in the 1170s and 1180s. John, the youngest son, joined Richard I's alliance with Philip II of France when it became clear that the old king was dying in 1189. The betrayal allegedly caused Henry II to despair of life on his deathbed at Chinon.[1] If this was a recognition of political reality, John proved a greater threat to his family during Richard I's early years as monarch. The crusader king provided his younger brother with a lavish landed endowment, but John was at once a potential heir and a possible threat. The Lionheart showed his awareness that his brother might seek the throne for himself by retaining key castles in the hands of loyal servants, excluding John from the regency council, and initially making him swear an oath to stay out of England for a period of three years (his anticipated absence on crusade). The latter demand was rescinded, but John failed to live up to his elder brother's trust. Eleanor of Aquitaine, said to have intervened to secure John's release from his oath, was forced to act to prevent his alliance with Philip II when the French king returned from the crusade. John then attempted to seize the throne during the period of his brother's captivity.[2]

Critics of the Angevins were well aware of this apparent lack of family unity and its destabilising consequences. Bishop Hugh of Lincoln was credited with the ability to prophesy the dynasty's future. He blamed what he regarded as the unlawful marriage of Henry II to Eleanor of Aquitaine, following the annulment of her union with Louis VII of France (1152). On his deathbed in 1200, the bishop is said to have declared: 'the words of the Bible must inevitably be fulfilled in the case of the descendants of King Henry, "Bastard shoots will not have deep roots" and "the offspring of an adulterous union shall be destroyed"'. Three sons had already

---

[1] Warren, *Henry II*, pp. 116-38, 584-626; Gillingham, *Richard*, pp. 41-51, 66-100; J. A. Everard, *Brittany and the Angevins: Province and Empire 1158-1203* (Cambridge, 2000), pp. 131-42.

[2] Warren, *John*, pp. 39-46; Gillingham, *Richard*, pp. 120, 227-9, 235-6, 239-53; J. Flori (trans O. Classe), *Eleanor of Aquitaine: Queen and Rebel* (Edinburgh, 2007), pp. 139-40, 156-61. For John's release from his oath: *Gesta Regis Henrici Secundi Benedicti Abbatis. The Chronicle of the Reigns of Henry II and Richard I. A.D. 1169-1192; Known Commonly under the Name of Benedict of Peterborough*, ed. W. Stubbs, RS 49, 2 vols (London, 1867), vol. II, p. 106. Also barred from England was Richard and John's illegitimate half-brother, Geoffrey. Richard had sought to neutralise any threat he posed by securing his election, and crucially his consecration, as archbishop of York. Geoffrey's ban was not lifted, resulting in his arrest on his attempted return: *EEA* 27, pp. xxxvii-xlii.

'been destroyed by the French'. John's turn would come.³ Such comments sought to explain Henry II's apparently imploding relationship with sons competing for an increased inheritance. Yet a deceased Angevin sometimes attracted more sympathy from his or her siblings or successors. John regularly sought to provide for the souls of a host of direct relatives and kinsmen. This chapter examines King John's 'family' religious activity, considering how the Angevin kinship network influenced his devotional activity.

Several instances of engagement with family tradition have been discussed in preceding chapters. John continued and perhaps expanded his predecessors' practice of hearing the *Laudes Regiae* on religious and regnal occasions. In establishing masses, provision extended to the souls of his kinsmen. At Lichfield, this included the souls of Henry II, Eleanor of Aquitaine, and Richard I, whilst Bishop Geoffrey Muschamp made arrangements for masses for John, his father, and deceased brothers. At Salisbury and at St Paul's, London, provision was made for marking the anniversary of Henry II's death. Chaplains sponsored by the king fulfilled their duties for the wellbeing of his soul and those of his ancestors and heirs. Likewise we have seen that at Fontevraud – a house central to discussion in the first part of this chapter – John reinforced his mother's largesse, referring to the wellbeing of his soul and the salvation of the souls of Eleanor of Aquitaine, his father and brothers. Elsewhere, the chaplains at Falaise performed masses for John and his ancestors, those at Argentan for John, Henry II, and their ancestors and successors.⁴

A similar picture has been seen in royal devotion to the saints. At Canterbury, John inherited and initially continued the tradition of pilgrimage to the shrine of St Thomas begun by his father and continued by his brother. Like Henry and Richard he combined this with going to Bury St Edmunds. He renewed Richard's grant for tapers at St Edmund's shrine, and confirmed possessions granted to the abbey by his eleventh- and twelfth-century predecessors. Meanwhile, association with the king's canonised kinsman, St Edward the Confessor, was inherent in royal links to Westminster Abbey. Here, John confirmed Richard's grants for the souls of their parents. In devotion to the Virgin Mary, he followed Henry I, Henry II, and Richard I. His patronage of the relics at Reading Abbey involved John in a regnal tradition originating under his great-grandfather. In supporting the canonisation of Gilbert of Sempringham, he associated with an order much favoured by his father.⁵

Likewise, John emulated his kinsmen in founding religious communities. Beaulieu continued longstanding patterns of royal largesse to the Cistercians. The foundation charter referred to the souls of Henry II, Eleanor of Aquitaine, Henry the Young King, Richard I, and all John's ancestors and heirs. For the smaller

---

3   *Magna Vita*, vol. II, pp. 184–5. For the biblical quotations: Wisdom 4:3 and 3:16. On the annulment of Eleanor's first marriage, and her second marriage: Turner, *Eleanor of Aquitaine*, pp. 99–112.
4   See above, Chapter 1.
5   See above, Chapter 2.

foundations for which he is sometimes claimed as founder, his grants were often made for the souls of relatives. He also emulated his father, Henry II, in associating (or making a gift that led him to be associated) with a community as effective co-founder. This happened at the Augustinian Priory of Newstead (Nottinghamshire) and the Gilbertine house of the same name (Lincolnshire). John also established tradition. His benefaction was emulated by his heirs. Other houses successfully argued before John's successors that he had been their founder.[6]

Though they often combined in rebellion, the male children of Henry II and Eleanor of Aquitaine all took steps to commemorate family members. This is particularly evident in the case of Henry the Young King, who died in 1183 whilst at war with his father. Henry II quickly ensured that his son was buried in Rouen Cathedral. The dying man had apparently asserted that this was his wish, turning down burial at Grandmont in the Limousin and adding that he wanted to lie alongside his uncle William. Young Henry was also interred alongside his earliest predecessors as duke of Normandy, Rollo and William Longsword.[7] Provision for his soul gradually followed. In 1184, his brother Geoffrey, duke of Brittany, Young Henry's ally in his last campaign, was joined by his wife Constance in establishing a chaplain at Rouen Cathedral to pray for Henry. In around 1185, similar provision was made by the Young King's widow Margaret, who promised three hundred marks, which the abbot of Clairvaux was to use to establish further chaplains at Rouen.[8]

In 1189, the release of Eleanor of Aquitaine, whose independence had been curtailed by her husband following her part in the Great Rebellion (1173-74), sparked a further wave of provision for Young Henry's soul. His mother was said to have experienced visions of his salvation before she knew of his death in 1183, and may have had the opportunity to visit his tomb when she accompanied Henry II in Normandy in 1185-86.[9] Freed after the old king's death in 1189, Eleanor directed her sons Richard and John, and even Henry II's illegitimate son Geoffrey, to give up churches and lands, or to grant their approval, for establishment of chantry chaplains in Rouen Cathedral in the Young King's memory.[10] Eleanor's influence may also explain why, in 1199, Richard I ordered his heart to be buried

---

[6] See above, Chapter 3.

[7] R. J. Smith, 'Henry II's Heir: The Acta and Seal of Henry the Young King 1170-83', *EHR*, 116 (2001), 297-326 (p. 322 no. 21); *CDF*, pp. 9-10 (nos 35-8); *The Chronicle of Robert of Torigni, Abbot of the Monastery of St Michael-in-Peril-of-the-Sea*, ed. R. Howlett, *Chronicles of the Reigns of Stephen, Henry II, and Richard I*, RS 82, 4 vols (London, 1884-89), vol. IV, p. 306. Henry II's brother William allegedly pined to death in 1164, after Archbishop Becket refused to licence his marriage to the widowed Countess of Warenne: Vincent, 'Murderers', p. 246.

[8] *The Charters of Duchess Constance of Brittany and her Family 1171-1221*, ed. J. Everard and M. Jones (Woodbridge, 1999), pp. 14 (Plate 1), 16 (Ge7), 47 (C4); *CDF*, pp. 10-11 (nos 39-41). On Geoffrey's role in the 1183 rebellion: Everard, *Brittany*, pp. 131-6.

[9] Turner, *Eleanor*, pp. 244, 250; Flori, *Eleanor*, p. 126.

[10] *CDF*, pp. 12-13 (nos 47-8, and see also nos 49-52), 17 (no. 62). For John's grants, see below. For relevant *acta* of Geoffrey, as archbishop-elect then archbishop of York, including one issued in 1207, after the loss of Normandy, and when Geoffrey was living in exile,

at Rouen, opposite his brother's tomb, in front of the high altar. Also that year, Eleanor's daughter Joanna died in childbirth at Rouen. The son she bore lived barely long enough to be baptised, and was buried in the cathedral. So too, briefly, was Joanna, before her body was transferred to Fontevraud.[11]

John's contribution in 1189, discussed above in relation to his establishment of masses, was made for his wellbeing, and for the souls of his father Henry II, his brother the Young King, and his ancestors. He gave the collegiate chapel of Blyth (Nottinghamshire), to establish two prebendary priests.[12] In part, this confirmed an earlier gift (in 1174) by Henry II to Walter of Coutances, made before the latter became archbishop of Rouen.[13] However, John's grant was made both to Walter and to Rouen Cathedral. Provision for the soul of the Young King was entirely new. The document refers to cathedral canons who served for the dead man's soul, performing services on the anniversary of his death. John provided £10 for poor canons present at his brother's annual obit (and in time the obit of John himself). He went on to confirm the grant as king, in September 1200.[14] This was part of his response to the fire which swept Rouen on Easter Day that year, causing substantial damage to several churches, including the cathedral.[15] He had already promised two thousand *livres Angevin* for repairs, and went on to issue protection for the cathedral's messengers. These envoys were to be well received. Alms was to be given for work on their church. John mentioned its dedication to the Virgin Mary and his own devotion. Although his gift was not all paid at once (in 1203, John ordered payment of the remaining 460 *livres*), clearly the king was keen to support one of the principal churches of the duchy of Normandy, important as the seat of the archbishopric, site of ducal inauguration, and a developing Angevin burial church.[16]

Eleanor of Aquitaine's influence is unsurprising, and can be seen in particular at the royal abbey of Fontevraud. In 1199, she was present at Richard I's deathbed,

---

apparently at Henry II's foundation of Notre-Dame-du-Parc at Rouen: *EEA* 27, pp. 65–9 (nos 58–60).

[11] Turner, *Eleanor*, pp. 278, 285–6; *Histoire des ducs de Normandie*, pp. 83–4; C. Bowie, 'To Have and Have Not: The Dower of Joanna Plantagenet, Queen of Sicily (1177–1189)', *Queenship in the Mediterranean: Negotiating the Role of the Queen in the Medieval and Early Modern Eras*, ed. E. Woodacre (New York, 2013), pp. 27–50 (pp. 38–9); *CDF*, pp. 392–3 (no. 1105). In her final testament, Joanna gave fifty marks to the cathedral.

[12] *CDF*, pp. 12 (no. 46), 16–17 (no. 61); also discussed above, Chapter 1. The text of John's grant will appear in: *Mortain*. Later tradition has it that Blyth was founded by his mother: Turner, *Eleanor*, pp. 129, 276.

[13] Vincent, 'Jean', p. 43; *Recueil des actes de Henri II*, vol. II, pp. 11–12 (no. 462). The Young King himself confirmed this grant in the late 1170s: Smith, 'Henry II's Heir', p. 319 (no. 13). See also *EEA* 27, p. 66 (no. 58 n).

[14] *RC*, pp. 75b–76a.

[15] Howden, vol. IV, p. 116; F. M. Powicke, *The Loss of Normandy 1189–1204: Studies in the History of the Angevin Empire*, 2nd edn (Manchester, 1960, first published 1913, reprinted 1999), p. 262 and n. 72; Webster, 'King John and Rouen', pp. 328–32.

[16] *RN*, pp. 33, 86; *RC*, p. 100b.

then oversaw his burial at Fontevraud and wider provision for his soul.[17] In that year, John was also called upon to approve bestowal of substantial funds to his sister Joanna, who spent time at the abbey following her flight from the county of Toulouse. These arrangements allowed her to make her testament, most probably with Eleanor's close supervision. Fontevraud features prominently. Joanna had spent some of her early years there, and entered the order on her deathbed. The testament made substantial gifts to the abbey, contributing to paying the abbess's debts, to building work, to Fontevraudine daughter-houses, and to marking the anniversary of her death and that of her first husband, King William II of Sicily. She left a rent of one thousand shillings to the abbey's kitchen. In addition, Joanna provided for chantry chaplains performing services for her soul. As noted above, she was buried at Fontevraud, having died at Rouen in childbirth.[18] John's commitment to her memory extended to providing for members of her entourage. Joanna's servants Beatrice and Alice, who took the veil at Fontevraud, received a rent of twenty-five *livres Angevin* in Saumur. After their deaths, one hundred shillings were to be given annually to the abbey. All of this was done for Joanna's soul. John was still honouring his commitment to fund his sister's testament as late as 1212.[19]

Eleanor's other offspring followed her lead in sponsoring religious activity at Fontevraud. Her daughter Eleanor, who had married Alfonso VIII of Castile (1170), commemorated her father, Henry II, in 1190 by inaugurating payment of one hundred gold coins annually.[20] Richard I made several grants, and is credited with funding construction of the cloister.[21] John issued documents approving and associating with his mother's arrangements for her soul at Fontevraud, in particular the chantry chaplain serving the chapel of St Laurence there.[22]

Much of the evidence for John's family piety discussed above involved Eleanor of Aquitaine. It seems that she was a primary influence on her children's religious activity. Eleanor and Fontevraud are inextricably linked.[23] However, there were additional factors that made the abbey an appropriate focus of Angevin religious

---

17 Flori, *Eleanor*, pp. 184-5; Turner, *Eleanor*, p. 278; CDF, p. 389 (no. 1097, issued on the day of Richard's burial).
18 CDF, pp. 391-3 (nos 1102-5); Bowie, 'To Have and Have Not', pp. 36-40. On Joanna's infancy at Fontevraud: Lewis, 'Birth and Childhood of King John', pp. 166-8.
19 RC, p. 25b; RLC 1204-24, p. 125b.
20 C. M. Bowie, 'The Daughters of Henry II and Eleanor of Aquitaine: A Comparative Study of Twelfth-Century Royal Women' (unpublished PhD thesis, University of Glasgow, 2011), p. 213. The younger Eleanor also requested prayers for the Castilian royal family.
21 CDF, pp. 382 (no. 1083), 384-6 (nos 1085-6, 1088); L. Grant (trans. B. Duchet-Filhol), 'Le patronage architectural de Henri II et de son entourage', *Cahiers de Civilisation Médiévale*, 37 (1994) 73-84 (p. 77); J.-M. Bienvenu, 'Aliénor d'Aquitaine et Fontevraud', *Cahiers de Civilisation Médiévale*, 29 (1986), 15-27 (p. 23).
22 RC, pp. 72a, 127b; RL, p. 92. On Eleanor's chantry: CDF, p. 390 (no. 1100). For later payments, perhaps to the chantry chaplain: RLC 1204-24, pp. 125b, 153b, 176a.
23 For further material: CDF, pp. 375-6 (no. 1061), 381-2 (no. 1080), 387 (no. 1090), 388 (nos 1092, 1094), 388-9 (no. 1096), 390-1 (no. 1100-1), 394 (no. 1108); Bienvenu, 'Aliénor', pp. 15-27; Wood, 'Fontevraud', pp. 414-16.

expression. By 1199, when John became king, Fontevraud had an especially wide range of links with his Anglo-Norman and Anglo-Angevin heritage, more so than any other house in his lands. The abbey respected this tradition, marking the anniversaries of the deaths of its benefactors. Its *martyrologium* (calendar of saints and benefactors, and book of obits) recorded:

30 March	'the lady Eleanor queen of the English our most illustrious mother'
7 April	'our most illustrious friend' Richard I
10 June	Henry the Young King, son 'of our most pious father' Henry II
7 July	Henry II
4 September	Queen Joanna of Sicily
30 October	another of John's sisters, Eleanor of Castile
10 November	Fulk V of Anjou

Updated into the fourteenth century, the document noted the dates of death of queens of England, including Berengaria (23 December) and Eleanor of Provence (26 June), who had entered the Fontevraudine order in later years. In terms of kings of England, it also noted Edward I, 'the most powerful and excellent' (10 July), and Henry III (15 November).[24]

John's name is conspicuously absent. However, he is included amongst the epitaphs recorded at Fontevraud, along with Fulk V, Henry II, Richard I, Henry III, John's younger son Richard of Cornwall, Edward I, Queen Joanna of Sicily, Eleanor of Aquitaine, Isabella of Angoulême, and Eleanor of Provence.[25] John's obituary is briefer than the record of those kings and queens buried at the abbey, but equally he was not excluded. It suggests provision for his soul, recalling his benefaction of Fontevraud. The obituary reveals that John spent much of his first five years at the abbey, allegedly as an oblate.[26] From then on, he would have become aware of the abbey's heritage (see Figure 1), its close connection to his Aquitainian lineage (for instance, Eleanor's grandmother Philippa of Toulouse and her father Duke William X), and its long-standing links with the counts of Anjou (including Fulk IV le Réchin, his wife Bertrade de Montfort, and their son Fulk V).[27] Contact with

---

[24] B. Pavillon, *La Vie du Bienheureux Robert d'Arbrissel, patriarche des solitaires de la France et instituteur de l'ordre de Fontevraud* (Saumur and Paris, 1666), pp. 577-81. On Eleanor of Provence as a Fontevraudine nun at Amesbury: M. Howell, *Eleanor of Provence: Queenship in Thirteenth-Century England* (Oxford, 1998), pp. 300-6.

[25] Pavillon, *La Vie*, pp. 583-90. Isabella of Angoulême's name is given as Elizabeth. On the obituaries of Henry II and Eleanor: Bienvenu, 'Aliénor', pp. 26-7 and n. 98; J.-M. Bienvenu, 'Henri II Plantagenêt et Fontevraud', *Cahiers de Civilisation Médiévale*, 37 (1994), 25-32 (pp. 31-2 and n. 86).

[26] Pavillon, *La Vie*, p. 585; Lewis, 'Birth and Childhood of King John', pp. 166-8. John's name – perhaps linked to his birth on or near the feast of St John the Evangelist (27 December) – may have been chosen for religious reasons. As youngest son, he was perhaps so named because he was intended to pursue a life in the Church: Bowie, 'Daughters of Henry II', p. 205.

[27] Bienvenu, 'Aliénor', pp. 16-17; Bienvenu, 'Henri II', pp. 25-32; Bowie, 'Daughters of Henry II', pp. 218-19; K. A. Dutton, 'Geoffrey, Count of Anjou and Duke of Normandy, 1129-51' (unpublished PhD thesis, University of Glasgow, 2011), pp. 157, 162; Flori, *Eleanor*, p. 20;

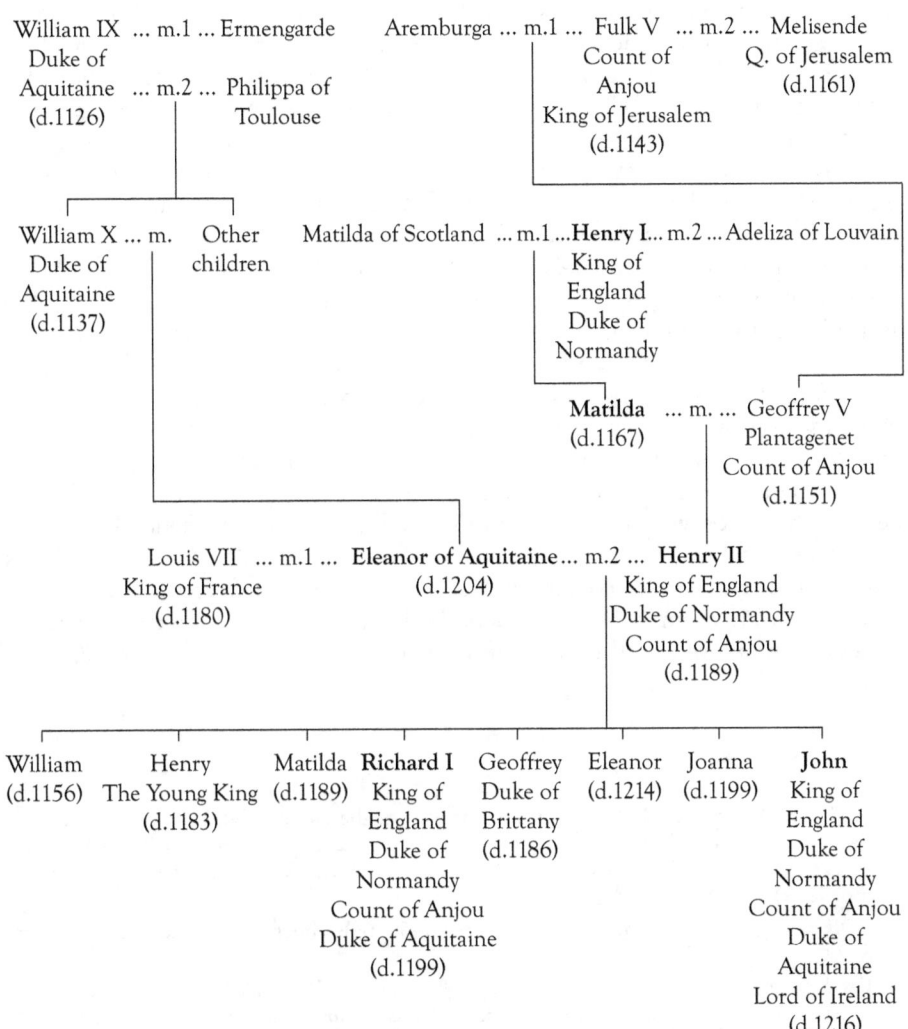

Figure 1 The Angevin dynasty in the twelfth century

the kings of England had been established after Henry I forged the Anglo-Angevin alliance through the marriage of his daughter, the Empress Matilda, to Geoffrey of Anjou (1128). Henry I's gifts linked the abbey to prayers for his own salvation, and for William the Conqueror and Queen Matilda, amongst other relatives.[28] The Empress confirmed many of these gifts. She and Geoffrey made additional grants of their own, although the latter was not remembered in its necrology. Instead his rule was recalled as a period of 'great poverty' for the house.[29] Nonetheless, his sister Matilda, widow of Henry I's son William, became a nun there in 1122, and abbess from 1149 until her death in 1155. Amongst her late twelfth-century successors was a niece of Count Geoffrey, another Matilda, in 1189.[30] Even King Stephen confirmed one of Henry I's grants to Fontevraud, suggesting the importance he attached to being seen to maintain dynastic interests.[31]

In her discussion of Anglo-Norman royal monastic patronage, Emma Mason argues that, prior to 1154, rulers sought a religious house 'which would symbolise and enhance the stability of their dynasty'.[32] Prior to 1204, Fontevraud fulfilled this function for the Angevins: a religious symbol of the territorial inheritance Henry II had forged and which he and his successors hoped to maintain.[33] It was appropriate for his offspring to continue what their predecessors had begun. It was said to have been at Fontevraud that Henry II's respect for the religious was impressed upon John, shortly after Richard I's death in 1199. He was initially refused entry because the abbess was absent. The nuns asked him not to be offended: '"Rather your father ought to be imitated ... since what he especially admired in monks was that they should observe strictly and with undeviating devotion the customs handed down to them by their founders".' John apparently respected their wishes, requested the prayers of the nuns, and stated 'his intention of conferring many

---

L. Grant, 'Aspects of the Architectural Patronage of the Family of the Counts of Anjou in the Twelfth Century', *Anjou: Medieval Art, Architecture and Archaeology*, ed. J. McNeill and D. Pringent, *British Archaeological Association Conference Transactions*, 26 (2003), pp. 96-110 (pp. 98-9).

[28] CDF, pp. 372-3 (nos 1052-3), 539-40 (nos 1459-69); Green, 'Piety and Patronage', pp. 8-9.

[29] For Matilda: *Regesta Regum Anglo-Normannorum 1066-1154. Vol. III. Regesta Regis Stephani ac Mathildis Imperatricis ac Gaufridi et Henrici Ducum Normannorum 1135-1154*, ed. H. A. Cronne and R. H. C. Davis (Oxford, 1968), p. 124 (no. 328); CDF, pp. 372 (no. 1052), 374 (no. 1056); M. Chibnall, *The Empress Matilda: Queen Consort, Queen Mother and Lady of the English* (Oxford, 1991), pp. 58-9, 127. For Geoffrey: Dutton, 'Geoffrey', pp. 157-68, 229-31, and Appendix 1, pp. 26-8 (nos 46-50); Grant, 'Aspects', p. 98.

[30] Dutton, 'Geoffrey', p. 162. Henry II issued a charter for the souls of Geoffrey V and his aunt Matilda before he became king: CDF, p. 375 (no. 1060).

[31] CDF, pp. 373-4 (no. 1055).

[32] Mason, '*Pro statu et incolumnitate regni mei*, p. 99.

[33] For Henry's grants and confirmations to Fontevraud: CDF, pp. 374-5 (nos 1058-60), 377 (nos 1063-5), 378 (no. 1068), 379-81 (nos 1071, 1073-6, 1078); Grant, 'Le patronage architectural', p. 77.

favours on them', and presumably therefore of continuing and augmenting his predecessors' largesse.³⁴

The author of this account, Adam of Eynsham, was clearly convinced that John would break his promises. However, he continued to support Fontevraud even after the loss of swathes of his continental inheritance in 1204.³⁵ This was in part achieved through support for Fontevraudine houses in England, where John made regular payments that evolved into the endowment for the alien priory of Grovebury by the time of Henry III.³⁶ Under John's son, Fontevraud continued to receive alms, with efforts made to address a backlog of payments. Henry ultimately ordered his heart to be taken there for burial alongside his forebears.³⁷

All this points towards a conclusion that John's family-related religious activity was dictated by inherited obligations which he was expected to maintain. To what extent did he make further provision for the souls of his relatives? Here, it is worth beginning by looking at John's gifts – beyond Fontevraud – for his mother's soul, before considering his wider kin group. When Eleanor died in 1204, John moved quickly to honour her. All prisoners in England were released, 'for the love of God and for the salvation of the soul of our dearest mother'.³⁸ This was unusual for a queen, but perhaps acknowledged the years of Eleanor's life in which Henry II had kept her in confinement, and her own actions when Henry II died. There were also echoes of actions of John's predecessors. William Rufus ordered the release of prisoners shortly after his coronation in 1087, amidst various provisions made for the soul of William the Conqueror.³⁹

Soon after his mother's death, John also ordered masses for her salvation. In May 1204, he confirmed the foundation of Gilbertine Marmont (Cambridgeshire) by Ralph de Hauvill and his wife Matilda. Daily mass for Queen Eleanor was to be celebrated there.⁴⁰ Intercessory prayers or services are also likely to have been

---

34 *Magna Vita*, vol. II, pp. 138–9.
35 In addition to grants and confirmations discussed above: *RC*, p. 72; *RLC 1204–24*, pp. 125b, 153b, 170b, 176a.
36 *PR 1 John*, p. 105; *PR 2 John*, p. 254; *PR 3 John*, p. 163; *PR 4 John*, p. 21; *PR 5 John*, p. 89; *PR 6 John*, p. 8; *PR 7 John*, p. 68; *PR 8 John*, p. 35; *PR 9 John*, p. 151; *PR 10 John*, p. 128; *PR 11 John*, p. 177; *PR 12 John*, pp. 10–11; *PR 13 John*, p. 139; *PR 14 John*, p. 123; *PR 16 John*, p. 13; *PR 17 John*, p. 22; B. M. Kerr, *Religious Life for Women c. 1100–c. 1350: Fontevraud in England* (Oxford, 1999), p. 73.
37 *RLC 1204–24*, pp. 411a, 442b, 473a, 494b, 509b, 512b, 546b, 573b, 627b, 653a; *CLR 1226–1240*, p. 55; *CLR 1240–1245*, pp. 270–1; *FR 27 Henry III*, no. 821; Carpenter, 'Burial', p. 428.
38 Turner, *Eleanor*, p. 296; *RLP*, p. 54a–b. The exceptions were prisoners taken in war, those captured in Normandy who had been sent to England, and Jews.
39 J. Martindale, 'Eleanor, suo jure Duchess of Aquitaine (c. 1122–1204)', *ODNB* (Oxford, 2004, online edn, 2006) [http://www.oxforddnb.com/view/article/8618, accessed 10 December 2013]; *Medieval England 1000–1500: A Reader*, ed. E. Amt (Peterborough Ontario, 2001), p. 66.
40 *RC*, p. 129a. The exact date of foundation is unclear. Matilda de Hauvill allegedly experienced a vision of Gilbert of Sempringham being taken to heaven, on the day the saint died in 1189. Golding argues that the house was not founded until c. 1204, the date of John's confirmation charter. The foundation presumably dates to after Matilda's marriage to Roger

expected after John pardoned the church of St Mary, Oxford, 32¼d in perpetuity for his mother's soul.[41] Meanwhile, there was substantial royal almsgiving in early May. Varying numbers of paupers (between one hundred and five hundred; overall some 2,200) were fed across the country over a period of fifteen weeks leading up to the feast of the Assumption (15 August). It seems highly likely that this was in Eleanor's honour.[42] Might the king have believed that, on the feast of the Assumption, his mother would be admitted to heaven? This tempting but ultimately speculative conclusion is probably not sustainable. John made longer-term arrangements for prayers for his mother, wishes that continued to be fulfilled under Henry III. In 1241, the Knights of the Temple received £4, in fulfilment of letters of King John, to sustain four chaplains performing masses (*celebrantium*) for Eleanor's soul.[43]

John also commissioned intercessory activity for the souls of his father, Henry II, and his brother, Richard I. Arrangements at Salisbury and St Paul's Cathedrals have already been discussed.[44] Before he became king, John instructed the Premonstratensian canons of Durford to mark the anniversary of his father's death.[45] As king, similar activity for the salvation of Henry II was ordered in various castle chapels, including Argentan (Normandy), Clipstone (Nottinghamshire), and Horston (Derbyshire), with further masses celebrated by a chaplain ministering on the bridge at Lincoln.[46] Provision for Richard I does not survive so frequently, although five marks were granted to the hospital of Brackley (Northamptonshire) 'for the soul of King Richard'.[47] On the feast of the Exaltation of the Cross (14 September) 1212, John ordered one hundred poor to be given alms for his brother's soul.[48] Feeding the poor to commemorate deceased relatives is a trend associated with the piety of John's son, Henry III, and extensively studied by Sally Dixon-Smith.[49] The above examples suggest that John's reign is not entirely devoid of evidence for this trend.

It is far less clear that the king provided for the soul of the third of his brothers who survived to adulthood: Geoffrey of Brittany. The two men were allies in

---

de Hauvill, likely to have taken place after the death of her father, Roger le Gros, in 1202, after which Matilda was recorded as a royal ward. Golding, *Gilbert*, pp. 246-8; Knowles and Hadcock, pp. 197, 198.

[41] *RL*, p. 94; *RC*, p. 126a-b; Harvey, 'Piety', p. 22.

[42] *RL*, pp. 95-6. This cost some £306 12s 10d: *PR 6 John*, pp. 80, 94, 106, 121, 146, 176, 177, 187, 248. For a link between this alms distribution and John's itinerary: Harvey, 'Piety', pp. 22-3. For the grants as part of his response to famine, see below, Chapter 5.

[43] *Receipt and Issue Rolls for the Twenty-Sixth Year of the Reign of King Henry III, 1241-2*, ed. R. C. Stacey, PRS, 87, ns 49 (London, 1992), p. 84.

[44] See above, Chapter 1.

[45] *Earldom of Gloucester Charters*, pp. 68-9 (nos 59-61); *Mortain*. This confirmed Countess Hawisa's arrangements for masses for various souls, including Henry II, Richard I, and John.

[46] *RC*, pp. 53b, 69a; *RLC 1204-24*, p. 182b.

[47] *PR 1 John*, p. 4.

[48] *RM*, p. 241. A further one hundred received alms on 3 October 1212 for Henry II's soul: *RM*, p. 243.

[49] Dixon-Smith, 'Feeding the Poor'; Dixon-Smith, 'Image and Reality', pp. 79-96.

attacking Richard's lands in Poitou in 1184.⁵⁰ Like Henry the Young King, Geoffrey ended his life in opposition to Henry II. He died in August 1186, whilst at the French court in Paris, either from fever, or having been trampled to death during a tournament.⁵¹ There is strikingly little evidence that Geoffrey was mourned by his wider family. Provision for his soul was made by his wife Constance and son Arthur and, as was appropriate for a man of royal blood who had died at his court, by the French king. Philip II supervised the duke of Brittany's burial before the high altar in Notre-Dame Cathedral in Paris, and endowed priests to pray for his soul.⁵²

Where John established chaplains and made gifts for the souls of his brothers Henry the Young King and Richard, similar arrangements for Geoffrey were almost non-existent. They appear to be limited to his inclusion amongst the royal relatives for whom chaplains were to pray at Lichfield, arrangements made not by John but by Bishop Geoffrey Muschamp in 1206.⁵³ There may have been good reason for this lack of attention. Those for whom John made provision were anointed kings and queens who died within the Angevin lands. Geoffrey died in Paris. John does not seem to have provided for the souls of his sisters Matilda, who died in Saxony (1189), and Eleanor, who died in Castile (1214). Yet John could hardly have known these sisters, who left the Angevin lands in 1167 and 1170.⁵⁴ He did know Geoffrey, whose final rebellion, unlike that of the Young King, was not in alliance with his brothers. His death was also to John's advantage, increasing his chances of becoming king. John was in direct competition with the duke of Brittany's son Arthur for the succession. He may have preferred not to commemorate Geoffrey.⁵⁵

This trend is further confirmed by naming patterns.⁵⁶ In naming his legitimate children, John largely followed the example of his own parents, except that Geoffrey, a traditional Angevin name, was absent, as were two names with

---

50 For differing views of this campaign: Everard, *Brittany*, p. 137; Turner, *Eleanor*, p. 248.
51 Everard, *Brittany*, pp. 138-45; Flori, *Eleanor*, pp. 130-2. For description of his death as due to illness: *Giraldi Cambrensis de Principis Instructione*, p. 176; *Oeuvres de Rigord*, vol. II, pp. 68-9. For description of his death as occurring in a tournament: *Gesta Regis Henrici Secundi*, vol. I, p. 350.
52 *Charters of Duchess Constance of Brittany and her Family*, pp. 52-3 (C 17), 55-6 (C 20), 62-3 (C 31), 68-9 (C 38, C 39), 89 (C 72), 123-4 (A 11, A 12); *Oeuvres de Rigord*, vol. I, pp. 68-9; 'Diplôme de Philippe Auguste instituant deux chapellenies pour l'âme de Geoffroy, comte de Bretagne', ed. A. de Bouard, *Le Moyen Age*, 35 (1924), 63-70 (pp. 66-7); Everard, *Brittany*, pp. 144-5.
53 *EEA* 17, pp. 96-7 (no. 113).
54 K. Norgate, 'Matilda, Duchess of Saxony (1156-1189)', rev. T. Reuter, *ODNB* (Oxford, 2004) [http://www.oxforddnb.com/view/article/18339, accessed 17 December 2013]; Bowie, 'Daughters of Henry II', pp. 90, 285. John probably first encountered Matilda when she was in exile in England in 1182-85.
55 On the claims to the throne of John and Arthur: J. C. Holt, 'King John and Arthur of Brittany', *Nottingham Medieval Studies*, 44 (2000), 82-103.
56 On Angevin dynastic nomenclature: Bowie, 'Daughters of Henry II', pp. 200-11. More broadly, see: J. C. Holt, 'What's in a Name? Family Nomenclature and the Norman Conquest', *Colonial England 1066-1215*, J. C. Holt (London and Rio Grande, OH, 1997), pp. 179-96.

Anglo-Norman, Angevin, and (or) Aquitainian pedigree: William and Matilda. The eldest son Henry was probably named for John's father, but choice of name could commemorate several relatives, in this case evoking the memory of the king's brother and great-grandfather. The second son, Richard, took the name of John's late brother, and of some of the earliest dukes of Normandy – an interesting choice, given that John lost Normandy but is unlikely to have accepted this as permanent. His daughter Eleanor shared her name with John's mother and sister, with his eldest daughter Joan taking the name of the king's closest sibling in age, with whom he apparently spent some of his formative years at Fontevraud. Could this suggest that he prioritised her commemoration over that of his mother or wife?

Following a similar pattern to the children of Henry II, John's second daughter Isabella took his wife's name.[57] However, there is only limited evidence of the king acting with his wives, first Isabella of Gloucester, then Isabella of Angoulême, in soliciting the prayers of the religious. In the case of his first wife, this is perhaps unsurprising. John seems to have been estranged from her by 1193, when a marriage to Alice, sister of Philip II of France, was proposed. However, in a charter in favour of the canons of St Augustine's, Bristol, Isabella does refer to the wellbeing of John's soul.[58] The marriage was annulled following John's accession, although it appears that, for much of his reign, Isabella was treated as a ward, prior to marrying Geoffrey de Mandeville in 1214. Indeed, the king's provision for his first wife's household was at times similar to that for his queen. At times they may even have resided together.[59] Fleeting glimpses suggest that John made some provision for religious activity linked to his second wife, including money for offerings and vestments for use in her chapel.[60] On at least one occasion, Isabella of Angoulême was mentioned as expected beneficiary of the prayers of the organised religious – the bishop, dean, and canons of Chichester – in 1204. The relevant charter was issued for God (*pro Deo*), for John's wellbeing and that of his queen, and for the souls of the king's ancestors and heirs. Isabella confirmed this after her husband's death, but absence of further evidence implies that this was not a regular occurrence.[61]

The names chosen for John's illegitimate children, most of whom were born

---

[57] Nicholas Vincent's pedigree of Isabella of Angoulême gives Isabella as an 'alias' of Elizabeth de Courtenay, grandmother of John's queen: Vincent, 'Isabella', p. 180. This might suggest that Isabella's heritage had some impact on naming her second daughter.

[58] *Earldom of Gloucester Charters*, p. 52 (no. 33). John did not reciprocate: *Earldom of Gloucester Charters*, pp. 49–50 (nos 31–2); *Mortain*.

[59] R. B. Patterson, 'Isabella, suo jure Countess of Gloucester (c. 1160–1217)', *ODNB* (Oxford, 2004, online edn 2005) [http://www.oxforddnb.com/view/article/46705, accessed 18 December 2013]; Vincent, 'Isabella', pp. 196–7.

[60] *RLC 1204–24*, pp. 34a, 103a; *PR 9 John*, p. 31; 'Rotulus de Praestito – Anno Regni Regis Johannis Septimo', ed. H. Cole, *Documents Illustrative of English History in the Thirteenth and Fourteenth Centuries*, RComm (London, 1844), pp. 270–6 (p. 274).

[61] Vincent, 'Isabella', pp. 189, 198; *RC*, p. 129a–b.

before he became king, should also be noted.⁶² Some were also used for legitimate offspring: Henry, Richard, Joan, and Isabel.⁶³ Two took traditional Angevin names, Geoffrey and Maud or Matilda. Another was named John. Of these, in the early thirteenth century, Geoffrey fitz Roy was old enough to lead mercenaries and to hold the honour of Perche. When he died in 1205, he cannot have been much older than twenty-five, possibly some years younger, so he may have been named in memory of the duke of Brittany.⁶⁴ Matilda's name evoked the Empress, Henry I's queen Matilda of Scotland, William the Conqueror's spouse Matilda of Flanders, and John's own sister, the wife of Henry the Lion and mother of Otto IV.⁶⁵ Several of these women were noted for their religious activity, so perhaps it is no coincidence that John's Matilda became a nun. She was abbess of Barking from 1247 to c. 1252, following in the footsteps of a natural daughter of Henry II, another Matilda, abbess from the late 1170s until her death in the early thirteenth century.⁶⁶ John's remaining illegitimate children took names which are harder to explain: Eudo (or Ivo), Oliver, Osbert Giffard, Bartholomew, and – perhaps most surprising in view of John's fortunes as king – Philip.⁶⁷

More broadly, John's benefaction of the organised religious favoured institutions founded or supported by his predecessors. This suggests acceptance that strategies favoured by his forebears, either for salvation or for demonstration of religious largesse, would work for him as well, indicating a king whose giving was shaped by established trends. This may in itself have been an Angevin tradition. In a document issued in 1133 to the abbey of Saint-Florent at Saumur, Count Geoffrey V of Anjou noted that: 'It is most salutary ... for princes to care with affection for those churches and abbeys founded by their antecessors, and to take their lands, men and buildings under the shadow of their protection.'⁶⁸

There is widespread evidence from John's lifetime that suggests that this was still

---

62 Painter, *Reign*, p. 232; Gillingham, 'John'. For a list: R. V. Turner, 'Bastards of King John, Chart' [http://www.academia.edu/3100660/Bastards_of_King_John_Chart, accessed 3 July 2013].

63 On whom, see: Painter, *Reign*, pp. 232–3; S. D. Church, *The Household Knights of King John* (Cambridge, 1999), pp. 42, 127, 133 n. 133; S. Lloyd, 'Chilham, Sir Richard of (d. 1246)', *ODNB* (Oxford, 2004, online edn 2008) [http://www.oxforddnb.com/view/article/46706, accessed 3 July 2013]; K. Norgate, 'Joan (d. 1237)', rev. A. D. Carr, *ODNB* (Oxford, 2004) [http://www.oxforddnb.com/view/article/14819, accessed 3 July 2013]; Turner, 'Bastards'.

64 Painter, *Reign*, p. 232; Warren, *John*, p. 112.

65 Bowie, 'Daughters of Henry II', pp. 201–3.

66 *CPR 1232–1247*, pp. 506, 507; *CPR. Henry III. 1247–1258*, HMSO (London, 1908), p. 128; Turner, *Eleanor*, pp. 110–11; Knowles, Brooke and London, *Heads*, p. 208.

67 Turner, 'Bastards'; Painter, *Reign*, p. 232; Warren, *John*, p. 189 n; S. Lloyd, 'Oliver (d. 1218/19)', *ODNB* (Oxford, 2004) [http://www.oxforddnb.com/view/article/20717, accessed 3 July 2013]. Bartholomew, a Dominican, received papal dispensation to minister in Holy Orders, and to be promoted to the episcopate, in 1252. A year later, he was appointed as a papal chaplain. In 1254, he was permitted to converse with Dominicans or Franciscans at table. In each case, he was described as Henry III's brother or kinsman: *Calendar of Entries in the Papal Registers. Papal Letters 1198–1304*, pp. 281, 286, 305.

68 Grant, 'Aspects', p. 97.

the case. Many of the monastic houses he supported had a heritage of royal, ducal, or comital involvement. These included houses founded by his early predecessors as duke of Normandy, such as the mausoleum established by Dukes Robert I and Robert II at Fécamp; Cerisy-la-Forêt, founded by William the Conqueror's father Robert; and St-Etienne, Caen, established by William himself.[69] John confirmed his mother, Queen Eleanor's gifts to the latter community, and issued a charter reciting grants of the Conqueror and Henry I to the abbey of St Martin at Troarn in the Calvados region.[70]

John's support for religious houses associated with his predecessors also includes a cluster of institutions established by King Henry I. Augustinian Cirencester (Gloucestershire), effectively re-founded by Henry in 1117, had received backing from successive members of the Angevin family. During Richard I's reign, styling himself count of Mortain although acting in the capacity of earl of Gloucester, John took the community into his protection, granted quittance of tolls, and quitclaimed alms the canons had received from Henry I in Somerset.[71] He renewed his protection as king and confirmed charters and gifts of Henry II and Richard I. He did so in 1199, for his wellbeing and that of Queen Eleanor his mother, and for the souls of Henry I, Henry II, Richard I, his brothers, and all the faithful dead. Despite this, the abbey paid £100 for its charter.[72] Later royal grants added to this endowment, giving further land and a fair. The abbot received custody in 1208 when church property was restored after the seizures accompanying the imposition of the interdict. Although this suggests a community with royal favour, the relationship was variable. The canons were subjected to seizure of lands in 1204 and 1205, and at the hands of Gerard d'Athée, sheriff of Gloucestershire, c. 1208-10.[73]

Other Augustinian foundations by Henry I received John's support. At Dunstable (Bedfordshire), founded in 1131-32, he made routine confirmations of his predecessors' gifts, 'for the sake of God' (*intuitu Dei*) for his wellbeing and the souls of his ancestors and successors. John also granted the right to hold a three-day annual fair.[74] Meanwhile, the house of St Denys, at Portswood by Southampton, founded by Henry in the 1120s, received confirmation of a charter of John's brother Richard I. Again, this was issued for the souls of the king's ancestors and successors, for the wellbeing of John's soul, and 'for the love of God'

---

[69] For evidence linking John to these houses: *RC*, p. 69b; *RLP*, pp. 15b, 56b, 73a, 90a, 106b; *RN*, pp. 32, 65, 74, 79; *Magni rotuli scaccarii Normanniae*, vol. II, pp. 506, 512, 515, 572, 573; Mortain.

[70] *RC*, pp. 6b, 124b-125a. For Troarn, see also: *CDF*, pp. 164-81 (nos 463-510), esp. pp. 167 (no. 468), 168-9 (no. 475); *Regesta Regum Anglo-Normannorum. The Acta of William I (1066-1087)*, ed. D. Bates (Oxford, 1998), p. 855 (no. 281, version III).

[71] *Cartulary of Cirencester*, vol. I, p. 62 (nos 81/11, 82), vol. III, p. 737 (no. 9).

[72] *RC*, p. 10a-b; *Cartulary of Cirencester*, vol. I, pp. xxxiv, 30 (no. 33/5), 63-4 (nos 84-5); *PR 1 John*, p. 31; *PR 2 John*, p. 123.

[73] *RC*, pp. 132b, 218a; *RLC 1204-24*, pp. 113a, 220a; *Cartulary of Cirencester*, vol. I, pp. xxxiv, 33-4 (nos 37-8), 36-7 (no. 41/6), 38 (no. 43/7), 63 (no. 83/10), 64-5 (no. 87), 119 (no. 133); *RLP*, p. 149a; Vincent, 'Athée, Girard d''.

[74] *RL*, pp. 38, 40; *RC*, pp. 107a, 115a; Dunstable, p. 28.

(*pro Dei amore*).⁷⁵ Likewise, Wellow (Lincolnshire), received confirmation of its possessions in 1201, in pure and perpetual alms, for the souls of John's father and brothers, for his wellbeing and for that of his kingdom.⁷⁶

Foundations by his grandmother, the Empress Matilda, also received royal alms, as when John paid one hundred shillings to the abbot of Cistercian La Noë in the Evrecin.⁷⁷ Likewise her foundation of Notre-Dame-du-Voeu, Cherbourg. As count of Mortain, John witnessed a charter of Richard I to this community, confirming their father's gifts when the abbey was dedicated, of the Cotentin churches of Barfleur and Gatteville. In turn, John confirmed this grant as king.⁷⁸

John also supported houses founded by his father. We have already seen how his support for the Gilbertine order, including Henry's foundation at Newstead (Lincolnshire), tapped into a heritage of royal involvement.⁷⁹ It also included foundations linked to Henry II's penance for his perceived role in the murder of Archbishop Becket.⁸⁰ In terms of houses traditionally linked to Henry's activity, John supported the Augustinian canons of Waltham (Essex) and Amesbury (Wiltshire), where his charters were given 'for the decency of religion' (*pro ... religionis honestate*), referring to his wellbeing, the salvation of his father and mother, and that of his ancestors and successors.⁸¹ John also issued documents in favour of several communities established by Henry and dedicated (or re-dedicated) to Becket. The leper house of Mont-aux-Malades, outside Rouen, dedicated to St Thomas by Henry II at its re-foundation in c. 1174, was taken into John's protection, in accordance with his father's letters patent, in 1200.⁸² John also issued documents in favour of Carthusian Le Liget in the Touraine, supported by his father in the post-Becket phase of his reign, and the Augustinian house of St Thomas the Martyr, Dublin, founded by Henry in 1177.⁸³

Houses established by Richard I are not unrepresented in John's family largesse. The Cistercian monks of Bonport received quittance of customary dues, as the Lionheart had granted. They also received dues from a widow (Ermengarde, wife

---

75 RC, p. 83b; Green, *Henry I*, p. 279; Knowles and Hadcock, p. 172.
76 RC, p. 94a–b.
77 RLC 1204–24, p. 182a.
78 RC, p. 36a. See also *CDF*, pp. 334–40 (nos 933–56).
79 See above, Chapter 3.
80 Duggan, 'Diplomacy', pp. 285–7; Hallam, 'Henry II as a Founder', pp. 113–14, 117–18.
81 RLC 1204–24, pp. 140b, 158a; RC, pp. 13b–14b, 65b–66a; *Early Charters of the Augustinian Canons of Waltham*, pp. 27 (no. 38), 127 (no. 201), 197–8 (nos 294–5), 435 (no. 637). John's support for Henry II's post-Becket foundations will be discussed further in: P. Webster, 'Crown Versus Church After Becket: King John, St Thomas and the Interdict', *The Cult of St Thomas Becket in the Plantagenet World, c. 1170–c. 1250*, ed. P. Webster and M.-P. Gelin (Woodbridge, forthcoming).
82 RC, p. 76a; Grant, 'Le patronage architectural', p. 76. On Mont-aux-Malades: E. Brenner, *Leprosy and Charity in Medieval Rouen* (Woodbridge, forthcoming); and below. Brenner notes that the grant of protection was confirmed by Philip II of France in 1207.
83 RC, p. 63a; RN, p. 77; *Chartae, Privilegia et Immunitates*, pp. 4–6, 8–9; *Register of the Abbey of St Thomas, Dublin*, ed. J. T. Gilbert, RS 94 (London, 1889), pp. 6–7; RL, p. 71; Duggan, 'Diplomacy', p. 287; Hallam, 'Henry II as a Founder', pp. 117–20.

of William de Folbec) permitted to reside there, and were taken into royal protection. John visited his brother's foundation, issuing documents there (including the grant of protection) in late June and for much of July 1202.[84] There is an overall sense of it being appropriate for John to associate himself with houses founded by his royal predecessors, updating the religious sentiments expressed in documents so that he was also included.

Meanwhile, houses founded by others, but which had received support from John's royal kinsmen, in particular his father and brothers, are also prominent amongst institutions where he linked his confirmations to the souls of his relatives. Perhaps these communities were concerned to secure the gifts of past kings. They appear not to have had difficulty securing documents from John, who issued them noting that this had been done for him and his heirs. Three examples – Osney (Oxfordshire), Lenton (Nottinghamshire), and Bradsole (Kent) – illustrate a wider pattern.

At Augustinian Osney, John renewed documents issued by the Empress and by Henry II, confirming a gift made by Adeliza of Louvain, second wife of Henry I. John referred to the wellbeing of himself and those around him (*nostra et nostrorum*), and to the soul of Henry I, specified as his father's grandfather. John's own grandfather (*avi nostri*) is then listed, seemingly a rare reference to Geoffrey of Anjou. *Inspeximus* charters of Henry III and Edward II show that in other grants to Osney, John also referred to his wellbeing, and to the souls of his father, grandfather, and kinsmen.[85]

Henry II's gifts to Cluniac Lenton Priory were also confirmed by John, again for the wellbeing of his soul and his heirs, for his father's salvation, that of Henry I, royal ancestors, and all the faithful.[86] Here, he added to his father's benefaction, giving heathland to the monks before he was king, and in 1212 giving dead wood and a tenth of his hunting in Nottinghamshire and Derbyshire.[87] Thirdly, at Premonstratensian St Radegund, Bradsole, John acted partly to fulfil Richard I's wishes, and also on his own initiative. In 1199, he confirmed the site of the house, and land in the town of River, next to Dover. A subsequent royal grant of the church of St Peter, given in 1208 and confirmed in 1215, was to support the canons and poor pilgrims. These grants were made for John's wellbeing, and for the salvation of his ancestors and heirs. Richard I had given the house one hundred acres of waste adjoining the monastery. In the early years of John's reign, a project was in hand, with royal support, to relocate the community to River. Ultimately, this did not take place.[88]

Under John, a long-standing royal tradition of supporting leper communities continued. Queen Matilda, first wife of Henry I, was noted as a patron of

---

84 *Cartulaire de l'abbaye royale de Notre-Dame de Bon-Port de l'Ordre de Cîteaux au diocèse d'Evreux*, ed. J. Andrieux (Evreux, 1862), pp. 29–31 (nos 30, 32–3); *RLP*, p. 14b; 'Itinerary'.
85 *RC*, pp. 81b–82a; *CChR 1226–1257*, p. 113; *CChR 1300–1326*, p. 419.
86 *RC*, pp. 56a, 56b.
87 J. Throsby (ed.), *Thoroton's History of Nottinghamshire: Republished with Large Additions*, 3 vols (Nottingham, 1797), vol. II, p. 252; Mortain; *RLC 1204–24*, p. 120a; *RC*, p. 189b.
88 *RC*, pp. 12a–b, 131a–b, 176b, 215b; *RLC 1204–24*, p. 107b; Colvin, *White Canons*, p. 147.

lepers, reputedly inviting sufferers into her chamber and washing their feet.[89] The Empress Matilda continued her family's largesse to the lepers of Rouen and attracted a reputation as the 'consoler of the poor'.[90] Henry II continued these trends. Indeed, he has been described as 'almost obsessed with the leper'. He was a prominent supporter of the hospital of Mont-aux-Malades, outside Rouen, and the benefactor of numerous other leper communities.[91] The association again passed to the next generation. Henry the Young King issued documents both for Mont-aux-Malades and other Rouen hospitals. Richard I granted an annual £10 of alms to the lepers of Les Andelys, next to Château-Gaillard.[92] Just as John extended his protection to Mont-aux-Malades, so too he confirmed his brother's arrangements at Les Andelys.[93]

King John 'is sometimes regarded as the conspicuous patron of lepers'.[94] The claim does not seem entirely far-fetched when his support for hospitals is considered. In terms of those that received benefaction from his forebears, he issued documents in favour of various hospitals that claimed Henry I, his first wife Matilda, or his second wife Adeliza, as founder. In 1200, John took the lepers of St Bartholomew, Oxford, into his protection. In 1205, he did the same for the lepers of Holy Innocents, Lincoln, where Henry I had paid for chaplains to intercede for his spiritual wellbeing. Henry expected the hospital to admit anyone in the royal household who contracted leprosy. Similar arrangements existed in John's reign. In 1213, St Bartholomew, Oxford, were required to receive and provide for a sick clerk, Adam of Brill, who was to be given their first available prebend.[95] Elsewhere, the king appears to have inaugurated a new payment to the lepers of St Giles, Wilton (Wiltshire), the foundation of Adeliza of Louvain.[96]

Further dynastic continuity is shown by instances in which John tapped into a tradition begun by Henry I and continued by Henry II. St Giles, Shrewsbury, probably founded by Henry I, received confirmation of John's father's alms of a handful of corn and flour from each sack brought to Shrewsbury market.[97] In

---

[89] E. J. Kealey, *Medieval Medicus: A Social History of Anglo-Norman Medicine* (Baltimore, MD, and London, 1981), pp. 20, 89-91.

[90] Michel Mollat (trans. A. Goldhammer), *The Poor in the Middle Ages: An Essay in Social History*, (New Haven, CT, and London, 1986), p. 97. See also: Brenner, *Leprosy*.

[91] Grant, 'Le patronage architectural', p. 76 (my translation); Hallam, 'Aspects', pp. 120-3; E. H. O. Brenner, 'Charity in Rouen in the Twelfth and Thirteenth Centuries (With Special Reference to Mont-aux-Malades)' (unpublished PhD thesis, University of Cambridge, 2008); Brenner, *Leprosy*.

[92] *Recueil des actes de Henri II, roi d'Angleterre et duc de Normandie, concernant les provinces françaises et les affaires de France: Introduction*, ed. L. Delisle (Paris, 1909), pp. 257-8 (no. V); Smith, 'Henry II's Heir', p. 324 (no. 29, where the Young King's charter is discussed as one for the house of Ste Katherine-du-Mont, Rouen); Brenner, *Leprosy*; Hallam, 'Aspects', p. 134.

[93] *RC*, pp. 76a, 97a.

[94] Clay, *Mediaeval Hospitals*, p. 72.

[95] *RC*, p. 99a; *RLP*, p. 54a; *RLC 1204-24*, p. 139a; Rawcliffe, *Leprosy*, pp. 150, 296.

[96] *PR 7 John*, p. 169; *PR 8 John*, p. 187; *PR 9 John*, p. 205; *PR 10 John*, p. 196; *PR 11 John*, p. 82; *PR 12 John*, p. 78; *PR 13 John*, p. 164; *PR 14 John*, p. 148; *PR 16 John*, p. 39.

[97] *RC*, p. 122b; Knowles and Hadcock, p. 391.

1204, the king confirmed a charter of Henry II to the leper nuns of St James, Westminster. John did this for his wellbeing, and for the souls of Henry I (referred to as John's father's grandfather), Queen Matilda, his ancestors and successors.[98] Letters close issued in 1213 and 1214 provided sixty shillings alms to Matilda's hospital dedicated to St Giles, Holborn. Again, this reflected arrangements made by Henry II, who had given the money to fund better clothing there.[99]

John's support for provision for lepers by his father can also be seen at Preston (Lancashire), where Henry II had taken the hospital of St Mary Magdalene into his protection in the late 1170s or early 1180s. John did so in 1207.[100] In 1215, whilst John was at Northampton, orders were issued to protect the town's leper house, St Leonard's, their messengers and their possessions. This was probably sought due to the impending likelihood of civil war between crown and barons. The hospital had perhaps been founded by William the Conqueror, and John's protection echoed arrangements made by his father, who had also given permission to receive alms.[101] The king's backing for leper hospitals extended to those supported by his mother. In 1199, her gift of land to the leper nuns of St Mary de Pré, by St Albans (Hertfordshire), was confirmed by John. The community was granted the right to hold a fair on the vigil and feast of the Nativity of the Virgin Mary (7-8 September). This was done for John's soul, for that of Henry II, and for those of all his ancestors and successors. In 1204, John added forest rights in free, pure, and perpetual alms, 'for the sake of God' (*intuitu Dei*), and again for his soul and those of his ancestors and heirs. The community was taken into the king's protection in 1215.[102] These examples are by no means exhaustive, but illustrate this aspect of family trends in royal religious activity.

Earlier discussion of John's foundation of religious houses noted that he made no noticeable effort to associate himself with a religious house in his county of Mortain.[103] However, he did engage with communities established by previous counts. The nunnery of Les Blanches (or Mortain) had been begun in 1105 by Count William and supported by his successors, including King Stephen, the latter's son William, Henry II's younger brother William, and Henry II himself.[104] John issued a charter 'for the love of God' (*pro amore Dei*), for his soul and those of his ancestors and successors. The house received confirmation of various revenues

---

[98] RC, p. 117b.

[99] RLC 1204-24, pp. 153b, 176a; Rawcliffe, *Leprosy*, pp. 330-1 n. 128, and see also p. 341 n. 184, revealing that Henry II endowed lights at St Giles.

[100] *Lancashire Pipe Rolls*, pp. 333-4, where it is suggested that the hospital was possibly founded by John's predecessor as holder of the honour of Lancaster, Stephen, Count of Mortain (and later king); RLP, p. 59b.

[101] RLP, p. 129a; Knowles and Hadcock, p. 380; Serjeantson and Atkins, VCH *Northampton*, vol. II (1906), pp. 159-60.

[102] *Cartae Antiquae Rolls 11-20*, pp. 54-5 (nos 374-6); RC, p. 127a; RLP, p. 131a.

[103] See above, Chapter 3.

[104] CDF, p. 58 (nos 787-91); King, *King Stephen*, p. 26; N. Vincent, 'New Charters of King Stephen with Some Reflections upon the Royal Forests During the Anarchy', EHR, 114 (1999), 899-928 (pp. 906-7, 924-5 (Appendix, no. 9)).

given by one Ralph the priest for an annual pittance on St Andrew's Day (30 November). The community also received wheat and alms in 1203.[105]

Savigny in western Normandy, a community which had influenced Stephen as count of Mortain, also received a charter from Count John, confirming churches given to the community along with all donations, gifts, liberties, and quittances given within John's lands. Here, however, the link to Stephen is debatable, as the charter specifically stated that it followed the tenor of documents issued by Henry I and Henry II.[106] As king, John confirmed annual rents to the abbey, and gave forest lands in pure and perpetual alms. Again, the emphasis was on the Angevin line, referring to John's wellbeing, the soul of his father, and those of all his ancestors. Royal favour is also suggested following the seizure of Norman lands in England, with orders issued for the abbot to receive full seisin of lands taken from the community in Rutland.[107]

Similarly, Furness Abbey (Lancashire) had clear links to Stephen, John's predecessor as lord of Lancaster, but the latter's documents invoked his Angevin heritage. In the 1190s, John confirmed charters to the abbey issued by Stephen (as count of Mortain and Boulogne), Henry I, and Henry II. He issued further confirmations as king, and gave land in Cumbria in 1215, for God, in free, pure, and perpetual alms, for his wellbeing and for the souls of his ancestors and heirs.[108] Likewise, John confirmed the monks of Stoneleigh (Warwickshire) in possession of the site given by Henry II in exchange for their initial home, Radmore (Staffordshire). This was originally given by Stephen to a group of hermits, who prudently also sought a charter from the Empress Matilda, John's paternal grandmother, who persuaded them to become Cistercian.[109] The king also confirmed charters of the foundations made by King Stephen and Queen Matilda at Coggeshall and Faversham.[110] Here, he may simply have acted within a tradition of support for houses established by royal predecessors.

Religious communities clearly had an important part to play in building and recalling an association with the ruler and his dynasty. Yet the rights and privileges involved could be withheld or withdrawn as well as bestowed. This was particularly the case when a ruler fell into dispute with the church.[111] Conversely, the commitment to pray for royal donors and their kinsmen was one that religious communities themselves took seriously. In the late 1240s, the canons of Evreux protested (unsuccessfully) against the sale of one of their English manors by their bishop, John de La Cour. Their objection highlighted that the manor had been given over a century earlier, in return for annual masses at Evreux, in atonement for Henry

---

[105] *Mortain*; *Magni rotuli scaccarii Normanniae*, p. 538.

[106] *Mortain*. For grants by Henry I, Stephen, Geoffrey of Anjou, Henry II, Geoffrey duke of Brittany and Richard I: *CDF*, pp. 287–308 (nos 792–851).

[107] *RC*, p. 114a; *CDF*, pp. 304–5 (nos 844–5); *RLC 1204–24*, p. 60b.

[108] *Mortain*; *Lancashire Pipe Rolls*, pp. 315–16; *RC*, pp. 41a-b, 52b, 53a, 53b, 213b. In 1200, the abbot paid £100 for his privileges: *ROF*, p. 55.

[109] *RC*, pp. 130b–131a; Knowles and Hadcock, pp. 124, 125–6.

[110] *RC*, pp. 114b, 150a; Dugdale, *Monasticon*, vol. IV, pp. 573b–574a.

[111] See below, Chapter 6.

I's sins, and for his forebears and heirs. The sale went ahead, but the purchaser, Hugh, bishop of Ely, used revenues from the manor to pay for prayers for Henry III and Eleanor of Provence.[112]

There is a further dimension to John's support for 'family' religious projects: his involvement with foundations by prominent members of the *familia regis*. Religion and provision for the soul were not neglected by members of the court, who received royal backing for their activity. The king's support for Archbishop Hubert Walter's projected re-foundation of the secular college at Wolverhampton as a Cistercian abbey has already been discussed, as has John's backing for Halesowen Abbey, established by Peter des Roches.[113] These are not isolated examples. At Hubert's Premonstratensian community at West Dereham (Norfolk), the archbishop successfully petitioned for confirmation of gifts of numerous donors.[114] It was a similar situation at the hospital at Portsmouth, established with the support of des Roches by William de Wrotham, keeper of the king's ships. The royal charter here was issued 'for the sake of God' (*intuitu Dei*), for John's wellbeing, for the souls of his ancestors and successors, and for all the Christian faithful. It noted that the hospital, dedicated to the Trinity, the Virgin Mary, the Holy Cross, and St Nicholas, was for support of the poor in Christ.[115] Other houses established by central figures within royal government benefited in similar ways. Around four months after the death of his justiciar, Geoffrey fitz Peter, John confirmed charters for a hospital founded on land Geoffrey had given to William de Wrotham for the purpose at Sutton-at-Hone (Kent).[116] Meanwhile, Geoffrey's foundation of a hospital or pilgrim hostel at East Tilbury (Essex) received ten marks in alms in 1212, 1213, and 1214, although in the first case this payment seems to have been authorised by the justiciar (and others) acting on behalf of the king.[117]

Further examples concern communities of Augustinian canons. In Normandy, Peter de Préaux was granted one hundred *livres Angevin* from various fairs, to confer on men of religion as he wished. He gave this to the canons of Nôtre-Dame de Beaulieu. In return, the canons were to pay twenty shillings annually to the hospital of St Mary Magdalene for the soul of John's eldest brother, Peter's former lord, Henry the Young King.[118] In England, Bradenstoke Priory (Wiltshire)

---

[112] J. Peltzer, 'The Slow Death of the Angevin Empire', *Historical Research*, 81 (2008), 553–84 (pp. 571–2).

[113] See above, Chapter 1.

[114] RC, pp. 21b–22a, and see also p. 93a. John is said to have granted the right to hold a fair: F. Blomefield, *An Essay Towards the Topographical History of the County of Norfolk*, 11 vols (London, 1805–10), vol. VII, pp. 331–2.

[115] RC, p. 202a; Vincent, *Peter des Roches*, pp. 70, 110, 114; EEA IX, p. 133 (Appendix 2, no. 4).

[116] *Cartae Antiquae Rolls 11–20*, pp. 48–9 (no. 362); PR 16 John, pp. 26–7; PR 17 John, p. 29; Turner, Men, p. 88.

[117] RLC 1204–24, pp. 125b, 153b, 176a; Turner, Men, p. 65. The hostel was founded in part commutation of Geoffrey's unfulfilled crusading vow.

[118] RC, pp. 70b–71a; *Norman Charters from English Sources*, pp. 115–17 (no. 7). The canons also agreed to celebrate masses and burn candles for Peter and his brother Roger. John's charter was issued on the same day as the second of his charters relating to lordship of the Channel

received forty cows and two bulls, given by William de Briouze whilst he still had the king's favour, in 1205. A royal charter, issued 'for the love of God' (*pro amore Dei*), for John's soul, and for those of his ancestors and successors, granted pasture for this herd.[119] These were just two of the royal *acta* in favour of this house. A general confirmation was issued in 1207. The king's itinerary brought him to Bradenstoke in 1215, where he acted to ensure that land was conferred on the house in alms along with daily rights to timber.[120]

Linked to Bradenstoke through the family of William Marshal, John also confirmed charters of Augustinian Cartmel Priory (Lancashire). William's father was buried at Bradenstoke, which provided canons for the Marshal's foundation at Cartmel in 1189-90. As lord of Lancaster during Richard I's reign, John confirmed Cartmel to William, granting leave to establish a house for whatever religious he wished.[121] His confirmation as king demonstrates how he and the founder could differ in their specificity in regards to members of the royal dynasty for whom prayers were expected. John's first charter states that the Marshal's foundation was for the souls of Henry II, Henry the Young King, and John. The confirmation was for his soul and those of his ancestors and successors. The Marshal's documents emphasise the importance he attached to intercession for his first royal master, the Young King, who he describes as 'my lord'.[122]

Meanwhile, John supported several religious houses founded by William Brewer. At Augustinian Mottisfont (Hampshire), founded in 1201, the king gave confirmation 'for the sake of God' (*intuitu Dei*), for his soul's wellbeing, and for those of his ancestors and heirs.[123] The same combination of souls was referred to when John confirmed gifts of various donors to Brewer's Cistercian foundation at Dunkeswell (Devon). The house also received royal protection.[124] The king also issued confirmations and gave a church to Torre, William's Premonstratensian

---

Islands, which Peter was to receive pending marriage to Mary de Vernon, heiress to the Isle of Wight. If John were to die before this could take place, Jersey, Guernsey and Alderney were to pass to Peter in hereditary right: *RC*, pp. 33b, 71a; Everard and Holt, *Jersey 1204*, pp. 76-7; D. Power, 'Les Dernières années du régime angevin en Normandie', *Plantagenêts et Capétiens: confrontations et héritages*, ed. M. Aurell and N.-Y. Tonnerre (Turnhout, 2006), pp. 163-92 (p. 179); *Norman Charters from English Sources*, pp. 150-3 (no. 39).

[119] *RLC 1204-24*, p. 19b; *RC*, p. 152. For the rise and fall of de Briouze: R. V. Turner, 'Briouze, William (III) de (d. 1211)', *ODNB* (Oxford, 2004, online edn 2006) [http://www.oxforddnb.com/view/article/3283, accessed 18 December 2013].

[120] *RC*, pp. 169b-170b, 212b; *RLC 1204-24*, pp. 219b, 220a; *The Cartulary of Bradenstoke Priory*, ed. V. C. M. London, Wiltshire Record Society, 35 (Devizes, 1979), pp. 117-18 (no. 372), 162-3 (nos 552-3), 165-8 (no. 565); 'Itinerary'.

[121] *Lancashire Pipe Rolls*, pp. 343-5.

[122] *RC*, pp. 8a-b, 215b-216a. The second of these was given in exchange for a palfrey, and agreement that two hundred marks taken during the interdict would not be repaid by the king: *Lancashire Pipe Rolls*, p. 247. See also: D. Crouch, *William Marshal: Knighthood, War and Chivalry, 1147-1219*, 2nd edn (London, 2002), pp. 73, 211-12; Farrer and Brownbill, *VCH Lancaster*, vol. II, p. 144.

[123] *RC*, p. 139a-b. On Brewer and his foundation: Turner, *Men*, pp. 71-90 (esp. p. 87); S. Wood, *English Monasteries and their Patrons in the Thirteenth Century* (Oxford, 1955), p. 132.

[124] *RC*, pp. 164b-165a; Turner, *Men*, pp. 75, 87-8.

foundation in Devon, and for the hospital of St John the Baptist established by Brewer at Bridgwater (Somerset).[125]

Further examples include Premonstratensian Langley (Norfolk), established in 1195 by Robert fitz Roger. Here, alongside the health of his soul and those of his ancestors and successors, the king's confirmation specifically mentions the salvation of Henry II. John also granted the right to hold a weekly market and an annual fair on the vigil and feast of the Apostles Philip and James (30 April–1 May).[126] Other instances may also have been inspired by an individual's service to the crown, such as John's grant of one hundred shillings a year to Croxden Abbey (Staffordshire) in 1201, for the soul of a knight named Roger Caperon, buried in their church.[127]

However, John did not always favour his courtiers' benefaction. Hubert Walter's brother Theobald was a constant presence in the count of Mortain's entourage between 1185 and 1193. In c. 1192, Theobald was prominent in re-founding the hospital at Cockersand (Lancashire) as a Premonstratensian house. Whether the count supported this is unclear, but he judged in favour of the Augustinian canons of Leicester in a dispute over the manor of Cockerham in which the community was based. Theobald granted a new site for his abbey, using part of Amounderness (Lancashire) which he had been granted by John.[128] Thereafter, Theobald appears not to have supported John's attempted seizure of the throne in 1193–94. Richard I rewarded him with the sheriffdom of Lancaster. He apparently fell from grace when John became king. Nonetheless, as Theobald gradually negotiated his way back into royal favour, or perhaps because Cockersand wanted greater certainty over its holdings, in 1201 the king confirmed the canons' possession of the site and the gifts of donors.[129] In 1215, further charters were issued, invoking the king's wellbeing and the souls of his ancestors and successors.[130]

The evidence suggests that, in many cases, John was prepared to support religious activity by leading courtiers, usually by issuing confirmation charters to houses established by the *familia regis*. This presented further opportunities to solicit prayer for his spiritual needs and for the souls of his kinsfolk. He might also hope that this would help to sustain political support. If so, he was not always successful. William de Wrotham, for example, joined the rebellion of 1215, although he returned to the royalist camp after John's death.[131]

---

[125] *RC*, pp. 70a–b, 168b, 204b; Turner, *Men*, p. 87.

[126] *RC*, pp. 6a–b, 51a.

[127] *RL*, p. 13. Roger cannot be identified with certainty. A man of that name held land at Burton (Norfolk) of Earl Hugh of Chester (d. 1181): F. West, *The Justiciarship in England 1066–1232* (Cambridge, 1966), p. 99. This subsequently passed to Geoffrey fitz Peter's custody. The letter enrolled on the liberate rolls is addressed to the justiciar.

[128] Farrer and Brownbill, *VCH Lancaster*, vol. II, p. 154; *Mortain*.

[129] *RC*, p. 91a; M. T. Flanagan, 'Butler, Theobald (d. 1205)', *ODNB* (Oxford, 2004) [http://www.oxforddnb.com/view/article/4207, accessed 19 December 2013]. For the regularity with which Theobald witnessed John's charters as Count of Mortain: Vincent, 'Jean', p. 59.

[130] *RC*, pp. 216a–b, 218a; *ROF*, p. 564.

[131] B. Golding, 'Wrotham, William of (d. 1217/18)', *ODNB* (Oxford, 2004) [http://www.

The family dimension to John's religious activity spanned his lands, both before and after he became king. His critics argued that this extended no further than superstition. The *Life of St Hugh* recounts a conversation between John and the bishop, in which the former displayed a stone held in a gold mount, which he wore around his neck. He asserted that this 'had been given to one of his ancestors, and that God had promised him that none of his descendants who were fortunate enough to possess it should ever lose any part of their vast domains'. As befits the purpose of the *Life*, Hugh is said immediately to have issued a rebuke: '"Do not put your trust in an inanimate stone, but in the living true and heavenly stone, our Lord Jesus Christ".' It seems that the writer, Adam of Eynsham, was suggesting that the loss of large parts of John's continental inheritance was due to lack of faith. That said, there is evidence that John carried precisely such a good luck token. On one occasion it was lost. The finder, Bartholomew, received a reward of twenty shillings.[132]

The link between family religion and territory, however, is highlighted by more than good luck tokens. Marjorie Chibnall highlights the shifting horizons of benefactors in the century following the Norman Conquest. Leading families acquired lands that would become new centres of family piety and founded churches to establish roots in their new territories. At 'all times the royal family helped to point the way'.[133] As kings of England and dukes of Normandy, the rulers developed association, through direct foundation and support for houses founded by the nobility and members of the court, with religious institutions across their territories. The geographical span of such bonds increased with the wider expanse of territory under Angevin control. This is reflected in the range of houses from which documents issued by King John have survived.

Much of the evidence discussed in this chapter has focused on the *pro anima* clauses of John's charters. These reveal the extent to which he expected prayers for his kin-group, in particular his parents, and his predecessors as king. Similar conclusions have been reached by Stephen Marritt in assessing late eleventh- and early twelfth-century Anglo-Norman charters: 'it is not always possible to define what liturgical practices would result, but such clauses did commit institutions to seeking divine support for king, dynasty and kingdom in their religious observance in perpetuity'. Such clauses could be used to emphasise links with the past and the continuity of kingship.[134] In John's case, his father and mother feature prominently, but the references to kindred extended much more widely. In addition, the king associated with a wide range of religious communities established by members of his extended kin group.

This chapter has revealed how John sought prayers for the ruling dynasty. It might be suggested that this was in part a declaration and emphasis of his authority

---

oxforddnb.com/view/article/30087, accessed 20 December 2013]; Vincent, *Peter des Roches*, p. 110.

[132] *Magna Vita*, vol. II, pp. 139-40; *RL*, p. 23; *PR 4 John*, p. 276; Warren, *John*, p. 140.
[133] Chibnall, 'Monastic Foundations', pp. 37, 45-7.
[134] Marritt, 'Prayers', pp. 187, 193-4.

and right to rule, an opportunity to broadcast the titles he held or claimed. Before 1199, this was as count of Mortain, lord of Ireland, and holder of various lands in England. After 1199 it involved all the Angevin lands: England, Ireland, Normandy, Greater Anjou, and Aquitaine. Thus, on the one hand a king might show straightforward concern for the souls of his relatives. On the other, he could hope to consolidate spiritual support for the dynasty across his territories. This was perhaps of heightened importance for John, whose claim to England, and to the ducal and comital titles of the continental lands, was disputed. Invocation of the names and grants of predecessors could be used to emphasise continuity of rulership.[135] Here, future research might explore the way in which the *laudatio parentum* – the practice of relatives granting approval of a donor's gifts, usually to a religious house – was respected and sustained by successor generations.[136]

The Angevin family was not always united in life, but John's behaviour seems to suggest that they were more cohesive in provision for family members in death. The influence of Eleanor of Aquitaine on her offspring is striking. However, in his largesse to Rouen, Fontevraud, and many other religious houses, and in evidence such as the names of his children, John showed a wide understanding of the dynastic links that made up his family tree. The principal exception to this pattern of family commemoration was Geoffrey of Brittany. His exclusion may relate either to his death in a rebellion in which other family members did not participate or to the fact that, for John, acknowledgement of Geoffrey might give legitimacy to the rival claims of Geoffrey's son, John's nephew, Arthur.

Elsewhere, John showed wide-ranging recognition of his relatives' wishes and concern to confirm their provision. This was not confined to kings. Kinswomen were strongly represented, notably Henry I's queens, Matilda and Adeliza, and John's paternal grandmother, Empress Matilda. Coupled with the influence of Eleanor of Aquitaine, the impact of royal women on the family traditions transmitted to John seems clear.[137] Equally, a range of traditions acted simultaneously: Anglo-Norman, Angevin, Aquitainian. That said, John clearly failed to integrate Isabella of Angoulême into dynastic benefaction. Whilst this was not dissimilar to Richard I's marginalisation of Queen Berengaria, it contrasts markedly with a number of the royal women discussed here, not least Eleanor of Aquitaine and the Empress Matilda.

The impact on Henry III's family benefaction is another area worthy of further research. Patterns of religious activity in which John was involved were continued by his successor. Henry's piety was without doubt exceptional, but elements of it were not without precursors. Thus, he continued hearing the *Laudes Regiae*.[138] We have seen that King John paid respects to many saints, whether Anglo-Saxon,

---

[135] For similar possibilities in relation to the twelfth-century kingdom of Jerusalem: Gerish, 'Ancestors', pp. 127–50.

[136] On the *laudatio parentum*: S. D. White, *Custom, Kinship and Gifts to Saints: The Laudatio Parentum in Western France, 1050–1150* (Chapel Hill, NC, and London, 1988).

[137] On women as transmitters of family tradition: E. M. C. van Houts, *Memory and Gender in Medieval Europe, 900–1200* (Basingstoke and London, 1999), pp. 65–92.

[138] See above, Chapter 1.

saints whose cults had developed during his lifetime, or major Christian cults such as that of the Virgin Mary. This aspect of royal religion proved of central importance to Henry III, who continued a tradition of which his father had been part, albeit on a grander scale. It was to their father's foundation at Beaulieu that Henry III and Richard of Cornwall turned for monks to populate their own abbeys at Netley and Hailes.[139] We will see later how John engaged in charitable giving which bears comparison with that of Henry, in its nature if not in its scale.[140] Henry also continued and augmented his father's benefaction of the Cistercian Abbey of Beaulieu.[141] The family was an element of John's personal religion which he inherited and which he passed to his descendants.

---

[139] See above, Chapter 3.
[140] See below, Chapter 5.
[141] See above, Chapter 1, and below, Chapter 8.

5

Charity and Almsgiving

Charity and aid for the poor are aspects of royal religion for which King John's son, Henry III, is rightly renowned. Under Henry, 'a new chapter opens in the history of almsgiving'. The king regularly fed thousands of paupers, honouring the saints or the souls of his relatives.[1] His largesse took the form both of lavish, one-off events, such as feeding 102,000 individuals for the soul of his sister Isabella in 1242, and of daily giving, as with the distributions to several hundred paupers that occurred at various times during the reign.[2]

There are precursors for Henry's activity in his father's actions. Evidence is at times patchy, but suggests that John displayed charitable instincts across his reign. Writers and preachers active in this period highlighted the difficulties facing the rich man who hoped to gain entry to Heaven and the value of giving alms. It seems likely that royal charity responded to such a message, reflecting the contemporary notion that just as water extinguishes fire, so almsgiving counteracted sin.

Charity and almsgiving is one area of John's religious activity that has attracted attention from historians. Hilda Johnstone highlights that for elite households 'almsgiving was as much a part of daily ceremonial as sleeping or eating'. In John's case, 'the compensatory aspect of almsgiving was what he chiefly dealt in'. This 'was almost entirely on the principle of a debit and credit account with Heaven'.[3] Charles Young argues that, whilst 'there is little about King John's gifts to charity to suggest that spontaneous generosity or voluntary piety were characteristic of the man', he nonetheless accepted contemporary expectations and made appropriate responses.[4] Most recently, Sally Dixon-Smith's seminal study of Henry III's almsgiving observes that John's reputation conformed to the stereotype of 'a leader who did not fulfil the age-old duty of generosity and rightful reward'.[5] Whilst this is indisputable in the political sphere, it does not reflect the picture presented by the evidence to be discussed here. The king's almsgiving was an important element of his religious activity. He did more than go through the motions.

Before examining John's giving itself, it is important to consider how the twelfth- and thirteenth-century elite was encouraged to view charity to the poor.

---

[1] Johnstone, 'Poor-Relief', pp. 153-4.
[2] Dixon-Smith, 'Feeding the Poor', pp. 133, 160, 179-80, 212; CLR 1240-1245, p. 124; Dixon-Smith, 'The Image and Reality of Almsgiving'; *The Wardrobe Accounts of Henry III*, ed. B. L. Wild, PRS, 96, ns 58 (London, 2012).
[3] Johnstone, 'Poor-Relief', pp. 150, 153.
[4] Young, 'King John', p. 270.
[5] Dixon-Smith, 'Feeding the Poor', pp. 50-1.

Gratian's *Decretum*, which cannot have been completed before the Second Lateran Council (1139), argued that all property belonged to all men by natural law. The rich should use their surplus goods to help others.⁶ Alan of Lille (c. 1130–1203) argued that Christ dwelt in the poor alone. This drew on Matthew's gospel, where Jesus described the Last Judgement, and explanation to the righteous and the damned of how they had reached their respective fates: 'For I was hungry and you gave me meat, I was thirsty and you gave me drink, I was a stranger and you took me in, naked and you clothed me, I was sick and you visited me, I was in prison and you came to me.' When the saved asked when they had done this, Christ responded, 'Inasmuch as you have done it to one of these the least of my brethren, you have done it to me.' The fate of the damned was sealed when they failed to perform such charities.⁷ This passage influenced the sixth-century Rule of St Benedict, which noted: 'Let special care be taken in the reception of the poor and of strangers [or pilgrims], because in them Christ is more truly welcomed', adding:

> Let all guests that come be received like Christ Himself, for He will say: 'I was a stranger and ye took me in.' ... At the arrival or departure of all guests, let Christ – who indeed is received in their persons – be adored in them, by bowing the head or even prostrating on the ground.⁸

In the Anglo-Norman world this can also be seen in Lanfranc's *Monastic Constitutions*. These instructed communities that during the Maundy of the poor in Easter week, 'genuflecting and bowing down they shall adore Christ in the poor'.⁹

Charitable giving was also influenced by the concept of the seven corporal works of mercy. By the second half of the thirteenth century these were identified by St Thomas Aquinas as 'feeding the hungry, giving drink to the thirsty, clothing the naked, giving hospitality to strangers, visiting the sick, ransoming prisoners, and burying the dead'.¹⁰ Aquinas discussed almsgiving and the way in which charity should be bestowed. Thus, 'as long as the rich gave alms in the right spirit, they could enjoy their wealth, maintain their social status, and still fulfil their Christian obligations': welcome news to rulers with multiple demands on their finances.¹¹ The *Summa Theologiae* was written in the late 1260s and early 1270s, the era of King Henry III,¹² yet it reflects longer-term concerns.

---

6   M. Rubin, *Charity and Community in Medieval Cambridge* (Cambridge, 1987), p. 59. On Gratian and the *Decretum*: F. L. Cross and E. A. Livingstone, *The Oxford Dictionary of the Christian Church*, 3rd edn (Oxford, 1997), pp. 700–1; B. Tierney, *Medieval Poor Law: A Sketch of Canonical Theory and its Application in England* (Berkeley and Los Angeles, CA, 1959), pp. 7, 37.
7   Rubin, *Charity*, p. 59; Mollat, *The Poor*, pp. 112–13; Matthew 25, verses 31–46.
8   *The Rule of St Benedict*, ed. D. O. Hunter-Blair, 4th edn (Fort Augustus, 1934), pp. 138–43 (chapter 53).
9   *Monastic Constitutions of Lanfranc*, p. 49.
10 St Thomas Aquinas, *Summa Theologiae. Volume 34. Charity (2a2ae, 22–33)*, ed. and trans. R. J. Batten (Cambridge, 2006), pp. 240–1; Dixon-Smith, 'Feeding the Poor', pp. 68–70.
11 Dixon-Smith, 'Feeding the Poor', pp. 68–78 (esp. pp. 77–8).
12 Cross and Livingstone, *Oxford Dictionary of the Christian Church*, pp. 1614–15.

Such concepts would have circulated in religious preaching during John's lifetime. They also influenced figures active within Angevin government. The *Dialogue of the Exchequer*, written in the late 1170s, argued that in peacetime 'though arms are laid down, devout princes build churches, they feed and clothe Christ by giving alms to the poor, and they distribute money by practising other works of mercy'.[13] During John's reign, one of his closest advisers, Peter des Roches, bishop of Winchester, quoted the teaching of Matthew's gospel in an indulgence issued to contributors to the hospital of St Thomas, Southwark.[14]

These ideas created a sense in which the poor had been 'created and placed in the world for the sake of the rich man's salvation'.[15] In the early twelfth century, Honorius Augustodunensis, a preacher for a time active in England, claimed that 'God wanted the rich to be fathers to the poor'.[16] At the turn of the twelfth and thirteenth centuries, the Parisian master Peter the Chanter and his followers were of particular importance in their teaching on social obligations.[17] These men 'maintained that a secular ruler should enforce the rich people's duties to relieve the poor', implying that they thought it important for kings to set an example as almsgivers.[18] Emphasis was placed on the argument that the rich man was certain of damnation if he did not give to the poor. The parable of Dives and Lazarus was cited as evidence. Such associations clearly shaped Henry III's religious giving and the iconography of the residences from which his largesse was issued.[19]

Again, such arguments probably found favour with churchmen active in John's reign. In attitudes to almsgiving and fasting there is *some* similarity between the king and Archbishop Stephen Langton, one of the Chanter's most important followers, whose appointment John worked so hard to prevent. After Stephen was finally accepted into his see, it seems likely that at some point he preached before the king. Langton regarded 'a man's relation with the poor the test of true religion'. At least one of his sermons can be compared with John's attitude to almsgiving and fasting. Here, the theologian argued that '"alms without fasting are

---

[13] *Dialogus de Scaccario. The Dialogue of the Exchequer. Constitutio Domus Regis. The Establishment of the Royal Household*, new edn, ed. and trans. E. Amt and S. D. Church, OMT (Oxford, 2007), p. 5; Dixon-Smith, 'Feeding the Poor', pp. 78-9.

[14] *EEA IX*, pp. 50-1 (no. 58).

[15] Mollat, *The Poor*, p. 106.

[16] Rubin, *Charity*, p. 83: V. I. J. Flint, 'Honorius Augustodunensis (d. c. 1140)', *ODNB* (Oxford, 2004) [http://www.oxforddnb.com/view/article/53485, accessed 31 July 2013].

[17] On the schoolmen and the relationship between temporal power and society: J. W. Baldwin, *Masters, Princes and Merchants: The Social Views of Peter the Chanter & his Circle*, 2 vols (Princeton, NJ, 1970); P. Buc, '*Principes Gentium Dominantur Eorum*: Princely Power between Legitimacy and Illegitimacy in Twelfth-Century Exegesis', *Cultures of Power: Lordship, Status and Process in Twelfth Century Europe*, ed. T. N. Bisson (Philadelphia, PA, 1995), pp. 310-28 (summarising fuller discussion in: P. Buc, *L'ambiguïté du livre: Prince, pouvoir et peuple dans les commentaires de la bible au moyen âge* (Paris, 1995)); K. Chambers, '"When We Do Nothing Wrong, We Are Peers": Peter the Chanter and Twelfth-Century Political Thought', *Speculum*, 88 (2013), 405-26.

[18] Rubin, *Charity*, p. 62.

[19] Luke 16, verses 19-25; Dixon-Smith, 'Image and Reality', esp. pp. 81-3, 91.

more valuable that fasting without alms'" and that '"fasting without almsgiving is of no good'". The king, it may be argued, subscribed to this opinion. It could be seen to justify his policy of not fasting and giving alms instead. That said, he did not always follow, and perhaps lacked the willpower to observe, Langton's further injunction: '"fasting with almsgiving is of double goodness'".[20]

The most plentiful evidence for John's charity concerns the poor. As he travelled, and at the stopping points on his itinerary, paupers would have sought his alms, either money or scraps from the rich man's table. Few narrative accounts highlight this aspect of royal religious activity. However, the *Life of St Hugh* describes the bishop's efforts to instruct John in the virtues required to secure the salvation of his soul and for the exercise of good kingship. After this:

> For the next few days both in speech and in action he [John] made a parade of meekness and humility. When the beggars he met wished him prosperity, he bowed to them and thanked them most assiduously, and graciously returned the greetings of ragged crones. After three days, however, his completely different words and behaviour grieved the bishop and others much more than they had been pleased at what they had previously witnessed.[21]

The author Adam of Eynsham wanted Hugh of Lincoln to be seen as a devoted man of God. Thus he contrasted the holy bishop with his impious pupil by portraying John's behaviour as a 'parade' which he could not sustain. Nonetheless, in its references to 'beggars' and 'ragged crones' the account highlights that the poor were a group whom John could expect to encounter, and that there were expectations of how he should react. These responses, especially the idea of bowing before them, are suggestive of the contemporary belief that Christ was in some way present in the poor.

Sources such as the *Misae* rolls, which record daily expenditure by the royal household, reveal that John did more than go through the motions in his almsgiving. These documents bring us closer to the king's personal religion than other surviving evidence. They include numerous payments in alms and provision for the poor and sick. Unfortunately, only two household rolls survive for John's reign, covering his eleventh and fourteenth years as king. Nonetheless, they provide an insight into the life of the king and his entourage at the height of the interdict. Further evidence can be drawn from the *Liberate* Rolls and the Pipe Rolls, in particular those covering the fifth and sixth years of John's rule.[22] Meanwhile, three surviving *Praestita* Rolls, covering the seventh and twelfth regnal years, and the period from 14 to 18 John, record advance payments to royal officials covering numerous purposes, such as military provisioning. They sometimes

---

20 Rubin, *Charity*, pp. 63–4.
21 *Magna Vita*, vol. II, pp. 141–2.
22 RL (for Liberate Roll 5 John and Misae Roll 11 John); *PR 6 John*; RM (for Misae Roll 14 John). The *Liberate* Rolls in John's reign are essentially the same as the Close Rolls. They re-emerged as a separate administrative entity under Henry III, when they record substantial royal almsgiving.

record sums issued in advance for alms payments.[23] More broadly the Pipe Rolls, like those of earlier reigns, demonstrate continuity in maintenance of payments in alms and tithes from the county farms. Historians have deemed these to be 'royal contributions to charity', in this case directed to the organised religious, the institutionalised poor. Indeed, Bynum argues that paying tithes was an element of the 'minimal definition' of a Christian in this period.[24]

King John gave regular alms to feed the poor, sometimes also ordering clothes to be distributed. We do not always know the purpose; for example, in August 1203, when he was at Alençon in Normandy, he ordered payment of £510 9s 10½d to the Rouennais merchant Laurence du Donjon to finance feeding the poor.[25] Similarly, in 1208, no reason was stated in a charter granted to one Robert Ruffus of Kimbolton (Cambridgeshire) confirming possession of lands which Elena of Papworth had held of the king's alms. This was in return for feeding two paupers a day, forever, for the king's soul and for the souls of his ancestors and heirs.[26]

Like Henry III, although not as regularly, John fed the poor to commemorate or to seek intercession for the dead. This has been shown in the case of John's giving in 1204, shortly after the death of his mother, Eleanor of Aquitaine.[27] Feeding the poor at this time may also have been a response to agricultural dearth. Several chroniclers recorded famine in 1203 which 'killed a multitude of the poor'. Waverley Abbey dispersed its community amongst other houses.[28] Historians have argued that this was a period of bad harvests, with the price of wheat unusually high.[29] Other high-status figures, such as Peter des Roches, increased their almsgiving during such times.[30] In 1203, Archbishop Hubert Walter directed Herbert Poor, bishop of Salisbury, to admonish the clergy of his diocese to follow specific instructions relating to poor relief. A further letter, purporting to be from

---

[23] 'Rotulus de Praestito' (Praestita Roll 7 John); *RL* (Praestita Roll 12 John); *PR 17 John*, pp. 89–100 (Praestita Roll 14–18 John); Bartlett, *England*, p. 698.

[24] Young, 'King John', pp. 264–5; Bynum, *Holy Feast*, p. 40; Harvey, 'Piety', p. 8.

[25] *RL*, p. 57. On Laurence: A. Sadourny, 'Une famille rouennaise à la fin de la période ducale: les Du Donjon', *La Ville Médiévale en deçà et au-delà de ses murs: Mélanges Jean-Pierre Leguay*, ed. P. Lardin and J.-L. Roch (Rouen, 2000), pp. 183–8; M. Six, 'The Burgesses of Rouen in the Late Twelfth and Early Thirteenth Centuries', *Society and Culture in Medieval Rouen, 911–1300*, ed. L. V. Hicks and E. Brenner (Turnhout, 2013), pp. 247–78 (pp. 257–8); Webster, 'King John and Rouen', pp. 321–3.

[26] *RC*, p. 180a; *RLC 1204–24*, pp. 95b–96a; W. Farrer, *Feudal Cambridgeshire* (Cambridge, 1920), p. 97.

[27] He also fed the poor for the souls of Henry II and Richard I in 1212: see above, Chapter 4.

[28] *Annales de Margan*, p. 26; *Waverley*, p. 255; Cheney, 'Levies', p. 580.

[29] J. Z. Titow, *English Rural Society 1200–1350* (London and New York, 1969), pp. 100–1; C. Dyer, *Standards of Living in the Later Middle Ages: Social Change in England c. 1200–1520* (Cambridge, 1989), p. 264; P. Latimer, 'Early Thirteenth-Century Prices', *King John: New Interpretations*, ed. S. D. Church (Woodbridge, 1999), pp. 41–73. For a chronicler's account: *Annales de Theokesberia (A.D. 1066–1263)*, ed. H. R. Luard, *Annales Monastici*, RS 36, 5 vols (London, 1864–69), vol. I, p. 57.

[30] N. Vincent, 'The Politics of Church and State as Reflected in the Winchester Pipe Rolls, 1208–1280', *The Winchester Pipe Rolls and Medieval English Society*, ed. R. Britnell (Woodbridge, 2003), pp. 157–81 (pp. 172–3).

Hubert to Geoffrey Muschamp, bishop of Coventry, complained that famine had increased due to neglect of charity. Society was urged to help the poor, with clergy to take steps on a parish level to ensure that the needy did not die of starvation. Non-resident priests were to be compelled to give a quarter of their revenue in alms. Special prayers were to be said, including supplication for good weather and plentiful crops. Cheney sees John's giving in this period as directly linked to the suffering the famine had caused.[31]

If this was the case, then the payment which John made in Normandy in 1203 may indicate that supplies from the duchy were sent to England to feed the starving. The impression that provision was needed is sustained by the evidence of the Pipe Roll for 1203–04. Two payments provided alms for one hundred poor from the Friday after Easter until the feast of St Peter in Chains (1 August). Three others do the same, beginning on the second Sunday after Easter. If this relates to 1203, then they began on 11 and 20 April, a month in which Ralph of Coggeshall recorded widespread flooding.[32]

The poor were also fed in reaction to transgressions by the king and members of his entourage, notably their regular failure to fast when this was a requirement. There appears to have been a consistent penalty: payment of 9s 4½d for one hundred paupers. This usually occurred because of non-observance of Friday fasts, which was the case on some thirty-two occasions in 1209–10 and thirty-one occasions in 1212–13.[33] These often coincided with or happened shortly before or after feast days (Table 1).

In 1209, John's failure to fast included two Fridays during Advent, whilst, in 1212, he did not fast on any Fridays in the month leading up to Christmas.[34] Amongst the feast days noted, that of the Ascension, one of major significance in the religious calendar, also marked the anniversary of John's coronation, whilst some, notably those of St James and St Philip, were feasts of saints whose cults played an important part in the king's religious activity. Perhaps this suggests why he was keen to atone for his error. One problem to note here is that the sources record the king making amends for transgressions. Arguments from silence are dangerous, but it was not the purpose of the accounts to record occasions when John did what was expected. Meanwhile, the pauper at the king's gate must often have been greeted with welcome news: the king had broken his fast and undertaken to make amends.

Coincidentally, at much the same time as the *Misae* Rolls record these regular failures to fast, the *Life of St Hugh* was written.[35] This also highlighted the king's reluctance to abstain from eating in recounting his Easter observance in 1199. On

---

[31] Cheney, 'Levies', pp. 578–84; *Royal Commission on Historical Manuscripts. Reports. 15. Report on Manuscripts in Various Collections. Vol. 1. Berwick-upon-Tweed, Burford and Lostwithiel Corporations; The Counties of Wilts and Worcester, the Bishop of Chichester; and the Deans and Chapters of Chichester, Canterbury, and Salisbury*, HMSO (London, 1901), pp. 233–4.

[32] PR 5 John, pp. 59, 71, 80; Coggeshall, p. 142.

[33] Harvey, 'Piety', p. 10.

[34] Harvey, 'Piety', p. 10.

[35] *Magna Vita*, vol. I, pp. xi–xii, vol. II, p. 74; Gransden, *Historical Writing*, pp. 312–13, 317.

Table 1 John's non-observance of fasts on Friday feast days, the eve of feast days, or the day following a feast day

Year	Friday	Date of feast day
1209	Eve of St Mark the Evangelist	25 April
	Apostles Philip and James	1 May
	Ascension	7 May
	Eve of St James the Apostle	25 July
1212	Day after Ascension	3 May
	Apostles Peter and Paul	29 June
	St Margaret the Virgin	20 July
	St Laurence	10 August
	St Bartholomew	24 August
	Eve of the Nativity of the Virgin Mary	8 September
	Exaltation of the Cross	14 September
	St Andrew	30 November
	Day after St Lucy	13 December
	St Thomas the Apostle	21 December
	Holy Innocents	28 December
1213	Conversion of St Paul	25 January
	St Peter *in Cathedra*	22 February

Source: Misae Roll 11 John and Misae Roll 14 John: *RL*, pp. 110–11, 117, 120, 122, 124, 136–7, 159–60, 162; *RM*, pp. 231, 232, 233, 234, 235, 236, 237, 240, 242, 244, 246, 247, 251, 252, 254, 255, 262, 264, 266

this occasion, Hugh preached on the subject of good and bad rulers, a provocative theme which made John impatient, repeatedly sending a messenger asking the bishop 'to wind up his sermon and celebrate mass, as he [John] wished to eat after such a prolonged fast'. Hugh ignored him, and 'continued to feed his vast audience with the meat of sound doctrine'. Adam of Eynsham was clear in his opinion of the king, 'rejecting both foods ... the word and the sacrament ... eager to fill his belly with meat'. The evidence suggests that the anecdote, which has parallels with late twelfth-century criticism of kings who left church before the sermon had ended, was plausible. John apparently disliked fasting, lacking the willpower to go without food on a regular basis. That said, the instance highlighted by the *Life of St Hugh* was apparently one on which the king had, for once, observed the required fast.[36]

[36] *Magna Vita*, vol. II, p. 143; Stephen Langton, *Commentary on the Book of Chronicles*, ed. A. Saltman (Ramat-Gan, 1978), pp. 42–3, 199–200; K. Harvey, 'An Un-Christian King? King John and the Lenten Fast', *Magna Carta Research Project Blog* (12 March 2014) [http://magnacartaresearch.blogspot.co.uk/2014/03/an-un-christian-king-king-john-and.html, accessed 19 June 2014].

Vincent argues that this passage shows that the king was 'sufficiently pious to fast during Holy Week'.[37] This was not always the case. John transgressed on Good Friday, 1209. Afterwards, his almsgiving was five times his usual amount.[38] This failure to fast on the holiest day in the Christian calendar might seem a damning reflection on his religious observance. Bynum suggests that 'to violate the Friday fast was the clearest, most visible way of rejecting the faith'.[39] Here, there is perhaps a distinction between church teachings and their observance. As will be seen, John's courtiers joined him at his table. Nor was he the last king of England to demonstrate such failings. Both Edward I and Edward III gave alms when they failed to attend mass or fast.[40] Tanner and Watson write of a 'general relaxation in interpretation and practice' in the period 1100-1500. Travellers might be exempted. Given John's near-ceaseless itineration, it seems possible that he regarded almsgiving as an appropriate compensatory act.[41]

Generally, John did observe religious requirements during Holy Week, including fasting. Likewise, in terms of the period for which records survive, during Lent there were no payments for fast-breaking in 1210, 1212, or 1213.[42] He was also particular, on occasion, about what he would receive during Lent. An entry on the Fine Rolls notes payment of two hundred chickens by Joan de Neville, so that she could lie for a night with her husband Hugh, chief justice of the forest. Sir James Holt highlights the final sentence: 'The chickens are to be handed over before the beginning of Lent; any then outstanding are to be delivered at the following Easter.' Thus, they were not to be received during Lent.[43] Equally, on Good Friday 1209 John knew he had transgressed. The fact that he gave such extensive alms suggests that he was well aware of the extent of his fault. It seems that the king believed that he could balance his sins with the performance of reparatory good works.

John's religious activity at Easter also included giving to the poor on Maundy Thursday, which marked Christ's final meal with his disciples on the eve of the Crucifixion. This was seen to symbolise the institution of the Eucharist. On Maundy Thursday, penitents expelled from the church on Ash Wednesday were readmitted. Ceremonial included the *pedilavium*, or washing of feet. We cannot be sure whether John washed the feet of the poor, but it is possible. Later thirteenth-century kings did so, including Henry III and Louis IX of France.[44] John certainly

---

[37] Vincent, 'Pilgrimages', p. 21.
[38] RL, p. 110.
[39] Bynum, *Holy Feast*, p. 41; Harvey, 'Piety', pp. 10-11.
[40] Prestwich, 'The Piety of Edward I', p. 122; Ormrod, 'Personal Religion', p. 854.
[41] Tanner and Watson, 'Least of the Laity', p. 417. On King John's religious observance and his itineration: Webster, 'Making Space'.
[42] Harvey, 'Piety', p. 12; Harvey, 'An Un-Christian King?'
[43] Holt, *King John*, pp. 6-7; ROF, p. 275. The entry is usually discussed in terms of John's lack of respect for leading courtiers, in choosing to sleep with their wives: Painter, *Reign*, pp. 231-2. See also: D. Crouch, 'Baronial Paranoia in King John's Reign', *Magna Carta and the England of King John*, ed. J. S. Loengard (Woodbridge, 2010), pp. 45-62 (p. 53).
[44] Cross and Livingstone, *Oxford Dictionary of the Christian Church*, pp. 953, 1059, 1247-8;

made gifts to the poor on Maundy Thursday. On 15 April 1210, when he was in Knaresborough, 3s 1d was allocated for the poor, with 2s 2d spent on robes for them, and 4s 4½d provided for buying thirteen belts, knives and girdles.[45] The latter sum suggests the number of poor involved, further implying that the robes cost two pence each. This looks like some kind of commemoration or invocation of the Last Supper. Perhaps the king washed the feet of the poor, or bowed before them (as Lanfranc's *Constitutions* suggested), as an act of humility and in recognition of the presence of Christ, before conferring his gifts. The next day, Good Friday, John spent £4 13s 9d on feeding one thousand paupers.[46] This was at the rate of 9s 4½d per hundred poor.

These observances have added significance. Although Henry I's queen, Matilda, engaged in something similar in the early twelfth century, in imitation of her mother, Queen (St) Margaret of Scotland, the 1210 example is the first known occasion on which a king of England marked Maundy Thursday.[47] John was able to perform his act of charity despite the sentences of interdict and personal excommunication in place at the time. Arnold Kellett suggests that due to a gap in the roll, the first sum of 3s 1d can be expanded to read 14s 1d, suggesting that thirteen paupers received thirteen pence each. Meanwhile, £28 14½d paid for cloth, linen, hoods, and shoes for the king's alms, recorded in the Yorkshire section of the Pipe Roll, could include the royal gifts made at Knaresborough on Maundy Thursday and Good Friday.[48]

Indeed, the poor regularly received royal alms in Easter week. On Palm Sunday (15 April) 1207, the abbot of Forde was charged with issuing instructions for thirty robes for thirty paupers. John's Maundy almsgiving in 1210 was no one-off. Similar provision occurred at Rochester on Maundy Thursday (10 April) 1213, when 14s 1d was allocated for thirteen poor at a rate of thirteen pence per person. There is no record of distribution of robes, but the allocation suggests fulfilment of the expectations of the occasion. Good Friday provision can be found in 1205, when John paid for bread and shoes for thirteen 'brothers'. In 1211, he was at the Tower of London on Good Friday. Brother Thomas the almoner was provided with one hundred shillings for the king's alms.[49]

Just as John often failed to fast on Fridays, but provided for the poor in recompense, so too he consistently failed to respect Wednesday as a day of abstinence, again even when these coincided with feast days of important saints. In 1212 this included the feast of St James the Apostle (25 July) and that of St Peter in Chains (1 August). Compensatory almsgiving and non-observance on Wednesday 8 August are recorded on the rolls in an entry dating to the feast of the Assumption (15

Hicks, *Religious Life*, p. 43; Dixon-Smith, 'Feeding the Poor', pp. 93–6.

[45] *RL*, p. 161. It is unclear how the first sum was to be spent, as part of the entry is missing. The significance of this event is explored in Kellett, 'King John', pp. 69–90.

[46] *RL*, pp. 161–2.

[47] L. L. Huneycutt, *Matilda of Scotland: A Study in Medieval Queenship* (Woodbridge, 2003), pp. 104–5; Harvey, 'Piety', p. 14.

[48] Kellett, 'King John', pp. 80–2; *PR 12 John*, p. 149.

[49] *RLC 1204–24*, pp. 38a, 81b; *RM*, p. 258; *RL*, p. 244.

August). Perhaps this was an appropriate occasion to recognise that he had erred. Later in the year, Wednesday payments covered the eve of the feast of St Luke (18 October). Here, as in August, John paid 16s 3d to feed 120 paupers to cover his transgression.[50]

There is some variation in payments for oversights on Wednesdays. The standard tariff appears to have been 13s 6½d for feeding one hundred paupers. Double this sum was paid, feeding two hundred paupers, on Wednesday 3 October 1212, half for the soul of King Henry II and half because Geoffrey fitz Peter and William Brewer had eaten meat that day. Later that year, 30s 9½d was paid for feeding 120 poor for the transgression of courtiers, whilst thirteen paupers were fed at Hereford at the king's expense, costing some 20½d. Eighty paupers were fed for 10s 10d in May 1213, and at around the same time the poor at Dover were fed on a Saturday. The latter payment notes that the sum had not been accounted for in the household.[51] Could this reflect a daily gift otherwise unknown to us?

The poor were also fed following regular occasions when King John and his followers went hunting on feast days, a practice frowned upon by the religious. In 1209, one hundred paupers received food because John had been hunting on the feast of St Mary Magdalene (Wednesday 22 July). In 1212, he hunted on Tuesday 6 November, the feast of St Leonard, and later fed one hundred poor with bread, meat, and ale. A few days later, on Friday before the feast of St Martin (11 November), the king enjoyed the thrill of the chase until Vespers. Another hundred paupers were fed in recompense. This happened again on Thursday 6 December, the feast of St Nicholas. The sums paid usually followed the pattern for broken fasts. On a Friday, non-observance cost 9s 4½d. On other days it cost 13s 6½d.[52]

Again, there are variations. On Friday 28 December 1212, the feast of Holy Innocents, the king went hunting for cranes, returning successful, with seven. He fed fifty paupers for each bird: 350 paupers at a rate of one penny each, totalling 29s 2d. Once more, this was a repeated offence: on 2 February 1213 (the feast of the Purification of the Virgin), John caught nine cranes whilst hunting with his gerfalcons. The penalty was not so severe. Provision was made for one hundred poor. The offence took place on a Wednesday, thus costing 13s 6½d.[53]

Such almsgiving was not solely linked to the king's sins of omission. Just as he supported religious houses established by members of his entourage, John also fed the poor on behalf of courtiers who joined him in breaking required fasts. Two of his closest lay associates in the government and administration of the kingdom, Geoffrey fitz Peter, the justiciar, and William Brewer, ate meat with John on Wednesday (8 April) after the Octave of Easter in 1209, at Laxton (Nottinghamshire). Eighty paupers were fed at a cost of 10s 5½d. Another, Richard Marsh, at

---

50 RM, pp. 238, 244. For other payments linked to failure to abstain on Wednesdays: RL, p. 110; RM, pp. 236, 264. On the significance of Wednesday: Cross and Livingstone, *Oxford Dictionary of the Christian Church*, p. 1724.
51 RL, p. 111; RM, pp. 235, 243, 248, 264. The Saturday feeding cost the standard 9s 4½d.
52 RL, p. 124; RM, pp. 246, 251.
53 RM, pp. 250, 253.

this stage one of the king's most senior Chancery clerks, broke his fast with John at some point soon after Easter in 1210.⁵⁴

Geoffrey (on four occasions), William (three times), and Thomas Basset (twice) proved repeat offenders. In addition, the poor were fed following single instances when Thomas de Samford, Henry fitz Count, and Hugh de Boves ate with the king when supposed to be fasting or abstaining. The number of pauper recipients varied. When Thomas Basset, a long-standing adviser of John, involved in his affairs from the early 1190s onwards, broke his fast with the king, twenty poor were fed on both occasions.⁵⁵ Thirty obtained food because Geoffrey fitz Peter consumed meat on the Wednesday after the octave of the feast of St Peter and St Paul (29 June) 1212. At other times, the rate was forty or fifty paupers per courtier. In October 1212, a hundred were fed for the household knight Thomas de Samford, whose duties at around this time included guardianship of Richard, second son of William Marshal.⁵⁶ Likewise in May 1213, when non-observance involved Henry fitz Count, a prominent courtier, and Hugh de Boves, the king's favoured mercenary captain.⁵⁷ There is no obvious pattern to the numbers involved, but apparently on certain occasions fast-breaking was more serious, so larger numbers of paupers received alms to counteract the sin committed. One pattern is, however, clear: all the courtiers concerned were close, often long-standing, counsellors or servants of John.⁵⁸

At times, it is difficult to be sure whether the king's charitable provision was for the poor or the organised religious. In March 1205, the Knights Hospitaller were given a gold crown from the royal regalia, 'for the sake of piety' (*pietatis intuitu*). Its value was to be used for the benefit of the poor overseas. A few months later, the barons of the Exchequer were instructed to recompense William de Cornhill for expenditure feeding three hundred 'brothers' at Farnham from Palm Sunday (3 April) until a month after the feast of St John the Baptist (24 June).⁵⁹

Meanwhile, John's almsgiving was not confined to those defined as 'the poor'. He made several payments to small religious communities, often nunneries, and to the solitary religious – hermits and anchorites. In 1212–13, regular gifts

---

⁵⁴ *RL*, pp. 110, 162. Part of the latter entry is missing, but falls immediately after payment for feeding one thousand paupers on Good Friday. It can be suggested that one hundred poor were fed when Richard ate with the king. As 9s 4½d was paid in recompense, the transgression probably took place on a Friday. Kellett suggests that Marsh was to provide the food, rather than that he had failed to fast: Kellett, 'King John', p. 82. However, comparison with similar entries in the rolls suggests this is unlikely. On Marsh: R. C. Stacey, 'Marsh, Richard (d. 1226)', *ODNB* (Oxford, 2004) [http://www.oxforddnb.com/view/article/18061, accessed 6 August 2013].

⁵⁵ On Basset: N. Vincent, 'Basset, Thomas (d. 1220)', *ODNB* (Oxford, 2004) [http://www.oxforddnb.com/view/article/47245, accessed 6 August 2013].

⁵⁶ Crouch, *William Marshal*, pp. 101–2 esp. n. 10, p. 118.

⁵⁷ On Henry: S. Lloyd, 'Henry fitz Count (b. in or before 1175, d. 1221)', *ODNB* (Oxford, 2004) [http://www.oxforddnb.com/view/article/47207, accessed 6 August 2013]. On John's need for mercenaries and the role of Hugh de Boves: Painter, *Reign*, pp. 264–8.

⁵⁸ For payments discussed in this paragraph: *RM*, pp. 236, 243, 244, 248, 264, 266.

⁵⁹ *RLP*, p. 51b; *RLC 1204–24*, p. 38a; Webster, 'Military Orders', p. 217.

Map 3 Nunneries in receipt of alms 1212–13

to nunneries are recorded, ranging from twenty shillings to five marks, paid to communities close to the areas through which the king passed. This included a cluster in northern England, in midlands counties, and occasional houses further south (see Map 3).[60] Historians have sometimes been sceptical of this. Painter only grudgingly acknowledges that we should probably discount 'the scandalous explanation ... that John's reputation suggests'.[61] There are surely more likely reasons: response to famine or to difficulties such houses faced in maintaining resources during the interdict. Some, such as Armathwaite and Hinchingbrooke, may have claimed royal associations. In the later Middle Ages, these houses asserted links to

[60] RM, pp. 233–5, 237, 240, 247, 249–52, 258; 'Itinerary'.
[61] Painter, *Reign*, pp. 152–3.

John's predecessors. Others, such as Moxby and Newcastle, had received grants or confirmations from John's forebears.[62]

Equally, this information is drawn from the infrequent records of the royal household. It could reflect a type of payment made regularly, but for which evidence only fleetingly survives. Some of these houses received royal grants at other times during the reign. Keldholme, Lambley, and Nun Cotham obtained confirmation charters in 1201.[63] Cook Hill was given money to purchase herrings.[64] Henwood received alms (along with Brewood and Farewell) in 1204 and confirmation of possession of a church in 1206.[65] Alms were paid to the nuns of Keldholme, Pinley, and Wroxall.[66] Broomhall was given a church in 1200, and pardoned dues from land in Windsor, in perpetuity, four years later.[67] Also in 1204, the leper nuns of St Mary de Pré received forest rights. They were taken into the king's protection in 1215.[68]

In terms of hermits and the solitary religious, John's support provides further evidence for Angevin respect for holy men, discussed by Karl Leyser in relation to St Hugh of Lincoln.[69] 'St' Robert of Knaresborough, 'the last of the notable hermits who flourished in post-Conquest England', provides a prime example. Robert established himself (initially without permission) in the forest of Knaresborough by the early thirteenth century. Here he attracted the attention, and ultimately the support, of the royal sheriff William de Stuteville (d. 1203), and of Brian de l'Isle, who had custody and then retained control of Knaresborough after Stuteville's death.[70] John visited the hermit in 1216. Sources for the saint's life present an instructional tale contrasting earthly and heavenly power. Robert is said first to have ignored the monarch, remaining at prayer. He then challenged him, if he really was king, to make an ear of corn. Whether or not this exchange occurred, John gave nearby woodland to Robert. It was later said that this was at the instigation of Brian de l'Isle.[71] The hermit died in 1218. Henry III transferred John's gift

---

[62] Thompson, *Women Religious*, pp. 10, 29, 45, 65-6, 164.

[63] *RC*, pp. 85a-86a, 87a-b.

[64] *PR 13 John*, p. 251; *PR 14 John*, p. 58

[65] *RL*, p. 84; *RC*, p. 164b.

[66] *RLC 1204-24*, pp. 125b-126a, 153b, 176a; *MR 1 John*, p. 7; *Cartae Antiquae Rolls 1-10*, p. 23 (no. 43); *PR 6 John*, pp. 192, 209.

[67] *RC*, pp. 48b, 136a. See also above, Chapter 3.

[68] *RC*, p. 127a; *RLP*, p. 131a; Thompson, *Women Religious*, p. 40.

[69] Leyser, 'Angevin Kings'.

[70] B. Golding, 'The Hermit and the Hunter', *The Cloister and the World: Essays in Medieval History in Honour of Barbara Harvey*, ed. J. Blair and B. Golding (Oxford, 1996), pp. 95-117; B. Golding, 'Robert of Knaresborough (d. 1218?)', *ODNB* (Oxford, 2004) [http://www.oxforddnb.com/view/article/23733, accessed 26 July 2014]; T. Licence, *Hermits and Recluses in English Society, 950-1200* (Oxford, 2011), pp. 94, 102-3; S. D. Church, 'Lisle, Brian de (d. 1234)', *ODNB* (Oxford, 2004, online edn 2007) [http://www.oxforddnb.com/view/article/47250, accessed 26 July 2014].

[71] *The Metrical Life of St Robert of Knaresborough, Together with the other Middle English Pieces in British Museum Ms. Egerton 3143*, ed. J. Bazire, Early English Text Society Original Series, 228 (London, 1953), pp. 64-6 (lines 735-806), Appendix A, pp. 124-5, Appendix B, pp.

to the hermit's companion and successor, Ivo, in 1227. The honour of Knaresborough passed to Richard, earl of Cornwall, in 1235, and the late king's younger son supported the Trinitarian community that inherited Robert's legacy and lands.[72] An enduring popular cult developed, with prose and verse lives penned between the thirteenth and fifteenth centuries.[73]

Other hermits received royal largesse. Some, such as the hermits of Clipstone and St Werburg, celebrated services for the wellbeing of the king and for the souls of his ancestors.[74] Elsewhere, in 1213, 'a certain monk who lives in a certain cell next to Tickhill' was paid half a mark, and 'two monks living at the hermitage of Tickhill' were given one mark.[75] William, hermit of Finmere, obtained one penny a day in exchange for land next to the king's house at Finmere (Oxfordshire). Perhaps the chapel here was referred to in 1216, when Brother William the monk was presented to the living. John ordered that provision was to be made for the decrepit hermit dwelling there, so long as he lived.[76] Evidence from the early years of Henry III's reign indicates the difficulties of making alms payments during the crises of the final phase of his father's reign. For example, in 1217, it was ordered that a hermit named Benedict should receive the forty shillings annually granted him by John, with arrears covering the previous three years.[77]

However, the solitary religious did not always win royal support. The self-styled 'prophet' Peter of Wakefield came to a grisly end after forecasting the king's demise during the interdict.[78] Meanwhile, Ann K. Warren argues that John was reluctant to support anchorites, granting their revenues to other recipients when they died. Thus, he reduced support for anchorites within the honour of Gloucester before he became king, although thereafter revenues were conferred on a hermit named Godwin.[79] Similarly, in Herefordshire, the deaths of anchorites at Newnham and St Audoenus (Ouen) saw their allowance conferred on others, albeit that money given to Richard, anchorite of St Sepulchre, was conferred on another, Margaret, following his death.[80] John also endowed a cell after the interdict. Eve of Preshute

---

139-40; *Chronicon de Lanercost. MCCI-MCCCXLVI. E codice Cottoniano nunc primum typis mandatum*, ed. J. Stevenson, Bannatyne Club, 65, and Maitland Club, 46 (Edinburgh, 1839), pp. 26-7; *RLC 1204-24*, p. 249a; Church, *Household Knights*, p. 141; A. K. Warren, *Anchorites and their Patrons in Medieval England* (Berkeley and Los Angeles, CA, and London, 1985), pp. 152-3; Golding, 'Hermit', pp. 100-1 and n. 26, suggesting that John's grant may have been a confirmation of a gift of one of Robert's early followers.

[72] *CChR 1226-1257*, p. 66; *CChR 1257-1300*, pp. 240-1; Golding, 'Hermit', pp. 107-8.
[73] Golding, 'Hermit', pp. 97-8; Licence, *Hermits*, pp. 193-5.
[74] See above, Chapter 1.
[75] *RM*, pp. 240, 255.
[76] *RLC 1204-24*, pp. 155a, 179b, 258b.
[77] *RLC 1204-24*, p. 344a.
[78] See below, Chapter 7.
[79] Warren, *Anchorites*, pp. 151, 153. For an anchorite whose payments ceased in the second regnal year: *PR 1 John*, p. 36; *PR 2 John*, p. 128. For Godwin: *PR 1 John*, p. 36; *PR 2 John*, p. 128; *PR 3 John*, p. 55; *PR 4 John*, p. 280; *PR 5 John*, p. 41; *PR 6 John*, p. 230.
[80] Warren, *Anchorites*, p. 154. For payments to the anchorites of Newnham and St Audoenus, and to Richard: *PR 1 John*, p. 215; *PR 2 John*, p. 240; *PR 3 John*, p. 265; *PR 4 John*, p. 273;

(Wiltshire) took the sum of a penny per day previously allocated to a recluse at Marlborough.[81]

Without apparently making gifts himself, John regularly issued letters of protection for religious institutions – usually hospitals – whose representatives sought to travel the country preaching and raising alms. In 1207, such protection was granted to the leper hospital of St Leonard at Bedford, to apply wherever their messengers went in England preaching in aid of the sick of that house.[82] Equally, the king might stipulate that a hospital should not be impeded from receiving alms, as he did for the lepers of St Leonard, Northampton, and their messengers, whilst he was in the town in 1215. This renewed a right first conferred by Henry II, whilst tradition ascribed the foundation to William the Conqueror.[83] The deteriorating political situation suggests why the community sought such renewal. In January 1215, it was agreed that on 26 April (the Sunday after Easter), at Northampton, John would respond to the barons demanding reform of the realm. In the event he did not. Civil war was imminent. This was a region where much of the 'action' seemed set to take place.[84]

On other occasions, the king's protection stipulated that those to whom the letters were presented should give generously. In March 1209, he ordered that brothers of the leper house of Dunstable were to be well received 'for the sake of God and of us' (*intuitu Dei et nostri*) and goods bestowed upon them.[85] In the cases of the hospitals of St Mary in Sassia at Rome, and St Anthony, in the province of Vienne, these instructions related to continental houses which had sent representatives to England to seek charitable gifts. The house in Rome was founded by Pope Innocent III. It was given the church of Writtle (Essex) by John in 1204, along with annual revenues of one hundred marks until the church fell vacant. The king's protection in 1213 was issued as negotiations to resolve the interdict moved towards their conclusion. The hospital regarded itself as holding a reciprocal obligation, according John a place in its necrology. His successors renewed the protection for the order of St Anthony, whilst Henry III promised the order a church for his father and mother's souls.[86]

The evidence for John's charity also reveals glimpses of the infrastructure that

---

PR 5 John, p. 55. For Margaret: PR 5 John, p. 55; PR 6 John, p. 16; PR 7 John, p. 271; PR 8 John, p. 65; PR 9 John, p. 157; PR 10 John, p. 190; PR 11 John, p. 60; PR 12 John, p. 145; PR 13 John, p. 232; PR 14 John, p. 158.

[81] RLP, p. 152a; MR 10 John, p. 139; Warren, *Anchorites*, p. 155.

[82] RLP, pp. 71b, 131b–132a. This is apparently the first known record of the house, possibly founded by the Basset family: H. A. Doubleday (ed.), VCH Bedford, vol. I (London, 1904), p. 398.

[83] RLP, p. 129a; Knowles and Hadcock, p. 380; Serjeantson and Atkins, VCH Northampton, vol. II, pp. 159–60.

[84] Holt, *Magna Carta*, p. 232; C. R. Cheney, 'The Eve of Magna Carta', *Bulletin of the John Rylands Library*, 38 (1955–56), 311–41 (esp. pp. 312–24).

[85] RLP, p. 90a.

[86] RC, p. 123a; RLP, pp. 106a, 108a; Cheney, *Innocent*, p. 237; R. Graham, 'The Order of St Antoine de Viennois and its English Commandery, St Anthony's, Threadneedle Street', *Archaeological Journal*, 84 (1927), 341–406 (pp. 349–50).

underpinned it. Royal benefaction, especially almsgiving, must have required officials charged with ensuring that grants reached intended recipients. Some of this must have fallen to the king's servants in the localities, as the itinerant court moved on its way. Equally, John's household is likely to have initiated distribution of his largesse. A number of men served as royal almoner during John's reign, revealing how his charity was not based on *ad hoc* response to the needs of moment, but was underpinned by a clear structure and process. Religious expression was recognised as a regular aspect of royal business.

An itinerant king needed an almoner to respond to the demands of the poor and needy encountered on the road. The earliest evidence for such an official comes from Henry I's reign, when Brother William the almoner fulfilled the role.[87] The charitable duties of the position were stipulated by John's father, in 1177, when he appointed a Templar brother named Roger. Henry II ordered him to hear those cries of the poor which could not be heard in the royal presence, and to deal with them benevolently and effectively. The almoner was to receive the full tenth of food and drink from the king's household to aid his work.[88] Yet this official could hold a range of roles in royal service. Thus, Roger is thought to have served on a diplomatic embassy to the French court in 1187. Likewise Thomas Brown, regularly described as royal almoner between 1164 and 1175, was also an Exchequer official closely trusted by Henry II.[89]

Aspects of the role must have remained constant. Malcolm Vale notes how elite members of late thirteenth- and fourteenth-century royal courts 'were especially exposed to the solicitations of paupers, hermits, anchorites, mendicants, widows, orphans, and other indigent people as they travelled'.[90] This is just as likely to have been the case in John's reign. The records provide a sense that the royal almonry was in operation, but precise details of provision and the reasons for it remain elusive. In February 1206, an unnamed official referred to as almoner was paid six marks for alms to cover days when the king was '*ad alienum custum*'.[91] Quite how this phrase translates is uncertain. Tentatively, 'on other business' might be suggested. It is equally unclear what this might have been.

However, we can identify some officials involved. Brother Thomas the almoner served in various capacities, including receipt of payments to cover royal alms, in 1209, 1210, 1212, and 1213.[92] He fulfilled this role whilst John was in Ireland

---

[87] *Regesta Regum Anglo-Normannorum 1066–1154. Vol. II. Regesta Henrici Primi 1100–1135*, ed. C. Johnson and H. A. Cronne (Oxford, 1956), p. 31 (no. 643); Dixon-Smith, 'Feeding the Poor', p. 31.

[88] *Gesta Regis Henrici Secundi*, vol. I, p. 169; Young, 'King John', p. 266.

[89] Dixon-Smith, 'Feeding the Poor', pp. 31–3; D. J. A. Matthew, 'Brown, Thomas (d. 1180)', *ODNB* (Oxford, 2004) [http://www.oxforddnb.com/view/article/27202, accessed 7 August 2013].

[90] M. Vale, *The Princely Court: Medieval Courts and Culture in North-West Europe 1270–1380* (Oxford, 2001), p. 237.

[91] 'Rotulus de Praestito', p. 275.

[92] *RL*, pp. 117, 122, 234, 242, 245; *RM*, pp. 235, 236, 240, 242, 247, 251; *PR 17 John*, p. 88; Young, 'King John', p. 266; L. E. Tanner, 'Lord High Almoners and Sub-Almoners, 1100–1957', *Journal of the British Archaeological Association*, 20-1 (1957–58), 72–83 (p. 74).

during the summer of 1210 and on important religious occasions, notably Good Friday (1 April) 1211. He seems to have been in charge of a group of men in dispensing the king's alms. In 1213 he was paid five marks for buying robes for 'his' twelve men.[93] In 1212 and 1213, Brother William the almoner is also recorded, perhaps the same man acting as a royal envoy, but described as 'of the almonry' in 1216, a description which furthers the possibility of several men acting in this role.[94]

The religious order to which Thomas and William belonged is never stated, although royal almoners in this period were often members of the Templar order.[95] In 1205, a royal letter noted that the king had received a gold crown and ornate items of clothing from Brother Alan [Martel], Preceptor of the New Temple in London, and Brother Roger the almoner, presumably a Templar from this community.[96] He was presumably the namesake, not the same man, as the official who served Henry II. In John's final years, Brother Roger the Templar is regularly referred to as royal almoner. He was active in a number of ways. Strikingly, few of these relate to almsgiving. He is recorded as an envoy and messenger, as receiving or paying out money, in numerous letters relating to preparation and movements of boats, and in orders to acquire and distribute food, wine, and goods.[97] However, he was involved in feeding the poor in 1212, when John atoned for having eaten twice on the feast of the Apostles Peter and Paul.[98]

Templars did not act alone in distribution of royal charity. Richard I appointed the Cistercian abbot of Le Pin, near Poitiers, as his almoner.[99] The white monks fulfilled a similar role for John. Abbot Henry of Bindon and Abbot John of Forde were both prominent. Neither is specifically referred to as royal almoner, but both were involved in the king's almsgiving. On Palm Sunday 1207, John of Forde received orders for robes to be made for thirty paupers and instructions to take thirty robes and pairs of shoes from Marlborough to London, where presumably they were to be handed out.[100] Henry of Bindon was given monies for the poor following several of John's failures to fast in 1209 and was paid to provide for

[93] RL, pp. 196, 227, 244; RM, p. 262.
[94] RM, pp. 244, 254; RLP, p. 179a.
[95] Dixon-Smith, 'Feeding the Poor', pp. 31-3; H. Nicholson, 'The Military Orders and the Kings of England in the Twelfth and Thirteenth Centuries', *From Clermont to Jerusalem: The Crusades and Crusader Societies 1095-1500*, ed. A. V. Murray (Turnhout, 1998), pp. 203-18 (pp. 205-6). Dixon-Smith argues that this was the case until 1255 in England, and until 1285 or 1286 in France.
[96] RLP, pp. 54b-55a; Bent, 'Early History of the English Chapel Royal', vol. II, p. 209. Roger is not specifically referred to as the king's almoner in this letter. On Alan Martel: Webster, 'Military Orders', pp. 211, 213-16.
[97] RLC 1204-24, pp. 197a, 214b, 218a, 227a-234b, 236b-243b, 244a, 253a, 255b, 266b, 267b; RLP, pp. 159a, 190b; Nicholson, 'Military Orders', pp. 211-12.
[98] RM, p. 234. It is assumed that 'Brother R' refers to Roger. See also: Johnstone, 'Poor-Relief', p. 153.
[99] Coggeshall, p. 98.
[100] RLC 1204-24, pp. 81b, 82a.

paupers on Maundy Thursday 1210. Later that year, he was provided with one hundred shillings for alms on Christmas Day.[101]

As in the case of Abbot Hugh of Beaulieu, association with the king brought with it the expectation of serving as his envoy. Henry of Bindon represented King John in Rome in 1209 and 1210.[102] Yet the two abbots were also rewarded. John's relations with both may have begun before he became king. He gave Bindon Abbey a mill in this period and confirmed grants of the founder Roger of Newburgh and his wife Matilda. He also gave land to Forde.[103] After John inherited the throne, Bindon was given a mill outside Dorchester, part of a house in London, and building materials for the abbey's roof. The king made the latter grant whilst at Bindon in 1213.[104] Forde Abbey received confirmation of donors' grants in 1204, and sixty cows and ten bulls a year later. John also ordered that the community should not be distrained relating to a precious Cistercian commodity, sheep.[105] Both houses benefited from royal gifts of wine.[106]

The overall impression is that the royal almonry was staffed by multiple officials – 'there were certainly two and even three almoners at the same time'. Historians have classified these as almoners and sub-almoners.[107] In the case of the Cistercian abbots and Templars, their primary role probably lay outside court. In some instances payments may have been made to individuals in the service of men who surrounded the king, such as Simon of Tallington, who received John's payments for the poor after the king caught cranes on the feast of Holy Innocents in 1212. Simon was a clerk of Richard Marsh, serving him from his career as chancery clerk through to his elevation to the bishopric of Durham.[108]

For men such as Brother Thomas and Brother William the role of almoner did not extend far beyond the job description: a distributor of alms. For others, the role was one part of duties carried out either within or outside court on behalf of the king. It was likely to have been advantageous, during John's near ceaseless itineration, to have a range of alms officials available. Some could be sent ahead, and some left behind, to arrange or carry out the king's giving to the poor. John's

---

[101] *RL*, pp. 110, 115, 161, 235, 236; *PR 13 John*, p. 38.

[102] Cheney, *Innocent*, pp. 36, 323.

[103] *Cartae Antiquae Rolls 1–10*, p. 68 (no. 125); *Cartae Antiquae Rolls 11–20*, pp. 117–18 (no. 498); *Mortain*. John perhaps encountered both men at Bindon. John of Forde was Abbot of Bindon prior to 1191. Henry of Bindon appears to have succeeded him: Knowles, Brooke, and London, *Heads*, p. 127.

[104] *RL*, p. 102; *RC*, p. 135b; *RLC 1204–24*, pp. 88b, 148a, 150a. Revenues from the mill were credited to Bindon from 6 John onwards: *PR 6 John*, p. 176; *PR 7 John*, p. 133; *PR 8 John*, p. 125; *PR 9 John*, p. 54; *PR 10 John*, p. 103; *PR 11 John*, p. 96; *PR 12 John*, p. 68; *PR 13 John*, p. 221; *PR 14 John*, p. 113; *PR 16 John*, p. 96; *PR 17 John*, p. 19.

[105] *Cartae Antiquae Rolls 1–10*, p. 120; *RLC 1204–24*, p. 25a; *RC*, p. 153a.

[106] *RLC 1204–24*, pp. 18a, 230a; *PR 6 John*, p. 176.

[107] Tanner, 'Lord High Almoners', p. 72.

[108] *RM*, p. 250; *RL*, pp. 233, 239. For Simon as witness to Marsh's charters as bishop: *EEA 25. Durham 1196–1237*, ed. M. G. Snape (Oxford, 2002), pp. 242–3 (no. 253), 246–9 (nos 260–1), 258–9 (no. 276), 261–2 (no. 279).

castellans, sheriffs, and bailiffs are also likely to have been involved, as occurred during the reigns of his predecessors and successors.

In addition, almonries were probably maintained at locations on the king's itinerary, from which his largesse could be dispensed. Dixon-Smith lists those maintained by Henry III which existed before he became king: Clarendon, Guildford, Havering, Kempton, Marlborough, Nottingham, Westminster, Winchester, Windsor, and Woodstock. Many of these were frequented by John. It seems reasonable to suppose that the almonries would have been used during his visits.[109]

The king's orders leave much unsaid about the logistics of feeding the poor, much as for Henry III's reign.[110] We do not know how officials carried out their task. How did they identify and assemble eligible paupers? Lanfranc's *Constitutions* suggested that the monastic almoner seek out the poor.[111] Was this a requirement for the royal almoner or did poor people flock to the king's court when he passed through a region? Certainly the royal entourage made a significant impact on areas through which it travelled, due to its size and resultant requirements.[112] Although we do not know whether paupers waited outside royal residences when the king arrived, or by the time he left, hoping for scraps from the rich man's table, leading abbots found this to be the case at monastic gatehouses. William of Trumpington, abbot of St Albans (1214–35), could rely on finding the poor at the monastery entrance on returning from a journey.[113] Royal courtiers may have been designated to oversee the feeding of the poor. Under Henry III, on Christmas Day and the feast of Holy Innocents in 1239, orders were issued for the poor to be fed at Windsor 'by the view of Hugh Giffard'. Even here, it is impossible to know how Hugh oversaw operations. In an example from 1245, Henry acknowledged that 'it may not be possible to find so many poor at once'. They were therefore to feed paupers in turns over several days, until the specified number (ten thousand) had been reached.[114]

Instructions of this sort do not survive for John's reign. Although he fed smaller numbers of poor than his son, no firm conclusions can be reached as to how they were found. Nonetheless, further aspects of his giving can be examined, such as what was provided when the poor were fed: bread, fish or meat, and ale.[115]

---

[109] Dixon-Smith, 'Feeding the Poor', pp. 31–41; 'Itinerary'; J. E. Kanter, 'Peripatetic and Sedentary Kingship: The Itineraries of the Thirteenth-Century English Kings' (unpublished PhD thesis, King's College London, 2010), pp. 125–6.

[110] Dixon-Smith, 'Feeding the Poor', p. 165.

[111] *Monastic Constitutions of Lanfranc*, pp. 132–3. See also Dixon-Smith, 'Feeding the Poor', pp. 166–70; B. Harvey, *Living and Dying in England 1100–1540: The Monastic Experience* (Oxford, 1993), pp. 16–23.

[112] S. D. Church, 'Some Aspects of the Royal Itinerary in the Twelfth Century', *TCE* 11, ed. B. Weiler, J. Burton, P. Schofield, and K. Stöber (Woodbridge, 2007), pp. 31–45.

[113] *Gesta Abbatum*, vol. I, p. 303; Harvey, *Living and Dying*, p. 17.

[114] *CLR 1226–1240*, p. 433; *CLR 1240–1245*, p. 324; Dixon-Smith, 'Feeding the Poor', pp. 153, 174–5. To reach the target in 1245, Dominicans, Franciscans, the sick in hospitals, and anchoresses, in and around London, were to be fed.

[115] For bread, fish, and ale: *RL*, p. 159; *RM*, pp. 237, 248, 251, 252, 254, 255, 262, 264,

How much was spent per person can sometimes be calculated, such as when one hundred poor were paid one hundred shillings for food.[116] Comparison with Henry III's reign can suggest how money grants were spent. Under John's son, provision for the poor usually amounted to a penny per person per day.[117] When Henry purchased bread for particular feast days (notably those of St Edward the Confessor), perhaps for distribution to the poor, he did so at a rate of four loaves to the penny.[118] Sources from John's reign provide less detail, but the sums of money and numbers of paupers are comparable. The figure of 9s 4½d for one hundred poor, John's most regular alms gift, can be expressed in pennies as 112½d. The first hundred pence would provide one penny per person. The remaining 12½d would purchase fifty loaves of bread, or half a loaf per person, if one penny would purchase four loaves. On a similar basis, payments of 13s 6½d for one hundred poor would provide 1½d per person, and fifty loaves. These figures are speculative. The money may have been spent in other ways. Nonetheless, there is a possible parallel with the organisation of royal giving during the reign of John's son. It also bears comparison with the 1½d per pauper consistently allocated by Edward I's household in the late thirteenth and early fourteenth centuries.[119]

Overall, King John's charity and almsgiving suggest a concern to accumulate 'good works' to stand in his favour at the Last Judgement. He seems to have hoped to counterbalance his frequent failure to fast when required and his inability to resist the temptation to hunt on major feast days. Thus, his almsgiving corresponds to the contemporary notion that, just as water extinguishes fire, so almsgiving counteracted sin, 'the most common proverb on the efficacy of almsgiving' for which 'occurrences range from Aelfric to late medieval writers'.[120] If the proverb was commonplace, this implies that the king's attitude was not unusual.

Deeper motivation is ultimately impossible to determine. In the absence of hard evidence we cannot be sure whether John believed that Christ was present in the poor. Nor can we be sure whether he felt that the act of giving was sufficient, or if he expected a return. His establishment of masses and payments for chaplains to perform them, his patronage of the saints, and his foundation and benefaction of religious houses all suggest a perception of the importance of establishing a body of intercessory activity. In the monastic context, this created a reciprocal association between the king and those whose 'profession' was a life of poverty. Did he try to do something similar in making gifts to the destitute? Patterns of twelfth- and thirteenth-century thought at least suggest the possibility. Honorius Augustodunensis argued that when the poor received alms they could 'reciprocate by offering

---

266. For bread, meat, and ale: RM, pp. 235, 236, 238, 243, 246, 248, 251, 253, 264. One payment refers to provision of bread and ale: PR 14 John, p. 149.

[116] PR 6 John, p. 248.

[117] Dixon-Smith, 'Feeding the Poor', pp. 133, 175–7; Johnstone, 'Poor-Relief', pp. 155–6.

[118] CR 1247–1251, pp. 89–90; CR 1251–1253, HMSO (London, 1927), pp. 438, 504; CR 1254–1256, HMSO (London, 1951), pp. 150-1, 152, 226, 378; CR 1256–1259, HMSO (London, 1932), pp. 114-15, 153; CR 1259–1261, HMSO (London, 1934), pp. 40-1, 121-2.

[119] Prestwich, 'Piety of Edward I', p. 122.

[120] Rubin, Charity, p. 64 and n. 2.

prayer in return'.[121] Peter the Chanter stated that Count Theobald of Champagne justified his decision to give alms to the poor in person by arguing that this would '"excite among them greater devotion and gratitude so that they will pray for me more frequently and fervently"'.[122] Modern commentators view the obligations incurred by the recipients of charity in similar terms. Rubin writes of the poor as 'intercessors for the benefactor's soul'. Mollat notes that 'the position of the pauper was one of waiting for others to discharge their duty toward him; this gave him a claim upon others, in exchange for which he incurred the obligation to pray for their souls'.[123] It seems possible that King John thought in these terms. In the absence of documents stating that he expected prayers in return for his gifts, it cannot be proven.

Whether or not there was a conscious underlying theory, John's charitable giving is significant. This was an important element of royal religious practice prior to the similar, though more substantial, largesse of Henry III. The sheer scale of Henry III's almsgiving should surely be viewed as exceptional. That said, John did occasionally feed large numbers of poor at a single sitting. In November 1212, one thousand paupers were provided with bread, meat, and ale.[124] This is some way short of the 102,000 fed by Henry III in 1242, but, nevertheless, father and son appear to have shared the belief that such almsgiving was an important part of royal religious activity. John provided for large numbers of paupers on a regular basis, even at the height of the interdict. It seems reasonable to conclude that he conformed to contemporary expectations of a king: the concept that charity, perhaps conceived as a work of mercy, was necessary to salvation; and that it was the duty of the rich man – and of the king as the wealthiest of the wealthy – to provide for the poor.

---

[121] Rubin, *Charity*, p. 83.
[122] Baldwin, *Masters*, vol. I, pp. 255–6.
[123] Rubin, *Charity*, p. 10; Mollat, *The Poor*, p. 107.
[124] *RM*, p. 248.

6

Religion, Politics, and Reputation
The Interdict and King John's Excommunication

Despite his attendance at and provision for masses, his veneration of the saints, his religious foundations, provision for prayers for his wellbeing and for the souls of his relatives, and his almsgiving, King John is primarily remembered as a king who lacked respect for religion and the church. That this is the case is largely due to the long-running dispute over who would succeed Hubert Walter as archbishop of Canterbury. As with Richard I's dealings with the Church, 'religious motives had no place' in John's attitude to the dispute. He was concerned to protect what he perceived to be his rights. Nonetheless, 'whilst it would be rash to accuse these kings of atheism or of denying the tenets of the Catholic faith', John's 'treatment of the English clergy and his reaction to the pope explain how his reputation in medieval historiography was formed'.[1]

Archbishop Hubert Walter died in July 1205, depriving John of a lynch-pin of government and a principal religious advisor. The king reacted quickly, making 'all speed to Canterbury', where he adopted a conciliatory attitude. He 'made arrangements concerning the archbishop's affairs in fatherly fashion', and 'said with sufficient kindness many things with the monks concerning the putting in place of another pastor'. The community had 'no small hope' that Hubert's successor would be one of their own.[2]

If the Canterbury monks thought they would be allowed to choose a new archbishop, this quickly became the subject of contention. In July 1205, the election was postponed whilst the cathedral monks and the suffragan bishops of the archiepiscopal province of Canterbury appealed to Pope Innocent III to determine who had the right to elect Hubert's successor.[3] The monks argued that this was their exclusive right. The bishops claimed precedent for their involvement. They had played a part in the elections of 1191 and 1193. John should have been aware of this. In 1191, he had acted alongside Walter of Coutances, archbishop of Rouen, in communicating King Richard's wishes to the assembled company.[4] In 1205, he may have used the postponement to seek a papal guarantee that, when royal

---

1   Cheney, *Innocent*, pp. 14–15.
2   Coggeshall, pp. 159–61; *GR*, p. 98; Webster, 'Crown, Cathedral and Conflict', pp. 211–12. On the course of the Canterbury election: M. D. Knowles, 'The Canterbury Election of 1205-6', *EHR*, 53 (1938), 211–20.
3   *EEA* 26, pp. 88–9 (no. 91). See also *RLP*, p. 56b.
4   *EEA* 26, pp. 13–14 (nos 11A–12); Turner and Heiser, *Reign of Richard Lionheart*, pp.

licence to elect was granted, the chosen candidate would receive Pope Innocent's approval.[5]

The Canterbury monks appear to have been petrified of being encumbered with an archbishop who would revive the efforts of Archbishops Baldwin and Hubert to establish a collegiate church at Hackington or Lambeth. They feared that this would lead to the transfer of the archiepiscopal seat and all its accompanying rights. Worse still, in the period before the 1220 translation of St Thomas' bones to their new shrine, the monks feared the loss of their most prized (and lucrative) relics.[6] Therefore, before dispatching their delegation to Rome, the monks conducted a secret election, choosing Reginald, their sub-prior. He swore only to reveal his election if it appeared that the monks' claims were about to be thwarted, but upon arrival at the papal curia he promptly requested consecration. When the bishops' proctor protested, Innocent III delayed his confirmation.

Meanwhile, John returned to Canterbury in December 1205. The monks denied holding a secret election. They then elected the king's preferred candidate, John de Gray, bishop of Norwich. Innocent III later cleared John of intimidating the electors, but there can be little doubt that the monks followed the king's instructions.[7] Gray had effectively acted as John's 'chancellor' before he became king. At Norwich, he had proved an efficient administrator, had resolved a long-running dispute between bishop and cathedral chapter, and had been employed on papal business by Pope Innocent.[8] John probably saw him as an effective choice as Archbishop Hubert's successor. The bishops were urged to voice support by adding their seals to a letter to Rome on behalf of the archbishop-elect.[9]

Gray's arrival in Rome prompted Innocent III to take matters into his own hands. He rejected the suffragan bishops' claim to a role in the election, quashed the two elections he had been asked to confirm, and summoned new electors from the ranks of the Canterbury monks. At the pope's prompting, these men elected the English cardinal, Stephen Langton, a notable master of the Paris schools as one

---

133-5; Z. N. Brooke, *The English Church and the Papacy from the Conquest to the Reign of John* (Cambridge, 1952), pp. 224-5.

[5] C. R. Cheney, 'A Neglected Record of the Canterbury Election of 1205-6', *Bulletin of the Institute of Historical Research*, 21 (1946-48), 233-8 (p. 233).

[6] J. Sayers, 'Peter's Throne and Augustine's Chair: Rome and Canterbury from Baldwin (1184-90) to Robert Winchelsey (1297-1313)', *JEH*, 51 (2000), 249-66 (pp. 254-7, 259-61). On the aborted foundation at Hackington or Lambeth: Cheney, *Innocent*, pp. 208-20; M.-P. Gelin, 'Gervase of Canterbury, Christ Church and the Archbishops', *JEH*, 60 (2009), 449-63; S. Sweetinburgh, 'Caught in the Cross-Fire: Patronage and Institutional Politics in Late Twelfth-Century Canterbury', *Cathedrals, Communities and Conflict in the Anglo-Norman World*, ed. P. Dalton, C. Insley and L. J. Wilkinson (Woodbridge, 2011), pp. 187-202. For aspects of the dispute after John's reign: C. R. Cheney, 'Magna carta beati Thome: Another Canterbury Forgery', *Medieval Texts and Studies*, C. R. Cheney (Oxford, 1973), pp. 78-110.

[7] Cheney, 'Neglected Record', p. 234 n. 1.

[8] R. M. Haines, 'Gray, John de (d. 1214)', *ODNB* (Oxford, 2004) [http://www.oxforddnb.com/view/article/11541, accessed 19 August 2013]; Vincent, 'Jean', p. 58; Harper-Bill, 'John and the Church of Rome', p. 294; Cheney, *Innocent*, pp. 29-30.

[9] *EEA* 26, p. 89 (no. 93); *RLP*, p. 57a; Cheney, *Innocent*, pp. 148-9.

of the leading theologians of the era.[10] King John objected. He refused to accept Langton's appointment or to admit him to England. He allegedly threatened to hang Stephen should he travel to Canterbury to assume office.[11] In 1207, the king expelled the monks of Canterbury Cathedral, numbered by the Winchester annalist at sixty-four individuals. They were driven into exile overseas, first at St Omer, at the Abbey of St Bertin, before most of the community were sent to other religious houses in France and Flanders. The exiles were followed in 1208 by those blind or incapacitated monks who had previously been exempted.[12] Meanwhile, the pope conferred the pallium upon his choice.[13]

Innocent III then threatened, and imposed, sentences of interdict on England (1208-14) and excommunication of the king (1209-13). The interdict came into force on Monday 24 March 1208. Its meaning was summarised by the chronicler Gervase of Canterbury: 'nowhere on Easter Sunday or Good Friday were divine services celebrated, but a silence, unheard of by the laity, was imposed on all, both clerics and monks'. Meanwhile, the dead could only be buried 'in unseemly and unholy places'. The Durham chronicler Geoffrey of Coldingham also bemoaned the silence that fell upon the church and the denuding of the altars which accompanied the cessation of services. Similar observations were made by the Cistercian Matthew of Rievaulx.[14] In other words, services were suspended, in particular the sacraments, with the exception of baptism of the new-born, hearing the confession of the dying and, from 1212, allowing those at death's door to receive final communion (although administering the consecrated oil of extreme unction remained forbidden). Burial with religious ceremony, in consecrated ground, was not permitted. Yet there was considerable uncertainty about the precise terms of the sanction. Innocent III issued a number of letters clarifying those to whom the sentence applied. There are likely to have been local variations. The silence that fell within churches may have been counterbalanced by elements of religion practised outside: preaching, its accompanying prayers and bible readings. Observance of feasts and fasts was encouraged. Penitents may have made confession outside church and (although forbidden) *panis benedictus*, bread set aside for the mass but not consecrated, appears to have been distributed in churchyards on Sundays. Pilgrimage was encouraged, along with almsgiving and payment of sums

---

[10] C. Holdsworth, 'Langton, Stephen (c. 1150-1228)', ODNB (Oxford, 2004) [http://www.oxforddnb.com/view/article/16044, accessed 19 August 2013]; N. Vincent, 'Stephen Langton, Archbishop of Canterbury', *Étienne Langton, Prédicateur, Bibliste, Théologien*, ed. L.-J. Bataillon, N. Bériou, G. Dahan and R. Quinto (Turnhout, 2010), pp. 51-123.

[11] *Annales de Burton*, pp. 209-11.

[12] GR, pp. 100-1; *Annales Monasterii de Wintonia (A.D. 519-1277)*, ed. H. R. Luard, *Annales Monastici*, RS 36, 5 vols (London, 1864-69), vol. II, p. 80; Stanley, p. 509; *Annales S. Edmundi*, p. 145; RLP, p. 74a; N. Vincent, 'Master Simon Langton, King John and the Court of France', unpublished.

[13] Sayers, 'Peter's Throne', p. 252.

[14] GR, p. 101; *Liber Gaufridi Sacristae de Coldingham de statu Ecclesiae Dunhelmensis*, ed. J. Raine, *Historiae Dunelmensis Scriptores Tres, Gaufridus de Coldingham, Robertus de Graystanes, et Willielmus de Chambre*, Surtees Society, 9 (London, 1839), p. 25; Clarke, p. 134.

due to the church.[15] The uncertainty was in all likelihood due to the fact that, in imposing an interdict, the papacy did not anticipate it would be long-lasting. John was expected to realise his error. The faithful were supposed to persuade him to do so and make terms. Beyond the claims of the *Deeds of Pope Innocent*, there is little sense that this was the case.[16]

Excommunication was pronounced on John in November 1209.[17] Here, the individual sinner was targeted: to be excluded completely from the church, and indeed from Christian society. To a certain extent, however, interpreters of canon law recognised some rights to the excommunicate person, for instance their right to interact with family and servants and to draw up contracts. However, for kings, not only were their souls in peril, but their earthly authority too. It was no longer clear that subjects were obliged to obey. Innocent III stopped short of formally deposing John, although it is likely that he considered it. Certainly the threat existed.[18]

Given the hostility provoked by King John's actions, and his ultimate climb-down, it is easy to view the interdict from either the papal perspective or that of the Canterbury monks. John's approach, and justification for his actions, is sometimes lost, but is worth considering.[19] The Church argued that the royal will had no part to play in the electoral process.[20] This was the direct opposite to the traditional attitude of the Angevin kings. When Hubert Walter died in 1205, John did not apparently anticipate that the vacant archbishopric would cause him trouble. He had dealt with episcopal appointments before, visiting sees which fell vacant, or if he could not be present, ensuring that elections were overseen by his officials. In particular, he was quick to assert what he perceived to be his rights. In 1200, the canons of Lisieux were instructed that John expected his wishes to be respected, and that he saw it as his role to approve the election of a new bishop. Just as the chapter expected their rights to be respected, so too did he. The king appealed to the pope, and the community was apparently quick to comply. The archdeacon of Lisieux, Jordan du Hommet, was duly elected. In having his instructions enrolled

---

[15] Clarke, pp. 130-68; Cheney, 'Papal Interdict', pp. 297-300, 314-16; Cheney, 'Recent View', pp. 161-2.

[16] Clarke, p. 45; *The Deeds of Pope Innocent III, by an Anonymous Author*, trans. J. M. Powell (Washington DC, 2004), pp. 240-1.

[17] Warren, *John*, p. 169.

[18] Tanner and Watson, 'Least of the Laity', pp. 420-1; Cheney, *Innocent*, pp. 319-22; C. R. Cheney, 'The Alleged Deposition of King John', *Studies in Mediaeval History Presented to Frederick Maurice Powicke*, ed. R. W. Hunt, W. A. Pantin, and R. W. Southern (Oxford, 1948, reprinted 1969), pp. 100-16.

[19] For an exception: H. G. Richardson and G. O. Sayles, *The Governance of Mediaeval England from the Conquest to Magna Carta* (Edinburgh, 1963), pp. 337-63; critically discussed in Cheney, 'Recent View', pp. 159-68. See also: Webster, 'Crown, Cathedral and Conflict', pp. 212-16.

[20] J. Peltzer, *Canon Law, Careers and Conquest: Episcopal Elections in Normandy and Greater Anjou, c. 1140-c. 1230* (Cambridge, 2008), pp. 31-6, 81-2.

on the charter roll, John sought to establish written precedent for his claimed right to intervene.[21]

The king had a habit of getting his way in the early years of his reign. The royal choice William Tolomeus was elected at Avranches in 1198-1200 (in an election begun under Richard I, but not concluded due to dispute that prolonged it into John's). In 1201-02, John secured his preferred appointment, Vivian de l'Etang, at Coutances. In 1202 the royal candidate William de Beaumont was elected at Angers. Here, electoral dispute probably reflected the rival claims of John and Arthur of Brittany to rule Anjou. Meanwhile, with papal approval, the king conferred the bishopric of Carlisle on Bernard, want-away archbishop of Ragusa (Dubrovnik). Elsewhere, after two previous elections were quashed by the pope, Geoffrey of Henlaw, prior of Llanthony and Archbishop Hubert's physician, became bishop of St David's. His election, supervised by Geoffrey fitz Peter, the justiciar, occurred at the royal palace of Westminster.[22]

The contentious results of John's intervention can be seen particularly clearly at Sées in Normandy, between 1201 and 1203, where he faced his first major setback. Both the canons and the king were determined to secure their own man. John attempted to bully the community into submission, persuading one party amongst the divided chapter to elect Herbert, son of Ralph L'Abbé (one of the most senior officials at the Norman Exchequer). However, another group of canons, headed by the prior, sought to elect one of their own number, first Ralph de Merle (who died travelling to Rome to seek papal confirmation), then the archdeacon of Sées, Silvester. Innocent III confirmed the latter's election in June 1201. Much as later happened at Canterbury, John refused to back down. His position was based on what he believed were his rights and those of his lands. This was a 'well prepared attack', which 'indicates the availability of great expertise in canon law at the royal court', illustrative of the king's determination to protect what he saw as his right to involvement. This was very much his stance when it came to choosing Hubert Walter's successor at Canterbury. At Sées, however, Innocent III instructed Walter de Coutances, archbishop of Rouen, to impose an interdict on Normandy if John did not back down. This threat persuaded John to fall into line, although he was careful to claim that he did so only out of respect for the pope. Bishop Silvester was not apparently moved to a spirit of compromise, styling John as 'once king of England' as early as 1203.[23]

John was fighting against the tide. In Normandy, where he also reaped the whirlwind of his diminishing authority as duke, he increasingly found that 'cathedral chapters no longer considered him an authority on electoral matters'. The Sées election was a prelude of the larger crisis to come. The early years of the reign

---

21   Peltzer, *Canon Law*, pp. 113-14, 135, 148-9; Cheney, *Innocent*, pp. 126-7 and n. 18; *RC*, p. 99a.
22   Peltzer, *Canon Law*, pp. 148-9, 161-3, 203-8; Cheney, *Innocent*, pp. 74-5, 126, 135-40; Summerson, 'Bernard'.
23   Peltzer, *Canon Law*, pp. 124-32, 245 n. 34. See also D. Power, 'Angevin Normandy', *A Companion to the Anglo-Norman World*, ed. C. Harper-Bill and E. van Houts (Woodbridge, 2003), pp. 63-85 (pp. 78-9); Cheney, *Innocent*, pp. 127-8; *RL* p. 72; *RLP*, p. 16a-b.

were also marked by ongoing dispute over the election at Armagh in Ireland. In 1206, the king proved unable to prevent the chapter making their own choice of Eugenius as archbishop.[24]

The king's efforts to influence episcopal appointments prompted a strong response from Pope Innocent III in 1203, admonishing John for his behaviour in various elections since becoming king, notably at Lincoln, Sées, and Coutances.[25] However, in 1205, at the time of Hubert Walter's death, the choice of Peter des Roches for the see of Winchester must have been fresh in the minds of both the king and those at the papal curia. This election gave John cause to hope for success at Canterbury. The choice of his preferred candidate had been disputed, but Innocent III's judgement in favour of Peter expressed willingness to meet the king's desires, in so far as was proper. The caveat probably received scant attention at the royal court. John quite probably thought that his wishes regarding Canterbury would be respected.[26]

In taking a stand against the church over what he perceived as his rights, John was not unique amongst kings of England. The tenth-century Anglo-Saxon King Eadwig had driven Abbot (later Archbishop and Saint) Dunstan into exile in 956. Since the Norman Conquest, William Rufus and Henry I had been involved in long-running disputes with Archbishop Anselm of Canterbury. The latter was exiled from England twice, and Henry was on the verge of excommunication in 1105 because of his failure to restore archiepiscopal lands and revenues.[27] King Stephen had also fallen into dispute with Archbishop Theobald, whilst Henry II's dispute with Thomas Becket is too well known to need further discussion here.[28] All these disputes occurred between kings and recognised archbishops, whereas under John conflict centred on that official's right to hold his office. However, some of the sentiments expressed during the earlier stand-offs were echoed in John's reign. Henry I's observation 'What have I to do with the pope about things that are mine?' would not seem out of place if it had been made by his early thirteenth-century successor. More recently, Richard I had reacted in angry astonishment when the monks of Durham attempted an unauthorised election in 1195, writing that this was an offence to the royal majesty and that action should be taken to ensure that the rights and dignities enjoyed by his predecessors were not infringed in the future.[29]

---

[24] Peltzer, *Canon Law*, p. 168; Cheney, *Innocent*, pp. 153–4.

[25] *SLI*, pp. 48–53 (no. 17); Peltzer, *Canon Law*, p. 131; Cheney, *Innocent*, p. 128.

[26] Harper-Bill, 'John and the Church of Rome', p. 303; Cheney, *Innocent*, pp. 144–7; Vincent, *Peter des Roches*, pp. 47–55; Webster, 'Crown, Cathedral and Conflict', pp. 212–13.

[27] Weiler, 'Bishops and Kings', p. 121; S. N. Vaughn, *Archbishop Anselm of Canterbury 1093–1109: Bec Missionary, Canterbury Primate, Patriarch of Another World* (Farnham, 2012), pp. 73–152.

[28] King, *King Stephen*, pp. 244–50; J. Truax, *Archbishops Ralph d'Escures, William of Corbeil and Theobald of Bec: Heirs of Anselm and Ancestors of Becket* (Farnham, 2012), pp. 125–6; Duggan, *Thomas Becket*.

[29] Cheney, *Innocent*, pp. 13, 126–7; Vaughn, *Archbishop Anselm*, p. 140; *Radulfi de Diceto*, vol. II, pp. 128–9.

Nor was John unique amongst late twelfth- and early thirteenth-century European kings. William I of Scotland found himself in a similar situation in relation to the bishopric of St Andrews between 1178 and 1186, 'a fierce dispute which weakened his hold on the Scottish church not a whit'.[30] John's cousin and ally, the Emperor Otto IV, incurred an interdict after invading the papal state in 1211. Observers commented that this boosted the king of England's position, as he 'began less to abhor the sentence inflicted on him long since, because he had such and so great an ally'.[31] Other European kingdoms and their rulers experienced sentences of interdict or the threat of sanctions at around this time, including Armenia, Léon, Navarre, and Portugal. The population of Venice was excommunicated in 1202. Rulers reacted similarly to John in 1208: exiling those who had pronounced sentence and seizing their property, with similar treatment for men of religion who refused to perform the sacraments. Sometimes this worked. In Portugal, the sentence was apparently lifted after King Sancho I threatened to blind clergymen who refused to celebrate in front of their friends and families.[32]

Elsewhere, John's great rival, Philip II of France, also experienced an interdict in 1200, albeit one that lasted only eight months, due to his determination to secure an annulment of his marriage to Ingeborg of Denmark. Philip took severe action against bishops who obeyed the sentence, including his cousin Odo of Paris, expelling them from their sees and seizing their property. Lower clergymen and canons faced similar reprisals. In France, at least one bishop (of Auxerre) argued cannily that the sentence did not apply to his diocese, as the French king held no land there. The sentence had some impact on John's affairs. The marriage of the French king's son and heir, Louis, to the English king's niece, Blanche of Castile, agreed as part of the Treaty of Le Goulet (1200), took place in Normandy in order to get around the sentence that lay on the French kingdom. Although Philip argued that this interdict was invalid, having been proclaimed outside his kingdom, he quickly accepted that nothing would be gained from a protracted dispute, and that Pope Innocent III could be a valuable ally in European power politics. That said, Ingeborg was not reinstated as queen of France until 1213. Again, this may have suited Philip's diplomatic needs at the time.[33]

In terms of the interdict imposed on England in 1208, the narrative sources present a picture of widespread discontent. As Holt observes, most are the work

---

[30] A. A. M. Duncan, 'John King of England and the Kings of Scots', *King John: New Interpretations*, ed. S. D. Church (Woodbridge, 1999), pp. 248-71 (p. 248).

[31] Clarke, p. 118; Barnwell, p. 202: N. Fryde, 'King John and the Empire', *King John: New Interpretations*, ed. S. D. Church (Woodbridge, 1999), pp. 334-46. Otto also incurred sentence of deposition: Cheney, 'Alleged Deposition', p. 108.

[32] Clarke, pp. 20, 41, 81, 172, 174, 181-2; Cheney, *Innocent*, p. 303; Cheney, 'Alleged Deposition', p. 108; Tanner and Watson, 'Least of the Laity', p. 420.

[33] Peltzer, *Canon Law*, pp. 240-1, 255; Clarke, pp. 60, 84, 89, 91, 107, 117, 153, 179-80, 237, 239; Cheney, *Innocent*, p. 343; J. W. Baldwin, *The Government of Philip Augustus: Foundations of French Royal Power in the Middle Ages* (Berkeley and Los Angeles, CA, and Oxford, 1986), pp. 84-7, 178-9; J. Bradbury, *Philip Augustus: King of France 1180-1223* (Harlow, 1998), pp. 184-5; J. E. M. Benham, 'Philip Augustus and the Angevin Empire: The Scandinavian Connection', *Mediaeval Scandinavia*, 14 (2004), 37-50 (pp. 44-5, 49).

of monastic writers 'understandably prejudiced against the king because of his quarrel with Rome and consequent treatment of the monastic order'. Yet they should not be dismissed: 'contemporary condemnation is too varied and widely based ... nor can it be explained by pointing to the differences between medieval and modern standards of judgement'.[34] There were clear grounds for criticism. Interdict and personal excommunication were the severest sanctions the medieval church could impose. John had reacted with severity against those who attempted to observe them.

Nevertheless, it is important to examine John's reaction. On the one hand, he sought to build a united response to Pope Innocent III's intervention. As we have seen, the bishops were urged to write to the pope in support of John de Gray. In May 1206, royal letters urged bishops and abbots in the Canterbury province to increase their efforts. Their episcopal colleagues at London, Winchester, Rochester, Ely, and Bath had written to Innocent III, John noted, concerning his dignity and that of his realm. He urged the recipients to do the same. The king sent his own messengers to the pope to inform him about the rights John's ancestors had held in relation to Canterbury and other cathedral sees, as the letters of the bishops and other faithful men would bear witness.[35]

On the other hand, those who defied the king's authority could expect trouble. During the disputed Canterbury election and its aftermath, John carefully targeted those who went against him. The prior and monks of Canterbury Cathedral bore the brunt. The king clearly felt that they had deceived him. Sub-Prior Reginald was seen as 'odious to king and kingdom', a view apparently relayed to the pope. Indeed Innocent III complained about the Canterbury community's duplicity when he intervened in 1206.[36] The king's candidate had been elected in such a way as to cause the pope to step in to direct proceedings. Seen from the king's perspective, this deprived John of what he perceived as his right to involvement, creating a precedent, which he felt bound to resist.[37] It did not help that Langton had spent the bulk of his career in Paris, the capital of Capetian France. In this sense, it did not matter to John that the pope's choice was 'a venerable man and of good repute'. Stephen could be seen as too close to the king's principal enemy, Philip II.[38] Other aspects of his career history may not have helped. In the 1190s, perhaps earlier, he appears to have served as a canon of York. When Archbishop Geoffrey of York returned to England in 1200, Stephen was amongst the Parisian masters who accompanied him, perhaps on the orders of Pope Innocent III.[39]

---

[34] Holt, *King John*, pp. 16–17.
[35] *RLP*, pp. 64a–b, 65b; Cheney, *Innocent*, p. 151.
[36] *Liber Gaufridi Sacristae de Coldingham*, p. 24, *LPI*, p. 116 (no. 699); Cheney, 'Neglected Record', p. 234.
[37] J. Sayers, *Innocent III: Leader of Europe 1198–1216* (London and New York, 1994), p. 45; Webster, 'Crown, Cathedral and Conflict', p. 214.
[38] Holdsworth, 'Langton, Stephen'; Stanley, p. 509.
[39] *EEA* 27, pp. lii, lxiii, 62–3 (no. 55); Vincent, 'Master Simon Langton'; Holdsworth, 'Langton, Stephen'. Langton possibly appears as a charter witness in *EEA* 20. *York 1154–1181*, ed. M. Lovatt (Oxford, 2000), pp. 54–5 (no. 46), 138–40 (nos 125–6); *EEA* 27, pp. 97–100 (nos 93–4).

York's Angevin archbishop rarely saw eye-to-eye with the legitimate sons of King Henry II. Thus his advisers could easily have incurred John's suspicion.

Evidence from an earlier dispute, involving the monks of St Augustine's, Canterbury, and the parish church of Faversham, suggests that John felt well within his rights to expel clergy from churches.[40] In the case of the archiepiscopal election, the king's anger led him to believe that the Canterbury Cathedral monks had committed treason. Therefore, he drove them into exile and allowed ruthless exploitation of their lands and possessions. In 1208, the pope acknowledged, in letters to Stephen Langton, that John felt 'in many ways aggrieved'. During negotiations, the king had conceded that the monks could return, but had done so reluctantly, because 'he believes that they plotted treasonably against him'. An anonymous Canterbury chronicle, which cannot have been penned before 1213, noted that John held the Christ Church monks responsible for usurping his rights and disobeying his orders.[41] Meanwhile, the Canterbury monk Gervase observed that all those 'connected with the monks ... [were] a public enemy'.[42] Even Roger of Wendover noted how John accused the monks of treachery, outlining the successive stages of their 'iniquity', including the election of Langton, seen by the king as his 'public enemy'. For Wendover, John's orders for the expulsion of the Canterbury community were issued as if the monks 'were guilty of a crime against his injured majesty'. Thus, they were 'to depart immediately from the kingdom of England as traitors'.[43]

Other sources noted the king's show of force. He sent crossbowmen and mercenary troops to Canterbury, and 'directed terrible threats' against the community. The monks departed with 'weeping and lamentation ... into grievous and insupportable exile'. Wendover noted the violence of their expulsion, writing that John, 'in the fury of his anger and indignation', sent 'two most cruel and inhuman knights' to expel the community, 'or else to consign them to capital punishment'. These men, Fulk de Cantilupe and Reginald of Cornhill, Sheriff of Kent, arrived at the cathedral, and allegedly threatened to burn it down with the monks inside. Even so the brothers of Christ Church were not necessarily united in dutiful departure. Some 'deserted their brothers', who consequently saw them as outcasts: 'in the manner of Cain, wandering and fugitive they dwelt on the earth'.[44] We

---

[40] *Historiae Anglicanae Scriptores* X, ed. R. Twysden (London, 1652), col. 1852; *EEA 42. Ely 1198-1256*, ed. N. Karn (Oxford, 2013), pp. 35-6 (no. 38). See also: Cheney, *Hubert Walter*, pp. 85-7; Gransden, *History of the Abbey of Bury*, pp. 73-4; E. Fernie, 'The Litigation of an Exempt House, St Augustine's Canterbury, 1182-1237', *Bulletin of the John Rylands Library*, 39 (1957), 390-415 (pp. 397-406).

[41] *Deeds of Pope Innocent*, pp. 240-1; *Fragmentary Chronicle, with Appendix of Letters, Relating to the Events Connected with the Election of Archbishop Langton to the See of Canterbury*, ed. W. Stubbs, *The Historical Works of Gervase of Canterbury*, RS 73, 2 vols (London, 1879-80), vol. II, p. lxiii; Knowles, 'Canterbury Election', p. 212; Webster, 'Crown, Cathedral and Conflict', pp. 214-15.

[42] GR, p. 101.

[43] Wendover, vol. II, pp. 38-9; Webster, 'Crown, Cathedral and Conflict', pp. 217-18.

[44] Barnwell, p. 199; Wendover, vol. II, p. 39. Wendover names Fulk's associate as Henry of Cornhill (d. 1192/93), a mistake for his brother Reginald.

might question how far some exiles went. Gervase of Canterbury was presumably amongst those expelled. According to G. H. Martin, he died in around 1210, 'undoubtedly at Canterbury', aged over sixty.[45] If so, it seems that he had not joined his comrades overseas.

The extent to which John held the monks' behaviour against them is shown by his treatment of their estates whilst they were exiled. The king set out to make an example of those he perceived as his enemies. Substantial sums were consistently raised from the Canterbury lands and possessions. Assets, especially crops and animals, were systematically sold off. Woodland was treated as a source of income once other stocks had been auctioned.[46] However, a certain amount of contemporary opinion appears to have been on his side. Although the 'Barnwell' annalist described how 'God did not desert those who had hope in Him, rousing both lay and Church people' to support the monks, the same commentator observed that in the eyes of 'the mob', the exiles were viewed as outlaws.[47]

The king found no difficulty in finding people to enforce his orders. His knights 'were not slow to obey the commands of their lord'.[48] Auctions require buyers, and the king's agents apparently had little difficulty finding purchasers for the goods being sold. Archbishop Langton seemed aware that such action would be condoned. On the eve of the interdict, he dispatched letters urging resistance, if not directly against the king then against his policy. Accepting attacks on the church, joining in, or simply turning a blind eye, would be seen as participating in the king's sins. These letters were addressed to all the faithful in England. There is a sense that the archbishop felt that he was unlikely to be preaching to the converted. He reminded the community of knights that they had received their insignia from, and undertaken to protect, the church. John's household knights, as regular recipients of lands that came into the king's hand due to the interdict, were amongst those who apparently took little notice.[49]

If the king dissipated the possessions of those he had exiled, he also acted to ensure that religious services continued in Canterbury Cathedral. Replacement monks were brought in from nearby houses – St Augustine's Canterbury, Rochester, and Faversham – 'to perform the duties'. Monks from Dover Priory administered, and presumably also maintained, the shrine of St Thomas.[50] Again, there is no sense that these communities refused.

---

[45] Martin, 'Canterbury, Gervase of'.

[46] *Interdict Documents*, ed. P. M. Barnes and W. R. Powell, PRS, 72, ns 34 (London, 1960), pp. 37–85; PR 13 John, p. 244; PR 14 John, pp. 40–2; Waverley, p. 265; RLP, p. 75b; Cheney, 'Papal Interdict', pp. 301–6; Cheney, *Innocent*, pp. 146–8; Webster, 'Crown, Cathedral and Conflict', p. 216.

[47] Barnwell, pp. 199, 211. For an example of religious largesse to the community whilst in exile: *Norman Charters from English Sources*, pp. 239–40 (no. 112).

[48] Wendover, vol. II, p. 39.

[49] *Acta Stephani Langton Cantuariensis Archiepiscopi A.D. 1207–1228*, ed. K. Major, Canterbury and York Society, 50 (Oxford, 1950), pp. 2–7 (no. 2); Clarke, pp. 42, 170–1; Cheney, *Innocent*, p. 301; Vincent, 'Stephen Langton', pp. 69–70; Church, *Household Knights*, pp. 51–3.

[50] Wendover, vol. II, p. 39; *Annales S. Edmundi*, p. 145; Webster, 'Crown, Cathedral and Conflict', p. 218; Nilson, *Cathedral Shrines*, p. 148.

Similar targeting of those who defied John's authority is found in the wider seizure and retention of church holdings. This focused principally on those who chose exile, to obey pope rather than king. When the interdict was imposed, John singled out the relatives and possessions of its executors, emulating Henry II's response to Becket's flight from England in 1164.[51] This included attacks on property: 'the king ordered the houses of the bishops, the executors of the interdict, to be destroyed, their groves to be cut down and their livestock destroyed'.[52] This seemingly extended to other bishops who went into exile. In 1215, Hugh of Wells, bishop of Lincoln, received a wood in compensation for damage done to his park at Stow during the interdict.[53]

Beyond this, only those who refused to administer the sacraments were forced to leave. The king ordered that 'he who was unwilling to sing [perform religious services] should leave his land'. John presumably believed them guilty of something akin to dereliction of duty. Even here, royal orders directing expulsions do not survive, and the opportunity to make money from fines for restoration of seized property may have trumped concern to restore the sacraments.[54] However, the fate of the Canterbury monks may well have persuaded churchmen who remained loyal to the pope that there would be repercussions of opposing the king. The memory of Thomas Becket provided precedent for royal behaviour during protracted disputes with the church. Thus, the executors of the interdict probably chose to go overseas before being forced out. They knew that care was needed in any attempted return. Ahead of negotiations in 1209, they were scrupulous in seeking safe-conducts in a correct and approved form.[55] Perhaps hoping to force their hand, in 1211 John allegedly threatened that, if the exiles did not come back by midsummer, they would lose all their English revenues. If the threat was made, it did not apparently work, but the king was keen that the will of the exiled prelates should not be respected in England. Further orders in 1212 required those appointed by churchmen living abroad to be deprived of their livings. They should leave John's lands 'without delay'.[56]

Prior to the pronouncement of the interdict, the attitude of several bishops was perhaps open to question. The pope criticised their lack of commitment. Gradually the number of bishops in England dwindled. Most were absent following the king's excommunication in 1209.[57] Peter des Roches, bishop of Winchester,

---

[51] Wendover, vol. II, p. 48; Duggan, *Thomas Becket*, pp. 96-7.
[52] Coggeshall, p. 163.
[53] RLC 1204-24, p. 217a; Cheney, *Innocent*, p. 354 n. 135. Stow Park was probably a favoured episcopal retreat. Bishop Hugh retired there in 1233, remaining until his death in 1235: D. M. Smith, 'Wells, Hugh of (d. 1235)', *ODNB* (Oxford, 2004) [http://www.oxforddnb.com/view/article/14061, accessed 30 September 2013].
[54] Dunstable, p. 30; Cheney, 'Papal Interdict', p. 304; Cheney, 'Recent View', p. 164.
[55] *EEA 34. Worcester 1186-1218*, ed. M. Cheney, D. Smith, C. Brooke, and P. M. Hoskin (Oxford, 2008), p. xxxvii.
[56] Waverley, p. 266; RLC 1204-24, p. 130b; Cheney, 'Papal Interdict', pp. 304-5; C. R. Cheney, 'King John's Reaction to the Interdict on England', *Transactions of the Royal Historical Society*, 4th ser., 31 (1949), 129-50 (pp. 147-8); Cheney, *Innocent*, p. 309.
[57] Clarke, p. 170; Cheney, 'Papal Interdict', p. 311.

remained, perhaps relying on the immunity from sanctions secured from Innocent III when his election was confirmed in 1205. Critics observed that Peter 'did not defend church matters so much as administer the king's business'.[58] John de Gray, bishop of Norwich and the king's preferred candidate for Canterbury, also stayed, and was appointed justiciar of Ireland in 1208.[59] Bishop Bernard of Carlisle probably stayed, whilst Philip of Poitou, bishop of Durham, was not in exile when he died in April 1208, a month after the interdict commenced. Philip was probably therefore buried in unconsecrated ground, although he was later reinterred in the chapter house at Durham. Likewise, in 1212, Bishop Robert of Bangor was not in exile when he died. His burial in the marketplace at Shrewsbury occurred 'just as he had wished during his life'.[60]

Amongst other bishops, attitudes were to a certain extent ambiguous. Those who went into exile overseas were later criticised for deserting their flock and living a life of luxury.[61] Both the veteran bishop of Salisbury, Herbert Poor, and Gilbert Glanville, bishop of Rochester, whose relations with his monks suggest that he might have sympathised with the king's struggle with the Canterbury community, chose exile in Scotland in 1209. One source suggests that they had John's permission, and they seem not to have fulfilled papal instructions directed to them in this period. Perhaps they felt they could no longer remain in England, but did not feel the need to take any further action against the king. During the dispute over Langton's election, John apparently accepted Glanville's claim to act as deputy within the archiepiscopal see. Gilbert's death (1214) came just days before the interdict was lifted, meaning that he was buried in unconsecrated ground, although later moved to Rochester Cathedral.[62] Two noted theologians also went into exile. William de Montibus, chancellor of Lincoln Cathedral, went to Scotland, also dying whilst the sentence was still in force in England. Herbert Poor's brother Richard, who later became bishop of Chichester (1215), Salisbury (1217), and Durham (1228), and was named as an arbiter and administrator of John's testament in 1216, returned to Paris, where he had previously been taught by Langton, and where he now taught theology himself.[63]

---

58 Vincent, *Peter des Roches*, p. 52; Barnwell, p. 202.
59 Haines, 'Gray, John de'.
60 Summerson, 'Bernard'; *Liber Gaufridi Sacristae de Coldingham*, p. 26; M. G. Snape, 'Poitou, Philip of (d. 1208)', *ODNB* (Oxford, 2004) [http://www.oxforddnb.com/view/article/22100, accessed 14 January 2014]; Clarke, p. 163; Waverley, p. 273.
61 Wendover, vol. II, p. 48; Cheney, *Innocent*, p. 313.
62 Dunstable, p. 31. For the treatment of the bishop of Salisbury's lands: *Interdict Documents*, pp. 3-32. On the two bishops: C. L. Kingsford, 'Poor, Herbert (d. 1217)', rev. B. R. Kemp, *ODNB* (Oxford, 2004, online edn 2009) [http://www.oxforddnb.com/view/article/22524, accessed 27 August 2013]; M. N. Blount, 'Glanville, Gilbert de (d. 1214)', *ODNB* (Oxford, 2004) [http://www.oxforddnb.com/view/article/10792, accessed 27 August 2013]; Cheney, 'Recent View', pp. 163-4.
63 *Chronicon de Lanercost*, p. 10; *Chronica de Mailros, e codice unico in bibliotheca Cottoniana servato*, ed. J. Stevenson, Bannatyne Club, 49 (Edinburgh, 1835), p. 114; Clarke, p. 163; J. Goering, 'Montibus, William de (d. 1213)', *ODNB* (Oxford, 2004) [http://www.oxforddnb.com/view/article/29471, accessed 15 January 2014]; *EEA* 22, p. xxvii; P. Hoskin, 'Poor,

Below the ranks of the bishops, it is likely that whilst some church officials and clerks went into exile, there were equally those who stayed. The regular presence of men of religion as litigants in the king's court seems to suggest continuity.[64] Raymond, archdeacon of Leicester, was portrayed as an exception in choosing to go overseas: 'almost the only one who of his own free will chose a long exile rather than be responsible for the cowardly betrayal of the liberty of Holy Church, the bride of the heavenly king, to the dictation of an earthly ruler'.[65] For others, the situation is harder to determine. Eustace de Fauconberg, future bishop of London, served as a royal justice from 1199 until John's excommunication in 1209, when he apparently left royal service. He reappeared in 1214, as 'the right hand man' of Peter des Roches, when the latter was justiciar. In all probability, however, he refused to serve the king in person, as he again disappears after John returned from his failed overseas campaigns, and during the Magna Carta civil war.[66] Amongst those who stayed in royal service during the interdict, some were rewarded after the dispute was settled, when Pope Innocent and his legates generally proved amenable to the king's candidates for bishoprics. Thus, Henry of London, who had sought to prevent publication of John's excommunication and played an important part in negotiating the king's peace with the church, became archbishop of Dublin in 1212. Like many of the royal followers discussed here, he was a longstanding associate of John.[67]

More widely, the extent to which churchmen went into exile is harder to gauge, even at the level of the heads of religious houses. Cheney notes that, during the period of sanctions, John allowed a number of monastic houses to make an election when vacancies arose. These included four Benedictine abbeys (Lancaster, Chertsey, Chester, and Durham), five Cistercian communities (Byland, Fountains, Meaux, Rievaulx, and Sallay), and one house each of the Augustinian and Premonstratensian canons (Nostell and Alnwick). Some seventeen monasteries were in the king's hand during the interdict, but some or all may have been without a head for the duration of the sentence. Ralph, abbot of St Benet Holme, provides an example of one who remained in England. When he died in 1210, he was buried outside the priory's cemetery, although his successor Reginald later transferred his remains to the church.[68]

Richard (d. 1237)', *ODNB* (Oxford, 2004, online edn 2009) [http://www.oxforddnb.com/view/article/22525, accessed 29 July 2014]; S. D. Church, 'King John's Testament and the Last Days of his Reign', *EHR*, 125 (2010), 505-28 (pp. 523-5).

[64] Cheney, 'Papal Interdict', pp. 307-8, 312.

[65] *Magna Vita*, vol. II, pp. 154-5.

[66] F. A. Cazel Jr, 'Fauconberg, Eustace de (c. 1170-1228)', *ODNB* (Oxford, 2004, online edn 2008) [http://www.oxforddnb.com/view/article/9202, accessed 16 June 2014]; Vincent, *Peter des Roches*, pp. 101-2.

[67] M. Murphy, 'London, Henry of (d. 1228)', *ODNB* (Oxford, 2004) [http://www.oxforddnb.com/view/article/17036, accessed 27 August 2013]; Turner, *Men*, pp. 91-106; Cheney, *Innocent*, p. 133.

[68] Cheney, *Innocent*, pp. 158-9; Cheney, 'King John's Reaction', pp. 142-5; *Chronica Johannis de Oxenedes*, ed. H. Ellis, RS 13 (London, 1859), p. 296; Clarke, p. 163.

Similarly, it is difficult to assess how widely the sentence was observed. Various religious orders might have expected papal exemption from interdicts to apply, in particular the Cistercians, but also the Templar, Hospitaller, and Premonstratensian orders, all of whom had received this immunity by the late twelfth century. The Cistercians and the Military Orders were soon informed by the pope that they were expected to obey his sanction. For the white monks, observance not only annoyed the king, but also incurred the wrath of the General Chapter. At some communities – John's foundation of Beaulieu, as well as Margam and Meaux – initial observance apparently gave way to resumption of services. The Meaux chronicle records celebration behind closed doors throughout the interdict, noting that other houses did the same. Those subject to interdict or excommunication were excluded. The dead were not buried in the abbey cemetery. Reports reached the pope, however, suggesting that some Cistercian abbeys operated an open-door policy, heralding services with bell-ringing, and performing them with loud chants. After 1209 religious houses observing the interdict were permitted to hold weekly masses behind closed doors, perhaps providing a *modus vivendi* for those who had not already incurred royal or papal wrath. The Military Orders, meanwhile, seemingly sought a compromise enabling them to work with and on behalf of the king.[69]

Clarke notes that 'positive evidence of the offices ceasing during interdicts is generally hard to find; the violation of an interdict was usually thought more worthy of comment than its observance'. In c. 1210, the Cistercian Abbot John of Forde bemoaned the danger of faltering faith amongst those deprived of the sacrament of mass for a prolonged period, suggesting that the sentence was being observed. In other cases, we can infer observance because a chronicler notes when services resumed, as at Tewkesbury (on 5 July 1214).[70] In their analysis of charter evidence, Gervers and Hamonic argue that a hiatus in use of the term 'serving God there' (*deo ibidem servientibus*) highlights recognition of the cessation of services: 'one could not serve God when the country was under interdict'.[71] Thus, the likelihood is that services ceased and many churches fell silent. However, possible exceptions now lost to us cannot be discounted. The Margam annalist observed that the laity, nearly all the clergy, and some of the organised religious supported John.[72]

Royal seizure of church property appears initially to have been almost universal, and was enforced on the first day of the interdict (24 March 1208). A second

---

[69] Clarke, pp. 121-2, 131, 193-4; *SLI*, p. 96 (no. 31); *LPI*, p. 138 (no. 835); *Chronica Monasterii de Melsa, a fundatione usque ad annum 1396, auctore Thoma de Burton, abbate. Accedit continuatio ad annum 1406 a monacho quodam ipsius domus*, ed. E. A. Bond, RS 43, 3 vols (London, 1866-68), vol. I, p. 381; Cheney, *Innocent*, p. 306; Cheney, 'Recent View', pp. 163-4; Webster, 'Military Orders', pp. 210-13.

[70] Clarke, pp. 133-4, 171; *Annales de Theokesberia*, p. 61. On John of Forde's role in distribution of King John's alms prior to the interdict: see above, Chapter 5. For his wider career: C. Holdsworth, 'Forde, John of (c. 1150-1214)', *ODNB* (Oxford, 2004) [http://www.oxforddnb.com/view/article/53109, accessed 16 January 2014].

[71] Gervers and Hamonic, '*Pro Amore Dei*', pp. 245-7.

[72] *Annales de Margan*, p. 28; Clarke, p. 169; Cheney, *Innocent*, p. 312.

seizure, of the clergy's corn, followed by its sale, was said to have taken place in 1209. Cheney highlights the scale of the task, involving local men – four from each community – requisitioning church barns in the name of the king. Commentators remarked on the spiritual consequences for those involved – excommunication. Yet this appears to have been ignored, suggesting that the English church managed a less than obedient flock. The laity were apparently disposed to follow John's instructions, with the wealth of clergy and monks seen as a legitimate target. The king's instructions to arrest the partners of clergymen who struggled to maintain a life of celibacy may also have been widely observed, given that it attracted contemporary comment. This was not new, having been adopted during Henry I's and Stephen's reigns. John had also used it before, probably at Hubert Walter's prompting, against Welsh clergy supporting Gerald of Wales' candidature for the bishopric of St David's. Meanwhile, royal prohibition of church cases being heard on the authority of papal mandates seems to have been observed.[73]

There may have been exceptions to the policy of confiscation. At Winchester Cathedral, no doubt linked to the influence of the king's closest advisor, Bishop Peter des Roches, the community received a charter dated 23 March 1208, the day before the interdict came into effect. The king confirmed to God, the church of Winchester, its bishop, and his successors all their lands, possessions, holdings, and fees, for 'the sake of God's charity' (*divini karitatis intuitu*), for John's wellbeing, and for the souls of his father, ancestors, and successors.[74] More widely, the seizures may have been tempered according to the king's understanding of the extent to which religious houses would observe the sanction of interdict. This is the implication of the letters announcing that confiscations would take place sent a few days before the sentence was enforced. These referred specifically to those who would not celebrate religious services.[75] Elsewhere, one commentator observed that the royal anger abated. Another remarked that 'afterwards' the king made restitution.[76]

In some instances, this may have been linked to the king's devotion to saints whose relics were preserved in a particular church. At Bury St Edmunds, John mitigated his confiscations 'on account of his reverence for St Edmund', doing so when he marked the Easter festival at Guildford.[77] In other cases, the return of property perhaps reflected which communities were favoured by the king. Amongst the first to receive their lands were the archbishop and canons of Rouen, with whom John sought to maintain good relations.[78] A number of letters close

---

[73] Cheney, 'Papal Interdict', pp. 302–3, 306; Cheney, 'King John's Reaction', pp. 146–8; Cheney, *Innocent*, pp. 108, 308–11.

[74] RC, p. 183a–b; Vincent, *Peter des Roches*, pp. 78–9.

[75] RLP, p. 80b; Cheney, 'Papal Interdict', pp. 301–2.

[76] Dunstable, p. 30; Worcester, p. 396. It is not clear what timeframe the Worcester annalist meant when he wrote 'afterwards' (*postea*). His house regained its possessions within three weeks of the imposition of the sanction: *RLC 1204–24*, p. 111b; Cheney, 'King John's Reaction', pp. 132–3.

[77] *Annales S. Edmundi*, pp. 146–7; Cheney, 'King John's Reaction', pp. 131–2.

[78] Peltzer, 'Slow Death', pp. 560–1; Webster, 'King John and Rouen', pp. 326–32.

dealt with the return of property seized from the religious. Restorations were made to entire religious orders, such as the Hospitallers, Cistercians, and Gilbertines. In other cases, individuals took custody of religious houses where they were patron, such as William Marshal at Cartmel, or of religious communities and clerks within their fees. In other cases, the abbot or prior of a religious community received custody of his house, suggesting their presence in England and perhaps that they had convinced the king that religious services would continue. Thus, the abbots of St Peter's, Gloucester, Cirencester, Winchcombe, and Tewkesbury, and the priors of Llanthony and Beckford, all regained their communities and possessions.[79]

Equally, however, the king may have been fully aware of the money-making potential of fining religious communities for return of their property, following the precedent established after the loss of Normandy, when the English lands of continental houses were seized and then returned.[80] The Meaux chronicler described his house as the sole exception when John demanded that religious houses pay for return of their possessions.[81] It is clear that a large amount of religious property was only temporarily in the king's hand. In all probability houses paid or promised substantial fines (perhaps proportionate to their perceived wealth) to recover their holdings.[82] Arrangements relating to such fines were still being made in Henry III's reign.[83] As Cheney notes, it is now impossible to reconstruct the revenues the king drew from the church during the interdict, but a summary of receipts preserved in the *Red Book of the Exchequer* gives a sum in excess of one hundred thousand marks.[84]

If all this suggests that John sought to ride out the sentence of interdict, and to enter a trial of strength with the papacy, he was clearly much more concerned with the threat of excommunication. In September 1209, when this was imminent, the king commanded assemblies to be held across the land, in which 'all the men of England' performed oaths. In part, this emulated Henry II's response to sanctions threatened in 1169. However, the ceremonies held under John went further, demanding freemen to swear fealty and perform homage to the king and to his heir, the future Henry III.[85] Similar efforts to emphasise unity in the face of

---

[79] RLC 1204–24, pp. 107b–115b.

[80] For a similar conclusion: Clarke, p. 180. See also Cheney, 'Papal Interdict', p. 305; Peltzer, *Canon Law*, pp. 245–6; Peltzer, 'Slow Death', pp. 558–61; Matthew, *Norman Monasteries*, pp. 72–5.

[81] *Chronica Monasterii de Melsa*, vol. I, p. 326; Cheney, 'King John's Reaction', p. 132.

[82] Cheney, 'King John's Reaction', pp. 133–40. For a counter-argument: Gervers and Hamonic, 'Pro Amore Dei', pp. 233–7.

[83] FR 5 Henry III, no. 220; FR 6 Henry III, Henry III Fine Rolls Project [http://www.finerollshenry3.org.uk/content/calendar/roll_016.html, accessed 15 May 2014], no. 250; FR 32 Henry III, Henry III Fine Rolls Project [http://www.finerollshenry3.org.uk/content/calendar/roll_045.html, accessed 16 May 2014], no. 470.

[84] Cheney, 'King John's Reaction', p. 129; *The Red Book of the Exchequer*, ed. H. Hall, RS 99, 3 vols (London, 1896), vol. II, pp. 772–3. Cheney notes the difficulties of interpretation the figure poses.

[85] J. R. Maddicott, 'The Oath of Marlborough, 1209: Fear, Government and Popular Allegiance in the Reign of King John', EHR, 126 (2011), 281–318 (pp. 281, 299–307). Maddicott

papal policy can be seen in 1212, when John secured letters from the English and Irish barons expressing 'grief and astonishment' that Innocent contemplated the deposition of the king.[86]

After the mass oath-taking of 1209, John continued carefully to target those who opposed his will, beginning when he determined to tax the English church in 1210. The chroniclers criticised this levy as 'heavy and unheard of', universally applied 'so that not even lepers were spared'. The Worcester annalist wrote that his house paid two hundred marks, with the king demanding a wagon and four horses.[87] John's actions were opportunistic. The English church had failed to follow his lead, and he needed money. As Cheney observes, chroniclers and modern historians 'have tended to represent these measures too exclusively as the depredations of a king at war with the church rather than as the financial devices of a ruthless fiscal expert'.[88] Thus, there were severe repercussions for those who refused to pay, notably the Cistercian order. As in 1200, the white monks argued that they required the consent of the General Chapter.[89]

In 1210, the interdict, and the lack of a mediator of the stature of Hubert Walter, probably made the king markedly less inclined to back down. The monks nonetheless took a stand. The year saw royal campaigning in Ireland, and John hoped to use the money to fund attempts to regain his lost lands in France. The abbots, however, argued that:

> they were the guardians and dispensers of the alms of the faithful, which they [the faithful], for the benefit of their souls and [those] of all their predecessors and children, bestowed on all-powerful God and the blessed Virgin Mary for the use of monks and men of religion, of the poor and the weak, of orphans and the destitute and widows, and not for the revenues of kings or the wages of soldiers.

John responded by annulling their charters, allegedly ordering that 'whoever wished to do them evil or injury would do it without penalty'. The king's sanctions extended to grants made by members of his own family, including goods, lands, and forest rights conferred by Henry II.[90]

The chroniclers are united in giving details of the oppression. John 'did many bad things against the holy church', according to the Stanley annalist, whilst Ralph of Coggeshall complained that he 'oppressed most of all the Cistercians'.[91] Some houses were forced to disperse: 'scattered through the various churches in

---

quotes (p. 281) Gervase of Canterbury. On parallels with oaths of Henry II's reign: Webster, 'Crown Versus Church'.
[86] *CDI 1171–1251*, pp. 73–4 (no. 448); Cheney, 'Alleged Deposition', p. 109 n. 1.
[87] Worcester, p. 398; Dunstable, p. 32; *Annales S. Edmundi*, p. 149; Stanley, p. 512; Waverley, p. 264.
[88] Cheney, 'Papal Interdict', pp. 305–6; Cheney, *Innocent*, p. 309.
[89] C. Holdsworth, 'John of Forde and the Interdict', *EHR*, 78 (1963), 705–14 (pp. 706, 709). See also above, Chapter 3.
[90] Stanley, pp. 510–11.
[91] Stanley, p. 510; Coggeshall, p. 163. See also: *Annales de Margan*, pp. 29–30; Waverley, p. 264; Dunstable, p. 33; Barnwell, p. 201.

England, they were forced to beg for the necessities of nourishment'. The abbots, including the head of John's own foundation, were forbidden from attending the General Chapter, although Beaulieu, along with Margam (where the king stayed on his journey to Ireland) were exempted from the king's revenue raising.[92] This suggests that the ports were closed to the organised religious. Going into exile needed a certain amount of compliance from the authorities. In 1210, it does not seem to have been an option for the beleaguered white monks. Ultimately, they paid a higher levy than John had originally demanded, and the royal anger temporarily abated. However, in 1212, the king demanded £22,000 from the Cistercians, arguing that their collusion was responsible for the sufferings of Raymond VI, count of Toulouse (who had previously been married to John's sister Joanna), at the hands of the Albigensian crusaders.[93]

The sources highlight how royal activity, in particular taxation of the church, was portrayed as oppression characteristic of an irreligious tyrant. The sanctions 'naturally threw a shadow over John's reputation as a Christian king'.[94] Sadly, the account of this phase of the reign by one of the king's staunchest critics, Ralph of Coggeshall, is brief. Although the death of Hubert Walter apparently provided Ralph with a spur to resume writing, the folios covering 1206 to 1212 have been excised in the surviving manuscript. In all likelihood, Ralph's initial views on the interdict years have been lost. The replacement text proceeded 'in bare annalistic fashion'.[95]

Nonetheless, other narratives leave us in no doubt as to their opinion. Gervase of Canterbury described the exiles as 'many and numberless, both rich and poor, not bearing the tyranny of the king'. Meanwhile, John acted as if 'he neither feared God nor respected men'. There is a sense of disbelief or of lack of understanding of a king who 'made light of the lord pope's chastisement' and 'spurned' his instructions. The chronicler argued that the people felt deprived of their faith, and fearful for the future. John led an army north in 1209, a campaign that culminated in the Treaty of Norham. However, the *Gesta Regum* notes the soldiers' complaint: 'We are like pagans, without the law of God, without Christianity', by contrast to King William I of Scotland, 'for whom He [God] had worked several miracles'.[96]

Other writers saw matters in similar terms. The Worcester annalist twice described the king as 'disturbed': first in recounting the expulsion of the Canterbury monks, the sale of their stock, and the seizure of their lands and of archiepiscopal property; and second in describing the 'grievous exile' of the executors of the interdict (the bishops of London, Ely, and Worcester), along with the bishop of Hereford. The annalist complained of the impact of the sanctions: 'almost all

---

[92] GR, p. 105; Stanley, p. 512; Waverley, p. 265; Coggeshall, p. 163; Barnwell, p. 201; *Annales de Margan*, pp. 29–30.

[93] Barnwell, p. 201; Coggeshall, p. 164; P. Webster, 'King John and the Crusades' (in preparation). They were also ordered to supply John with wagons and horses.

[94] Harper-Bill, 'John and the Church of Rome', p. 298.

[95] Carpenter, 'Abbot Ralph', pp. 1213–14, 1227–8.

[96] GR, pp. 99–100, 102–3; Duncan, 'John King of England and the Kings of Scots', pp. 255–61.

the laity turned away from the care of Christianity'. Others portrayed laity and churchmen as 'plagued beyond measure', and described the seizure of church property as an 'enormous sin'.[97] Some saw natural phenomena as divine warnings of the trouble that would beset the kingdom if the king did not reach a settlement. The Dunstable annalist opened his account of 1208 with ominous news: 'portents were seen in England; for the sun and the moon fought at the same time. And further a terrible eclipse became visible.' It was not uncommon to see events in terms of tyranny. John was 'the tyrant of England'. His agents held the Canterbury lands in their 'tyrannical custody'.[98]

The seeds of John's later reputation were being sown. They influenced those at work in the 1220s and 1230s, notably Roger of Wendover, creating a highly credible portrayal. The St Alban's chronicler described how the king reacted to the bishops' warning, before they imposed the interdict, that he should have 'God in his sight'. If he accepted Langton and recalled the Canterbury monks, 'the Disposer of rewards would ... multiply his temporal honours, and after his death would bestow lasting glory upon him'. In response, according to Wendover, John became 'nearly mad with rage', uttering 'words of blasphemy against the pope and his cardinals, swearing by God's teeth' that if an interdict was imposed he would expel churchmen and confiscate their property. Papal clerks in his lands would be sent back to Rome 'with their eyes plucked out and their noses slit'. Perhaps Wendover knew of a precedent here: slitting of the noses of those employed by the pope or cardinals had been ordered by Emperor Henry VI when he invaded the papal lands in 1196. It is not recorded under John. Nonetheless, with masterful understatement, Roger observed that the bishops departed to pronounce their sentence, 'not finding any repentance in the king.'[99]

Wendover went further, arguing that John condoned the murder of churchmen. Roger described the arrest in 1208, on the Welsh border, of a highway robber who had attacked and murdered a priest. This man was brought before the king for sentencing. John ordered his release, arguing that '"he has slain an enemy of mine"'. John of Forde also noted that the clergy needed to be wary of attack.[100] However, this runs directly contrary to royal letters issued in 1208. The recipients are unspecified, but the tone is that of letters which could have been issued to sheriffs across the land:

> we command you that you should cause [public] declaration to be made ... that no-one, as he loves his person and chattels, should do or speak ill to the men of religion or clergy, against our peace, and if we can convict anyone of that we will have him hanged at the next quarter [sessions].[101]

---

[97] Barnwell, p. 200; Waverley, p. 261.
[98] Worcester, pp. 395-7; Dunstable, p. 30; *Annales de Margan*, p. 28; Waverley, pp. 259-61.
[99] Wendover, vol. II, pp. 45-7; Cheney, *Innocent*, p. 302 n. 38.
[100] Wendover, vol. II, pp. 47-8; Clarke, p. 176.
[101] *RLC 1204-24*, p. 111a.

Later sources were more sceptical. The London annals, which show an interest in legal procedure but which equally drew on sources originating at St Albans, suggest that coroners were not allowed to investigate the murder of clerks.[102] Nevertheless, the wording of the letters issued by John's government seems clear.

This is not the only instance in which Wendover's accusations do not completely withstand scrutiny. In his account of the fate of Geoffrey of Norwich, Roger described an exchequer clerk who argued that those who held benefices – that is, trained priests – could not continue in royal service. Geoffrey announced this at the Exchequer and then 'went to his own house without asking the king's permission'. John's disproportionate reaction was to have Geoffrey imprisoned, where he died under a weight of metal. The account is problematic. Roger misidentifies his subject as one of the two archdeacons of Norwich, Geoffrey de Buckland and Geoffrey de Burgh, who later became bishop of Ely (1225).[103] Meanwhile, whilst he cannot have helped his cause if he indeed made these remarks, his crime included leaving court without royal permission. Again, this would suggest that John targeted those who deserted their posts. Others saw Geoffrey's fate in a different light, linking his death to complicity in baronial conspiracy against the king. Painter suggests that John's excommunication in 1209 provided later rebels with a convenient excuse for their defiance.[104]

Wendover's successor as St Alban's chronicler, Matthew Paris, went further, suggesting that John considered abandoning the Christian faith. Paris took Roger's account of the royal submission to the pope and the king's absolution from excommunication, and inserted claims that envoys were sent to the North African emir, Muhammad al-Nasir. John offered to surrender his kingdom to the emir, and to 'abandon the Christian faith, which he considered false, and [that he] would faithfully adhere' to Islam. The messengers found the emir studying the works of St Paul. He expressed disappointment that the apostle did not '"stand firm to the faith in which he was born"'. John, he said, was similar, showing a '"flexible and unstable"' attitude. Matthew claimed personally to have heard the tale from one of the envoys, the royal clerk Robert of London, who acted as the king's custodian at St Albans during the interdict.[105]

---

[102] *Annales Londonienses*, ed. W. Stubbs, *Chronicles of the Reigns of Edward I and Edward II*, RS 76, 2 vols (London, 1882-83), vol. I, p. 8; Cheney, 'Papal Interdict', pp. 300-1; Gransden, *Historical Writing*, pp. 508-9.

[103] Wendover, vol. II, pp. 52-3; S. Painter, 'Norwich's Three Geoffreys', *Speculum*, 28 (1953), 808-13; J. Hudson, 'Buckland, Geoffrey of (d. 1225)', *ODNB* (Oxford, 2004) [http://www.oxforddnb.com/view/article/2749, accessed 23 August 2013]; N. Karn, 'Burgh, Geoffrey de (d. 1228)', *ODNB* (Oxford, 2007) [http://www.oxforddnb.com/view/article/95140, accessed 23 August 2013].

[104] Coggeshall, p. 165; Dunstable, pp. 32-3; Painter, 'Norwich's Three Geoffreys', pp. 808-10. The Dunstable annalist later describes Geoffrey of Norwich as a martyr, but attributes his death to the king's half-brother, William, earl of Salisbury.

[105] *Matthaei Parisiensis*, vol. II, pp. 559-64; *Gesta Abbatum*, vol. I, pp. 236-42; *RLP*, p. 81a; N. Barbour, 'The Embassy Sent by King John of England to Miramolin, King of Morocco', *Al-Ándalus. Revista de las escuelas de estudios árabes de Madrid y Granada*, 25 (1960), 373-81 (p. 373); N. Barbour, 'Two Christian Embassies to the Almohad Sultan Muhammad al-Nasir

As it stands, the account is clearly a fiction, 'a vehicle for the expression of Paris' petty prejudices against King John'.[106] It principally provides a satire on the royal submission to Pope Innocent III. Satire, however, often contains a grain of truth. Without giving credence to the idea that John sought to deny his faith, it may be possible to envisage such an embassy taking place. The king needed allies in his efforts to defend his remaining lands on the continent and to regain his losses.[107] Cheney observes that whilst Matthew's narrative on this theme contains 'a lot of nonsense', such an embassy was in keeping with the policy adopted by contemporary rulers when expediency demanded: 'few would have regarded it as a mark of outrageous infidelity'. In 1201, John had agreed a treaty with King Sancho VII of Navarre in which he promised to safeguard the latter's agreement with the king of the Moroccans. The English monarch also received an envoy from the Sultan of Egypt in 1207. The possibility that a mission to the North African ruler took place is probably as far as Paris' account can be believed.[108] John was clearly not an apostate. The accusations were similar to those levelled against Henry II by John of Salisbury during the Becket conflict, and against Raymond VI of Toulouse (another of John's allies against the French king and the pope) by writers of the southern French territories during the Albigensian crusade.[109]

Matthew's portrayal of John's supposed irreligion included various observations he alleged the king to have made. On one level, this amounted to critique of the wealth of churchmen, for instance the king's mocking comment '"how fat this animal has grown without ever hearing mass"' when he captured a particularly well-proportioned stag. More seriously, Paris suggested that John developed heretical ideas. The king 'conceived evil thoughts about the resurrection of the dead, and other matters connected with the Christian religion, and gave utterance to some unmentionable foolish sayings'. Such allegations are clearly unfounded. John's orthodox credentials can be seen throughout the interdict. Shortly afterwards he issued letters ordering suppression of heresy in his lands in south-western France.[110]

---

at Seville in 1211', *Congreso de Estudios Árabes e Islámicos* (Madrid, 1964), pp. 189-213 (p. 195); R. Vaughan, *Matthew Paris* (Cambridge, 1958), p. 14; A. Taylor, 'Robert de Londres, Illegitimate Son of William, King of Scots, c. 1170-1225', *Haskins Society Journal*, 19 (2007), 99-119 (p. 115). Taylor notes that the royal clerk Robert was different from the illegitimate son (of the same name) of William I of Scotland.

[106] Church, *Household Knights*, p. 66. By contrast to the historians discussed below, Church argues that the story 'in no way can be taken seriously'. Efforts to see it as credible therefore constitute a 'hopeless task'.

[107] Vincent, 'Isabella', pp. 200-1; Vincent, 'England and the Albigensian Crusade', pp. 72-8.

[108] Cheney, *Innocent*, pp. 14-15. For efforts to prove that it occurred: Barbour, 'Embassy', pp. 373-81; Barbour, 'Two Christian Embassies', pp. 189-213.

[109] Barbour, 'Two Christian Embassies', p. 190; Vincent, 'England and the Albigensian Crusade', p. 75.

[110] *Matthaei Parisiensis*, vol. II, p. 565; RLP, p. 124a; N. Vincent, 'Simon of Atherfield (d. 1211): A Martyr to his Wife', *Analecta Bollandiana*, 113 (1995), 349-61 (p. 355).

The image of King John created by the St Albans chroniclers is well known.[111] Examples from early thirteenth-century monastic annals also shed light on the evolving perception of the king in the context of the Canterbury dispute. The Worcester and Tewkesbury annalists include brief reference to letters purportedly from the Virgin Mary, delivered to John by an unnamed cleric in 1206.[112] In both sources, the reference comes amidst discussion of the relationship between England and the papacy and, in the Tewkesbury account, immediately precedes description of Langton's election to Canterbury. We have no information as to what the letter contained, but as John's reputation worsened during the thirteenth century, the Virgin was invoked in material hostile to the king. The so-called *Invectivum contra regem Iohannem*, a forthright condemnation penned in the 1250s or 1260s, thus itself the product of a period of sustained opposition to royal government, was set out in the form of a letter from Christ to his mother. It is therefore possible to see how those noting the letters allegedly produced in 1206 might assume that they criticised John for his attitude towards church and people, rather than offering the comfort of saintly protection.[113]

Despite the tidal wave of criticism, some writers highlighted how those involved in the dispute appealed to the king's religious sensibilities, expressing the view that John could make amends, and redeem the damage to his soul, by reaching a settlement. Gervase of Canterbury commented that many hoped that the king 'would correct in the church of God those things which he had done ill, and would put right his mistakes', though he adds that instead John hardened his oppression of the Cistercians. Roger of Wendover noted Innocent III's observation that by accepting Langton, John would be able to call upon a man whose 'character would be of no small advantage to the king's soul', not to mention his potential contribution to the king's temporal affairs. This echoes a papal letter sent in August 1207 to the bishops charged with pronouncing the interdict, stating that the king should realise that acceptance of Langton was the best means of provision for his honour and salvation.[114] That process of acceptance (despite the king's outlook and his effort to undertake religious activity during the interdict), and the impact on the king's reputation in the final months of his rule, will provide the focus for the next chapter.

---

[111] Galbraith, *Roger of Wendover and Matthew Paris*, pp. 17–19, 34–7; Gransden, *Historical Writing*, pp. 368–9; Warren, *John*, pp. 11–16.
[112] *Annales de Theokesberia*, p. 58; Worcester, pp. 393–4; Gransden, *Historical Writing*, pp. 318, 405 and n. 13.
[113] Vincent, 'Mary', p. 132. On the *Invectivum*: Vincent, 'Master Simon Langton'.
[114] *GR*, p. 105; Wendover, vol. II, p. 38; *SLI*, p. 93 (no. 30).

7

Peace with the Pope
Diplomacy, Personal Religion, and Civil War

King John was no stranger to ecclesiastical sentences. His first marriage (1189), to his second cousin, Isabella of Gloucester, was deemed consanguineous, prompting an interdict imposed by Archbishop Baldwin of Canterbury. The count of Mortain incurred excommunication when he attempted to seize the throne in 1194. Here, he was attempting to violate the rights and possessions of a sworn crusader, his brother Richard. The sentence was pronounced by Archbishop Hubert Walter and his fellow bishops.[1] In 1203 Hubert, acting alongside Eustace, bishop of Ely, was again charged with sanctioning John. This time, an ambulatory interdict was to be imposed if John Cumin, archbishop of Dublin, was not allowed to return from exile. This had begun in 1197, when Cumin fell into dispute with the Irish justiciar, Hamo de Valognes, a close associate of John both as count of Mortain and king. After 1199, the archbishop of Dublin was barred from the realm, whereupon he sought papal support. Hubert and Eustace did not enforce the interdict they had been ordered to impose, incurring papal rebuke, although a settlement allowed Cumin to return to Dublin in 1206.[2] Meanwhile, whilst engaged in dispute with the pope over the appointment of Langton, and whilst England was under interdict from 1208–14, John was also threatened with a local interdict, to be applied to the lands he refused to surrender to Richard I's widow, Berengaria, as settlement of her dower. A further sentence was contemplated because the king would not restore property to his half-brother Geoffrey, archbishop of York.[3]

This cannot have been a promising track record for those who hoped for a quick solution to the Canterbury dispute. John must have appeared intent on achieving peace on his terms or not at all. Contemporary observers saw little hope of resolution. At one point, the *Life of St Hugh* noted that 'we have now endured [John] for fourteen years and three months', suggesting that the author, Adam of Eynsham, was at work in September 1213.[4] The king seemed to have forgotten the promises made when he succeeded Richard I. Adam hoped nonetheless that John

---

[1] Venables, 'Lucy, Godfrey de'.
[2] Clarke, p. 89; M. Murphy, 'Cumin, John (d. 1212)', *ODNB* (Oxford, 2004) [http://www.oxforddnb.com/view/article/6043, accessed 14 January 2014]; C. A. Empey, 'Valognes, Hamo de (d. 1202/3)', *ODNB* (Oxford, 2004) [http://www.oxforddnb.com/view/article/50032, accessed 19 August 2014]; Vincent, 'Jean', pp. 48, 58.
[3] Clarke, p. 63; Cheney, *Innocent*, pp. 24, 296–7.
[4] *Magna Vita*, vol. I, pp. xi–xii, vol. II, p. 74; Gransden, *Historical Writing*, pp. 312–13, 317.

'might be roused at last to do his best to avoid damnation', but gloomily observed that the king did not comprehend the fate that awaited him:

> the wrongs and enormities committed by him against God appear indeed irremediable and irreparable. He however, owing to his darkened mind, does not realise or understand the reason for his present misfortunes, or what he will justly have to suffer after the short span of this life, or the certainty of his shame and damnation.[5]

Yet perhaps it was not too late. Adam hoped that the threat of deposition: 'would cause him [John] to take pains to avoid eternal damnation, so that ... he may endeavour to transfer himself from the left hand to the right hand of the supreme judge'.[6] The king's efforts to negotiate a settlement form the focus of this chapter. The evidence reveals that John saw his dispute with the church rather differently to many of the commentators of the day. It also demonstrates that elements of royal religious observance continued during the period of sanctions, despite the way in which they were perceived.

Firstly, let us consider the king's perspective. For much of the period, John kept diplomatic avenues open. The bishop-executors of the interdict fulfilled the pope's orders to impose the sanction.[7] Nonetheless, they were keen to listen and make proposals for peace, perhaps aware that their exile left them open to criticism. Wendover accused them of living a life of luxury, 'instead of placing themselves as a wall for the house of God'. For Roger, John would have been excommunicated sooner, but the bishops were 'like dumb dogs not daring to bark'.[8] Equally, however, the threat persuaded John that negotiation was worthwhile. He was presented with demands that he was always likely to find difficult to accept. Everything Archbishop Hubert had held when he died was to be 'restored' to Langton. Restitution was to be made to the Canterbury monks, to the executors of the interdict, and to other churchmen in exile. The king was to receive the archbishop and bishops, guaranteeing their safety. Langton, after receiving his regalia, would swear fealty to the king. The Canterbury community would be allowed to return unmolested. In other words, John was to condone most if not all of what he had refused to accept in the process of choosing Hubert's successor. He was particularly unlikely to favour the suggestion that Archbishop Langton would swear to uphold royal rights 'saving the honour of the Church'. Such phraseology had been employed by Stephen's martyred archiepiscopal predecessor, causing deadlock in the dispute between Becket and Henry II.[9]

In this atmosphere, it seems unsurprising that the executors of the interdict met a frosty reception when they arrived in England to attempt to negotiate in 1209. They quickly became concerned that royal guarantees of their safety were

---

5 *Magna Vita*, vol. II, p. 141.
6 *Magna Vita*, vol. II, p. 141. On possible deposition: Cheney, 'Alleged Deposition', pp. 100-16.
7 *EEA 26*, pp. 89-96 (nos 94-8).
8 Wendover, vol. II, pp. 48, 52.
9 *EEA 26*, pp. 97-8 (nos 99-100); Duggan, *Thomas Becket*, pp. 149-53, 260-1.

insufficient, so remained on neutral ground, probably at Temple Ewell near Dover, urging John's main episcopal ally, Peter des Roches, bishop of Winchester, to hurry to join the negotiations. In early autumn, they nearly reached a settlement. The *Deeds of Pope Innocent* closed its account of events at this point, noting that John 'not being able to maintain his position, offered satisfaction'. Excommunication was postponed on the proviso that the king restore church property and signify his acceptance of peace terms in writing. Differences soon resurfaced. The executors again complained that their safe-conducts were inadequate, adding that no protection had been extended to Stephen Langton's brother and procurator Simon, nor to the Canterbury monks, who clearly remained a target of royal anger. Discussions broke down and the executors returned to the continent. Unable to excommunicate John in England, the bishops of London and Ely announced the sentence at Arras on 8 November 1209. It is not clear whether Bishop Mauger of Worcester was present. He had perhaps already retired to Cistercian Pontigny Abbey, Becket's former home in exile, where he died in 1212.[10]

Whilst papal and episcopal letters preserve arguments advanced by the church, it is often difficult to know what case was put forward by the royal party. During the negotiations, and the regular exchange of envoys between the royal and papal courts, the king and his advisers surely presented a position of their own. This presumably countered the church's promotion of the ideal that the ruler's role in elections was simply to authorise them, and that the royal prerogative did not extend to nominating candidates. Peltzer notes that during the disputed election at Sées in 1201–03, considerable expertise in canon law was evident at the royal court. It seems likely that this was also the case during the Canterbury dispute.[11]

We can suggest that the king's men were sent to explain his position to those affected by the dispute or by the royal reaction to the imposition of sanctions. In 1208, shortly before the proclamation of the interdict, the men of Kent were instructed to give credence to the words of Reginald de Cornhill, the sheriff. He would explain what had occurred in negotiations between the king, the bishops, and Archbishop Langton's brother Simon. At the same time, Cornhill was issued with letters granting him custody of the lands of the archbishop and of the cathedral priory. A few days later, all those in the bishopric of Durham were instructed to have faith in Robert de Vieuxpont's description of the same matter and about the 'injury' inflicted on the king by Pope Innocent. Robert, a powerful royal agent in northern England, received custody of the bishopric of Durham when Philip of Poitou died, just weeks after the interdict was pronounced.[12]

John's supporters are likely to have emphasised the king's traditional role in appointments. A description of the case he developed is offered by the Burton

---

10   *EEA* 26, pp. 98–101 (nos 101–3); *Deeds of Pope Innocent*, pp. xliv–xlv, 240–1; *EEA* 34, p. xxxvii; Cheney, 'Alleged Deposition', pp. 107–8.
11   Peltzer, *Canon Law*, pp. 129, 254–5, and see above, Chapter 6.
12   *RLP*, p. 80a; Clarke, p. 171; H. Summerson, 'Vieuxpont, Robert de (d. 1228)', *ODNB* (Oxford, 2004) [http://www.oxforddnb.com/view/article/28276, accessed 16 January 2014].

annals, in recounting negotiations at Northampton in 1211.[13] The source, 'the work of an archivist rather than a historian', proceeds by linking sections of narrative with documents available to the writer. It becomes progressively more detailed from the late 1180s onwards, ending in 1262.[14] Whether it presents an account of events which actually happened is open to debate, but there is a sense of portrayal of the arguments the two sides found it possible to advance. Positions were entrenched. John threatened that Langton would be hung if he attempted to come to England. Yet the king also told the envoys, Pandulf and Durand, that he acknowledged the pope as his spiritual father, to be obeyed in matters of faith. However, such authority did not apply to earthly affairs that pertained to the crown. The king reiterated his view that the Canterbury monks had deceived him. He added that all his predecessors had collated archbishops, bishops, and abbots. They had done so within the setting of the royal court.[15]

John then recounted the legend of St Wulfstan's staff, which resonated with his attitude towards the extent of royal authority over episcopal appointments. He drew comparisons from the lives of other saints prominent in his devotional activity. Even his father's nemesis, St Thomas, was cited in support of his case. The archbishopric of Canterbury had been conferred on Becket by Henry II. Therefore, Pope Innocent was trying to deprive John of rights exercised by his predecessors. The arguments were consistent with the king's outlook on the dispute as a whole, and account for many of his actions. Indeed, Becket had associated himself with the cults of Edward the Confessor and Bishop Wulfstan in 1163, claiming the relic of the stone into which Wulfstan had plunged his staff as fee for participating in the translation of St Edward in Westminster Abbey.[16]

This viewpoint was hardly likely to prove acceptable to the papal envoys. The Burton annals credit Pandulf with a response summarising the papal perspective. He argued that the king's use of examples of English saints was invalid. St Edward had been the protector of the church. John was its destroyer. The latter's refusal to accept Langton was akin to William the Conqueror's initial hostility towards Wulfstan. Likewise, although Henry II had engineered Becket's election, the latter had resigned his see to Pope Alexander III. Following the martyrdom, Pandulf added, Henry had conceded, for the remission of all his sins, that forevermore the archbishop should be elected by the monks of Canterbury, according to the will of God, without recourse to the input of the bishops, and with the assent of the king, earls and barons in attendance.[17]

Clearly the two sides were deadlocked. Although probably written during Henry III's reign, the Burton annals nonetheless reflect a real and ongoing debate, both

---

[13] *Annales de Burton*, pp. 209–17. A shorter account, abridged from the same source of information, is included in: Waverley, pp. 268–71. For the pope's instructions to his envoys: *SLI*, pp. 125–7 (no. 43).

[14] Gransden, *Historical Writing*, pp. 408–9.

[15] *Annales de Burton*, pp. 209–11.

[16] *Annales de Burton*, pp. 211–12; Mason, *St Wulfstan*, p. 284. For further discussion of the legend of St Wulfstan's staff, see Chapter 2 above.

[17] *Annales de Burton*, pp. 212–15.

under John and later, about the role of the crown and the papacy in episcopal elections in England.[18] The popularised version of the legend of St Wulfstan's staff, reflected in the arguments attributed to John, held currency from the later twelfth century onwards. By extension, it can be suggested that the king felt that the limited education attributed (unfairly) to Wulfstan provided a useful contrast to his academic opponents, Langton and indeed Innocent III, whose challenge to the royal will might be countered with the Anglo-Saxon bishop's respect for Edward the Confessor's authority.[19] After John's death, the debate continued: the legend of St Wulfstan's staff was depicted at Worcester Cathedral and in court circles in the thirteenth and fourteenth centuries. In 1313, a sermon preached at Oxford showed awareness of the account preserved by the Burton annals. The issue of the appointment of an archbishop of Canterbury again provided the context, due to Edward II's elevation of Walter Reynolds from Worcester to Canterbury in the summer of that year.[20]

The notion that John invoked a sense of how churchmen were appointed in the late eleventh and twelfth centuries is sustained by letters issued by a group of his baronial supporters. These expressed surprise that Pope Innocent even considered absolving the king's subjects from their fealty, referring to the 'injury' John had suffered due to the Canterbury dispute. The barons asserted their right to defend their liege lord, indeed to live or die with him. There is a palpable sense that these letters were written with considerable input from the king and his advisers. Thus, the sentiments expressed reflect the royal position: his 'liberty and dignity', and that of his crown, had been attacked. 'Before the coming of the Normans the kings of England conferred at their will cathedral churches on many archbishops and bishops, now saints. But after this period the kings granted that elections should be made, as they have hitherto been made, by assent of the K[ing].' John had resisted in the Canterbury election in order to preserve the rights 'which the crown of England has hitherto enjoyed.'[21]

Other sources highlight – albeit critically – that John drew on the advice of those around him in formulating his policy. In describing the breakdown of negotiations in 1209, Gervase of Canterbury blamed the king's advisers, arguing that John had been 'inflamed by the tongues of evil-minded disparagers'. When John sought to maximise the revenue raised from the religious in 1210, he was said to have been inspired by Richard Marsh, an 'impious and hostile clerk', who the king 'did not fear to nominate as his god before men of religion and secular men'.[22]

Even amongst such hostility, there are hints that the king and his advisers were building a case. Perhaps this was the purpose of the books the king borrowed from

---

[18] The subject of: K. Harvey, *Episcopal Appointments in England, c. 1214–1344* (Farnham, 2014).
[19] Mason, 'Wulfstan's Staff', pp. 166–7.
[20] Mason, 'Wulfstan's Staff', pp. 162–3, 170; F. M. Powicke, *Stephen Langton* (Oxford, 1928), p. 87 n. 1; Harvey, *Episcopal Appointments*, p. 174; J. R. Wright, 'Reynolds, Walter (d. 1327)', *ODNB* (Oxford, 2004, online edn 2008) [http://www.oxforddnb.com/view/article/23443, accessed 8 March 2011].
[21] *CDI 1171–1251*, pp. 73–4 (no. 448); Cheney, 'Alleged Deposition', p. 109 n. 1.
[22] *GR*, pp. 103–5; Stanley, p. 512. On Marsh: Stacey, 'Marsh, Richard'.

Reading Abbey, days after the interdict came into effect. These included the whole of the Old Testament, works of the twelfth-century thinkers Hugh of St Victor and Peter Lombard, and writers of the early church, such as St Augustine and Origen. A further work, by the classical writer Pliny, described as 'our book', was recovered from the custody of the Reading community shortly afterwards.[23] Ultimately, we cannot know whether these were used to buttress the royal argument, but it is a tempting possibility. Elsewhere, John of Forde highlights that the king attempted to back up his position with evidence, recounting discussion about royal taxation of the Cistercians in 1210. Here, King John argued that it was appropriate for the white monks to pay, providing biblical examples such as Christ's utterance: 'Render therefore unto Caesar the things that are Caesar's; and to God the things that are God's.' The king also observed that relieving the Cistercians of their wealth would enable them to return to their founders' ideal of a life of poverty.[24] Again, there is a sense that during a dispute between secular and spiritual powers, the wealth of the religious was deemed fair game.

Roger of Wendover once more took this further, highlighting the case of Master Alexander the Mason, a 'pseudo-theologian' (*pseudo theologus*) who won royal favour 'by his iniquitous preaching' and 'incited the king to acts of cruelty'. Alexander argued that the interdict was the fault of the king's subjects. John, with the Canterbury monks and some of the bishops in mind, might well have agreed. The king's counsellor went much further, setting out a philosophy based on the notion that the ruler was ordained by God. Thus, John 'was the rod of God'. He 'had been made a prince in order to rule his people and those subject to him with a rod of iron, and to break them all "like a potter's vessel"'. For Alexander, the pope was meddling in matters that were none of his business. Matthew Paris added that the king's adviser counselled him not to surrender England to Pope Innocent. Wendover noted that Alexander was richly rewarded, receiving benefices taken from churchmen who took a different stance. Naturally, Roger also believed that 'the Mason' received his comeuppance: 'deprived of all his goods and benefices, and at length reduced to such wretchedness, that he was compelled by necessity, in the poorest of clothing, to beg his bread from door to door'.[25]

Although there was later confusion as to Alexander's identity, and his fall was apparently spectacular, the example again suggests entrenched positions, with the king's supporters arguing forcefully that divine providence was in fact on his side. Perhaps John's position was not as isolated as is traditionally assumed. Again, Wendover's description might seem like the words of a chronicler intent on negative portrayal of John, but it is not entirely without corroboration. Powicke identifies Master Alexander of St Albans in a royal letter of 1212. Further letters of 1215, displaying a knowledge of scripture not normally found in chancery documents,

---

[23] RLC 1204–24, pp. 108a, 108b. Whether this was Pliny the Elder or Younger is not specified.
[24] Holdsworth, 'John of Forde and the Interdict', pp. 705–14. For the bible quotation: Matthew, chapter 22, verse 21.
[25] Wendover, vol. II, pp. 53–4; *Gesta Abbatum*, vol. I, pp. 235–6; F. M. Powicke, 'Master Alexander of St Albans: A Literary Muddle', *Essays in History Presented to Reginald Lane Poole*, ed. H. W. C. Davis (Oxford, 1927), pp. 246–60 (p. 259); Cheney, *Innocent*, p. 18.

asked Innocent III to show mercy to Alexander should he appear before the pope. Perhaps he was one of those forced to travel to Rome for absolution having failed to observe John's excommunication.[26]

Serious charges were made against John for his treatment of the religious during the period of sanctions. Yet it is important also to consider the evidence for his personal religion during these years. He did not entirely neglect the church. The previous chapter noted that monks from other houses were installed at Canterbury, and that acts of lawlessness against churchmen were not allowed, despite what the chroniclers would have us believe. Seizure of church property was followed with some restitution. In assessing the evidence for John's religious activity during this part of his reign, historians are hampered by some of the poorest survival of documentary sources. The gaps fall in the middle of the interdict. The Charter, Close, and Patent Rolls are missing for the eleventh, twelfth, and thirteenth regnal years. Nonetheless, surviving evidence suggests that the pattern of royal religious activity identified in previous chapters continued during the interdict and even whilst John was excommunicate. The king 'continued active in devotional works and promoted Christian piety among his subjects'.[27]

It is unclear whether or not the king received the sacraments, but he is known to have requested that mass be performed (even if the abbot of St Albans, at least, refused).[28] He was involved in the commemoration of Easter, as shown by his almsgiving on Maundy Thursday or Good Friday in 1209, 1210, 1211, and in 1213, when at least one knight accompanied him in making offerings before the cross. It seems at least tentatively possible that mass would have been performed, even though the last three examples fall during the period of excommunication.[29] Meanwhile, various individuals served the royal chapel during the interdict, suggesting that this continued to operate. Godfrey *Spigurnell'*, the Chancery officer responsible for sealing writs, was described as a chapel servant in 1210, along with Job (or perhaps John) of the Chamber, and Adam Cat.[30] That said, royal chaplains appear to have ceased to perform the *Laudes Regiae*. Certainly it is not documented during this period. Whether or not the king heard mass, there seem to have been places where the sacraments were administered. Geoffrey fitz Peter established a chantry chaplain at Winchester Cathedral in 1210.[31] Later, between the end of the king's excommunication and the lifting of the interdict, so whilst administration of the sacraments was still suspended, John made a grant in support of a chaplain at Egerton for celebration of services for the souls of the dead, perhaps principally for the royal servant Robert of Thornham.[32]

---

[26] *RLC 1204–24*, pp. 121a, 203a-b; Powicke, 'Master Alexander', pp. 258-9; *LPI*, p. 161 (no. 969), and see also p. 150 (no. 908).
[27] Cheney, 'Papal Interdict', p. 307.
[28] *Gesta Abbatum*, vol. I, p. 235; discussed above, Chapter 1.
[29] *RL*, pp. 110, 161-2, 244; *RM*, p. 258; discussed above, Chapter 5. See also Cheney's words of caution: Cheney, 'Recent View', pp. 165-7.
[30] *RL*, p. 206.
[31] London, British Library, Additional Ms. 29436, ff. 31v-32; discussed above, Chapter 1.
[32] The chaplain had been given two bovates of land by Robert (d. 1211). The king issued quit-

John also made grants out of reverence to the saints. The relic collection which accompanied the king as he travelled was recorded in 1212, with candles burning before the relics at Winchester and Bridgnorth.[33] Whilst at Reading Abbey on Sunday after the feast of All Saints 1212, John made an offering of seven bezants. A further payment covered a knight who made gifts alongside the king 'when he saw the relics' on the following day.[34] Meanwhile, records of the royal household indicate the holy days respected at court in 1209–10 and 1212–13: the period of the interdict and the king's excommunication. Amongst the feast days mentioned, those of the Virgin Mary are prominent.[35] During the interdict, priests were urged to encourage observance of the religious calendar, and to promote pilgrimage.[36] Many of these responses fell outside the limitations of the interdict. It is nonetheless striking that John was involved, particularly during his excommunication, when he was supposed to be shunned by the faithful.

In 1213, four months before he was absolved from excommunication, John's religious activity included renewed investment in Beaulieu Abbey.[37] Royal promotion of work on religious buildings also occurred elsewhere. In January 1209, the canons of Lincoln were allowed to move timber and lead for construction work at their cathedral. This came shortly before the election of the royal servant Hugh of Wells as bishop, suggesting that John sought the canons' support for his candidate. In 1213, the Premonstratensian canons of Barlings (Lincolnshire), the canonesses at Broadholme (Nottinghamshire), and the Benedictine nuns of Romsey (Hampshire) received money on account of fires they had suffered.[38] Meanwhile, religious houses continued to request royal documents and to seek confirmation of gifts they had received. For example, in October 1209, when the king's excommunication was imminent, Bradenstoke Priory obtained confirmation of lands granted by William Crassy. John's itinerary suggests that he visited Bradenstoke in February 1211 and July 1212.[39]

The king's religious observance whilst under sanctions included provision for the souls of deceased relatives, such as feeding the poor for Henry II and Richard

---

tance of eight shillings due from this land: *RLC 1204–24*, p. 151b. *Eggeton*', referred to by John, could be Egerton (Kent), near Thurnham Castle, from which Robert's family took its name. However, the letter was addressed to Gilbert fitz Reinfrey, Sheriff of Lancashire, who had only just ceased to be Sheriff of Yorkshire, a county linked to Robert's affairs. Thus, the grant could refer to Egerton (Lancashire), or Egton (Yorkshire). The latter was within accessible range of John's itinerary in September 1213: 'Itinerary'. On Robert: H. Summerson, 'Thornham, Robert of (d. 1211), *ODNB* (Oxford, 2004) [http://www.oxforddnb.com/view/article/27884, accessed 29 August 2013].

[33] *RM*, p. 237; discussed above, Chapter 2.
[34] *RM*, pp. 246, 249. See also above, Chapter 2.
[35] Vincent, 'Mary', pp. 131–2 and n. 27; *RL*, pp. 127, 130, 141, 148, 158; *RM*, pp. 238, 240, 252. See also above, Chapter 2.
[36] Clarke, p. 144.
[37] *RM*, p. 257; discussed above, Chapter 3.
[38] *RLP*, p. 88b; *RM*, pp. 251, 257; Cheney, 'Papal Interdict', p. 310.
[39] *Cartulary of Bradenstoke*, p. 163 (no. 554) and see also p. 131 (no. 428); 'Itinerary'.

I in 1212.⁴⁰ He regularly gave alms, usually in recognition of failing to fast or abstain or on account of hunting on feast days. Such compensatory almsgiving can be found regularly in 1209-10 and 1212-13.⁴¹ Meanwhile, the Cistercian Abbot of Bindon acted as royal almoner. This provides an example of the head of a religious house present at the royal court, even perhaps at the king's table, whilst he was excommunicate.⁴² He was not the only abbot in royal service: Hugh of Beaulieu was regularly to be found travelling – usually to Rome – on the king's business.⁴³

John also encouraged religious communities who sought charity, such as the leper house of Dunstable in 1209. Messengers from Lichfield Cathedral were granted royal protection in 1210, to seek alms for repairs to their church. Protection was afforded to the monks of St Andrew at Northampton.⁴⁴ In the later stages of the interdict, such grants of protection were probably part of a diplomatic drive to win papal support. In late 1213, the hospital of St Mary in Sassia, Pope Innocent's foundation in Rome, received protection so that its envoys could seek alms in England.⁴⁵ The abbot of another Italian church, Cistercian St Martin al Cimino, at Viterbo, came to England with the papal legate Nicholas and received an annual pension of thirty marks from King John. This grant was issued a few weeks before the interdict was lifted.⁴⁶

From 1212 onwards, faced with the threat of domestic revolt, a possible papal sentence of deposition, and, with it, the prospect of French invasion, John became serious about reaching a settlement. Wendover, who argued that the invasion would be a crusade, suggested that, as a long-term excommunicate, John realised that he had gravely offended God and the church.⁴⁷ The king was persuaded to accept Stephen Langton as archbishop of Canterbury and to revoke the sentence of outlawry pronounced against churchmen. John acknowledged that he did not have the authority to impose such a sentence, and assured Langton and the returning bishops that they would exercise their offices without royal interference.⁴⁸ Initial compensation was paid. The papal envoy Pandulf received £8,000 for the returning exiles: £2,500 to be paid to Archbishop Stephen, £1,500 to the bishop of Ely, £1,000 to the Canterbury monks, and £750 each to the bishops of Bath, Hereford, Lincoln, and London. The Canterbury shrine accounts record receipt of just such a payment in 1214. Arrangements were made for lands to

---

40 RM, pp. 241, 243; discussed above, Chapter 4.
41 Discussed above, Chapter 5.
42 RL, pp. 110, 115, 161, 176, 235, 236; PR 13 John, p. 38; discussed above, Chapter 5.
43 Discussed above, Chapter 3.
44 RLP, p. 90a–b; Cheney, 'Papal Interdict', p. 310.
45 RLP, p. 106a; discussed above, Chapter 5.
46 LPI, p. 191 (no. 1171); RC, p. 198b; Cheney, *Innocent*, p. 95 and n. 72; N. Vincent, 'Pandulf (d. 1226)', ODNB (Oxford, 2004) [http://www.oxforddnb.com/view/article/21230, accessed 30 September 2013].
47 Warren, *John*, pp. 199–205; Cheney, 'Alleged Deposition', pp. 100–16; Cheney, *Innocent*, pp. 326–7; Wendover, vol. II, pp. 63–4, 69.
48 RLP, pp. 98b–99a, 100a.

be returned to the exiles. Estates were to be surrendered to their owners or the latter's representatives.[49] John later offered Langton, as further compensation, half the money he sought to extort from Geoffrey de Mandeville for his marriage to Isabella of Gloucester, the king's first wife. As Carpenter has shown, this was a 'toxic debt'. Transferring part of it to Langton 'got rid of a bad debt, compensated the church, and compromised the archbishop all in one go'.[50]

Central to the settlement was the royal submission of the kingdom of England and lordship of Ireland to Pope Innocent III, to be received back as a papal fief. This was initially set out by charter when negotiations concluded in May 1213, then re-issued, sealed with a golden bull, at a ceremony on 3 October 1213 at St Paul's Cathedral in London. Here, the king performed liege homage to the pope at the hands of the newly arrived papal legate Nicholas, cardinal bishop of Tusculum.[51] Oaths, seen as a necessary precursor for lifting ecclesiastical sanctions, were sworn by the king and several barons: William, earl of Salisbury, the king's half-brother, Reginald, count of Boulogne, William, earl of Warenne, and William, Earl Ferrars. These were on peril of John's soul, promising that he would adhere to the peace terms agreed. The king trod a delicate political tightrope. The settlement could be seen as 'ignominious to many and a huge yoke of servitude'. Equally, 'there was no shorter immediate way of avoiding danger'. Papal protection meant that foreign rulers would think twice about attacking England (at least in theory) 'because Pope Innocent was feared by everyone'. One writer observed that John's stock rose in the eyes of his people. The destruction of the French fleet at Damme a fortnight after the submission proved how 'God freed England from impending danger'.[52]

Several chroniclers saw the newly established papal overlordship as fulfilment of the prophecy of the pseudo-prophet Peter of Wakefield (also referred to as Peter of Pontefract), 'that most unwise, because most specific, of prophets', that the reign would come to an end.[53] Peter is said to have preached before John, perhaps when he was at Pontefract in late August 1212, warning the king that unless he corrected his faults and made peace with the church, he would not hold the throne beyond Ascension Day, the first day of the regnal year. John had Peter imprisoned, but apparently became increasingly concerned. The Stanley annalist noted that he 'was

---

[49] RC, pp. 193b-194a; RLP, p. 99b; Cheney, *Innocent*, p. 348; Clarke, p. 241; Nilson, *Cathedral Shrines*, p. 148.

[50] D. A. Carpenter, 'Archbishop Langton and Magna Carta: His Contribution, His Doubts and His Hypocrisy', EHR, 126 (2011), 1041-65 (pp. 1058-60); RLC 1224-27, p. 110b.

[51] LPI, pp. 156 (no. 941), 160 (no. 962); RC, p. 195a-b; RLC 1204-24, pp. 153b-154a; Wendover, vol. II, pp. 74-6. Nicholas had arrived in September 1213: Cheney, *Innocent*, pp. 39, 345.

[52] Barnwell, pp. 209-11; Wendover, vol. II, pp. 69-77; RLP, p. 139a; Clarke, p. 239.

[53] For a summary: J. C. Russell, 'The Development of the Legend of Peter of Pontefract', *Medievalia et Humanistica*, 13 (1960), 21-31. For the quotation: N. Vincent, 'The Strange Case of the Missing Biographies: The Lives of the Plantagenet Kings of England 1154-1272', *Writing Medieval Biography 750-1250: Essays in Honour of Professor Frank Barlow*, ed. D. Bates, J. Crick, and S. Hamilton (Woodbridge, 2006), pp. 237-57 (p. 240).

seriously afraid of death', fearing 'that demons were about to come and seize him', and, more plausibly, that the French king, Philip II, would receive a papal mandate to invade England.[54]

A further problem was that Peter was popularly held to be 'a foreteller of future events' and a wandering preacher. His imprisonment made him more notorious: 'his reputation grew to huge proportions and his name was made excessively famous'. As word spread, rumour made matters worse: 'as is the habit of the masses, lies were added to lies; daily new things were ascribed to him, and each person bringing forth a falsehood from his own heart declared that Peter had said this'. To counter speculation the king had the royal tent erected in an open field on Ascension Day. When no harm came to him, he ordered Peter and his son to be executed.[55] The sentence was apparently carried out in the vicinity of Corfe Castle and Wareham in May 1213. One source noted that they were first dragged through the fields by horses. Another suggests they were dragged from Corfe to Wareham and back.[56] There is, however, no record of opposition to the sentence, nor of Peter's body being secured for burial. He appears to have been notorious, but to have lacked followers.[57]

Nevertheless, he was significant in death. Several accounts describe Peter's prophecy alongside the king's peace with the pope. The benefit of hindsight allowed for the construction of something of a satire on the king's decision to surrender his kingdom of England and lordship of Ireland and to receive them back as papal fiefs. This led writers to argue either that the prophecy was true, because Peter had forecast misfortunes that John later suffered, or that it was shown to be correct because the king placed himself 'under tribute' to Rome.[58] One account argued not only that Peter's words frightened the king into submission but that the 'prophet' explained to his executioners why his words had been proved correct.[59]

It is possible that this can be linked to growing opposition to John, which openly emerged in 1212. Pontefract lay within the inheritance of John de Lacy, who joined the ranks of the king's opponents in 1215. However, prior to this, Lacy was assumed to be loyal to John, so perhaps this link should not be pushed too

---

54 Russell, 'Development of the Legend', p. 25; Stanley, pp. 514–15.
55 Barnwell, pp. 208–12; Wendover, vol. II, pp. 62–3.
56 *Annales Wintonienses in monasterio de Waverley adaucti a. 1201–60*, ed. F. Liebermann, *Ungedruckte Anglo-Normannische Geschichtsquellen* (Strasbourg, 1879), pp. 186–7; Waverley, p. 278; Stanley, p. 515. The latter suggests that Peter and his son were hanged at Wareham. Russell agrees: Russell, 'Development of the Legend', pp. 22–3, 26.
57 Russell, 'Development of the Legend', pp. 29–30; Vincent, 'Master Simon Langton'.
58 Dunstable, p. 34; *The Chronicle of Bury St Edmunds 1212–1301*, ed. and trans. A. Gransden, NMT (London, 1964), p. 1; *Liber Gaufridi Sacristae de Coldingham*, pp. 27–8; *Chronica de Mailros*, p. 113; Russell, 'Development of the Legend', p. 23; Cheney, *Innocent*, pp. 327–8.
59 *Histoire des ducs de Normandie*, pp. 123, 125–6; Russell, 'Development of the Legend', p. 25; Cheney, *Innocent*, p. 328.

far.⁶⁰ The tale came to be associated with the mid-thirteenth-century *Invectivum contra regem Iohannem*, suggesting that it contributed to the fast developing negative portrayal of the reign and, in the context of reaction against Henry III in the 1250s, of Plantagenet kingship more broadly. Certainly it found its place in descriptions of John's reign penned across the thirteenth century, as in the chronicle of Thomas Wykes.⁶¹ By the mid-fourteenth century, Peter was portrayed by Ranulf Higden's *Polychronicon* as a saintly man who had experienced a vision of Christ in the Eucharist. This 'taught him many things, that he told afterwards to bishops and people that were of evil life'.⁶² The legend was later used by Shakespeare.⁶³ Its longevity further demonstrates how chronicler accounts of the reign could evolve into an enduring part of the posthumous critique of John and his rule.

When negotiation finally led to acceptance of Langton as archbishop and the exiles' return, the king was absolved from his excommunication, at Winchester, on 20 July 1213. Although one chronicle considered John reluctant to meet Langton, Wendover writes in terms of outward contrition by the king, who went to meet the archbishop and bishops, 'prostrated himself at their feet, and besought them in tears to have compassion on him and the kingdom of England'. His behaviour was notable for its 'great humility'. The fiftieth psalm, concerning the repentance and confession of King David, was chanted.⁶⁴ Having received the 'customary discipline', John was absolved from excommunication, renewed his coronation oath, and promised to restore seized property. He was led into the cathedral church, where Langton celebrated mass and the king received the sacrament. During the service, he offered a gold mark at the high altar, for the supply of which Aimery de Saint-Maur, the Templar Grand Commander in England, was later reimbursed nine silver marks. The Winchester monks sang the *Te Deum laudamus*.⁶⁵

It seems noteworthy that the ceremony did not take place at Canterbury. John's continued anger with the monks of the cathedral priory there might be a possible reason, alongside Archbishop Langton's reputation as a mediator prepared, in this

---

⁶⁰ A. M. Cooke, 'Wakefield, Peter of (d. 1213)' rev. J. R. Whitehead, *ODNB* (Oxford, 2004) [http://www.oxforddnb.com/view/article/28419, accessed 30 August 2013]; N. Vincent, 'Lacy, John de, Third Earl of Lincoln (c. 1192–1240)', *ODNB* (Oxford, 2004, online edn 2010) [http://www.oxforddnb.com/view/article/15855, accessed 30 August 2013].

⁶¹ Vincent, 'Master Simon Langton'; Russell, 'Development of the Legend', pp. 26–7; *Chronicon vulgo dictum chronicon Thomae Wykes A.D. 1066–1289*, ed. H. R. Luard, *Annales Monastici*, RS 36, 5 vols (London, 1864–69), vol. IV, pp. 56–8.

⁶² *Polychronicon Ranulphi Higden Monachi Cestrensis Together with the English Translations of John Trevisa and of an Unknown Writer of the Fifteenth Century*, ed. C. Babington and J. R. Lumby, RS 41, 9 vols (London, 1865–86), vol. VIII, pp. 192–5; Cooke, 'Wakefield, Peter of'; Russell, 'Development of the Legend', p. 28.

⁶³ William Shakespeare, *King John*, ed. L. A. Beaurline (Cambridge, 1990), pp. 137 (Act 4, Scene 2, lines 147–57), 149 (Act 5, Scene 1, lines 25–9).

⁶⁴ Waverley, p. 276; Wendover, vol. II, pp. 81–2; Barnwell, p. 213; Cheney, *Innocent*, p. 346 n. 97; S. Ambler, 'The Penitent King: John Submits to Archbishop Langton, July 1213', *Magna Carta Research Project Blog* (16 July 2014) [http://magnacartaresearch.blogspot.co.uk/2014/07/the-penitent-king-john-submits-to.html, accessed 19 July 2014].

⁶⁵ Dunstable, pp. 37–8; Waverley, p. 276; Wendover, vol. II, pp. 81–2; *RLC 1204–24*, p. 148b.

instance, to accommodate the king in the interests of reconciliation.⁶⁶ Although the parallels are not exact, Winchester had previously been used for ceremonial linked to restoration of the *status quo* of rulership, when Richard I held a crown-wearing there shortly after returning from captivity (1194). Yet there was also precedent for Canterbury, where Stephen had been re-crowned following his release from captivity in 1141.⁶⁷ John had not been in captivity, but as an excommunicate he had theoretically been cast from the Christian flock. There may have been a sense of the 1213 ceremonial marking a reassertion, even a resumption, of kingly authority.

Where previously John had sought settlement with the church on his terms or not at all, from 1213 onwards he seems to have been engaged in damage limitation. Having been absolved from excommunication, and with the prospect of the interdict being lifted, he was keen to avoid a repeat. There was a danger that troubled relations with Archbishop Langton and the returning exiles would lead them to regard such penalties as a weapon against the king. Thus, John asked Pope Innocent for personal immunity from excommunication, and for a guarantee that his chapel could not be placed under interdict. Innocent responded with a verbal message, but later confirmed the king's wishes in writing in 1214. Such sentences could only be imposed on John by authority of the pope himself.⁶⁸ In addition to indicating the king's desire to avoid a repeat, perhaps this also suggests that he did pay attention to the significance of the sentences he had apparently ignored for so long. Again, there was European precedent. The pope confirmed similar rights to the Aragonese king and queen in 1213.⁶⁹

John also sought to minimise damage to his finances and (unsuccessfully) to his reputation. Religious houses were asked to issue charters stating that they had voluntarily given up property taken from them. Letters sent to communities in the bishopric of Ely referred to 'those things which you gave to us in the time of the interdict which are now called stolen'.⁷⁰ Some abbeys, such as Bath, complied with the king's instructions, but generally the notion that those affected would signify that they had returned their possessions to John out of sheer generosity would not wash with the church authorities. Innocent III ordered such charters to be annulled and seized property restored. If those dispossessed refused to claim their possessions, they were to be used for the benefit of the Holy Land.⁷¹

At Bury St Edmunds, the king's demands formed part of the protracted dispute over the election of the successor to Abbot Samson. The abbey received letters

---

66 J. W. Baldwin, 'Master Stephen Langton, Future Archbishop of Canterbury: The Paris Schools and Magna Carta', *EHR*, 123 (2008), 811–46 (pp. 835–6); Webster, 'Crown, Cathedral and Conflict', pp. 218–19.
67 Gillingham, *Richard*, pp. 271–2; King, *King Stephen*, pp. 176–8. King notes that Richard's second coronation followed the practice adopted at Stephen's.
68 *SLI*, pp. 168–70 (no. 63, at p. 170), 175–6 (no. 66); Cheney, *Innocent*, pp. 350–1.
69 Clarke, p. 124.
70 Coggeshall, p. 165; Waverley, p. 268; Dunstable, p. 34; Barnwell, p. 207; *RLP*, p. 140b.
71 *Two Chartularies of the Priory of St Peter at Bath*, ed. W. Hunt, Somerset Record Society, 7 (London, 1893), part ii, p. 18; *SLI*, pp. 137–8 (no. 46).

almost identical to those sent to religious communities within the bishopric of Ely, with the royal envoys playing off and pressurising the factions within the abbey in the hope of getting their way.[72] An alternative was to make concessions in return for writing off royal debts. Thus, rights offered in the king's confirmation charter to Cartmel Priory were extended to the community's tenants in return for a palfrey and agreement that John would not repay two hundred marks taken during the interdict.[73] This arrangement was made a few weeks after Magna Carta (1215), suggesting that the issue of repayments was still a live one, and that the king was prepared to make concessions to keep his allies onside. One of his most important supporters, William Marshal, was the abbey's founder and principal patron.

Ecclesiastical commentators, however, considered John's treatment of religious communities during the years of sanctions and concluded that he was little better than a thief, reflecting the damage to the royal image of apparently turning against the church. Coggeshall wrote that Langton and his fellow bishops had been robbed, noting arrangements made for payments to continue 'until the whole cost of the robbing has been compensated'. Other writers echoed this view. Richard de Morins, prior of Dunstable, was involved in investigating the losses sustained. Thus, the Dunstable annals concluded that twenty-three thousand marks' worth of damage had been done in the bishopric of Lincoln, whilst twenty thousand marks would be required to compensate the Canterbury monks. Dunstable Priory had incurred damage costing £443.[74]

John's compensatory activity, such as it was, says more about his need for allies and political stability than it does about a wish to pay. The returning exiles secured fifteen thousand marks in late 1213, but some commentators saw this as an effort to buy episcopal support.[75] In seeking the loyalty of Bishop Eustace of Ely, the king granted him the advowson of Thorney Abbey (Cambridgeshire). He imposed the 'curse of God' against anyone acting against his orders.[76] Ultimately, John's prevarication, coupled with the defeat of his continental ambitions in 1214, must have ensured that most of the compensation for his exploitation of church property during the interdict remained unpaid. This had been reckoned at one hundred thousand marks in a settlement imposed by the pope in early 1214, of which forty thousand marks were to be paid before the sentence was annulled, with the remainder to follow in annual instalments. Even the initial down-payment was postponed. The interdict was lifted on 2 July 1214.[77] The civil war that followed Magna Carta probably ensured that all chance of payment was lost.

---

72 *Chronicle of the Election*, pp. 132–47.
73 *Lancashire Pipe Rolls*, p. 247; *RC*, pp. 215b–216a; Farrer and Brownbill, *VCH Lancaster*, vol. II, p. 144.
74 Coggeshall, pp. 168–9; Dunstable, p. 39. See also: Stanley, p. 515; Worcester, p. 402; Cheney, *Innocent*, pp. 348–55. On the extent of Prior Richard's involvement in writing the Dunstable annals: Cheney, 'Notes on the Making of the Dunstable Annals', pp. 79–98.
75 *EEA 26*, p. 102 (no. 105); *RLP*, p. 106a–b; Waverley, p. 278; Cheney, *Innocent*, p. 351 n. 121.
76 *EEA 42*, pp. 76–7 (no. 84); *RLP*, p. 124a; *RC*, p. 204a–b; Cheney, *Innocent*, pp. 362–3. See also *Letters and Charters of Cardinal Guala*, pp. 129–33 (no. 158).
77 Cheney, *Innocent*, pp. 351–3; Clarke, p. 241; Warren, *John*, p. 210.

In many ways, the king was keen to return to business as usual in dealing with the church. Whilst under sanctions, he had treated elections as he had done in the past, indicating his belief in the continuity of royal rights. When Innocent III authorised elections to five vacant sees in 1209, the king quickly sought to secure the bishoprics for his own men. At Lichfield, he sought the election first of Henry of London, then of Abbot Henry of Bindon and Richard Marsh, before threatening force to secure the choice of the royal chancellor, Walter de Gray. Henry of London was then 'chosen' at Exeter. Both elections were promptly quashed when approval was sought from Archbishop Langton. Another royal appointee, Hugh of Wells, sought confirmation and was consecrated bishop of Lincoln by Langton, presumably having indicated that he would remain with the exiles.[78]

During the period of settlement of the interdict, John found the papal legate, Nicholas de Romanis, cardinal bishop of Tusculum, to be a willing ally. Once absolved from excommunication, John quickly sought to fill vacant positions, emphasising royal rights by referring to elections occurring according to the customs of England. Prior to the legate's arrival, the king's efforts were not notably successful. However, Nicholas was charged by the pope to handle the matter of elections, and with his compliance the king secured his preferred appointments to bishoprics and abbacies. This was not always straightforward. John de Gray, bishop of Norwich, died before he could be successfully translated to Durham. The king was unable to secure the translation of Peter des Roches to York, which in turn prevented Richard Marsh becoming bishop of Winchester. Marsh, who also failed to be 'elected' bishop of Ely, became bishop of Durham after John's death. Another royal candidate, the chancellor Walter de Gray, was again rejected at Lichfield, elected to Worcester, and then translated to York. Meanwhile, William of Cornhill, royal clerk and archdeacon of Huntingdon, became bishop of Lichfield. The papal sub-deacon Pandulf, who had not been active in England for some time, succeeded John de Gray at Norwich, although he was not consecrated until 1222.[79]

As his political problems mounted after his return to England in the autumn of 1214, following the military setback at La-Roche-aux-Moines and his allies' disastrous defeat at the battle of Bouvines, John issued his important charter granting the principle of free elections to cathedral and monastic communities. This was given forever, for the wellbeing of the king's soul, and for those of his predecessors and successors as king of England.[80] Whilst in part the product of John's immediate political circumstances, the concession perhaps owed much to the influence of the legate Nicholas. It reflected a European trend, similar concessions being made in Sicily, the Empire, Austria, and Aragon during Innocent III's pontificate.[81] The charter was reissued in January 1215 and included in Magna Carta in

---

[78] Cheney, *Innocent*, pp. 130-1, 133, 156-8.
[79] Cheney, *Innocent*, pp. 76-7, 131-2, 159-75, 394; Vincent, 'Pandulf'.
[80] *Councils and Synods with Other Documents Relating to the English Church. II. A.D. 1205-1313. Part I. 1205-1265*, ed. F. M. Powicke and C. R. Cheney (Oxford, 1964), pp. 38-41; Harvey, *Episcopal Appointments*, pp. 19-28.
[81] Harvey, *Episcopal Appointments*, pp. 21-2.

June. The commitment to free elections was not included in the re-issues of 1216 and 1217, probably due to the influence of Nicholas' successor as papal legate, Guala Bicchieri, whilst Langton was absent from England. Nonetheless, freedom of the church was part of the enduring re-issue of 1225. Carpenter sees this as Archbishop Langton's 'great work'.[82] In 1214–15, the grant helped cement support from Rome, but in England, few can have expected the influence of the royal will to decline in church 'elections'. At Bury St Edmunds, the king's envoys had instructed the electors that 'it behoves you to preserve his [John's] privileges and liberties unhurt and unimpaired', and that penalties would follow if they did not. The king himself visited the chapter, asking them to 'proceed in obedience to my customary rights'. Adopting a conciliatory tone, he nonetheless warned the monks that to ignore his advice would be to 'incur your ruler's hatred'.[83]

The charter of free elections followed these events within days. It addressed an issue at the heart of the Canterbury dispute. There was an implicit recognition that the methods John had previously employed, with their origins in the behaviour of his predecessors, would no longer work. The custom of summoning electors to make their selection under his watchful eye now lapsed, as did the practice of the king picking his preferred candidate from a list of nominees. Yet he retained substantial opportunity to influence proceedings. He could give licence to elect and agree to the choice, he could still hold episcopal revenues until a choice had been made, and he could still send representatives to an election. As Harvey points out, the charter did much to clarify the king's position. This was to John's advantage. It may even have been his choice to send the charter to Pope Innocent for his confirmation.[84]

The king's close alliance with Cardinal Nicholas did not go unnoticed. The legate was sent as 'an angel of peace and salvation' as the pope responded to 'the need to give absolution to a sinful but repentant ruler who asked for it'.[85] Nicholas had a near impossible task: balancing the interests of the victims of the king's exploitation, of John, and of the king's new overlord, the pope. For commentators in England, this did not mean allowing the monarch to have his way in ecclesiastical matters, which seemed to be happening all too often. The cardinal took the blame. He 'was too favourable to the king in settling causes and matters relating to the church', 'favoured the regal excesses', and 'greedily placed his relatives in ecclesiastical benefices'. Ultimately, this led to his recall to Rome, in December 1214. The chroniclers believed he had been summoned to explain his conduct, although Cheney notes that Nicholas' return meant that a cardinal sympathetic to John was at the curia precisely when Magna Carta came to the pope's attention. He was succeeded by Guala Bicchieri, cardinal priest of San Martino, who came to

---

[82] Harvey, *Episcopal Appointments*, pp. 24–6; Holt, *Magna Carta*, pp. 448–51; Cheney, *Innocent*, p. 169; Carpenter, 'Archbishop Langton', pp. 1050–7.
[83] *Chronicle of the Election*, pp. 84–5, 118–19; Cheney, *Innocent*, p. 127.
[84] Cheney, *Innocent*, pp. 168–75, 363–6; Harvey, *Episcopal Appointments*, pp. 19–21, 23–5.
[85] *SLI*, p. 154 (no. 55); Cheney, *Innocent*, p. 342.

England in May 1216 and became a central figure in the final weeks of John's reign and the first two years of Henry III's minority.[86]

The Canterbury dispute, interdict, and royal excommunication set the scene for consistently negative portrayal of John's kingship in the years that followed, in which evidence of his capacity for religious responses was overlooked. The observation that, after the settlement, the king 'began to be improved' is not characteristic of the general view.[87] As we have seen, this had an impact on opinions expressed about the insufficiency of reparations paid to the church. Meanwhile, there was considerable scepticism about the king's promise to crusade.

A new campaign to the east had been proclaimed in 1213.[88] Following Bouvines in 1214, a five-year truce had been drawn up between John and Philip II of France. Innocent III noted the king of England's claim that this was 'in order that relief may be brought more quickly to the Holy Land'. One chronicler observed that it was for 'those who had proposed to undertake the journey to Jerusalem'.[89] As his political problems mounted in England in 1215, John took the cross, on Ash Wednesday (4 March), at St Paul's Cathedral in London. He encouraged members of his household to join him, 'offering white crosses like his own, just like those of his brother or father'. The king's vow, widely recorded by the narrative sources, was made under the supervision of the bishop of London, William de Ste-Mère-Église, one of the former executors of the interdict.[90] It was made on a suitable religious occasion, with symbolic similarity between ceremonial for the beginning of Lent and that associated with the vow to crusade. Both involved participants being marked with the sign of the cross. Yet the writers of the day were not convinced. Even the Barnwell annalist, who was often less hostile than most, observed that many voiced doubts, arguing 'that he had done this not in respect of piety or from love of Christ, but to cheat them by design'. Others were less restrained. The Stanley annalist wrote that John 'had in his mind no reverence for God or for the holy church or for the people of England; but towards their destruction he prepared himself and his men'. Wendover felt that the king was 'induced to this more by fear than devotion'.[91]

Later historians agree: 'We may be pretty sure that the king had no intention of going to the land of Jerusalem ... There seems no particle of evidence that

---

[86] Coggeshall, pp. 167, 170; Barnwell, pp. 216-17; Cheney, *Innocent*, pp. 40-1, 368-9; B. M. Bolton, 'Guala (c. 1150-1227)', *ODNB* (Oxford, 2004) [http://www.oxforddnb.com/view/article/50349, accessed 1 October 2013]; *Letters and Charters of Cardinal Guala*, pp. xxxviii-xliii; F. A. Cazel Jr, 'The Legates Guala and Pandulf', *TCE* II, ed. P. R. Coss and S. D. Lloyd (Woodbridge, 1988), pp. 15-21.

[87] Barnwell, p. 210.

[88] J. Riley-Smith, *The Crusades: A Short History* (London, 1990), pp. 141-5.

[89] *SLI*, p. 192 (no. 72); Barnwell, p. 216.

[90] Barnwell, p. 219; Wendover, vol. II, p. 114; Worcester, pp. 403, 404; GR, p. 109; Coggeshall, p. 171; Cazel Jr, 'Ste Mère-Église, William de'. Wendover dates John's vow to the feast of the Purification of the Virgin (2 February). Other sources agree on Ash Wednesday (4 March). The Worcester annalist gives both 1214 and Ash Wednesday 1215.

[91] Barnwell, p. 219; Stanley, p. 518; Wendover, vol. II, p. 114.

King John was preparing for an expedition to the Holy Land.'[92] His dispute with the church, then with the barons, did nothing to suggest that John was a man of his word. The vow looked like a carefully timed political move. With a growing number of opponents, who would ultimately force him to agree to Magna Carta, it was to the king's advantage, having already granted his kingdom to Innocent III as a papal fief, to seek the protection traditionally offered to crusaders. John's assumption of the cross enhanced his ability to rely on papal support, which proved significant during the king's struggles with the barons. When Magna Carta was presented to Innocent, he is said to have read it carefully, before exclaiming:

> Are the barons of England endeavouring to drive from the throne of his kingdom a king who has taken the cross, and who is under the protection of the apostolic see, and to transfer to another the dominion of the Roman Church? By St Peter, we cannot pass over this insult without punishing it![93]

The chroniclers' scepticism seems to be justified by the limited evidence of John's provision for fulfilling his vow. A boat, the Hulk of Tykesfleet, under the command of Henry, the son of Reginald of Winchelsea, was prepared for the king's journey to the Holy Land. As Vincent observes, royal letters were written in a way which suggested that 'the king had a genuine intention of setting out'.[94] Magna Carta provided that, in certain cases, the king 'was to have respite for the usual crusader's term'. Even here, there is a sense of scepticism. Arrangements stipulated that justice was to be done immediately upon his return or, more tellingly, 'if perhaps we do not undertake' the expedition.[95] Overall, whilst John did not entirely ignore his promise, it can hardly be said that he was preparing a major military expedition.

The reign closed with the chroniclers accusing the king's troops of sacrilegious actions during the civil war that followed Magna Carta. A powerful sense of anti-royal feeling was combined with the impact of events taking place within chroniclers' churches and cloisters, perpetrated by those acting in John's name. Ralph of Coggeshall backed the king's opponents, describing them as the 'army of God'. He added that the barons took exception to their excommunication by the pope, since this 'had been brought through the instigation of a false accuser'. Ralph was particularly well informed about events in Essex (the site of his monastery), Kent, and East Anglia. He noted how mercenaries led by Savary de Mauléon embarked on a roving scorched-earth campaign. On Christmas Day 1215, 'they entered with violence the church and offices of Tilty, while the solemn mass after terce was being celebrated, and overturned all their goods, and destroying many storehouses, they seized and carried off the many things deposited there'. A few days later, at Coggeshall, again during terce, 'they entered the church with violence and took

---

[92] Cheney, *Innocent*, pp. 262-3.
[93] Wendover, vol. II, p. 139; Cheney, *Innocent*, pp. 382-6, 390-1.
[94] *RLP*, p. 186b; Vincent, *Peter des Roches*, pp. 118-19; S. Lloyd, *English Society and the Crusade 1216-1307* (Oxford, 1988), p. 209 n. 45.
[95] Holt, *Magna Carta*, pp. 464-9 (chapters 52, 53, and 57); Cheney, *Innocent*, p. 262.

away twenty-two horses'. An attack on the Isle of Ely targeted men and women, lay and religious: 'they destroyed churches, too, and stole what had been deposited in them'. For Ralph, it was principally John who was the problem. He switched his allegiance when Henry III became king, siding with the royalists against Louis of France and his baronial supporters.[96]

In their portrayal of sacrilege by those supporting John, the chroniclers reflected the assumptions of men of religion and the concerns of those faced with the horrors of war. They were particularly hostile to the king's use of mercenaries 'to the confusion and destruction of the Holy Church and all the people'. One writer estimated that John employed over 'fifteen thousand impious men who disregarded God and did not respect men'. Wendover all but celebrated the drowning of the mercenary captain Hugh de Boves in 1215 as an instance in which 'the grace of God altered their purpose for the better'. These hired soldiers were 'limbs of the devil' who 'ransacked towns, houses, cemeteries and churches, robbing everyone'. Churchmen were not exempt: 'even the priests while standing at the very altars, with the cross of the Lord in their hands, clad in their sacred robes, were seized, tortured, robbed and ill-treated'. Yet Roger contradicts himself, suggesting that church precincts were the only safe place: 'goods were exposed for sale only in churchyards ... no one dared to go beyond the limits of the churches'.[97] Nor were soldiers supposed to transgress these boundaries. A defendant at the York assizes in 1218–19 argued that he had lost his hand during the civil war, having unlawfully taken a cow from a churchyard.[98]

Unpalatably, the king may have justified his soldiers' action in terms of the military and political needs of the moment. The sacking of houses such as Coggeshall may well have been driven by the mercenaries' need for day-to-day finance. Elsewhere, as at Bury St Edmunds and Crowland, John's supporters sought either to deprive their opponents of supplies stored in these communities or targeted houses believed to sympathise with (or actively support) the king's opponents. Perpetrators might have argued that, in taking sides, a religious community had crossed the line between secular affairs and the seclusion of the cloister. The Worcester annalist felt that this explained the treatment of his community. The town had backed Louis of France. When it was captured by King John's supporters, the cathedral was plundered and three hundred marks exacted. Metalwork from St Wulfstan's shrine had to be handed over. The monks were treated 'as if excommunicated', having celebrated mass whilst John's enemies were in Worcester. They 'had scarcely been let off on the day of Assumption' (15 August), although the king was present in the city on the day after this feast.[99]

---

[96] Coggeshall, pp. 171, 177–9; Gransden, *Historical Writing*, p. 327.

[97] Stanley, pp. 520–1; Wendover, vol. II, pp. 147–8, 165–6.

[98] *Rolls of the Justices in Eyre, being the Rolls of Pleas and Assizes for Yorkshire in 3 Henry III, 1218–9*, ed. D. M. Stenton, Selden Society, 56 (London, 1937), pp. 310–11 (no. 851). See also: Poole, *From Domesday Book*, p. 481; S. McGlynn, *Blood Cries Afar: The Forgotten Invasion of England 1216* (Stroud, 2011), p. 158.

[99] M. Strickland, *War and Chivalry: The Conduct and Perception of War in England and Normandy, 1066–1217* (Cambridge, 1996), pp. 90, 268; Worcester, pp. 406–7; 'Itinerary'.

Some houses sought to avert damage. At St Albans, financial inducements were offered to stave off the forces both of John and Louis, although the latter pillaged the abbey in 1217. When Ely was attacked, the prior negotiated with the king's forces as they plundered the cathedral or its precincts. The burning of the church was prevented 'with difficulty' and the payment of nine silver marks. Stephen Ridel, who had served John before he became king and was now archdeacon of Ely, was dragged from the church. Through payment of one hundred marks his life was spared but 'he lost all he possessed, his horses, books, household goods and utensils'.[100] However, others escaped entirely. The church of St Peter and St Wilfrid at Ripon recorded that, during the civil war, nothing was taken from the community, either from its fee or liberty.[101] Meanwhile, a church such as Rochester Cathedral, where John allegedly stabled horses and billeted soldiers in 1215, was an ideal location for a besieging army to camp, given its immediate proximity to the town's castle. Nor was the king the first or last to pursue this strategy. His Norman kinsman, William the Conqueror's eldest son Robert Curthose, had turned nunnery buildings at Almenêches into stables in 1100. Nearly fifty years after John's siege of Rochester, the cathedral's potential utility to a besieging army was recognised in 1264 by Simon de Montfort, a man otherwise renowned for his respect for religion.[102]

Whatever the king's view of actions taken in his name, it is clear that the commentators of the day increasingly saw them as the sacrilegious actions of an irreligious king. Unlike Henry I, who lived for some thirty years after his dispute with Archbishop Anselm, and Henry II, who survived for eighteen years after the murder of Archbishop Thomas Becket, King John died during the crises generated by his rule. He had not convinced anyone that he was serious about making reparations to the church following the resolution of the Canterbury dispute. Nobody believed he would go on crusade. Nor did he seem to contemplate observing Magna Carta, hence the civil war and French invasion. Like William Rufus, John died before his reputation could be restored. The sheer quantity of setbacks he had suffered may in any case have made this impossible. The arbiters and administrators of his last testament made some effort to make reparation for damages inflicted in his name during the civil war.[103] Overall, however, John's treatment of the church created a reputation which overshadowed all evidence of his engagement with the religious during his lifetime.

---

[100] Strickland, *War*, p. 84; *Wendover*, vol. II, pp. 171-2; *EEA 31. Ely 1109-1197*, ed. N. Karn (Oxford, 2005), p. lxxix; Vincent, 'Jean', p. 57.

[101] *Memorials of the Church of SS Peter and Wilfrid, Ripon. Vol. I*, ed. J. T. Fowler, Surtees Society, 74 (Durham, London and Edinburgh, 1882 for 1881), p. 59; Holt, *Northerners*, p. 134 n. 1; McGlynn, *Blood Cries*, p. 158.

[102] Coggeshall, p. 176; Hicks, *Religious Life*, p. 129; W. M. Aird, *Robert Curthose: Duke of Normandy (c. 1050–1134)* (Woodbridge, 2008), p. 220. De Montfort's use of Rochester Cathedral is found in an excerpt from the so-called 'Matthew of Westminster', printed in *The Chronicle of William de Rishanger of the Barons' Wars. The Miracles of Simon de Montfort*, ed. J. O. Halliwell, Camden Society, Old Series 15 (London, 1840), pp. 126-8.

[103] Discussed below, Chapter 8.

8

King John's Deathbed and Beyond

King John died on the night of 18/19 October 1216, during a civil war very much of his own making, far from being master of his kingdom. Nonetheless, evidence for royal religion can be found up until the very end. Days before his death, part of the king's baggage train became trapped in quicksands whilst his entourage undertook a dangerous estuary crossing before the tide went out, in the so-called 'disaster in the Wash'.[1] Losses included John's chapel and the relics carried with it, suggesting that even amidst a crisis in which the king travelled the country at speed and on a war footing, he kept means of attending services close at hand.[2]

John was already ill at this time, and perhaps knew some days before his death that he was suffering his last illness, probably dysentery.[3] On 10 October, the king made a grant to Margaret de Lacy, for her Hospitaller foundation at Aconbury (Herefordshire).[4] Between 1208 and 1211, John had hounded Margaret's father, William de Briouze, into exile and ordered the deaths of her mother, Matilda, and her brother (also William). He had confiscated the lands of Walter de Lacy (Margaret's husband), who had supported Briouze, only restoring them in the period 1213–15. Walter could well have secured the concession from the dying king, as 'a constant presence in the royal entourage in the dog days of John's rule'. Equally, John's grant could have been motivated by political–religious reasoning: appearing to atone for his actions whilst seeking to regain and retain the Lacys' goodwill. A sense of reconciliation is suggested by Margaret's later comment, in correspondence with Pope Gregory IX, that the community had been founded in John's memory.[5] A further letter issued from John's deathbed, requesting final absolution from all his sins from Pope Honorius III, suggests his concern for the future of his soul.[6] These examples seem representative of the fears of a dying man, 'significant of the remorse awakened in him ... by the terror of approaching death'.[7] They were also in keeping with John's longer-term attitude. He realised the importance of provision for his soul.

---

[1] See above, Chapters 1 and 2.
[2] Coggeshall, pp. 183–4.
[3] Barnwell, p. 231; Church, 'King John's Testament', p. 519.
[4] *RLP*, p. 199b; H. J. Nicholson, 'Margaret de Lacy and the Hospital of St John at Aconbury, Herefordshire', *JEH*, 50 (1999), 629–51. Aconbury was re-founded in 1237 for Augustinian canonesses, at Margaret's instigation, following a bitter dispute.
[5] Church, 'King John's Testament', p. 523; Nicholson, 'Margaret de Lacy', p. 633.
[6] *Letters and Charters of Cardinal Guala*, pp. 105–6 (no. 140b).
[7] K. Norgate, *John Lackland* (London, 1902), p. 281.

Gillingham has identified provision for burial and the welfare of the soul, and concern for the succession, as principle concerns of post-Conquest kings at the point of death.[8] Few chroniclers provided detailed accounts of John's deathbed itself. However, Wendover gives the impression that John, like his predecessors, had a sense of these priorities. Despite referring critically to 'the sin of the father' which 'ought not to be charged to the son', Roger noted that in John's last hours he 'confessed himself and received the Eucharist'. Having named his heir, he was asked where he would like to be buried, and commended his body and soul to the care of God and St Wulfstan of Worcester. The biographer of William Marshal had been told 'that he was most truly repentant'. Even Matthew Paris offered some crumbs of comfort:

> it is, however, confidently to be hoped that some good works, which he performed in this life, may plead in his favour at the tribunal of Jesus Christ; for he founded a monastery of the Cistercian order at Beaulieu and, when dying, gave to the monastery of Croxton land worth ten pounds.

Nonetheless, Paris could not resist quoting a popular rhyme, which claimed that hell was made worse by John's presence.[9]

In terms of burial, earlier in the reign the king had expressed a wish to be buried at the Cistercian monastery he had founded at Beaulieu.[10] However, in 1216, John's last testament expressed a 'desire that my body be buried in the church of the Blessed Virgin and St Wulfstan at Worcester', where he was laid to rest, on or around 23 October 1216.[11] If Beaulieu objected, the community did not voice their opposition until 1228, when they petitioned Pope Honorius III to have the body transferred to their abbey church. At the time, they had the backing of Henry III, whose supporting letter wrote of the disturbance besetting the kingdom when John died, preventing burial at his preferred location. Nothing came of the petition. Henry was present at Worcester Cathedral in 1232 when his father's body was moved to its new tomb.[12]

Despite the civil war in 1216, due ceremony and reverence was accorded to John's funeral. The body was dressed in royal robes, perhaps including the king's 'coif of

---

[8] J. Gillingham, 'At the Deathbeds of the Kings of England, 1066–1216', *Herrscher- und Fürstentestamente im Westeuropäischen Mittelalter*, ed. B. Kasten (Cologne, Weimar, and Vienna, 2008), pp. 509–30 (p. 509).

[9] Wendover, vol. II, pp. 196, 198; *History of William Marshal*, ed. A. J. Holden, trans. S. Gregory, and historical notes by D. Crouch, Anglo-Norman Text Society, Occasional Publications Series, 4, 3 vols (London, 2002–06), vol. II, pp. 260–1 (lines 15199–200); *Matthaei Parisiensis*, vol. II, pp. 668–9.

[10] Howden, vol. IV, p. 145; Coggeshall, p. 109; *Annales de Margan*, p. 25.

[11] Church, 'King John's Testament', pp. 505, 516–18. On the process of royal burial between the Norman Conquest and John's accession: Church, 'Aspects of the English Succession'.

[12] *Foedera, Conventiones, Litterae et cujuscunque generis Acta Publica inter Reges Angliae et alios quosuis imperatores, reges, pontifices, principes vel communitates ab ingressu Gulielmi I in Angliam, A.D. 1066 ad nostra usque tempora habita aut tractate*, ed. T. Rymer, new edn ed. A. Clark and F. Holbrooke, 4 vols (London, 1816–69), vol. I, part 1, 1066–1272, p. 192; Draper, pp. 43–4; Jenkins, 'The King's Beaulieu', pp. 58–9; St John Hope and Brakspear, pp. 138–9.

unction'. William Marshal provided silk cloths to cover the tomb, suggesting that, in the years following John's death, it 'was marked with no more than a slab'.[13] The papal legate Guala joined Marshal in making reparation for damages inflicted on the prior and monks of Worcester earlier in the year. The community was granted part of the bailey of Worcester castle. Archbishops Walter of York and Henry of Dublin and Bishops Jocelin of Bath and Silvester of Worcester were also present, along with Ranulf, earl of Chester, William, Earl Ferrars, Walter de Lacy, John of Monmouth, Hugh de Mortemer, Walter Clifford, and Roger Clifford.[14] The location of the tomb, in front of the high altar, between the shrines of St Wulfstan and St Oswald, attracted comment, perhaps at the time of the funeral and certainly after remodelling of the east end of the cathedral during the thirteenth century. One of the so-called prophecies of Merlin, that the king would be stationed amongst the saints, had been fulfilled.[15]

Amongst John's predecessors, dispute over place of burial was not entirely unusual. Nor were they always interred where they had requested. Empress Matilda was buried at Bec in 1167, but when her death was feared imminent in 1134 had argued against her father's desire that she be buried in Rouen Cathedral. In 1183, John's eldest brother, Henry the Young King was buried at Le Mans, like his grandfather Geoffrey V of Anjou. Henry II, however, had his eldest son re-interred at Rouen. Henry II was himself entombed at Fontevraud, despite previously expressing a desire to lie at Grandmont. John's son and heir, Henry III, asked first to rest in the New Temple in London, before his ambitious plans for Westminster provided a new setting.[16]

A variety of reasons have been advanced for King John's choice of Worcester in 1216. Martindale argues that his pilgrimage of 1207, when he prayed at the shrine of St Wulfstan, provides the origin of his decision. Draper and Mason agree that attachment to the saint is likely to have determined his choice. Duffy argues that Beaulieu was rejected because the Cistercians complied with the interdict. This seems unlikely. The king resumed support for his foundation as the sanctions

---

[13] *History of William Marshal*, vol. II, pp. 262-3 (lines 15207-28); J. Martindale, 'The Sword on the Stone: Some Resonances of a Medieval Symbol of Power (The Tomb of King John in Worcester Cathedral)', ANS, 15 (1992), 199-241 (p. 204); Carpenter, 'Burial', pp. 435-6; *Roll of Divers Accounts*, p. 36.

[14] *Letters and Charters of Cardinal Guala*, p. 99 (no. 138); *Worcester Cartulary*, pp. 174-6 (nos 328, 328a, and see also 329). The respective rights of those holding land in the bailey of Worcester castle were subsequently disputed. In 1276, William de Beauchamp, Earl of Warwick, surrendered his family's rights there in return for services in memory of his father: *Worcester Cartulary*, pp. 287-8 (nos 534-5), 292 (no. 541).

[15] Wendover, vol. II, p. 196; Worcester, p. 407. Crook notes that John's known wishes do not mention burial between Oswald and Wulfstan – all such references are of later date: Crook, 'Physical Setting', p. 209 and n. 116, and pp. 211-12.

[16] Chibnall, *Empress Matilda*, pp. 190-2; Green, *Henry I*, p. 217; E. Hallam, 'Henry (1155-1183)', ODNB (Oxford, 2004, online edn 2006) [http://www.oxforddnb.com/view/article/12957, accessed 22 May 2014]; Wood, 'Fontevraud', pp. 413-14; C. T. Wood, 'La mort et les funérailles d'Henri II', *Cahiers de Civilisation Médiévale*, 37 (1994), 119-23; Carpenter, 'Burial', pp. 433-4.

came to an end. Mason further suggests that John's understanding of the legend of Wulfstan's staff explains his insistence on being buried next to the saint's tomb.[17]

Yet in many ways the choice was dictated by the territorial situation. One commentator observed that John was interred at Worcester 'not because he had chosen burial there, but because that place seemed more secure at that point of time'.[18] His actions during the civil war do not suggest that he was thinking of Worcester Cathedral as a potential burial church. In 1216 the community bore the brunt of punishment for the city's support for Louis of France, with the cathedral plundered and three hundred marks exacted, necessitating the handover of metalwork from Wulfstan's tomb.[19] We might expect a king who had planned to be buried in Worcester since as early as 1207 to have shown more concern for the shrine beside which he supposedly wished to be interred.

However, various alternatives were unavailable. Fontevraud, the Angevin mausoleum, had been so since 1204, as had Rouen, home of the body of John's brother Henry and the heart of his brother Richard.[20] In 1216, Louis of France controlled most of southern England, which ruled out Beaulieu. If the choice of Worcester was made out of military necessity, we should also consider the role of the courtiers who surrounded the dying king. Several churchmen were named in John's final testament: the papal legate Guala, Peter des Roches, bishop of Winchester, Richard Poor, bishop of Chichester, Silvester, bishop of Worcester, and Brother Aimery de St-Maur, Master of the Templars in England. Of these, the bishops of Winchester, Worcester, and Chichester are thought to have been present at the king's deathbed.[21] They are likely to have been charged with ensuring that John's body received safe and dignified burial. Abbot Adam of Croxton, also in attendance, may have harboured hopes. Premonstratensian Croxton (Leicestershire) was the foundation of one of John's predecessors as count of Mortain, William, second son of King Stephen. Adam obtained the right to bury the king's entrails. The abbey claimed to have John's heart in 1257, although several historians note the possibility that this ended up at Fontevraud.[22] Bishop Silvester of Worcester was a logical choice as custodian of John's body. Winchester and Chichester, like Beaulieu, lay in territory controlled by royal opponents. Likewise, Louis of France held London, so even had the Master of the Temple in England been present, burial at the New Temple – not inconceivable given the king's reliance on the order in his

---

[17] Martindale, 'Sword', p. 204; Draper, p. 48; Mason, 'Wulfstan's Staff', p. 157; M. Duffy, *Royal Tombs of Medieval England* (Stroud, 2003), p. 61; Mason, 'Wulfstan'.

[18] Barnwell, p. 232.

[19] Worcester, pp. 406-7; 'Itinerary'; discussed above, Chapter 7.

[20] Wood, 'Fontevraud', p. 422 n. 51; Draper, p. 43. The Rouen connection was maintained. Isabella of Angoulême's obit was inscribed in the cathedral's martyrology in 1251: Vincent, 'Mary', p. 144 n. 95.

[21] Church, 'King John's Testament', pp. 519-26.

[22] Barnwell, p. 232; CChR 1226-1257, p. 463; Binski, *Westminster Abbey*, p. 92; Mason, 'Westminster Abbey and the Monarchy', p. 215 n. 119; Palliser, 'Royal Mausolea', p. 2; Boase, 'Fontevraud', p. 7. On Croxton: Knowles and Hadcock, p. 187; Knowles, Brooke, and London, *Heads*, p. 194.

later years – was out of the question. It is nonetheless striking that at least three religious houses in England (Beaulieu, Croxton, and Worcester Cathedral) and perhaps one in the former Angevin lands in France (Fontevraud) can be associated with burial (or claims to burial) of all or part of King John, with the associated expectations linked to commemoration of his soul.

This perhaps helps to explain why Beaulieu felt that its claim should be respected after the civil war ended. It is questionable whether the abbey was sufficiently complete to receive a royal burial in 1216, when it seems that only the footings of the church were complete, so that any tomb would be open to the elements and a potential encumbrance on ongoing work.[23] In 1227, the monks moved into the choir of their church. They did not petition for John's body to be transferred until 1228, suggesting that there was nowhere suitable to receive it before then. The abbey acquired a significant tomb only in 1240, that of Isabella Marshal, first wife of John's younger son Richard of Cornwall. This burial negotiated clashing religious and family loyalties. Her heart was interred at Tewkesbury alongside her first husband, Gilbert de Clare. She did not otherwise favour Beaulieu, so that this was her body's final resting place presumably reflects the wishes of John's sons, either her second husband, Richard, or his brother Henry III. Her tomb before the high altar perhaps occupied the site originally earmarked for John. Even then, the monastery church was still incomplete. It was not dedicated until 1246.[24]

That Worcester Cathedral embraced the opportunity to house a royal burial is shown by the care taken in construction and maintenance of John's tomb and the area surrounding it. The king's reputation suffered following his death, but the community that cared for his body ensured that he was appropriately commemorated. Bishop Silvester provided annual revenues for lights around the tomb, suggesting that commemorative responsibilities were taken seriously.[25] From 1218, John lay at the devotional heart of the church. On 7 June of that year, Silvester translated St Oswald and St Wulfstan to their new shrines, which lay either side of the grave of King John, and rededicated the cathedral church. The ceremonies had the character of a state occasion. The boy-king Henry III was in attendance, with Archbishop Langton, ten bishops, numerous abbots and priors, and many leading men of the kingdom. Relics of St Wulfstan were distributed, with Langton taking a piece of the saint's right arm, and William of Trumpington, abbot of St Albans, obtaining a rib. Bishop Silvester was criticised for glorifying in cutting up relics with an axe.[26] On the one hand, 1218 was perhaps the first practical opportunity for consecration after the interdict and civil war. For Worcester, it provided an opportunity to advertise the cult of St Wulfstan. Equally, the government of

---

[23] Jenkins, 'The King's Beaulieu', p. 44; St John Hope and Brakspear, p. 137.

[24] Engel, 'Conversion', p. 324; Hockey, p. 29; Waverley, pp. 304, 337; B. Golding, 'Burials and Benefactions: An Aspect of Monastic Patronage in Thirteenth-Century England', *England in the Thirteenth Century: Proceedings of the 1984 Harlaxton Symposium*, ed. W. M. Ormrod (Grantham, 1985), pp. 64-75 (pp. 69-70).

[25] *EEA 34*, pp. 122-4 (no. 196).

[26] Worcester, pp. 409-10; *EEA 34*, p. xlii; Mason, *St Wulfstan*, pp. 283-4; Draper, p. 45; Waverley, p. 289.

Henry III's minority might have hoped that the ceremony would symbolise reconciliation, hoping to halt the damage that John's political actions had done to his posthumous reputation.[27]

Further major rebuilding, of the east end of Worcester Cathedral, was initiated in 1224 by Bishop William de Blois. The decoration scheme covered themes of central importance to the community: the Virgin Mary, St Wulfstan, and the tomb of King John. Work continued until the mid-1250s, with King Henry III combining with bishop and prior to secure a papal indulgence (1252) for relaxation of 140 days' penance for all donors to rebuilding of the church where John lay buried. Those collecting alms were granted royal protection to last for three years. The completed edifice 'rewarded the interest of their patron Henry III with a splendid architectural setting for his father's tomb'.[28]

Amidst the reconstruction, King John's body awaited a permanent resting place. It was translated from its original setting in 1232. A literal reading of the Tewkesbury annals suggests that a new sarcophagus was provided.[29] Two of John's children were present, Henry III and his sister Eleanor. The king granted timber to the cathedral, confirmed the grant within the bailey of Worcester castle made at his father's funeral, and gave the church of Bromsgrove to endow anniversary masses for John and, in time, himself.[30] Leading courtiers in attendance included Hubert de Burgh and possibly Peter des Roches, bishop of Winchester, whose short return to power reinstated the forceful methods of government traditionally associated with John. Elsewhere, des Roches honoured the kings he had served in gifts to his Premonstratensian foundation at Titchfield (Hampshire).[31] At Worcester, if the memory of John was being invoked in more ways than one, provision of services suggests ongoing concern for the late king's soul, in keeping with the religious activity of his lifetime.

Henry III proved keen to ensure that his father was appropriately honoured. His visits during the minority are likely to have forged an interest in his father's tomb. After 1232, for much of the remainder of the reign, Henry provided regular donations. Some supported rebuilding work. Others included gifts of vestments and privileges, such as the right to hold markets. Relevant documents regularly stated that they were issued for the king and his heirs, and for the soul of King John, or noted Worcester as the late king's burial place. Meanwhile, Henry's itin-

---

[27] Mason, 'Wulfstan's Staff', pp. 170-1; B. Singleton, 'The Remodelling of the East End of Worcester Cathedral in the Earlier Part of the Thirteenth Century', *Medieval Art and Architecture at Worcester Cathedral: British Archaeological Association Conference Transactions*, 1 (1978), 105-15 (pp. 105-6); U. Engel (trans. H. Heltay), *Worcester Cathedral: An Architectural History* (Chichester, 2007), pp. 112-13.

[28] Engel, *Worcester*, pp. 112-17; *Calendar of Entries in the Papal Registers. Papal Letters 1198-1304*, p. 282; *CPR 1247-1258*, p. 165; Engel, 'Conversion', pp. 327-8. On Henry III's contributions, see below.

[29] *Annales de Theokesberia*, p. 84; Martindale, 'Sword', p. 205. On the tomb's location prior to 1232: Crook, 'Physical Setting', p. 211.

[30] *Worcester Cartulary*, pp. 174-6 (nos 328, 330); *CChR 1226-1257*, pp. 154-5.

[31] Vincent, *Peter des Roches*, pp. 132, 291-2; *EEA IX*, pp. 59-61 (nos 67a, 69).

erary brought him to Worcester almost annually.³² In 1244, he gave a chasuble, specifying that this was for commemoration of his father, to be worn at celebration of high mass on Christmas Day.³³ With the possible exception of an embroidered cope given to the church of St Wulfstan in 1253, there is no evidence that Henry's interest was motivated by anything other than desire to honour his father.³⁴

Meanwhile, the Worcester community took their responsibility for John's soul seriously, marking the anniversary of his death. In 1236, at the petition of the king, Bishop William of Blois ordered revenues from the church of Bromsgrove, given by Henry III four years earlier, to be used to provide candles around the tomb, to fund a pittance on John's anniversary, for the infirmary at Worcester, and for hospitality and alms to the poor. The original purpose of Henry's gift – prayers and supplication for his father's soul – was still known in Edward III's reign.³⁵ The impression of care for John's grave is sustained by further fourteenth-century evidence. An officer responsible for the tombs at Worcester received payments for its maintenance. In 1349, fish costing 17s 6d were purchased for the convent for the obits of King John and Bishop William of Blois.³⁶

Due to the ongoing thirteenth-century building work, it may not have been until the 1250s (perhaps later) that John's remains could finally rest in peace. In the final arrangement, the royal body lay at foot of the high altar, with the shrine of St Oswald to the south and that of St Wulfstan to the north.³⁷ The effigy looked up to images of the two saints in the roof bosses, alongside Christ, Mary, and a holy king. The cohort of saintly overseers was completed by depictions of St John the Baptist and St John the Evangelist, the late king's name-saints, on the eastern transept vaults, whilst Old Testament kings and queens were depicted on the north of the choir. Finally, two figures bore the arms of the kings of England, perhaps invoking the Anglo-Saxon royal saints prominent in the devotions of both John and Henry III. All this set the royal body within 'a genealogy of holy kings' who 'would support the king's spiritual welfare'. Meanwhile, 'the eternal song of the angels to his left would echo the prayers of the Worcester monks in their stalls', a fascinating posthumous tribute to a ruler rarely seen in such terms in the centuries that followed.³⁸

---

32 In addition to grants already cited, see: Engel, 'Conversion', pp. 325–6; *Worcester Cartulary*, pp. 169 (nos 320–1), 237–8 (nos 458–9), 239 (no. 461), 244–5 (no. 468); CChR 1226–1257, p. 443; CChR 1257–1300, p. 7; CPR 1247–1258, p. 530; *The Beauchamp Cartulary Charters 1100–1268*, ed. E. Mason, PRS, 81, ns 43 (London, 1980), pp. 29–30 (no. 51). See also Engel, *Worcester*, pp. 160–2.

33 CR 1242–1247, p. 270.

34 CLR 1251–1260, p. 113. Further evidence for Henry's devotion to Wulfstan is found not at Worcester but at St Albans. Here he offered a pallium at an altar dedicated to the saint in 1256: Webb, *Pilgrimage*, p. 125.

35 *Worcester Cartulary*, pp. 177–8 (no. 322), 290–1 (no. 539).

36 *Early Compotus Rolls of the Priory of Worcester*, trans. and ed. J. M. Wilson and C. Gordon, Worcester Historical Society (Oxford, 1908), pp. 41, 60; Poole, *From Domesday Book*, pp. 428–9.

37 Engel, *Worcester*, pp. 114–17; Crook, 'Physical Setting', pp. 211–14.

38 Engel, 'Conversion', pp. 325 n. 21, 328–30. See also Engel, *Worcester*, pp. 211–18.

180   KING JOHN AND RELIGION

The black Purbeck marble effigy that lies on top of John's tomb post-dates the 1232 reburial. In the late twelfth and early thirteenth centuries, such royal effigies were not yet commonplace, making this tomb unusual, either by comparison with his Anglo-Norman predecessors or Capetian and Salian kings of the era. That said, it has clear parallels with the effigies of John's father, mother, and brother at Fontevraud, all probably installed in the years following 1200. In depicting these rulers as they might have appeared when laid out for burial, such tombs provided 'an ever-present reminder of the individuals for whom spiritual commemoration and intercession were requested'. It is therefore significant that such an effigy was commissioned at Worcester.[39]

The monument is also notable for elements of its iconography, including the unsheathed sword at the king's side. This naked blade is unique to royal effigies of the period. As an emblem signifying possession of the kingdom and the nature of kingship, its presence in an ecclesiastical setting is fraught with potential tensions in how it could and should be interpreted. Other details include the miniature statues either side of the king's head, depicting two bishops carrying censers, interpreted as St Oswald and St Wulfstan 'actively promoting the salvation of John's soul', and further reference to the notion that in death John would be in the company of the saints.[40]

The tomb was opened in 1529, revealing a body clad in regal robes, wearing a crown, sword, ring, and spurs, and carrying a staff and sceptre. The body remained on view for two days. A new base was created around the original stone coffin, described as 'recently renovated' when John Leland visited Worcester.[41] Ongoing desire to commemorate the king had perhaps experienced a revival linked to Henry VIII's dispute with the papacy. After the Reformation, obliteration of the cult of saints meant that John's tomb no longer stood between the shrines of Wulfstan and Oswald. The latter were taken down, either in 1538 or 1542.[42] By the early eighteenth century, misunderstanding both of the location of the bones of the two saints and of John's desire to be interred between them led to the conclusion that the king lay buried in the nave of the Lady Chapel. This was disproved in 1797, when the contents of the tomb were again inspected. The Tudor opening had apparently been forgotten, but comparison of the descriptions suggests that in 1529 much of the regalia had been removed. Only the sword remained. A number of bones (including the skull) had clearly not been replaced with care.[43]

In the nineteenth and twentieth centuries, treatment of the late king's effigy takes its place within lively debate about responsibility for care of royal tombs, indeed of historic monuments more broadly. Restoration was recommended and commissioned in 1872, including cleaning, repairs to defective masonry joints,

---

[39] Martindale, 'Sword', pp. 199–241; Nolan, 'The Queen's Choice', esp. pp. 382–95.
[40] Martindale, 'Sword', esp. p. 240; Engel, *Worcester*, p. 208; Mason, 'Wulfstan's Staff', p. 170.
[41] Engel, *Worcester*, p. 209; Martindale, 'Sword', p. 205 n. 15; Engel, 'Conversion', p. 325 n. 22; Crook, 'Physical Setting', p. 211.
[42] 'A Bailiff's List and Chronicle from Worcester', ed. D. MacCulloch and P. Hughes, *Antiquaries Journal*, 75 (1995) 235–53 (pp. 244a, 245a); Crook, 'Physical Setting', pp. 190–2.
[43] Engel, *Worcester*, p. 209; Crook, 'Physical Setting', pp. 194–6.

re-painting the shields, and re-gilding the effigy and the figures of the bishop-saints to either side of John's head. A new metal crown was to be made, and placed over the remains of the stone version. The work attracted considerable criticism. The new gilding was believed to have obliterated traces of original paintwork. Arguments rumbled on, not least over who would pay for removal of the offending gilding, so that renewed work was undertaken only in 1930. Any surviving original paint stood little chance against the chemicals then used. It was ultimately decided that the whole tomb should be polished, and the shields re-painted and re-gilded. During the Second World War, the effigy was moved to the crypt for protection in 1941. Work to protect the tomb base followed in 1942–3, with an ongoing exchange between the cathedral chapter and the Office of Works indicating the delay in achieving protection from the *Luftwaffe*. Today, the tomb remains one of the main historical attractions at Worcester Cathedral.[44]

John left only brief instructions for posthumous provision for his soul in his final testament of 1216. It is possible that he had made an earlier testament, before June 1207, when letters placed in safe-keeping at Reading Abbey were recalled by the king. They include the tantalising reference to letters in which 'the lord Hubert sometime archbishop of Canterbury confirmed our testament'.[45] Sadly, this text is now lost. The 1216 document, though brief, contains enough to offer 'a useful checklist of the kinds of thing we might expect to find in a ruler's testament': instruction for restitution to be made to the Church for wrongs committed, aid to be sent to the Holy Land, faithful servants to be rewarded, alms to be given to the poor and to religious houses for the salvation of his soul, and instructions regarding burial. This is in keeping with the king's religious outlook and the behaviour of his predecessors and successors, but tells us little in terms of specific intentions.[46]

The regency council moved quickly to honour John. They made reparation for his sins during the civil war, such as a grant in 1217 to atone for the burning of the church of St Peter and St Paul in Bedford.[47] Further payments, in 1228, were specified as alms to acquit the souls of Henry III and his father from association with damages inflicted by John and his men in Bristol.[48] Various pardons issued by assize judges, early in Henry III's reign, may also be linked to reparation for John's

---

[44] S. D. Church, 'The Care of the Royal Tombs in English Cathedrals in the Nineteenth and Twentieth Centuries: The Case of the Effigy of King John at Worcester', *Antiquaries Journal*, 89 (2009), 365–87; *Worcester Cathedral, King John* [http://www.worcestercathedral.co.uk/King_John.php, accessed 21 May 2014].

[45] *RLP*, p. 73b.

[46] Gillingham, 'Deathbeds', pp. 521–2; Church, 'King John's Testament', pp. 516–18.

[47] *CPR 1225–1232*, pp. 29, 173; Vincent, *Peter des Roches*, p. 132.

[48] *CLR 1226–1240*, p. 74. The recipients, the brethren of *Altubatia*, were probably the order of Altopascio, originally from Tuscany, dedicated to St James and the protection of travellers and pilgrims. See J.-M. Poisson, 'Altopascio, ordre de San Jacopo d'', *Prier et Combattre: Dictionnaire européen des ordres militaires au Moyen Age*, ed. N. Bériou and P. Josserand (Paris, 2009), pp. 84–5.

182 KING JOHN AND RELIGION

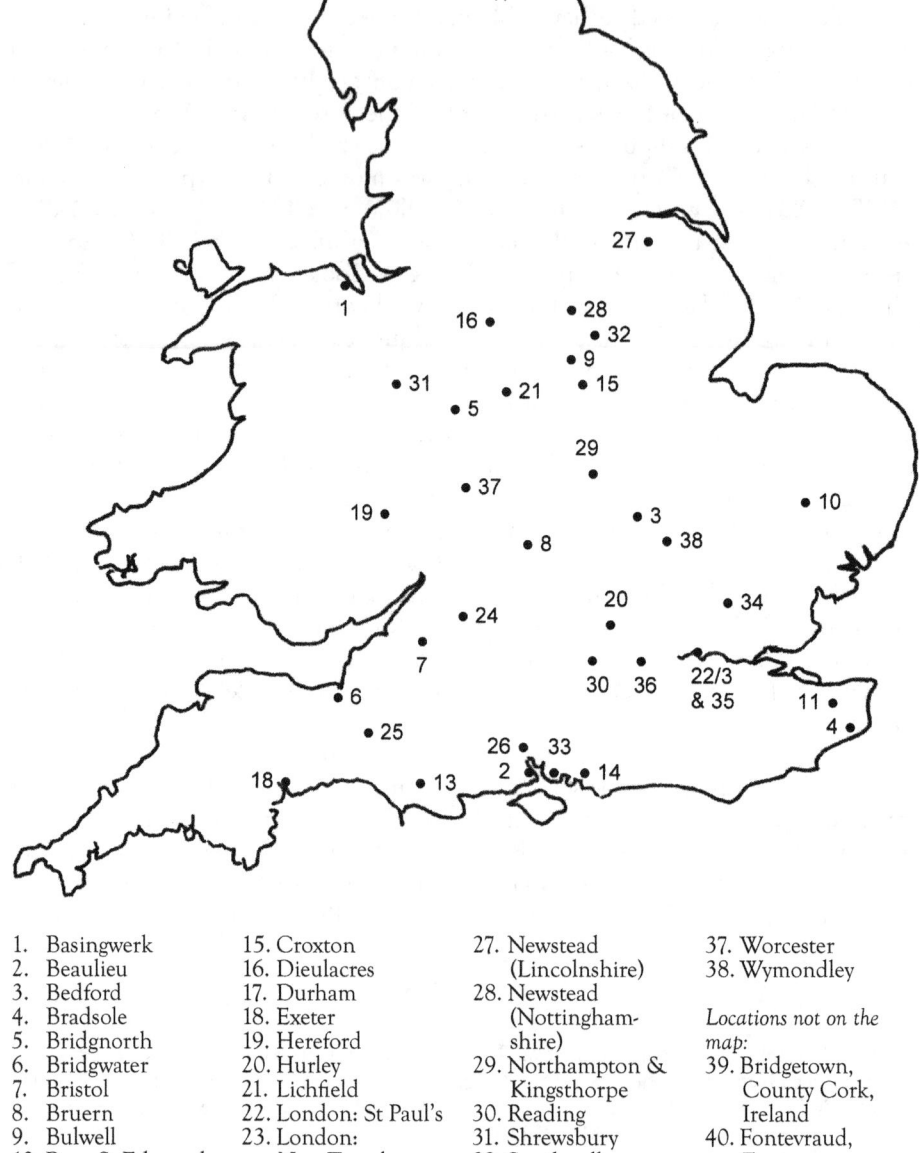

1. Basingwerk
2. Beaulieu
3. Bedford
4. Bradsole
5. Bridgnorth
6. Bridgwater
7. Bristol
8. Bruern
9. Bulwell
10. Bury St Edmunds
11. Canterbury
12. Carlisle
13. Cerne
14. Chichester
15. Croxton
16. Dieulacres
17. Durham
18. Exeter
19. Hereford
20. Hurley
21. Lichfield
22. London: St Paul's
23. London: New Temple
24. Malmesbury
25. Montacute
26. Mottisfont
27. Newstead (Lincolnshire)
28. Newstead (Nottinghamshire)
29. Northampton & Kingsthorpe
30. Reading
31. Shrewsbury
32. Southwell
33. Titchfield
34. Waltham
35. Westminster
36. Windsor
37. Worcester
38. Wymondley

Locations not on the map:
39. Bridgetown, County Cork, Ireland
40. Fontevraud, France
41. St Mary in Sassia, Rome

Map 4 Locations associated with posthumous provision for King John

actions. In one instance, at Shrewsbury, a chaplain named Laurence was ordered to perform thirty masses for the late king's soul.[49]

Elsewhere, in 1217, the manor of Bulwell (Nottinghamshire) was granted to the Grandmontines. It was stated that this was for John's soul, and that the manor was to be used to build a monastery of the order. However, a few years later the land was taken back into the king's hand.[50] More positively, the Knights Hospitaller received three pence a day, for the souls of Henry III's father and ancestors, and for that of Robert de Quincy. This was recorded from 1217, the year Robert, the eldest son of Saer de Quincy, earl of Winchester, died. Meanwhile, a chaplain of the Knights Templar celebrated masses for John at the New Temple. At Lichfield, where the late king had himself commissioned masses, the minority government gave twenty oaks for making timber for the work of the church, in a grant made for John's soul in 1221.[51]

Various other houses received material grants. In 1223, Cerne was given wood for the repair of the abbey dormitory, 'for the sake of God' (*intuitu Dei*) and for the soul of King John, with Henry III's wellbeing and his father's salvation referred to in letters issued to Basingwerk Abbey. In 1224, the leper hospital of St James at Bridgnorth was allowed to take a horse into the royal forest at Morville (Shropshire) for daily collection of dry and dead wood. Again, this was for the sake of God, the wellbeing of Henry III, and the soul of his father.[52]

Posthumous provision also included grants to Croxton Abbey, where John's entrails had been buried, including an annual payment of one hundred shillings apparently assigned by the late king himself. A cancelled letter of 1226 stated that this had been given to the abbey's infirmary for the poor. In 1231, the payment was replaced with an endowment of a series of rents.[53] Later confirmations were made with reference to the abbey as the burial place of John's heart. A spiritual return from the abbot and monks was presumably expected. This is further suggested by a commission by Henry III, made whilst he was at Croxton in 1244, for a chasuble

---

[49] *Rolls of the Justices in Eyre, being the Rolls of Pleas and Assizes for Gloucestershire, Warwickshire and Staffordshire, 1221, 1222*, ed. D. M. Stenton, Selden Society, 59 (London, 1940), p. 465 (no. 1050); *Rolls of the Justices in Eyre, being the Rolls of Pleas and Assizes for Lincolnshire 1218–9 and Worcestershire 1221*, ed. D. M. Stenton, Selden Society, 53 (London, 1934), pp. 606–7 (no. 1262); R. V. Turner, *The King and His Courts: The Role of John and Henry III in the Administration of Justice, 1199–1240* (Ithaca, NY, 1968), p. 156; Vincent, *Peter des Roches*, p. 132.

[50] *CPR 1216–1225*, p. 128; Vincent, *Peter des Roches*, p. 132; *FR 6 Henry III*, nos 213–14.

[51] *RLC 1204–24*, pp. 342b, 380b–381a, 394a; R. D. Oram, 'Quincy, Saer de, Earl of Winchester (d. 1219)', *ODNB* (Oxford, 2004, online edn 2005) [http://www.oxforddnb.com/view/article/22967, accessed 13 May 2014]; *The Register, or Rolls, of Walter Gray, Lord Archbishop of York*, ed. J. Raine, Surtees Society, 56 (Durham, 1872), p. 24 (no. 115); *RLC 1204–24*, p. 465a. For the masses of John commissioned at Lichfield, see also above, Chapter 1.

[52] *RLC 1204–24*, pp. 528b, 555a, 621b, 647a; Rawcliffe, *Leprosy*, p. 332.

[53] *RLC 1204–24*, pp. 300a, 331a, 364b, 381a, 540b, 596a; *RLC 1224–27*, pp. 175b, 176a; *CPR 1216–1225*, p. 41; *CPR 1225–1232*, pp. 55, 264–5; *CLR 1226–1240*, pp. 24, 76, 109, 126; *CChR 1226–1257*, p. 131; *FR 11 Henry III*, Henry III Fine Rolls Project [http://www.finerollshenry3.org.uk/content/calendar/roll_025.html, accessed 15 May 2014], no. 141.

to be made for the abbot. This was to be worn when performing services on the anniversary of John's death.[54]

Isabella of Angoulême also honoured her late husband. For her wellbeing and for John's soul, she confirmed the monks of Malmesbury in possession of the town's castle. She also issued a confirmation to the order of St Thomas of Acre, for her husband's soul, all her ancestors and heirs, and all the faithful dead. In granting the right to hold a fair to the monks of St Nicholas, Exeter, Isabella again referred to the late king's soul. However, there is no sense of a prolonged period of mourning. 'Thereafter, not a single charter issued by her during the remaining thirty years of her life, so much as mentions her late husband.'[55]

Others were more active. Within days of John's death, the regency council was honouring what were described as his alms payments.[56] Many of his courtiers provided for prayers and services in his name. This included men at the heart of the new administration, such as Hubert de Burgh.[57] William of Cornhill, bishop of Coventry, allowed the monks of Worcester to appropriate the church of West Bromwich for John's soul.[58] William Brewer, an administrator richly rewarded by the king and understood to have a close knowledge of John's mind, was especially active. At the rededication of Worcester Cathedral in 1218, he gave a gold chalice, which Turner links to the memory of his erstwhile master. At the hospital of St John the Baptist and St John the Evangelist at Northampton, Brewer supported a chapel where daily masses would be celebrated for the four kings he had served. Each was named: Henry II, Richard I, John, and Henry III. Services were also to be performed for William's ancestors, and all the faithful dead. At the Dissolution, provision by Brewer for himself and for John remained, through almsgiving to seven paupers and payment for a priest in the chapel at Bridgwater castle. The latter was an appropriate choice. The manor of Bridgwater had been given to Brewer in 1199. He rebuilt the castle, which became his centre of operations.[59]

Other courtiers joined in, including several bishops. Ralph Neville succeeded Richard Poor as bishop of Chichester in 1222, and provided for a chaplain celebrating masses for the late king's soul in c. 1227. Henry III supported this initiative,

---

[54] CChR 1226-1257, p. 463; CLR 1240-1245, p. 250.
[55] Vincent, 'Isabella', pp. 189, 198, 216-19 (Appendix, nos 1-3).
[56] RLC 1204-24, pp. 293a, 294a, 308a, 337a, 340b, 343b, 344a, 347b, 348b, 349b, 351a, 356b, 358a, 360a, 364a, 366a, 398b, 543a.
[57] Vincent, Peter des Roches, p. 132.
[58] Worcester Cartulary, pp. 105-6 (no. 196), and see also pp. 106-7 (nos 197-8, for confirmation by Prior Geoffrey of Coventry and Pope Honorius III), and p. 107 (no. 199, where Worcester granted West Bromwich to Sandwell Priory in return for six marks per year). On Cornhill: M. J. Franklin, 'Cornhill, William of (d. 1223)', ODNB (Oxford, 2004) [http://www.oxforddnb.com/view/article/6331, accessed 10 March 2011].
[59] Turner, Men, p. 88; The Percy Chartulary, ed. M. T. Martin, Surtees Society, 117 (Durham, 1911), pp. 384-5 (no. 898); Valor Ecclesiasticus, vol. I, p. 208; S. D. Church, 'Brewer, William (d. 1226)', ODNB (Oxford, 2004) [http://www.oxforddnb.com/view/article/3369, accessed 6 August 2013].

granting a garden, chapel, and graveyard.[60] In 1223, Eustace de Fauconberg, bishop of London, provided for performance of the obit John had commanded at St Paul's.[61] In the same year, Walter Mauclerk was elected bishop of Carlisle. Here, he made an endowment for his soul, those of his relatives, and that of the late king, confirmed by Henry III in 1230.[62] Even Archbishop Langton, so long at odds with John, could recall him with the phrase 'of good memory', in a charter issued to Mottisfont Priory between 1218 and 1228.[63]

Further members of the late king's entourage made similar arrangements. A knight in Ireland, Alexander fitz Hugh, made a gift for the king's soul to the community he founded at Bridgetown (County Cork) between 1206 and 1216.[64] By 1241, Robert de Lexinton had expanded chantry provision in the chapel of St Thomas Becket in Southwell Minster, so that the religious prayed for the souls of King John and Brian de Lisle. Robert's career had begun with service to Brian and John.[65]

Some chroniclers were sceptical. One described how a former royal priest set out to pray for John, but was instructed in a vision to read the fifty-first psalm, which included the injunction, 'Therefore will God destroy you forever', and ridicule for the man 'who did not make God his helper'. The clergyman abandoned his efforts.[66] Yet the evidence suggests that the late king's followers were more optimistic. Even Matthew Paris included the opinion that alms might ease John's passage through Purgatory, albeit in recounting a vision, said to have occurred in 1226, in which John, clad in burning robes of insupportable weight, appeared to a monk of St Albans.[67]

The late king's testament had referred to aid for the Holy Land. It is possible that attempts were made to offset the non-fulfilment of his vow to crusade. Bishop

---

[60] *Chartulary of the High Church of Chichester*, pp. 35 (no. 151), 106-7 (no. 410), 277-8 (no. 903), and see also pp. 51-2 (no. 211), 221-2 (no. 791); *EEA 23. Chichester 1254-1305*, ed. P. M. Hoskin (Oxford, 2001), p. 302 (appendix 2, no. 7); Poole, *From Domesday Book*, pp. 428-9; Vincent, *Peter des Roches*, p. 132; W. H. Blaauw, 'Letters to Ralph de Nevill Bishop of Chichester (1222-24) and Chancellor to King Henry III', *Sussex Archaeological Collections*, 3 (1850), 35-76 (p. 36); F. A. Cazel Jr, 'Neville, Ralph de (d. 1244)', *ODNB* (Oxford, 2004, online edn 2008) [http://www.oxforddnb.com/view/article/19949, accessed 23 July 2014].

[61] *EEA 26*, pp. 199-200 (no. 229); see also above, Chapter 1.

[62] *EEA 30. Carlisle 1133-1292*, ed. D. M. Smith (Oxford, 2005), pp. 54-5 (no. 71); *CChR 1226-1257*, p. 117. On Walter: N. Vincent, 'Mauclerk, Walter (d. 1248)', *ODNB* (Oxford, 2004) [http://www.oxforddnb.com/view/article/18355, accessed 23 April 2014].

[63] Vincent, 'Stephen Langton', p. 120 (Appendix no. 28).

[64] *CR 1254-1256*, p. 225; *CChR 1257-1300*, pp. 341-2; Gwynn and Hadcock, *Medieval Religious Houses Ireland*, p. 161.

[65] *Register, or Rolls, of Walter Gray*, pp. 195-8; J. A. K. Miller, 'The Building Programme of Archbishop Walter de Gray: Architectural Production and Reform in the Archdiocese of York, 1215-1255' (unpublished PhD thesis, University of Columbia, 2012), pp. 196-8, 223-4; D. Crook, 'Lexinton, Robert of (d. 1250)', *ODNB* (Oxford, 2004, online edn 2008) [http://www.oxforddnb.com/view/article/16616, accessed 12 June 2014].

[66] Carpenter, 'Burial', p. 457; Psalm 51, verses 7-9.

[67] *Matthaei Parisiensis*, vol. III, pp. 112-13; Harvey, 'Piety', p. 47.

Silvester of Worcester, who had overseen the burial of John's body, was the only English bishop to attempt to participate in the Fifth Crusade. He got no further than Ramsey Abbey, where he died. Before he set out in 1218, he obtained royal orders to the tenants of his bishopric ordering payment of an aid 'for the expenses which he made in the service of King John ... of the money which he should have spent in his pilgrimage'. The destination is omitted. Nor is it clear whether this refers to the pilgrimage of the king or the bishop, but the coincidence with Silvester's imminent departure raises the possibility that he had taken responsibility for fulfilling John's vow. He was also granted three years' revenue from the possessions of his see, and special protection.[68] Silvester was not alone. One of John's chaplains, referred to by his initial, H., was accorded crusaders' protection in c. 1219. At least two of the late king's illegitimate sons, Richard and Oliver, departed in 1218. Oliver died at Damietta. Richard returned to England in 1220 or 1221.[69]

Meanwhile, several religious communities recorded John's name in their obituary lists, including Pope Innocent III's foundation of St Mary in Sassia in Rome. Closer to home, Reading Abbey noted the anniversaries of Henry II and King John. The nuns of Fontevraud remembered him in their obituary as a benefactor of their church.[70] Perhaps most surprisingly, the monks of Canterbury Cathedral remembered John in their thirteenth-century obituary list.[71] Thus, he took his place in the community's provision for the souls of the dead, alongside other kings and their queens, including his immediate family, Henry II, Eleanor of Aquitaine, and Richard I. John's first wife, Isabella of Gloucester, was also listed. Posthumous care for souls at Canterbury did not apparently require a basis in smooth relations whilst they had been alive. On the same day (18 October) as they prayed for John, the monks honoured John de Gray, bishop of Norwich, whose candidacy for the archbishopric they had worked so hard to prevent.[72]

Prayers and almsgiving for the late king were still performed long after his death. At Durham, a late medieval obituary recorded him amongst those commemorated on 13 October.[73] Such provision continued until the Dissolution of the Monas-

---

[68] CPR 1216–1225, pp. 143, 144–5; EEA 34, pp. xli–xliii.

[69] London, National Archives, SC1/1/208; Cheney, Innocent, p. 266 n. 115; Lloyd, 'Chilham, Sir Richard'; Lloyd, 'Oliver'.

[70] Cheney, Innocent, p. 237; Cheney, 'Monastic Letter', p. 492; Pavillon, La Vie, p. 585.

[71] Preserved in: London, British Library, Ms. Cotton Nero C ix, folios 3r–18v, with a printed edition in R. Fleming, 'Christchurch's Sisters and Brothers: An Edition and Discussion of the Canterbury Obituary Lists', The Culture of Christendom: Essays in Medieval History in Commemoration of Denis L. T. Bethell, ed. M. A. Meyer (London and Rio Grande, OH, 1993), pp. 115–53 (pp. 130–48, esp. p. 143).

[72] Fleming, 'Christchurch's Sisters and Brothers', pp. 137 (Eleanor, Richard), 142 (Isabella), 143 (John, John de Gray). Part of the thirteenth-century list is missing, covering May–August. Henry II died in July 1189. However, like Richard, he is included in a further list, preserved in London, British Library, Ms. Cotton Galba E iii, 2, folios 32r–34r, with a printed edition in Fleming, 'Christchurch's Sisters and Brothers', pp. 126–30 (pp. 127–8).

[73] 'Excerpta ex obituario minori ecclesiae Dunelmensis', ed. A. H. Thompson, Liber Vitae Ecclesiae Dunelmensis; nec non obituaria duo ejusdem ecclesiae, Surtees Society, 136 (London, 1841), p. 152.

teries. In addition to William Brewer's endowment at Bridgwater (noted above), it can be seen across England (see Map 4 above). At Bradsole, the Premonstratensian canons of St Radegund's honoured his obit annually, as did the cathedral canons of Lichfield. Gilbertine Newstead made alms distributions for Henry II and John as co-founders, whilst two brothers prayed daily for John as founder of the hospital of St David at Kingsthorpe. At Montacute, 13s 4d was paid for distribution of bread and fish to the poor, at various times of year, for the king's soul. At Bury St Edmunds, ordinances in aid of the poor made by Richard I and John were still being honoured.[74] The list reflects the situation over three hundred years after John's death, and stands up to comparison with that for other twelfth- and thirteenth-century kings.[75]

Posthumous support for religious projects initiated by King John can be seen at Beaulieu. During Henry III's minority, his government soon provided for ongoing work. In 1217, the keeper of the king's horses in the New Forest was ordered, for the next three years, to hand over his profits to the monks. William Marshal explicitly stated that this was for the late king's soul.[76] Further contributions were not substantial, due to the political and financial constraints of the period. However, they were made. In November 1220, the works of the church of Beaulieu received fifty marks.[77] Further sums continued to be paid across the 1220s.[78] That building work continued is shown by difficulties experienced in 1224 by Durand the mason, who seemingly had to persuade the port bailiffs of Southampton that he had the abbot of Beaulieu's mandate to come to England. The bailiffs were ordered, without delay, to restore the materials he had brought with him.[79]

'The king's generosity to the Cistercians of Beaulieu continued year by year; it would be tedious to reiterate the specific benefactions.'[80] Yet this is worth exploring. Henry III's largesse reveals his concern to provide for his father's soul. The abbot was granted an annual two-day fair at the manor of Faringdon, the original location proposed for the house. This was to take place on 17 and 18 October, the vigil and feast day of St Luke, but also the anniversary of John's death.[81] In 1236, Henry confirmed all royal grants in the New Forest issued to

---

[74] *Valor Ecclesiasticus*, vol. I, pp. 59 (Bradsole), 196 (Montacute); vol. III, pp. 136 (Lichfield), 461-4 (Bury St Edmunds); vol. IV, p. 72 (Newstead); vol. V, p. 322 (Kingsthorpe); R. Dunning, *Somerset Monasteries* (Stroud, 2001), p. 61 (Montacute).

[75] Compared to the seven houses linked to commemoration of John, seven houses can be linked to Henry I, seven to Henry II, and six to Henry III: *Valor Ecclesiasticus*, vol. I, pp. 54, 56, 59, 207, 422; vol. II, pp. 79, 95, 97, 273, 412, 413, 468, 469, 499; vol. III, pp. 241, 287, 493; vol. IV, p. 72; vol. V, pp. 149, 154, 276, 282.

[76] *RLC 1204-24*, p. 299b; *CPR 1216-1225*, p. 28; Vincent, *Peter des Roches*, p. 132; Doubleday and Page, *VCH Hampshire*, vol. II (1903), p. 141.

[77] *RLC 1204-24*, p. 441b; St John Hope and Brakspear, p. 135.

[78] *CPR 1216-1225*, pp. 280-1; *RLC 1204-24*, pp. 457b, 486b, 521a, 592a; *RLC 1224-27*, pp. 36b, 64a, 84b, 91b, 138a, 138b, 140b, 196a; *CR 1227-1231*, p. 73; *CLR 1226-1240*, pp. 46, 132; St John Hope and Brakspear, pp. 135-6.

[79] *RLC 1204-24*, pp. 625b, 650b; St John Hope and Brakspear, p. 136.

[80] Doubleday and Page, *VCH Hampshire*, vol. II, p. 141.

[81] *RLC 1204-24*, p. 486a; *Beaulieu Cartulary*, p. 9 (no. 4); *CChR 1226-1257*, p. 60.

the house during his minority. He also confirmed John's foundation charter and compensated nearby Breamore Priory for losses sustained due to Beaulieu's establishment.[82] In 1236-37, the abbot was given a samite cloth from the king's wardrobe and in 1240 he received a chalice, suggestive of items used in performance of religious services.[83] Two letters close of 1243 granted Brother Hamo of Beaulieu a cask of wine. The second notes that this was for the abbey's infirmary, suggesting a concern to provide for sick members of John's foundation.[84]

Prayers for the royal family at Beaulieu appear to have continued long beyond this time. Edward III, whose gifts and visits to Beaulieu are probably due to the abbey's foundation by his ancestor, honoured Edward II's wish that the church of Ringwood be granted to the abbot and convent. Daily services were to be performed for Edward III, his mother Isabella of France, and his heirs, by four monks in addition to the thirty-two then resident there.[85]

Henry III's backing also included continued royal sponsorship of building work, in particular grants of timber and the right to quarry stone, not only for the church and the monks' accommodation but also for the lay brothers' buildings.[86] Crops, brushwood, and all manner of rights and liberties, in particular within the New Forest but also at locations including Faringdon, passed from the king to the monks.[87] On Henry's petition, Pope Gregory IX licensed appropriation of various churches, noting that Henry was the founder's son, or that Beaulieu had been begun by John. In the case of the licence of 1235, relating to the church of St Keverne (Cornwall), John's younger son, Richard, earl of Cornwall, had already granted Beaulieu patronage of the church, 'for the sake of charity' (*intuitu karitatis*), for the wellbeing of his soul, and for that of his father.[88]

---

[82] *Beaulieu Cartulary*, pp. 5-7 (no. 2); CChR 1226-1257, pp. 216-17, 219. John's foundation charter was confirmed again in January 1269: CChR 1257-1300, p. 115.

[83] *Wardrobe Accounts*, p. 29; CLR 1226-1240, p. 476. For wine given by John and Henry III for celebrating mass, see above, Chapter 1.

[84] CR 1242-1247, p. 12. For grants of wine for unspecified purposes: CLR 1226-1240, pp. 306, 447; CLR 1240-1245, p. 27; CLR 1245-1251, p. 63; CR 1261-1264, HMSO (London, 1936), p. 331.

[85] CPR. Edward III. 1327-1330, HMSO (London, 1891), p. 363; Doubleday and Page, VCH Hampshire, vol. II, p. 143; Ormrod, 'Personal Religion', p. 875. It appears that this was revoked: CPR. Edward III. 1330-1334, HMSO (London, 1893), p. 367.

[86] CR 1231-1234, pp. 58, 222; CR 1237-1242, pp. 74, 410, 513; CR 1242-1247, pp. 12, 107; CR 1247-1251, pp. 247, 494.

[87] *Beaulieu Cartulary*, pp. 247 (no. 297), 248 (no. 299), 249-50 (nos 301-2); CPR 1216-1225, pp. 285, 324; CPR 1232-1247, pp. 119-20, 280; CPR 1258-1266, pp. 316, 440; CPR 1266-1272, HMSO (London, 1913), pp. 192, 308; CR 1227-1231, pp. 10, 31, 303, 453; CR 1234-1237, HMSO (London, 1908), p. 212; CR 1237-1242, pp. 74, 194, 448; CR 1242-1247, p. 511; CR 1247-1251, pp. 68-9, 393, 396; CR 1251-1253, pp. 111, 281; FR 9 Henry III, no. 116; FR 34 Henry III, Henry III Fine Rolls Project [http://www.finerollshenry3.org.uk/content/calendar/roll_047.html, accessed 30 July 2013], no. 282; RLC 1204-24, pp. 471a, 559b; RLC 1224-27, p. 77b.

[88] *Calendar of Entries in the Papal Registers. Papal Letters 1198-1304*, pp. 129, 145; *Charters and Documents Illustrating the History of the Cathedral, City and Diocese of Salisbury in the Twelfth and Thirteenth Centuries*, ed. W. R. Jones and W. D. Macray, RS 97 (London, 1891), pp. 255-7

The royal itinerary also included Beaulieu, suggesting that Henry and his entourage came to inspect progress.[89] The abbey church was dedicated in 1246, with the king and queen in attendance, along with their eldest son Edward, and John's younger son, Richard, earl of Cornwall. The king provided six barrels of wine in honour of the occasion.[90] In 1247, Henry III recalled the event in a charter in which he gave the abbey 239 acres of land in the New Forest, lands the community had previously occupied without warrant.[91] That said, the dedication ceremony revealed the expectation incumbent upon the abbey to provide hospitality for the royal family. Henry III's son Edward fell ill and the boy and his mother, Eleanor of Provence, stayed at Beaulieu for three weeks. The prior and cellarer lost their positions for allowing this, their actions being deemed contrary to Cistercian statutes.[92] Further evidence that the relationship between the king and abbey was one in which reciprocal services were expected is shown by Beaulieu's contributions to overseas campaigns, and the continuing role of the abbot, monks, and even lay brothers as envoys.[93] During the early months of the baronial reform period, royal messengers were sent to the abbot on 'secret business', whilst for a time the abbey was used to deposit part of the wealth accumulated by the king's half-brother, Aymer de Lusignan, bishop-elect of Winchester.[94]

Henry III's commitment to his father's religious initiatives can be seen elsewhere. In 1232, the king followed up John's deathbed grant to Aconbury with a confirmation and gift of forest rights. The hospital of St Anthony of Vienne, who received royal protection for their preaching in 1214, were granted the advowson

---

(no. 225); Doubleday and Page, *VCH Hampshire*, vol. II, pp. 141-2. For Richard of Cornwall's grant: *Beaulieu Cartulary*, pp. 201-2 (no. 249), and see also pp. 203-7 (nos 251-3), 225-6 (no. 277).

[89] As shown by royal letters dated at Beaulieu or by references to gifts made to or by the king whilst he was there: *CLR 1245-1251*, p. 193; *CLR 1267-1272*, p. 58 (nos 537, 540); *CPR 1225-1232*, p. 426; *CPR 1232-1247*, pp. 88-9; *CPR 1266-1272*, pp. 307-8; *CR 1227-1231*, p. 483; *CR 1247-1251*, p. 389; *FR 19 Henry III*, Henry III Fine Rolls Project [http://www.finerollshenry3.org.uk/content/calendar/roll_034.html, accessed 30 July 2013], nos 89, 90; *FR 35 Henry III*, Henry III Fine Rolls Project [http://www.finerollshenry3.org.uk/content/calendar/roll_048.html, accessed 30 July 2013], no. 89.

[90] Hockey, p. 29; Waverley, p. 337; *CLR 1245-1251*, p. 51. For letters and charters issued whilst Henry was at the abbey: *CChR 1226-1257*, p. 294; *CPR 1232-1247*, p. 482.

[91] *Beaulieu Cartulary*, pp. 7-8 (no. 3), and see also pp. 9-10 (no. 5); *CChR 1226-1257*, p. 325.

[92] *CLR 1245-1251*, p. 65; St John Hope and Brakspear, p. 137; Waverley, p. 337.

[93] *CLR 1226-1240*, p. 228; *CLR 1240-1245*, pp. 141, 163, 180, 184, 192; *CPR 1225-1232*, pp. 24, 74-5; *CPR 1232-1247*, pp. 94, 99; *CR 1227-1231*, pp. 248-9; *CR 1231-1234*, p. 246; *CR 1237-1242*, pp. 430-1; *FR 27 Henry III*, no. 605; *RLC 1204-24*, p. 461b; *RLC 1224-27*, pp. 26b, 103b.

[94] *CR 1256-1259*, p. 317. Aymer and his Lusignan brothers were forced into exile in July 1258. He took with him three thousand marks: N. Vincent, 'Lusignan, Aymer de (c. 1228-1260)', *ODNB* (Oxford, 2004, online edn 2008) [http://www.oxforddnb.com/view/article/941, accessed 30 July 2013]. The funds lodged at Beaulieu were presumably all or part of the remainder. For uses to which the money was put: *CR 1256-1259*, pp. 253, 255; *CPR 1247-1258*, pp. 643-4; *CPR 1258-1266*, pp. 15, 17. In 1259, orders were issued for Aymer's treasure to be transferred to the Exchequer: *CPR 1258-1266*, p. 23.

of the church of All Saints, Hereford, in 1249. Henry III stipulated that this was for the souls of his father and his mother.⁹⁵ He also provided for marking the anniversary of John's death, notably at Fontevraud. This Angevin religious powerhouse received an annual grant of forty *livres Tournois* from Bordeaux for honouring Henry's anniversary and that of his father. Elsewhere, the prior and canons of the hospital of St Mary, Wymondley, were instructed to mark John's anniversary and Henry's as well. In 1242, the late king's demise was marked by feeding one thousand poor, costing £7 6s 10d. Daily mass for Henry III's father and mother were to be performed by a chaplain of the leper hospital of Windsor, under the terms of a royal gift of 1251.⁹⁶

Like John, Henry III's grants to the religious might include his father's name amongst family members for whom prayers were implicitly sought, for example confirmation to the brothers of the Holy Sepulchre in 1232. Here, charters of Henry II and Richard I were confirmed, with the souls of Henry III, John, his ancestors and successors, and Eleanor of Aquitaine all mentioned.⁹⁷ Similar instances can be found from Henry's minority, presumably at the instance of the regency government, and during his so-called 'Personal Rule'. Examples include Bruern, Dieulacres, Waltham, Westminster, the latters' dependency at Hurley, the Knights Templar, and confirmation to the Cistercians of Richard I's grant of the church of Scarborough.⁹⁸ Occasionally, grants to laymen referred to the late king's soul, or pardons were issued for his salvation. This was the reason given in early 1230, when one Frayo of Cuddington was pardoned a ten-mark fine for trespass of the royal forest, allegedly committed during John's reign.⁹⁹

In his later years, Henry III also showed concern for his father's sins (and indeed his own). In 1268, a grant to Amesbury was made for the souls of Arthur and Eleanor of Brittany, the former almost certainly murdered by John or on his orders, the latter in royal wardship from 1189 (perhaps earlier), thereafter if not imprisoned then certainly kept under close control by both John and Henry III for the remainder of her life. Amesbury was instructed to celebrate obits for both Arthur and his sister. The house was an appropriate recipient, as Eleanor had been buried there. Henry also endowed masses for her at Marlborough and Bristol castles.¹⁰⁰ Later, in 1272, John's grandson Edward obtained plenary indulgence

---

⁹⁵ *CChR 1226–1257*, pp. 172, 345; Vincent, 'Isabella', p. 214; Graham, 'Order of St Antoine', pp. 150-1.

⁹⁶ *CR 1231–1234*, p. 115; *CChR 1226–1257*, pp. 159, 357, 361; *FR 17 Henry III*, Henry III Fine Rolls Project [http://www.finerollshenry3.org.uk/content/calendar/roll_032.html, accessed 15 May 2014], no. 12; *CLR 1240–1245*, p. 151.

⁹⁷ *CChR 1226–1257*, p. 174.

⁹⁸ *RLC 1204–24*, p. 298a; *CChR 1226–1257*, pp. 208-9, 218, 325, 349-50; *CChR 1257–1300*, pp. 237-8; *Early Charters of the Augustinian Canons of Waltham*, pp. 28-31 (no. 41). For Scarborough, given to the Cistercians for the souls of both Richard and John, see also: Landon, *Itinerary*, p. 127 (no. 491); *RLP*, p. 24a.

⁹⁹ *CPR 1225–1232*, p. 112; *FR 14 Henry III*, Henry III Fine Rolls Project [http://www.finerollshenry3.org.uk/content/calendar/roll_029.html, accessed 15 May 2014], no. 146.

¹⁰⁰ *CChR 1257–1300*, p. 100; Vincent, 'Pilgrimages', p. 23. On Arthur and Eleanor: Holt, 'King John and Arthur of Brittany'; M. Jones, 'Eleanor, suo jure Duchess of Brittany

for the forgiveness of sins from the church of Jerusalem, encompassing Henry III, John, and Isabella of Angoulême.[101]

Despite his posthumous reputation, in the centuries that followed John could still be considered capable of founding religious communities, even though such a connection cannot always be sustained. Thus, under Edward I, John was thought to have established Augustinian St Katherine's at Waterford, whilst in Edward II's reign the king's great-grandfather was believed to have founded St Leonard's hospital, Lancaster. Investigations under Edward III suggested the possibility that John had founded Benedictine Otterton.[102]

Later still, John's religious activity was seen positively in the Reformation period, perhaps unsurprisingly given the standoff (this time permanent) with the papacy. In the play *Kynge Johan*, the Protestant John Bale flattered Henry VIII as John's natural successor. Where the earlier king was a 'faithful Moses', the Tudor monarch was both Joshua, leading his people to a land of milk and honey, and David, smiting Goliath (the pope) and restoring 'Christian liberty'. Yet John's treatment of the clergy meant that he was 'like to rue it sore', when they came to write the history of his reign. Bale described the thirteenth-century ruler as a champion of the poor: God had made him king to help the desolate. Having been poisoned, the dying king himself states that his 'pleasure was to help such as were needy'. Bale's character England pronounces that he would be mourned by the halt, sore, and lame, for whom no prince had made so much provision in the form of *maisons dieux*, hospitals, and 'spital houses', concluding 'of this noble king much was the godliness'.[103]

Nor did the late king's reputation make his name impossible to use when his relatives christened their children. His niece, Blanche of Castile, bore twins who died at birth in 1213. One was named John. Blanche and her husband Louis of France, who invaded England in 1216 claiming his wife's hereditary right to the throne, used the name again, in 1219. The boy was assigned Anjou and Maine, but he also died young (1227). John was also the name chosen for the third surviving son of Louis IX.[104]

(1182x4–1241)', *ODNB* (Oxford, 2004, online edn 2008) [http://www.oxforddnb.com/view/article/46702, accessed 21 May 2014]; G. Seabourne, 'Eleanor of Brittany and her Treatment by King John and Henry III', *Nottingham Medieval Studies*, 51 (2007), 73–110 (esp. pp. 105–9).

[101] Vincent, 'Pilgrimages', pp. 18–19.

[102] See above, Chapter 3.

[103] *Kynge Johan. A Play in Two Parts. By John Bale*, ed. J. P. Collier, Camden Society, Old Series 2 (London, 1838), pp. 7, 23, 43, 82–3, 85; Clay, *Mediaeval Hospitals*, p. 72; J. N. King, 'Bale, John (1495–1563)', *ODNB* (Oxford, 2004, online edn 2009) [http://www.oxforddnb.com/view/article/1175, accessed 11 November 2013]. Shakespeare also has John prefigure Henry VIII, declaring 'we under God are supreme head': Shakespeare, *King John*, p. 106 (Act 3, Scene 1, line 155).

[104] Bowie, 'Daughters of Henry II', pp. 209–10 n. 30; R. Fawtier (trans. L. Butler and R. J. Adam), *The Capetian Kings of France: Monarchy and Nation (987–1328)* (London, 1964), p. 164; J. M. Ferrante, 'Blanche of Castile, Queen of France', *Epistolae: Medieval Women's Latin Letters* [http://epistolae.ccnmtl.columbia.edu/woman/77.html, accessed 22 August 2014]; Hallam and Everard, *Capetian France*, pp. 280, 286, 319, 320.

In England, it was once thought that Henry III and Eleanor of Provence had a child named John in 1250, who died before his second birthday, although Howell has shown that the evidence here is problematic.[105] Significantly, Edward I and Eleanor of Castile chose the name for their eldest son. Born in 1266, as a period of baronial reactions against royal government drew to a close, the choice seems to make a clear statement. The child died in 1271, and was said to have been mourned in England.[106] In 1316, the centenary of King John's death, the second son of Edward II, a king whose reign was blighted by dispute with the nobility, also took the name.[107] Later examples – John of Gaunt, fourth son of Edward III and Philippa of Hainault, and Gaunt's grandson, John, Duke of Bedford – prove that the name remained useable, but are likely to be linked to other family members and allies who held the name.[108] The last medieval example is an illegitimate child of Richard III, a king who emulated John in acquiring the image of the wicked royal uncle.[109] Further instances are not found until the nineteenth century, leading historians to write of 'a centuries-old royal prejudice against the name', although there has been an equal dearth of royal Richards since 1485. After two short-lived princes, Alexander John (who lived for two days in 1871) and John Charles Francis (1905–19), the name has not be used by the monarchy.[110]

---

[105] M. Howell, 'The Children of King Henry III and Eleanor of Provence', *TCE* IV, ed. P. R. Coss and S. D. Lloyd (Woodbridge, 1992), pp. 57–72.

[106] Prestwich, *Edward I*, pp. 82, 125–7; J. C. Parsons, 'The Year of Eleanor of Castile's Birth and her Children by Edward I', *Mediaeval Studies*, 46 (1984), 245–65 (pp. 258–9).

[107] Phillips, *Edward II*, pp. 102, 279.

[108] S. Walker, 'John, Duke of Aquitaine and Duke of Lancaster, Styled King of Castile and León (1340–1399)', *ODNB* (Oxford, 2004, online edn 2008) [http://www.oxforddnb.com/view/article/14843, accessed 23 May 2014]; J. Stratford, 'John, Duke of Bedford (1389–1435)', *ODNB* (Oxford, 2004, online edn 2011) [http://www.oxforddnb.com/view/article/14844, accessed 23 May 2014].

[109] His date of birth is unknown. He apparently died in the Tower of London, c. 1499: R. Horrox, 'Richard III (1452–1485)', *ODNB* (Oxford, 2004, online edn 2013) [http://www.oxforddnb.com/view/article/23500, accessed 23 May 2014].

[110] K. D. Reynolds, 'John, Prince (1905–1919)', *ODNB* (Oxford, 2004) [http://www.oxforddnb.com/view/article/76928, accessed 11 June 2014]; H. C. G. Matthew, 'Edward VII (1841–1910)', *ODNB* (Oxford, 2004, online edn 2013) [http://www.oxforddnb.com/view/article/32975, accessed 11 June 2014]. For Richard, the modern exceptions are the present Prince Edward (whose third given name is Richard), and Prince Richard, present duke of Gloucester (youngest grandchild of George V).

Conclusion

This study has explored the range and extent to which personal religion was practised by King John. Ultimately, we cannot know what he thought about the religious rituals of his day. What can be shown, however, is that he realised that he needed to be seen to participate, that this was an aspect of kingship that he should acknowledge and harness. In his wider rulership, his political and military failures can rarely be attributed to lack of effort, despite the criticisms of the chroniclers. In terms of religion, he fell out with the church dramatically, but realised that the personal religion of a king needed to be demonstrated as part of his efforts to preserve an aura of authority.

Thus, we can reconstruct the religious calendar of King John's court across the year, including most of the major festivals of the church year and the major saints, notably the Virgin Mary (see Table 2, below). The extent to which each feast was observed yearly is unclear, but the annual pattern would also have included the principle moveable feasts: Palm Sunday, Easter (including Maundy Thursday and Good Friday), Ascension (also the anniversary of John's coronation), Pentecost (Whitsunday), and possibly Trinity Sunday. An important element of John's religious activity was focused around Holy Week, as seen in his combined pilgrimages to Bury St Edmunds, Canterbury, and Westminster in 1201. This is before one-off religious events are considered, such as the king's attendance and participation at the funeral of Hugh of Lincoln in 1200.

Amidst observance of the rhythms of the religious year, this was a ruler who attended mass when expected. As far as we can tell, he participated in the required elements of the religion of the time, from baptism through to confession and blessing on his deathbed. He visited shrines, acknowledged their feast days, and gave offerings in honour of the saints. John recognised the new religious phenomenon of the cult of St Thomas Becket and, like his father and brothers, sought to integrate this within wider devotion to the saints, in particular veneration of royal cults, notably St Edward the Confessor and St Edmund, King and Martyr, both regarded as exemplary kings. It also included the newly canonised St Wulfstan of Worcester and promotion of the canonisation of Gilbert of Sempringham. Major Christian saints, notably the Virgin Mary, but also Peter, Paul, James the Great, Philip, and possibly John the Baptist, had an important place. Intercessory possibilities of other cults were acknowledged when opportunity arose. Thus, there was wide-ranging combined devotion to the saints.

John ensured that the infrastructure of personal religion was maintained at court, enabling observance ranging from mass to the liturgical celebration of kingship, the *Laudes Regiae*. Chaplains were appointed, paid, and provided with 'tools

Feast Day	Date
Christmas	25 December
Holy Innocents	28 December
Circumcision	1 January
Epiphany	6 January
Conversion of St Paul	25 January
Purification of the Virgin	2 February
St Peter in *Cathedra*	22 February
Annunciation of the Virgin	25 March
St John the Baptist	24 June
Apostles Peter and Paul	29 June
Visitation of the Virgin	2 July
St Margaret the Virgin	20 July
St Mary Magdalene	22 July
St James the Apostle	25 July
St Peter in Chains	1 August
St Laurence	10 August
Assumption of the Virgin	15 August
St Bartholomew	24 August
Nativity of the Virgin	8 September
Exaltation of the Cross	14 September
St Michael	29 September
St Edward the Confessor	13 October
St Luke	18 October
All Saints	1 November
St Leonard	6 November
St Martin	11 November
St Andrew	30 November
St Nicholas	6 December
Conception of the Virgin	8 December
St Lucy	13 December
St Thomas the Apostle	21 December

Based on the evidence discussed in previous chapters.

Table 2 Suggested religious calendar of King John's court

of their trade'. The fabric of the royal chapel was maintained at locations across the king's lands and within the travelling household. A collection of relics accompanied John on the road. Meanwhile, a series of officials were employed to give alms to the poor. The principal royal almoner is often assumed to have been a Templar, although the Cistercian abbots of Forde and Bindon were also prominent in distributing the king's alms. This activity took place in John's presence or at his court. Yet royal religion did not always involve prayers and services, or celebration of feast days, by the king himself. He provided for those celebrating masses which he almost certainly did not attend, commissioning observance in his name, in his absence, performed by priests employed specifically for the purpose. Potentially this would occur in perpetuity, down to the last days, at locations ranging from castle chapels to monasteries, nunneries, and the great cathedrals of the Anglo-Norman world.

Churches where prayers were commissioned were supplemented by those which John founded. Born out of dispute with the Cistercians, the king showed sustained commitment for the abbey he established, eventually located at Beaulieu. Careful arrangements were made in setting up the new community, covering day-to-day necessities, building materials, and the wherewithal to celebrate services. The ground-plan at Beaulieu is indicative of its royal patronage. This provides a religious example of an aspect of John's career where his ambitions had not been fully fulfilled when he died. Yet instances of completion of such complexes in only a few years are rare, particular those founded by kings with pressing political or military concerns. It was also characteristic of John, as with other kings, that this was a give and take relationship. Abbot Hugh must have gained a weary familiarity of the roads to Rome.

Beyond Beaulieu, various religious communities are linked to John as founder. For many, the evidence is patchy, whilst in some cases, as at Broomhall, links can be refuted. However, some houses, such as St John the Evangelist, Waterford, and St Laurence's hospital, Bristol, seem to have been begun by John. Elsewhere, links remain unproven, as in the cases of the hospitals of St Leonard, Chesterfield, and St Nicholas, Carlisle. Meanwhile, he sought the status of co-founder, alongside his father, at Augustinian Newstead. Despite the emergence of his dark reputation, and its endurance since his death, some communities believed, or felt it beneficial to claim, that they owed their existence to King John. Such was the case at Otterton, Marlborough, at Gilbertine Newstead-on-Ancholme (where he was remembered as co-founder, alongside Henry II), at St Katherine's, Waterford, and at the hospitals of St Bartholomew in Newbury, Kingsthorpe, and St Leonard, Lancaster.

John is rarely seen to be the equal of his royal peers, yet all this sets him alongside other kings of England in his attitude to religion. Indeed, his activity emulated his Angevin predecessors, the Empress Matilda, Henry II, Eleanor of Aquitaine, and his brothers, in particular Henry the Young King and Richard I. This included endowment of intercession for his wellbeing whilst alive, and for his soul after death. John respected the religious wishes of his predecessors. His chantry foundations invoked their names alongside his own. He supported the churches family members had founded, confirming their grants and regularly invoking the salvation of their souls. This included the religious houses linked to

Henry II's penances for his part in the murder of Thomas Becket. Down to her death in 1204, the influence of John's mother, Eleanor of Aquitaine, is especially striking, in particular in relation to the royal abbey of Fontevraud. Nonetheless, these were aspects of John's personal religion evident across his lifetime, creating association with religious communities the length and breadth of the lands he held as lord of Ireland from 1185, count of Mortain from 1189, and as King of England, duke of Normandy and Aquitaine, and count of Anjou from 1199.

Where the king's family largesse focused on named relatives, these were primarily those who were crowned kings or queens. Others, notably John's brother Geoffrey, whose son Arthur had been an obstacle to a smooth succession, were almost entirely missing. Likewise, Queen Isabella of Angoulême had only limited involvement. Nor did John specifically honour his sisters Matilda and Eleanor, although he provided for the soul of Joanna, his closest sibling in age. Thus we are faced with a paradox: a king whose 'family' religion singled out some, but not others. Perhaps they were remembered through references to John's kinsmen, yet equally there are echoes of his wider failings here. His choice of officials was on the one hand too narrow, yet included many men from his continental lands. He could not inspire widespread loyalty, but had a few trusted followers (whose religious foundations he also supported). John did many things that kings were expected to do, but clearly failed to strike the right balance. Thus, despite apparent absentees amongst his immediate relatives, religious grants linked to royal kinsmen extended into the past, including early dukes of Normandy and the Anglo-Norman kings, principally Henry I. John, like Henry, venerated the Virgin Mary. He continued the trend of royal support for his great-grandfather's monastic foundations. His grants also included houses associated with Stephen, the ruler who had usurped the claims of John's grandmother, the Empress Matilda, but equally a predecessor both as king and count of Mortain. Continuity in religious trends associated with John's kinswomen, the Anglo-Norman queens, is also clear, in keeping with the role of royal women in the transmission of family tradition.

Like his forebears, charity formed an important part of John's personal religion. He continued long-standing royal traditions of charity for leprosy. His almsgiving responded to periods of dearth or famine, and during Easter week, charity on Maundy Thursday showed engagement with ceremonial invoking the Last Supper. Almsgiving followed the king's regular failure to abstain on Wednesdays and to fast on Fridays, and occasions when he hunted on feast days. Such oversights are not indicative of assiduous religious observance, but he did make reparation, feeding the poor with bread, fish or meat, and ale. In light of the extensive religious calendar identified above, we might speculate that fasting was difficult for a king in terms of the hospitality expected of his household, or which it was normal to provide for him. Certainly the records note how courtiers joined him in fast-breaking. Churchmen recognised that such behaviour took place. Archbishop Langton himself preached that '"alms without fasting are more valuable than fasting without alms"'.[1]

---

[1] Rubin, *Charity*, p. 64; discussed above, Chapter 5.

Just as John engaged with trends inherited from his predecessors, so too they passed on to his son. Alongside his deep attachment to St Edward the Confessor, Henry III followed longstanding tradition in demonstrating devotion to a wide variety of saints, both royal and episcopal, Anglo-Saxon and post-Conquest, and major saints such as Mary. It also fell to Henry to complete Beaulieu. Indeed, he began his own *magnum opus* at Westminster after John's abbey was largely complete. Fleeting examples of feeding the poor to commemorate the dead occasionally feature in John's religious practice and became a notable aspect of his son's piety. It was the scale of Henry III's giving which was exceptional. Overall, there is a sense of an accepted pattern of royal religious behaviour that kings inherited, continued, then passed to their successors. King John was no exception.

Such aspects of John's kingship are often overlooked. Events surrounding the loss of Normandy and Anjou, his all-encompassing efforts to maximise revenue to win them back, and the reaction after he failed, seen most strikingly in Magna Carta, all point to a ruthless, indeed merciless, king who irrevocably eroded trust. Later commentators simply did not look at John for engagement with religion. His reputation meant that they did not expect to find evidence. This is exacerbated by his dispute with the church. For the king this was in essence political. Nevertheless, sanctions of interdict and excommunication, and his reaction against those who obeyed them, provide powerful reasons why his ongoing religious observance went unnoticed or, if it was observed, deemed insincere.

John handled the Canterbury crisis with characteristically misplaced confidence. He thought he could orchestrate elections on his own terms and refused to accept alternative jurisdiction: the papacy. His attitude was in keeping with that of his predecessors and of other European rulers, and consistent with his hard-line response to opposition, questioning of his will or of what he perceived as his rights. With hindsight, he was fighting against the tide. He was almost certainly amongst the last to recognise it. His response to this crisis was not indiscriminate. John sought to present a united front and targeted those who opposed him. The Canterbury monks, seen as traitors, bore the brunt of reprisals, whilst the executors of the sanctions, and those who chose exile, were deemed fair targets. The king tried to pursue business as usual, seeking to secure bishoprics for his clerks when positions fell vacant. This attitude continued after the excommunication and interdict were lifted, although John conceded the principle of free elections in 1214, and again in Magna Carta.

With churchmen refusing to administer the sacraments, the king was typically alert to the revenue-raising opportunities presented by the boycott, seizing ecclesiastical property and imposing fines for its return. Nevertheless, John viewed excommunication with trepidation, if not religiously then due to the threat to his temporal authority. Mass oath-takings were ordered to attempt to ensure the loyalty of freemen, before the king resumed his financial exploitation by heavily taxing religious communities. This provided rich material for the chroniclers of the day and fed the more outlandish claims of their successors, notably Roger of Wendover and Matthew Paris.

The criticism obscures the evidence that the crown argued in favour of the king's role in elections during ongoing exchanges of envoys between the royal and papal courts. This standpoint was losing currency, but the case for the king's involvement was nonetheless advanced by John and his supporters. He ultimately admitted defeat, but his stance was not as isolated as traditionally assumed. However, his settlement with Pope Innocent seemed like a complete *volte-face*, and can hardly have added to his reputation for sincerity. Therefore, contemporary observers satirised the 'prophecy' of Peter of Wakefield in relation to John's surrender of his kingdom of England and lordship of Ireland to the pope. The king's damage limitation exercise thereafter, seen in his effort to pay minimal compensation, did nothing to redeem his overall reputation. Angry chroniclers described him as a thief. This hardly promised well for interpretation of his attitude to the charter of liberties (later named Magna Carta) to which he set his seal in June 1215.

Whilst John saw his dispute with the church in political terms, he viewed his personal religion as a separate matter during this period. Replacement monks were brought in at Canterbury. Favoured religious communities found that seized property was swiftly restored. Much of the evidence for the king's Easter observance comes from the years of interdict and excommunication. Servants continued their work in the royal chapel. The king engaged with the cult of the saints. Religious houses, including Beaulieu, received support for building works. Alms was distributed to the poor, both for the souls of John's forebears and because of his transgressions on holy days. Many of these actions were not expressly prohibited by the sanctions, but this remains religious activity by a king whose kingdom was under interdict and who, from 1209 to 1213, was personally excommunicate: in theory cast from the community of the faithful. When John finally reached a settlement, the formalities of absolution and readmission to the church were respected. Suitable observance can even be suggested when he vowed to go on crusade. That no-one saw this undertaking as genuine further demonstrates how John could make religious responses appropriate to a king which were increasingly seen as lacking substance.

The interdict of 1208-14 was the last to be laid upon England prior to the break with Rome.[2] Yet, just as John joined his forebears in holding his ground over the election of prelates, so his successors came into conflict with the church. Setting aside Henry VIII, who was clearly exceptional, this also included an indisputably devout king, Henry III. The latter was threatened with interdict when he failed to provide Pope Alexander IV with military support for the conquest of Sicily. Equally, however, John's submission in 1213-14 helped incline the papacy to use interdict and excommunication on behalf of his heir, both during Henry's minority and in response to the baronial reaction of the 1260s. Edward I also fell into dispute with the papacy over provision to benefices, though this was never allowed to escalate.[3] The legend of St Wulfstan's staff, deployed by John against Pope Innocent III's envoys, was invoked again during the reigns of Henry III, Edward I, and Edward II.

The scale of John's dispute with the church, and the cumulative nature of his

---

[2] Cheney, *Innocent*, p. 22.
[3] Clarke, pp. 118-19, 176-7.

political and military setbacks, can only lead to the conclusion that he failed as king, whether judged by medieval or modern standards. By holding out for his rights, and by continually losing, he condemned himself to the caricature created by the chroniclers. Over time, the assumptions and stereotypes that surround 'England's Evil King' magnified. Yet reconsideration of the evidence reveals that he engaged with the religious requirements of kingship, but his efforts were increasingly condemned by writers who could not believe him capable of the required attitude. Thus Adam of Eynsham, Roger of Wendover, Matthew Paris, and others believed what they said about John, but nonetheless offer a one-sided portrait. There are hints that some saw him differently, not least in the range of individuals who provided for his soul after death. Some people, apparently, did not see King John's soul as irredeemable, and continued efforts were made by courtiers at the heart of royal government – men such as Hubert Walter, Geoffrey fitz Peter, and Peter des Roches – to secure prayers for John during his reign. In many ways, John's court had too narrow a focus. There was insufficient place for those who felt they had a right to be involved, and who might in turn report the king's activity to the chroniclers. Perhaps this helps explain how the personal religion of King John failed to make an impact, either during his lifetime or after his burial in Worcester Cathedral.

Bibliography

Unprinted primary sources

Cambridge	St John's College	Ms. D 14.163.1
London	British Library	Additional Ms. 29436
		Cotton Ms. Domitian A. xii
		Cotton Ms. Galba E. iii, 2
		Cotton Ms. Nero A. xii
		Cotton Ms. Nero C. ix
London	College of Arms	Ms. Arundel 60
London	National Archives	C52/26
		SC1/1/208
		SC8/100/4954
		SC8/123/6135
		SC8/319/E372
		SC8/322/E517
London/Oslo	The Schøyen Collection	Ms. 610 [http://www.schoyencollection.com/palaeography-collection-introduction/latin-documentary-scripts/gothic-court-secretary/court-scripts/ms-610, accessed 28 February 2014]
Oxford	Bodleian Library	Ms. Rawlinson B 479

Printed primary sources

The Account-Book of Beaulieu Abbey, ed. S. F. Hockey, Camden 4th ser., 16 (London, 1975)

The Acta of the Bishops of Chichester 1075–1207, ed. H. Mayr-Harting, Canterbury and York Society, 56 (London, 1964)

Acta Stephani Langton Cantuariensis Archiepiscopi A.D. 1207–1228, ed. K. Major, Canterbury and York Society, 50 (Oxford, 1950)

Annales de Burton (A.D. 1004–1263), ed. H. R. Luard, *Annales Monastici*, RS 36, 5 vols (London, 1864-69), vol. I, pp. 181–500

Annales Londonienses, ed. W. Stubbs, *Chronicles of the Reigns of Edward I and Edward II*, RS 76, 2 vols (London, 1882-83), vol. I, pp. 3–251

Annales de Margan (A.D. 1066–1232), ed. H. R. Luard, *Annales Monastici*, RS 36, 5 vols

(London, 1864-69), vol. I, pp. 1-40

Annales Monasterii de Waverleia (A.D. 1-1291), ed. H. R. Luard, Annales Monastici, RS 36, 5 vols (London, 1864-69), vol. II, pp. 127-411

Annales Monasterii de Wintonia (A.D. 519-1277), ed. H. R. Luard, Annales Monastici, RS 36, 5 vols (London, 1864-69), vol. II, pp. 3-125

Annales Prioratus de Dunstaplia (A.D. 1-1297), ed. H. R. Luard, Annales Monastici, RS 36, 5 vols (London, 1864-69), vol. III, pp. 1-420

Annales Prioratus de Wigornia (A.D. 1-1377), ed. H. R. Luard, Annales Monastici, RS 36, 5 vols (London, 1864-69), vol. IV, pp. 353-564

'Annales Radingenses Posteriores, 1135-1264', ed. C. W. Previté-Orton, EHR, 37 (1922), pp. 400-3

Annales S. Edmundi a. 1-1212, ed. F. Liebermann, Ungedruckte Anglo-Normannische Geschichtsquellen (Strasbourg, 1879), pp. 97-155

Annales de Theokesberia (A.D. 1066-1263), ed. H. R. Luard, Annales Monastici, RS 36, 5 vols (London, 1864-69), vol. I, pp. 41-180

Annales Wintonienses in monasterio de Waverley adaucti a. 1201-60, ed. F. Liebermann, Ungedruckte Anglo-Normannische Geschichtsquellen (Strasbourg, 1879), pp. 173-202

Annals of Barnwell Priory, ed. W. Stubbs, Memoriale Walteri de Coventria. The Historical Collections of Walter of Coventry, RS 58, 2 vols (London, 1872-73), vol. II, pp. 196-279

Annals of Stanley, ed. R. Howlett, Chronicles of the Reigns of Stephen, Henry II and Richard I, RS 82, 4 vols (London, 1884-89), vol. II, pp. 501-83

The Antient Kalendars and Inventories of the Treasury of His Majesty's Exchequer Together with other Documents Illustrating the History of that Repository, ed. F. Palgrave, RComm, 3 vols (London, 1836)

'A Bailiff's List and Chronicle from Worcester', ed. D. MacCulloch and P. Hughes, Antiquaries Journal, 75 (1995), 235-53

The Beauchamp Cartulary Charters 1100-1268, ed. E. Mason, PRS, 81, ns 43 (London, 1980)

The Beaulieu Cartulary, ed. S. F. Hockey, with an introduction by P. D. A. Harvey and S. F. Hockey, Southampton Records Series, 17 (Southampton, 1974)

The Book of St Gilbert, ed. R. Foreville and G. Keir, OMT (Oxford, 1987)

Calendar of the Charter Rolls Preserved in the Public Record Office. Henry III. 1226-1257, HMSO (London, 1903)

Calendar of the Charter Rolls Preserved in the Public Record Office. Henry III-Edward I. 1257-1300, HMSO (London, 1906)

Calendar of the Charter Rolls Preserved in the Public Record Office. Edward I, Edward II. 1300-1326, HMSO (London, 1908)

Calendar of the Close Rolls Preserved in the Public Record Office. Edward I. 1302-1307, HMSO (London, 1908)

Calendar of the Close Rolls Preserved in the Public Record Office. Edward III. 1330-1333, HMSO (London, 1898)

Calendar of the Close Rolls Preserved in the Public Record Office. Edward III. 1360-1364, HMSO (London, 1909)

Calendar of the Close Rolls Preserved in the Public Record Office. Edward IV. 1461-1468, HMSO (London, 1949)

Calendar of Documents Preserved in France, Illustrative of the History of Great Britain and Ireland. Vol. I. 918-1206, ed. J. H. Round, HMSO (London, 1899)

Calendar of Documents Relating to Ireland Preserved in Her Majesty's Public Record Office, London, 1171-1251, ed. H. S. Sweetman (London, 1875)

Calendar of Documents Relating to Ireland, Preserved in Her Majesty's Public Record Office, London, 1285-1292, ed. H. S. Sweetman (London, 1879)

Calendar of Documents Relating to Scotland Preserved in Her Majesty's Public Record Office, London. Vol. I. 1108-1272, ed. J. Bain (Edinburgh, 1881)

Calendar of Entries in the Papal Registers Relating to Great Britain and Ireland. Papal Letters. Vol. I. A.D. 1198-1304, ed. W. H. Bliss, HMSO (London, 1893)

Calendar of Inquisitions Miscellaneous (Chancery) Preserved in the Public Record Office. Vol. II. Edward II-22 Edward III, HMSO (London, 1916)

Calendar of the Liberate Rolls Preserved in the Public Record Office 1226-1240, HMSO (London, 1916)

Calendar of the Liberate Rolls Preserved in the Public Record Office 1240-1245, HMSO (London, 1930)

Calendar of the Liberate Rolls Preserved in the Public Record Office 1245-1251, HMSO (London, 1937)

Calendar of the Liberate Rolls Preserved in the Public Record Office 1251-1260, HMSO (London, 1959)

Calendar of the Liberate Rolls Preserved in the Public Record Office 1260-1267, HMSO (London, 1961)

Calendar of the Liberate Rolls Preserved in the Public Record Office 1267-1272 with Appendices 1220-1267, HMSO (London, 1964)

Calendar of the Patent Rolls of the Reign of Henry III Preserved in the Public Record Office. 1216-1225, HMSO (London, 1901)

Calendar of the Patent Rolls of the Reign of Henry III Preserved in the Public Record Office. 1225-1232, HMSO (London, 1903)

Calendar of the Patent Rolls Preserved in the Public Record Office. Henry III. 1232-1247, HMSO (London, 1906)

Calendar of the Patent Rolls Preserved in the Public Record Office. Henry III. 1247-1258, HMSO (London, 1908)

Calendar of the Patent Rolls Preserved in the Public Record Office. Henry III. 1258-1266, HMSO (London, 1910)

Calendar of the Patent Rolls Preserved in the Public Record Office. Henry III. 1266-1272, HMSO (London, 1913)

Calendar of the Patent Rolls Preserved in the Public Record Office. Edward I. 1281-1292, HMSO (London, 1893)

Calendar of the Patent Rolls Preserved in the Public Record Office. Edward III. 1327-1330, HMSO (London, 1891)

Calendar of the Patent Rolls Preserved in the Public Record Office. Edward III. 1330-1334, HMSO (London, 1893)

Calendar of the Patent Rolls Preserved in the Public Record Office. Edward III. 1340-1343, HMSO (London, 1900)

Calendar of the Patent Rolls Preserved in the Public Record Office. Edward III. 1350-1354, HMSO (London, 1907)

Calendar of the Patent Rolls Preserved in the Public Record Office. Richard II. 1396–1399, HMSO (London, 1927)

Calendar of the Patent Rolls Preserved in the Public Record Office. Edward IV, Edward V, Richard III. 1478–1485, HMSO (London, 1901)

The Cartae Antiquae Rolls 1–10, ed. L. Landon, PRS, 55, ns 17 (London, 1939)

The Cartae Antiquae Rolls 11–20, ed. J. C. Davies, PRS, 71, ns 33 (London, 1960)

Cartulaire de l'abbaye royale de Notre-Dame de Bon-Port de l'Ordre de Cîteaux au diocèse d'Evreux, ed. J. Andrieux (Evreux, 1862)

The Cartulary of Bradenstoke Priory, ed. V. C. M. London, Wiltshire Record Society, 35 (Devizes, 1979)

The Cartulary of Cirencester Abbey Gloucestershire, ed. C. R. Ross and M. Devine, 3 vols (Oxford, 1964–77)

The Cartulary of Worcester Cathedral Priory (Register I), ed. R. R. Darlington, PRS, 76, ns 38 (London, 1968 for 1962–63)

The Chancellor's Roll for the Eighth Year of the Reign of King Richard the First, Michaelmas 1196 (Pipe Roll 42), ed. D. M. Stenton, PRS, 45, ns 7 (London, 1930)

Chartae, Privilegia et Immunitates, Transcripts of Charters and Privileges to Cities, Towns, Abbeys, and Other Bodies Corporate. 18 Henry II to 18 Richard II (1171 to 1395), Irish Record Commission (Dublin, London and Edinburgh, 1829–30)

Charters and Documents Illustrating the History of the Cathedral, City and Diocese of Salisbury in the Twelfth and Thirteenth Centuries, ed. W. R. Jones and W. D. Macray, RS 97 (London, 1891)

The Charters of Duchess Constance of Brittany and her Family 1171–1221, ed. J. Everard and M. Jones (Woodbridge, 1999)

'Chartes d'Otterton, Prieuré dépendant de l'abbaye de Mont-Saint-Michel', ed. L. Guilloreau, *Revue Mabillon*, 5 (1909) 169–206

The Chartulary of the High Church of Chichester, ed. W. D. Peckham, Sussex Record Society Publications, 46 (Lewes, 1946)

Chronica Johannis de Oxenedes, ed. H. Ellis, RS 13 (London, 1859)

Chronica Magistri Rogeri de Houedene, ed. W. Stubbs, RS 51, 4 vols (London, 1868–71)

Chronica de Mailros, e codice unico in bibliotheca Cottoniana servato, ed. J. Stevenson, Bannatyne Club, 49 (Edinburgh, 1835)

Chronica Monasterii de Melsa, a fundatione usque ad annum 1396, auctore Thoma de Burton, abbate. Accedit continuatio ad annum 1406 a monacho quodam ipsius domus, ed. E. A. Bond, RS 43, 3 vols (London, 1866–68)

The Chronicle of Bury St Edmunds 1212–1301, ed. and trans. A. Gransden, NMT (London, 1964)

The Chronicle of the Election of Hugh Abbot of Bury St Edmunds and later Bishop of Ely, ed. and trans. R. M. Thomson, OMT (Oxford, 1974)

The Chronicle of Robert of Torigni, Abbot of the Monastery of St Michael-in-Peril-of-the-Sea, ed. R. Howlett, *Chronicles of the Reigns of Stephen, Henry II, and Richard I*, RS 82, 4 vols (London, 1884–89), vol. IV, pp. 3–315

The Chronicle of the Reigns of Stephen, Henry II, and Richard I, by Gervase, the Monk of Canterbury, ed. W. Stubbs, *The Historical Works of Gervase of Canterbury*, RS 73, 2 vols (London, 1879–80), vol. I, pp. 1–594

The Chronicle of William de Rishanger of the Barons' Wars. The Miracles of Simon de Mont-

fort, ed. J. O. Halliwell, Camden Society, Old Series 15 (London, 1840)

Chronicon de Lanercost. MCCI-MCCCXLVI. E codice Cottoniano nunc primum typis mandatum, ed. J. Stevenson, Bannatyne Club, 65, and Maitland Club, 46 (Edinburgh, 1839)

Chronicon vulgo dictum chronicon Thomae Wykes A.D. 1066-1289, ed. H. R. Luard, *Annales Monastici*, RS 36, 5 vols (London, 1864-69), vol. IV, pp. 6-319

Chronique d'Ernoul et de Bernard le trésorier, ed. L. de Mas Latrie, Société de l'histoire de France (Paris, 1871)

Close Rolls of the Reign of Henry III Preserved in the Public Record Office. 1227-1231, HMSO (London, 1902)

Close Rolls of the Reign of Henry III Preserved in the Public Record Office. 1231-1234, HMSO (London, 1905)

Close Rolls of the Reign of Henry III Preserved in the Public Record Office. 1234-1237, HMSO (London, 1908)

Close Rolls of the Reign of Henry III Preserved in the Public Record Office. 1237-1242, HMSO (London, 1911)

Close Rolls of the Reign of Henry III Preserved in the Public Record Office. 1242-1247, HMSO (London, 1916)

Close Rolls of the Reign of Henry III Preserved in the Public Record Office. 1247-1251, HMSO (London, 1922)

Close Rolls of the Reign of Henry III Preserved in the Public Record Office. 1251-1253, HMSO (London, 1927)

Close Rolls of the Reign of Henry III Preserved in the Public Record Office. 1254-1256, HMSO (London, 1951)

Close Rolls of the Reign of Henry III Preserved in the Public Record Office. 1256-1259, HMSO (London, 1932)

Close Rolls of the Reign of Henry III Preserved in the Public Record Office. 1259-1261, HMSO (London, 1934)

Close Rolls of the Reign of Henry III Preserved in the Public Record Office. 1261-1264, HMSO (London, 1936)

Close Rolls of the Reign of Henry III Preserved in the Public Record Office. 1268-1272, HMSO (London, 1938)

Councils and Synods with Other Documents Relating to the English Church. II. A.D. 1205-1313. Part I. 1205-1265, ed. F. M. Powicke and C. R. Cheney (Oxford, 1964)

The Deeds of Pope Innocent III, by an Anonymous Author, trans. J. M. Powell (Washington DC, 2004)

A Descriptive Catalogue of the Manuscripts in the Library of Lambeth Palace, ed. M. R. James and C. Jenkins, 5 vols (Cambridge, 1930-32)

Dialogus de Scaccario. The Dialogue of the Exchequer. Constitutio Domus Regis. The Establishment of the Royal Household, new edn, ed. and trans. E. Amt and S. D. Church, OMT (Oxford, 2007)

'*Dialogus inter regem Henricum secundum et abbatem Bonnevallis*. Un écrit de Pierre de Blois réédité', ed. R. B. C. Huygens, *Revue Bénédictine*, 68 (1958), 87-112

Diplomatic Documents Preserved in the Public Record Office. Volume I. 1101-1272, ed. P. Chaplais, HMSO (London, 1964)

'Diplôme de Philippe Auguste instituant deux chapellenies pour l'âme de Geoffroy, comte de Bretagne', ed. A. de Bouard, *Le Moyen Age*, 35 (1924), 63-70

Disciplinary Decrees of the General Councils: Text, Translation and Commentary, ed. H. J. Schroeder (St Louis, 1937), pp. 236-96, from *Internet Medieval Sourcebook* [http://www.fordham.edu/halsall/basis/lateran4.html, accessed 16 November 2010]

Domesday Book. A Complete Translation, ed. A. Williams and G. H. Martin (London, 2002)

Dugdale, W., *Monasticon Anglicanum: A History of the Abbies and other Monasteries, Hospitals, Frieries, and Cathedral and Collegiate Churches, with their Dependencies, in England and Wales*, ed. J. Caley, H. Ellis and B. Bandinel, 6 vols (London, 1817-30)

Earldom of Gloucester Charters. The Charters and Scribes of the Earls and Countesses of Gloucester to A.D. 1217, ed. R. B. Patterson (Oxford, 1973)

The Early Charters of the Augustinian Canons of Waltham Abbey, Essex 1062-1230, ed. R. Ransford (Woodbridge, 1989)

Early Charters of the Cathedral Church of St Paul, London, ed. M. Gibbs, Camden 3rd ser., 58 (London, 1939)

Early Compotus Rolls of the Priory of Worcester, trans. and ed. J. M. Wilson and C. Gordon, Worcester Historical Society (Oxford, 1908)

English Episcopal Acta III. Canterbury 1193-1205, ed. C. R. Cheney and E. John (Oxford, 1991)

English Episcopal Acta VIII. Winchester 1070-1204, ed. M. J. Franklin (Oxford, 1993)

English Episcopal Acta IX. Winchester 1205-1238, ed. N. Vincent (Oxford, 1994)

English Episcopal Acta 14. Coventry and Lichfield 1072-1159, ed. M. J. Franklin (Oxford, 1997)

English Episcopal Acta 16. Coventry and Lichfield 1160-1182, ed. M. J. Franklin (Oxford, 1998)

English Episcopal Acta 17. Coventry and Lichfield 1183-1208, ed. M. J. Franklin (Oxford, 1998)

English Episcopal Acta 18. Salisbury 1078-1217, ed. B. R. Kemp (Oxford, 1999)

English Episcopal Acta 19. Salisbury 1217-1228, ed. B. R. Kemp (Oxford, 2000)

English Episcopal Acta 20. York 1154-1181, ed. M. Lovatt (Oxford, 2000)

English Episcopal Acta 22. Chichester 1215-1253, ed. P. M. Hoskin (Oxford, 2001)

English Episcopal Acta 23. Chichester 1254-1305, ed. P. M. Hoskin (Oxford, 2001)

English Episcopal Acta 25. Durham 1196-1237, ed. M. G. Snape (Oxford, 2002)

English Episcopal Acta 26. London 1189-1228, ed. D. P. Johnson (Oxford, 2003)

English Episcopal Acta 27. York 1189-1212, ed. M. Lovatt (Oxford, 2004)

English Episcopal Acta 30. Carlisle 1133-1292, ed. D. M. Smith (Oxford, 2005)

English Episcopal Acta 31. Ely 1109-1197, ed. N. Karn (Oxford, 2005)

English Episcopal Acta 33. Worcester 1062-1185, ed. M. Cheney, D. Smith, C. Brooke, and P. M. Hoskin (Oxford, 2007)

English Episcopal Acta 34. Worcester 1186-1218, ed. M. Cheney, D. Smith, C. Brooke, and P. M. Hoskin (Oxford, 2008)

English Episcopal Acta 42. Ely 1198-1256, ed. N. Karn (Oxford, 2013)

'Excerpta ex obituario minori ecclesiae Dunelmensis', ed. A. H. Thompson, *Liber Vitae Ecclesiae Dunelmensis; nec non obituaria duo ejusdem ecclesiae*, Surtees Society, 136 (London, 1841), pp. 149-52

Fine Roll 5 Henry III, Henry III Fine Rolls Project [http://www.finerollshenry3.org.uk/

content/calendar/roll_015.html, accessed 30 July 2013]
Fine Roll 6 Henry III, Henry III Fine Rolls Project [http://www.finerollshenry3.org.uk/content/calendar/roll_016.html, accessed 15 May 2014]
Fine Roll 9 Henry III, Henry III Fine Rolls Project [http://www.finerollshenry3.org.uk/content/calendar/roll_022.html, accessed 30 July 2013]
Fine Roll 11 Henry III, Henry III Fine Rolls Project [http://www.finerollshenry3.org.uk/content/calendar/roll_025.html, accessed 15 May 2014]
Fine Roll 14 Henry III, Henry III Fine Rolls Project [http://www.finerollshenry3.org.uk/content/calendar/roll_029.html, accessed 15 May 2014]
Fine Roll 17 Henry III, Henry III Fine Rolls Project [http://www.finerollshenry3.org.uk/content/calendar/roll_032.html, accessed 15 May 2014]
Fine Roll 19 Henry III, Henry III Fine Rolls Project [http://www.finerollshenry3.org.uk/content/calendar/roll_034.html, accessed 30 July 2013]
Fine Roll 20 Henry III, Henry III Fine Rolls Project [http://www.finerollshenry3.org.uk/content/calendar/roll_035.html, accessed 14 March 2011]
Fine Roll 27 Henry III, Henry III Fine Rolls Project [http://www.finerollshenry3.org.uk/content/calendar/roll_040a.html, accessed 16 July 2013]
Fine Roll 32 Henry III, Henry III Fine Rolls Project [http://www.finerollshenry3.org.uk/content/calendar/roll_045.html, accessed 16 May 2014]
Fine Roll 33 Henry III, Henry III Fine Rolls Project [http://www.finerollshenry3.org.uk/content/calendar/roll_046.html, accessed 16 July 2013]
Fine Roll 34 Henry III, Henry III Fine Rolls Project [http://www.finerollshenry3.org.uk/content/calendar/roll_047.html, accessed 30 July 2013]
Fine Roll 35 Henry III, Henry III Fine Rolls Project [http://www.finerollshenry3.org.uk/content/calendar/roll_048.html, accessed 30 July 2013]
Foedera, Conventiones, Litterae et cujuscunque generis Acta Publica inter Reges Angliae et alios quosuis imperatores, reges, pontifices, principes vel communitates ab ingressu Gulielmi I in Angliam, A.D. 1066 ad nostra usque tempora habita aut tractate, ed. T. Rymer, new edn ed. A. Clark and F. Holbrooke, 4 vols (London, 1816-69)
Fragmentary Chronicle, with Appendix of Letters, Relating to the Events Connected with the Election of Archbishop Langton to the See of Canterbury, ed. W. Stubbs, *The Historical Works of Gervase of Canterbury*, RS 73, 2 vols (London, 1879-80), vol. II, pp. liv-cxv
Gervase of Canterbury, *The Gesta Regum with its Continuation*, ed. W. Stubbs, *The Historical Works of Gervase of Canterbury*, RS 73, 2 vols (London, 1879-80), vol. II, pp. 1-106
Gervase of Canterbury, *Mappa Mundi*, ed. W. Stubbs, *The Historical Works of Gervase of Canterbury*, RS 73, 2 vols (London, 1879-80), vol. II, pp. 414-49
Gesta Abbatum Monasterii Sancti Albani, a Thoma Walsingham, regnante Ricardo Secundo, ejusdem ecclesiae praecentore, compilata, ed. H. T. Riley, RS 28, 3 vols (London, 1867-69)
Gesta Regis Henrici Secundi Benedicti Abbatis. The Chronicle of the Reigns of Henry II and Richard I. A.D. 1169-1192; Known Commonly under the Name of Benedict of Peterborough, ed. W. Stubbs, RS 49, 2 vols (London, 1867)
Giraldi Cambrensis de jure et statu Menevensis ecclesiae dialogus, ed. J. S. Brewer, *Giraldi Cambrensis Opera*, RS 21, 8 vols (London, 1861-91) vol. III, pp. 101-373
Giraldi Cambrensis de Principis Instructione Liber, ed. G. F. Warner, *Giraldi Cambrensis*

Opera, RS 21, 8 vols (London, 1861-91), vol. VIII

Giraldus Cambrensis de vita Galfridi Archiepiscopi Eboracensis: sive certamina Galfridi Eboracensis Archiepiscopi, ed. J. S. Brewer, Giraldi Cambrensis Opera, RS 21, 8 vols (London, 1861-91), vol. IV, pp. 357-431

The Great Roll of the Pipe for the Thirty-Fourth Year of the Reign of King Henry the Second, A.D. 1187-1188, PRS, 38 (London, 1925)

The Great Roll of the Pipe for the Seventh Year of the Reign of King Richard the First, Michaelmas 1195 (Pipe Roll 41), ed. D. M. Stenton, PRS, 44, ns 6 (London, 1929)

The Great Roll of the Pipe for the Ninth Year of the Reign of King Richard the First, Michaelmas 1197 (Pipe Roll 43), ed. D. M. Stenton, PRS, 46, ns 8 (London, 1931)

The Great Roll of the Pipe for the Tenth Year of the Reign of King Richard the First, Michaelmas 1198 (Pipe Roll 44), ed. D. M. Stenton, PRS, 47, ns 9 (London, 1932)

The Great Roll of the Pipe for the First Year of the Reign of King John, Michaelmas 1199 (Pipe Roll 45), ed. D. M. Stenton, PRS, 48, ns 10 (London, 1933)

The Great Roll of the Pipe for the Second Year of the Reign of King John, Michaelmas 1200 (Pipe Roll 46), ed. D. M. Stenton, PRS, 50, ns 12 (London, 1934)

The Great Roll of the Pipe for the Third Year of the Reign of King John, Michaelmas 1201 (Pipe Roll 47), ed. D. M. Stenton, PRS, 50, ns 12 (London, 1934)

The Great Roll of the Pipe for the Fourth Year of the Reign of King John, Michaelmas 1202 (Pipe Roll 48), ed. D. M. Stenton, PRS, 53, ns 15 (London, 1937)

The Great Roll of the Pipe for the Fifth Year of the Reign of King John, Michaelmas 1203 (Pipe Roll 49), ed. D. M. Stenton, PRS, 54, ns 16 (London, 1938)

The Great Roll of the Pipe for the Sixth Year of the Reign of King John, Michaelmas 1204 (Pipe Roll 50), ed. D. M. Stenton, PRS, 56, ns 18 (London, 1940)

The Great Roll of the Pipe for the Seventh Year of the Reign of King John, Michaelmas 1205 (Pipe Roll 51), ed. S. Smith, PRS, 57, ns 19 (London, 1941)

The Great Roll of the Pipe for the Eighth Year of the Reign of King John, Michaelmas 1206 (Pipe Roll 52), ed. D. M. Stenton, PRS, 58, ns 20 (London, 1942)

The Great Roll of the Pipe for the Ninth Year of the Reign of King John, Michaelmas 1207 (Pipe Roll 53), ed. A. M. Kirkus, PRS, 60, ns 22 (London, 1946)

The Great Roll of the Pipe for the Tenth Year of the Reign of King John, Michaelmas 1208 (Pipe Roll 54), ed. D. M. Stenton, PRS, 61, ns 23 (London, 1947)

The Great Roll of the Pipe for the Eleventh Year of the Reign of King John, Michaelmas 1209 (Pipe Roll 55), ed. D. M. Stenton, PRS, 62, ns 24 (London, 1949)

The Great Roll of the Pipe for the Twelfth Year of the Reign of King John, Michaelmas 1210 (Pipe Roll 56), ed. C. F. Slade, PRS, 64, ns 26 (London, 1951)

The Great Roll of the Pipe for the Thirteenth Year of the Reign of King John, Michaelmas 1211 (Pipe Roll 57), ed. D. M. Stenton, PRS, 66, ns 28 (London, 1953)

The Great Roll of the Pipe for the Fourteenth Year of the Reign of King John, Michaelmas 1212 (Pipe Roll 58), ed. P. M. Barnes, PRS, 68, ns 30 (London, 1955)

The Great Roll of the Pipe for the Sixteenth Year of the Reign of King John, Michaelmas 1214 (Pipe Roll 60), ed. P. M. Barnes, PRS, 73, ns 35 (London, 1962)

Histoire des ducs de Normandie et des rois d'Angleterre, ed. F. Michel (Paris, 1840)

Historiae Anglicanae Scriptores X, ed. R. Twysden (London, 1652)

History of William Marshal, ed. A. J. Holden, trans. S. Gregory, and historical notes by D. Crouch, Anglo-Norman Text Society, Occasional Publications Series, 4, 3 vols

(London, 2002–06)
'Inquisition of 1601 Regarding the Lazar or Leper House, Waterford', *Journal of the Waterford and South East Ireland Archaeological Society*, 1 (1895), 115–18
Interdict Documents, ed. P. M. Barnes and W. R. Powell, PRS, 72, ns 34 (London, 1960)
'The Irish Pipe Roll of 14 John, 1211–1212', ed. O. Davis and D. B. Quinn, *Ulster Journal of Archaeology*, 4, supplement (1941), 1–76
Issues of the Exchequer, Being a Collection of Payments made out of His Majesty's Revenue from King Henry III to King Henry VI Inclusive, ed. F. Devon (London, 1837)
Jean de Joinville, 'The Life of Saint Louis', *Joinville and Villehardouin. Chronicles of the Crusades*, trans. M. R. B. Shaw (Harmondsworth, 1963), pp. 161–353
Jocelin of Brakelond. *Chronicle of the Abbey of Bury St Edmunds*, trans. D. Greenway and J. Sayers (Oxford and New York, 1989)
Kynge Johan. A Play in Two Parts. By John Bale, ed. J. P. Collier, Camden Society, Old Series 2 (London, 1838)
Lancashire Inquests, Extents, and Feudal Aids. A.D. 1205–A.D. 1307, ed. W. Farrer, The Record Society for the Publication of Original Documents relating to Lancashire and Cheshire, 48 (Liverpool, 1903)
The Lancashire Pipe Rolls of 31 Henry I, A.D. 1130, and of the Reigns of Henry II, A.D. 1155–1189; Richard I, A.D. 1188–1199; and King John, A.D. 1199–1216. The Latin text extended and notes added. Also Early Lancashire Charters of the period from the Reign of William Rufus to that of King John, ed. W. Farrer (Liverpool, 1902)
Langton, Stephen, *Commentary on the Book of Chronicles*, ed. A. Saltman (Ramat-Gan, 1978)
The Letters and Charters of Cardinal Guala Bicchieri Papal Legate in England 1216–1218, ed. N. Vincent, Canterbury and York Society, 83 (Woodbridge, 1996)
The Letters and Charters of John Lord of Ireland and Count of Mortain, ed. N. Vincent (forthcoming)
Letters and Papers, Foreign and Domestic, Henry VIII, Volume III: 1519–1523, ed. J. S. Brewer, 2 vols (London, 1867)
The Letters of Pope Innocent III (1198–1216) Concerning England and Wales. A Calendar with an Appendix of Texts, ed. C. R. Cheney and M. G. Cheney (Oxford, 1967)
Liber Gaufridi Sacristae de Coldingham de statu Ecclesiae Dunhelmensis, ed. J. Raine, *Historiae Dunelmensis Scriptores Tres, Gaufridus de Coldingham, Robertus de Graystanes, et Willielmus de Chambre*, Surtees Society, 9 (London, 1839), pp. 3–31
Life of St Edward the Confessor by St Aelred of Rievaulx, trans. J. Bertram (Southampton, 1997)
Magna Vita Sancti Hugonis. The Life of St Hugh of Lincoln, ed. D. L. Douie and H. Farmer, NMT, 2 vols (London, 1961–62)
Magni rotuli scaccarii Normanniae sub regibus Angliae, ed. T. Stapleton, 2 vols (London, 1840–44)
Matthaei Parisiensis, Monachi Sancti Albani, Chronica Majora, ed. H. R. Luard, RS 57, 7 vols (London, 1872–83)
Medieval England 1000–1500: A Reader, ed. E. Amt (Peterborough Ontario, 2001)
The Memoranda Roll for the Michaelmas Term of the First Year of the Reign of King John, Together with Fragments of the Originalia Roll of the Seventh Year of King Richard I (1195–6), the Liberate Roll of the Second Year of King John (1200–1), and the Norman Roll of the

Fifth Year of King John (1203), with an introduction by H. G. Richardson, PRS, 59, ns 21 (London, 1943)

The Memoranda Roll of the Tenth Year of the Reign of King John (1207–8), Together with The Curia Regis Rolls of Hilary 7 Richard I (1196) and Easter 9 Richard I (1198) a Roll of Plate held by Hugh de Neville in 9 John (1207–8), and Fragments of the Close Rolls of 16 and 17 John (1215–16), ed. R. A. Brown, PRS, 69, ns 31 (London, 1957)

Memoriale Walteri de Coventria. The Historical Collections of Walter of Coventry, ed. W. Stubbs, RS 58, 2 vols (London, 1872–73)

Memorials of the Church of SS Peter and Wilfrid, Ripon. Vol. I, ed. J. T. Fowler, Surtees Society, 74 (Durham, London and Edinburgh, 1882 for 1881)

The Metrical Life of St Robert of Knaresborough, Together with the other Middle English Pieces in British Museum Ms. Egerton 3143, ed. J. Bazire, Early English Text Society Original Series, 228 (London, 1953)

'The Miracles of the Hand of St James', trans. B. R. Kemp, *Berkshire Archaeological Journal*, 65 (1970), 1–19

The Monastic Constitutions of Lanfranc, ed. and trans. D. Knowles, rev. edn C. N. L. Brooke, OMT (Oxford, 2002)

Monasticon Diocesis Exoniensis, ed. G. Oliver (Exeter and London, 1846)

Norman Charters from English Sources: Antiquaries, Archives and the Rediscovery of the Anglo-Norman Past, ed. N. Vincent, PRS, 97, ns 59 (London, 2013)

Northern Petitions Illustrative of Life in Berwick, Cumbria and Durham in the Fourteenth Century, ed. C. M. Fraser, Surtees Society, 194 (Gateshead, 1981)

Notitia Monastica: Or, an Account of all the Abbies, Priories, and Houses of Friers, heretofore in England and Wales; And also of all the Colleges and Hospitals founded before A.D. MDXL, ed. T. Tanner (London, 1744)

Oeuvres de Rigord et de Guillaume le Breton, historiens de Philippe-Auguste, ed. H. F. Delaborde, 2 vols (Paris, 1882–85)

The Parliament Rolls of Medieval England 1275–1504. I. Edward I 1275–1294, ed. P. Brand (Woodbridge and London, 2005)

The Percy Chartulary, ed. M. T. Martin, Surtees Society, 117 (Durham, 1911)

Pipe Roll 17 John. Praestita Roll 14–18 John. Roll of Summonses 1214. Scutage Roll 16 John, ed. R. A. Brown and J. C. Holt, PRS, 75, ns 37 (London, 1961)

Placita de quo warranto temporibus Edw. I. II. & III. in curia receptae scaccarii Westm. Asservata, ed. W. Illingworth, RComm (London, 1818)

Polychronicon Ranulphi Higden Monachi Cestrensis Together with the English Translations of John Trevisa and of an Unknown Writer of the Fifteenth Century, ed. C. Babington and J. R. Lumby, RS 41, 9 vols (London, 1865–86)

Radulphi de Coggeshall Chronicon Anglicanum, ed. J. Stevenson, RS 66 (London, 1875)

Radulfi de Diceto Decani Lundoniensis Opera Historica. The Historical Works of Master Ralph de Diceto, Dean of London, ed. W. Stubbs, RS 68, 2 vols (London, 1876)

Reading Abbey Cartularies. British Library Manuscripts: Egerton 3031, Harley 1708 and Cotton Vespasian E xxv. 1. General Documents and those relating to English Counties other than Berkshire, ed. B. R. Kemp, Camden 4th ser., 31 (London, 1986)

Reading Abbey Cartularies. British Library Manuscripts: Egerton 3031, Harley 1708 and Cotton Vespasian E xxv. 2. Berkshire Documents, Scottish Charters and Miscellaneous Documents, ed. B. R. Kemp, Camden 4th ser., 33 (London, 1987)

Receipt and Issue Rolls for the Twenty-Sixth Year of the Reign of King Henry III, 1241-2, ed. R. C. Stacey, PRS, 87, ns 49 (London, 1992)
Recueil des actes de Henri II, roi d'Angleterre et duc de Normandie, concernant les provinces françaises et les affaires de France: Introduction, ed. L. Delisle (Paris, 1909)
Recueil des actes de Henri II, roi d'Angleterre et duc de Normandie, concernant les provinces françaises et les affaires de France, ed. L. Delisle and E. Berger, 3 vols (Paris, 1909-27)
The Red Book of the Exchequer, ed. H. Hall, RS 99, 3 vols (London, 1896)
Regesta Regum Anglo-Normannorum. The Acta of William I (1066-1087), ed. D. Bates (Oxford, 1998)
Regesta Regum Anglo-Normannorum 1066-1154. Vol. II. Regesta Henrici Primi 1100-1135, ed. C. Johnson and H. A. Cronne (Oxford, 1956)
Regesta Regum Anglo-Normannorum 1066-1154. Vol. III. Regesta Regis Stephani ac Mathildis Imperatricis ac Gaufridi et Henrici Ducum Normannorum 1135-1154, ed. H. A. Cronne and R. H. C. Davis (Oxford, 1968)
Register of the Abbey of St Thomas, Dublin, ed. J. T. Gilbert, RS 94 (London, 1889)
The Register of John Kirkby. Bishop of Carlisle 1332-1352 and the Register of John Ross Bishop of Carlisle, 1325-32, ed. R. L. Storey, 2 vols, Canterbury and York Society, 79 and 81 (Woodbridge, 1992 and 1995)
The Register, or Rolls, of Walter Gray, Lord Archbishop of York, ed. J. Raine, Surtees Society, 56 (Durham, 1872)
Rogeri de Wendover liber qui dicitur Flores Historiarum ab anno domini MCLIV annoque Henrici Anglorum Regis Secundi Primo, ed. H. G. Hewlett, RS 84, 3 vols (London, 1886-89)
Roll of Divers Accounts for the Early Years of the Reign of Henry III, ed. F. A. Cazel Jr, PRS, 82, ns 44 (London, 1982), pp. 1-73
Rolls of the Justices in Eyre, being the Rolls of Pleas and Assizes for Gloucestershire, Warwickshire and Staffordshire, 1221, 1222, ed. D. M. Stenton, Selden Society, 59 (London, 1940)
Rolls of the Justices in Eyre, being the Rolls of Pleas and Assizes for Lincolnshire 1218-9 and Worcestershire 1221, ed. D. M. Stenton, Selden Society, 53 (London, 1934)
Rolls of the Justices in Eyre, being the Rolls of Pleas and Assizes for Yorkshire in 3 Henry III, 1218-9, ed. D. M. Stenton, Selden Society, 56 (London, 1937)
Rotuli Chartarum in Turri Londinensi asservati, Vol. I, pt. 1, 1199-1216, ed. T. D. Hardy, RComm (London, 1837)
Rotuli de Liberate ac de Misis et Praestitis regnante Johanne, ed. T. D. Hardy, RComm (London, 1844)
Rotuli Litterarum Clausarum In Turri Londinensi asservati, Vol. I, 1204-1224, ed. T. D. Hardy, RComm (London, 1833)
Rotuli Litterarum Clausarum in Turri Londinensi asservati, Vol. II, 1224-1227, ed. T. D. Hardy, RComm (London, 1834)
Rotuli Litterarum Patentium in Turri Londinensi asservati, Vol. I, Pt. 1, 1199-1216, ed. T. D. Hardy, RComm (London, 1835)
Rotuli Normanniae in Turri Londinensi asservati: Johanne et Henrico Quinto, Angliae Regibus. Vol. I. 1200-1205, necnon de anno 1417, ed. T. D. Hardy, RComm (London, 1835)
Rotuli de Oblatis et Finibus In Turri Londinensi asservati, tempore regis Johannis, ed. T. D. Hardy, RComm (London, 1835)
'Rotulus Misae - Anni Regni Johannis Quarti Decimi', ed. H. Cole, *Documents Illustra-*

tive of English History in the Thirteenth and Fourteenth Centuries, RComm (London, 1844), pp. 231–69
'Rotulus de Praestito – Anno Regni Regis Johannis Septimo', ed. H. Cole, Documents Illustrative of English History in the Thirteenth and Fourteenth Centuries, RComm (London, 1844), pp. 270–6
Royal Commission on Historical Manuscripts. Reports. 15. Report on Manuscripts in Various Collections. Vol. 1. Berwick-upon-Tweed, Burford and Lostwithiel Corporations; The Counties of Wilts and Worcester, the Bishop of Chichester; and the Deans and Chapters of Chichester, Canterbury, and Salisbury, HMSO (London, 1901)
The Rule of St Benedict, ed. D. O. Hunter-Blair, 4th edn (Fort Augustus, 1934)
St Thomas Aquinas, Summa Theologiae. Volume 34. Charity (2a2ae, 22–33), ed. and trans. R. J. Batten (Cambridge, 2006)
Selected Letters of Pope Innocent III Concerning England (1198–1216), ed. and trans. C. R. Cheney and W. H. Semple, NMT (London, 1953)
Shakespeare, William, King John, ed. L. A. Beaurline (Cambridge, 1990)
Statuta Capitulorum Generalium Ordinis Cisterciensis ab anno 1116 ad annum 1786. Tomus I. Ab anno 1116 ad annum 1220, ed. J.-M. Canivez, Bibliothèque de la revue d'histoire ecclésiastique, 9 (Louvain, 1933)
Two Chartularies of the Priory of St Peter at Bath, ed. W. Hunt, Somerset Record Society, 7 (London, 1893)
Valor Ecclesiasticus temp. Henr. VIII auctoritate regia institutus, ed. J. Caley and J. Hunter, RComm, 6 vols (London, 1810–34)
'La Vie de S. Edouard le Confesseur par Osbert de Clare', ed. M. Bloch, Analecta Bollandiana, 41 (1923), 5–131
Walter Map's 'De Nugis Curialium', trans. M. R. James, with historical notes by J. E. Lloyd, ed. E. S. Hartland, Cymroddorion Record Series, 9 (London, 1923)
The Wardrobe Accounts of Henry III, ed. B. L. Wild, PRS, 96, ns 58 (London, 2012)
Westminster Abbey Charters 1066–c.1214, ed. E. Mason, London Record Society Publications, 25 (London, 1988)
William of Malmesbury, Gesta Regum Anglorum, ed. and trans. R. A. B. Mynors, R. M. Thomson and M. Winterbottom, OMT, 2 vols (Oxford, 1998–99)

Secondary works

Aird, W. M., Robert Curthose: Duke of Normandy (c. 1050–1134) (Woodbridge, 2008)
Ambler, S., 'The Penitent King: John Submits to Archbishop Langton, July 1213', Magna Carta Research Project Blog (16 July 2014) [http://magnacartaresearch.blogspot.co.uk/2014/07/the-penitent-king-john-submits-to.html, accessed 19 July 2014]
Appleby, J. T., 'Richard of Devizes and the Annals of Winchester', Bulletin of the Institute of Historical Research, 36 (1963), 70–7
Augry, G., 'Reliques et pouvoir ducal en Aquitaine (fin X^{e}s.-1030)', Reliques et sainteté dans l'espace médiéval, ed. J.-L. Deuffic, PECIA, Ressources en médiévistique, vol. 8–11 (Saint-Denis, 2006), pp. 261–80
Badham, S., 'Edward the Confessor's Chapel, Westminster Abbey: The Origins of the

Royal Mausoleum and its Cosmatesque Pavement', *Antiquaries Journal*, 87 (2007), 197–219

Baines, E., *History of the County Palatine and Duchy of Lancaster*, 4 vols (London, Paris and New York, 1836)

Baldwin, J. W., *The Government of Philip Augustus: Foundations of French Royal Power in the Middle Ages* (Berkeley and Los Angeles, CA, and Oxford, 1986)

——, *Masters, Princes and Merchants: The Social Views of Peter the Chanter & his Circle*, 2 vols (Princeton, NJ, 1970)

——, 'Master Stephen Langton, Future Archbishop of Canterbury: The Paris Schools and Magna Carta', *EHR*, 123 (2008), 811–46

Barber, M., *The Two Cities: Medieval Europe 1050–1320*, 2nd edn (London and New York, 2004)

Barbour, N., 'The Embassy Sent by King John of England to Miramolin, King of Morocco', *Al-Ándalus. Revista de las escuelas de estudios árabes de Madrid y Granada*, 25 (1960), 373–81

——, 'Two Christian Embassies to the Almohad Sultan Muhammad al-Nasir at Seville in 1211', *Congreso de Estudios Árabes e Islámicos* (Madrid, 1964), pp. 189–213

Barlow, F., 'Apulia, Simon of (d. 1223)', *ODNB* (Oxford, 2007) [http://www.oxforddnb.com/view/article/94380, accessed 19 July 2013]

——, 'The King's Evil', *EHR*, 95 (1980), 3–27

——, 'Marshal, Henry (d. 1206)', *ODNB* (Oxford, 2007) [http://www.oxforddnb.com/view/article/94379, accessed 19 July 2013]

Bartlett, R., *England Under the Norman and Angevin Kings 1075–1225* (Oxford, 2000)

Benham, J. E. M., 'Philip Augustus and the Angevin Empire: The Scandinavian Connection', *Mediaeval Scandinavia*, 14 (2004), 37–50

Bent, I. D., 'The Early History of the English Chapel Royal, ca. 1066–1327', 2 vols (unpublished PhD thesis, University of Cambridge, 1969)

——, 'The English Chapel Royal before 1300', *Proceedings of the Royal Musical Association*, 90 (1963–64), 77–95

Bethell, D., 'The Making of a Twelfth-Century Relic Collection', *Popular Belief and Practice*, ed. G. J. Cuming and D. Baker, SCH 8 (Cambridge, 1972), pp. 61–72

——, 'Richard of Belmeis and the Foundation of St Osyth's', *Transactions of the Essex Archaeological Society*, 3rd ser. 2, part 3 (1970), 299–328

Bienvenu, J.-M., 'Aliénor d'Aquitaine et Fontevraud', *Cahiers de Civilisation Médiévale*, 29 (1986), 15–27

——, 'Henri II Plantagenêt et Fontevraud', *Cahiers de Civilisation Médiévale*, 37 (1994), 25–32

Binski, P., 'Abbot Berkyng's Tapestries and Matthew Paris's Life of St Edward the Confessor', *Archaeologia*, 109 (1991), 85–100

——, *The Painted Chamber at Westminster*, Society of Antiquaries Occasional Papers, ns, 9 (London, 1986)

——, 'Reflections on *La estoire de Seint Aedward le rei*: Hagiography and Kingship in Thirteenth-Century England', *JMH*, 16 (1990), 333–50

——, *Westminster Abbey and the Plantagenets: Kingship and the Representation of Power 1200–1400* (New Haven, CT, and London, 1995)

Bishop, E., 'On the Origins of the Feast of the Conception of the Blessed Virgin

Mary', *Liturgica Historica: Papers on the Liturgy and Religious Life of the Western Church*, E. Bishop (Oxford, 1918), pp. 238-59

Blaauw, W. H., 'Letters to Ralph de Nevill Bishop of Chichester (1222-24) and Chancellor to King Henry III', *Sussex Archaeological Collections*, 3 (1850), 35-76

Bloch, M., *The Royal Touch: Sacred Monarchy and Scrofula in England and France* (London, 1973)

Blomefield, F., *An Essay Towards the Topographical History of the County of Norfolk*, 11 vols (London, 1805-10)

Blount, M. N., 'Glanville, Gilbert de (d. 1214)', *ODNB* (Oxford, 2004) [http://www.oxforddnb.com/view/article/10792, accessed 27 August 2013]

——, 'Sawston, Benedict of (d. 1226)', *ODNB* (Oxford, 2004) [http://www.oxforddnb.com/view/article/24660, accessed 19 December 2012]

Boase, T. S. R., 'Fontevraud and the Plantagenets', *Journal of the British Archaeological Association*, 3rd ser., 34 (1971), 1-10

Bolton, B. M., 'Guala (c. 1150-1227)', *ODNB* (Oxford, 2004) [http://www.oxforddnb.com/view/article/50349, accessed 1 October 2013]

——, 'Philip Augustus and John: Two Sons in Innocent III's Vineyard?', *The Church and Sovereignty c. 590-1918: Essays in Honour of Michael Wilks*, ed. D. Wood, SCH, Subsidia 9 (Oxford, 1991), reprinted in B. Bolton, *Innocent III: Studies on Papal Authority and Pastoral Care* (Aldershot, 1995), pp. 113-34

Bowie, C. M., 'The Daughters of Henry II and Eleanor of Aquitaine: A Comparative Study of Twelfth-Century Royal Women' (unpublished PhD thesis, University of Glasgow, 2011)

——, 'To Have and Have Not: The Dower of Joanna Plantagenet, Queen of Sicily (1177-1189)', *Queenship in the Mediterranean: Negotiating the Role of the Queen in the Medieval and Early Modern Eras*, ed. E. Woodacre (New York, 2013), pp. 27-50

Bozoky, E., 'Prolégomènes à une étude des offrandes de reliquaires par les princes', *Reliques et sainteté dans l'espace médiévale*, ed. J.-L. Deuffic, PECIA, Ressources en médiévistique, vols 5-8 (Saint-Denis, 2006), pp. 91-116

Bradbury, J., *Philip Augustus: King of France 1180-1223* (Harlow, 1998)

——, 'Philip Augustus and King John: Personality and History', *King John: New Interpretations*, ed. S. D. Church (Woodbridge, 1999), pp. 347-61

Brenner, E. H. O., 'Charity in Rouen in the Twelfth and Thirteenth Centuries (With Special Reference to Mont-aux-Malades)' (unpublished PhD thesis, University of Cambridge, 2008)

——, *Leprosy and Charity in Medieval Rouen* (Woodbridge, forthcoming)

Brooke, C. N. L., 'Princes and Kings as Patrons of Monasteries: Normandy and England', *Il monachismo e la riforma ecclesiastica (1049-1122)*, Miscellanea del centro di studi medioevali, 6 (Milan, 1971), 125-42

Brooke, Z. N., *The English Church and the Papacy from the Conquest to the Reign of John* (Cambridge, 1952)

Brown, R. A. and H. M. Colvin, 'The Angevin Kings 1154-1216', *The History of the King's Works: Vol. I. The Middle Ages*, ed. R. A. Brown, H. M. Colvin and A. J. Taylor, HMSO (London, 1963), pp. 51-91

—— and H. M. Colvin, 'The King's Works 1272-1485', *The History of the King's Works: Vol. I. The Middle Ages*, ed. R. A. Brown, H. M. Colvin and A. J. Taylor,

HMSO (London, 1963), pp. 161–292

Buc, P., *L'ambiguïté du livre: Prince, pouvoir et peuple dans les commentaires de la bible au moyen âge* (Paris, 1995)

———, 'Principes Gentium Dominantur Eorum: Princely Power between Legitimacy and Illegitimacy in Twelfth-Century Exegesis', *Cultures of Power: Lordship, Status and Process in Twelfth Century Europe*, ed. T. N. Bisson (Philadelphia, PA, 1995), pp. 310–28

Bynum, C. W., *Holy Feast and Holy Fast: The Religious Significance of Food to Medieval Women* (Berkeley and Los Angeles, CA, and London, 1987)

Carpenter, D. A., 'Abbot Ralph of Coggeshall's Account of the Last Years of King Richard and the First Years of King John', *EHR*, 113 (1998), 1210–30

———, 'Archbishop Langton and Magna Carta: His Contribution, His Doubts and His Hypocrisy', *EHR*, 126 (2011), 1041–65

———, 'The Burial of King Henry III, the *Regalia* and Royal Ideology', *The Reign of Henry III*, D. A. Carpenter (London and Rio Grande, OH, 1996), pp. 427–61

———, '"In Testimonium Factorum Brevium": The Beginnings of the English Chancery Rolls', *Records, Administration and Aristocratic Society in the Anglo-Norman Realm: Papers Commemorating the 800th Anniversary of King John's Loss of Normandy*, ed. N. Vincent (Woodbridge, 2009), pp. 1–28

———, 'King Henry III and the Cosmati Work at Westminster Abbey', *The Reign of Henry III*, D. A. Carpenter (London and Rio Grande, OH, 1996), pp. 409–25

———, 'King Henry III and St Edward the Confessor: The Origins of the Cult', *EHR*, 122 (2007), 865–91

———, *The Struggle for Mastery: Britain 1066–1284* (London, 2003)

Cazel Jr, F. A., 'Fauconberg, Eustace de (c. 1170–1228)', *ODNB* (Oxford, 2004, online edn 2008) [http://www.oxforddnb.com/view/article/9202, accessed 16 June 2014]

———, 'The Legates Guala and Pandulf', *TCE II*, ed. P. R. Coss and S. D. Lloyd (Woodbridge, 1988), pp. 15–21

———, 'Neville, Ralph de (d. 1244)', *ODNB* (Oxford, 2004, online edn 2008) [http://www.oxforddnb.com/view/article/19949, accessed 23 July 2014]

———, 'Ste Mère-Église, William de (d. 1224)', *ODNB* (Oxford, 2004, online edn 2008) [http://www.oxforddnb.com/view/article/29474, accessed 21 March 2011]

Chambers, K., '"When We Do Nothing Wrong, We Are Peers": Peter the Chanter and Twelfth-Century Political Thought', *Speculum*, 88 (2013), 405–26

Cheney, C. R., 'The Alleged Deposition of King John', *Studies in Mediaeval History Presented to Frederick Maurice Powicke*, ed. R. W. Hunt, W. A. Pantin, and R. W. Southern (Oxford, 1948, reprinted 1969), pp. 100–16

———, 'The Eve of Magna Carta', *Bulletin of the John Rylands Library*, 38 (1955–56), 311–41

———, *Hubert Walter* (London, 1967)

———, 'King John and the Papal Interdict', *Bulletin of the John Rylands Library*, 31 (1948), 295–317

———, 'King John's Reaction to the Interdict on England', *Transactions of the Royal Historical Society*, 4th ser., 31 (1949), 129–50

———, 'Levies on the English Clergy for the Poor and for the King, 1203', *EHR*, 96 (1981), 577–84

———, 'Magna carta beati Thome: Another Canterbury Forgery', *Medieval Texts and Studies*, C. R. Cheney (Oxford, 1973), pp. 78-110

———, 'A Monastic Letter of Confraternity to Eleanor of Aquitaine', *EHR*, 51 (1936), 488-93

———, 'A Neglected Record of the Canterbury Election of 1205-6', *Bulletin of the Institute of Historical Research*, 21 (1946-48), 233-8

———, 'Notes on the Making of the Dunstable Annals A.D. 33-1242', *Essays in Medieval History Presented to Bertie Wilkinson*, ed. T. A. Sandquist and M. R. Powicke (Toronto, 1969), pp. 79-98

———, *Pope Innocent III and England* (Stuttgart, 1976)

———, 'A Recent View of the General Interdict on England, 1208-1214', *SCH*, 3 (1966), 159-68

Cheney, M. G., 'Roger (c. 1134-1179)', *ODNB* (Oxford, 2004) [http://www.oxforddnb.com/view/article/23960, accessed 14 March 2011]

Chibnall, M., 'The Changing Expectations of a Royal Benefactor: The Religious Patronage of Henry II', *Religious and Laity in Western Europe, 1000-1400: Interaction, Negotiation, and Power*, ed. E. M. Jamroziak and J. E. Burton (Turnhout, 2006), pp. 9-21

———, *The Empress Matilda: Queen Consort, Queen Mother and Lady of the English* (Oxford, 1991)

———, 'Monastic Foundations in England and Normandy, 1066-1189', *England and Normandy in the Middle Ages*, ed. D. Bates and A. Curry (London and Rio Grande, OH, 1994), pp. 37-49

Church, S. D., 'Aspects of the English Succession, 1066-1199: The Death of the King', *ANS*, 29 (2007), 17-34

———, 'Brewer, William (d. 1226)', *ODNB* (Oxford, 2004) [http://www.oxforddnb.com/view/article/3369, accessed 6 August 2013]

———, 'The Care of the Royal Tombs in English Cathedrals in the Nineteenth and Twentieth Centuries: The Case of the Effigy of King John at Worcester', *Antiquaries Journal*, 89 (2009), 365-87

———, *The Household Knights of King John* (Cambridge, 1999)

———, 'King John's Testament and the Last Days of his Reign', *EHR*, 125 (2010), 505-28

———, 'Lisle, Brian de (d. 1234)', *ODNB* (Oxford, 2004, online edn 2007) [http://www.oxforddnb.com/view/article/47250, accessed 26 July 2014]

———, 'Some Aspects of the Royal Itinerary in the Twelfth Century', *TCE* 11, ed. B. Weiler, J. Burton, P. Schofield, and K. Stöber (Woodbridge, 2007), pp. 31-45

Clanchy, M. T., *From Memory to Written Record: England 1066-1307*, 2nd edn (Oxford and Cambridge, MA, 1993)

Clarke, P. D., *The Interdict in the Thirteenth Century: A Question of Collective Guilt* (Oxford, 2007)

Clasby, M., 'The Abbot, the Royal Will and Magna Carta: The Amercement of the Abbot of St Albans for Non-Attendance at the Common Summons of the Yorkshire Forest Eyre in 1212', *Henry III Fine Rolls Project. Fine of the Month September 2009* [http://www.finerollshenry3.org.uk/content/month/fm-09-2009.html, accessed 7 November 2012]

Clay, R. M., *The Mediaeval Hospitals of England* (London, 1909)
Colvin, H. M., 'Henry III 1216-1272', *The History of the King's Works: Vol. I. The Middle Ages*, ed. R. A. Brown, H. M. Colvin and A. J. Taylor, HMSO (London, 1963), pp. 93-159
——, 'The Origin of Chantries', *JMH*, 26 (2000), 163-73
——, *The White Canons in England* (Oxford, 1951)
Constable, G., 'An Unpublished Letter by Abbot Hugh II of Reading Concerning Archbishop Hubert Walter', *Essays in Medieval History Presented to Bertie Wilkinson*, ed. T. A. Sandquist and M. R. Powicke (Toronto, 1969), pp. 17-31
Cooke, A. M., 'Wakefield, Peter of (d. 1213)' rev. J. R. Whitehead, *ODNB* (Oxford, 2004) [http://www.oxforddnb.com/view/article/28419, accessed 30 August 2013]
Cope, S. T., 'St Bartholomew's Hospital, Newbury', *Berkshire Archaeological Journal*, 39 (1935), 35-57
Crook, D., 'Lexinton, Robert of (d. 1250)', *ODNB* (Oxford, 2004, online edn 2008) [http://www.oxforddnb.com/view/article/16616, accessed 12 June 2014]
Crook, J., 'The Physical Setting of the Cult of St Wulfstan', *St Wulfstan and his World*, ed. J. S. Barrow and N. P. Brooks (Aldershot, 2005), pp. 189-217
Cross, F. L. and E. A. Livingstone, *The Oxford Dictionary of the Christian Church*, 3rd edn (Oxford, 1997)
Crouch, D., 'Baronial Paranoia in King John's Reign', *Magna Carta and the England of King John*, ed. J. S. Loengard (Woodbridge, 2010), pp. 45-62
——, 'The Culture of Death in the Anglo-Norman World', *Anglo-Norman Political Culture and the Twelfth Century Renaissance*, ed. C. W. Hollister (Woodbridge, 1997), pp. 157-80
——, *The Image of Aristocracy in Britain, 1000-1300* (London and New York, 1992)
——, 'The Origin of Chantries: Some Further Anglo-Norman Evidence', *JMH*, 27 (2001), 159-80
——, 'The Troubled Deathbeds of Henry I's Servants: Death, Confession, and Secular Conduct in the Twelfth Century', *Albion*, 34 (2002), 24-36
——, *William Marshal: Knighthood, War and Chivalry, 1147-1219*, 2nd edn (London, 2002)
Dendy, D. R., *The Use of Lights in Christian Worship*, Alcuin Club Collections, 41 (London, 1959)
Denton, J. H., *English Royal Free Chapels, 1100-1300: A Constitutional Study* (Manchester, 1970)
——, 'From the Foundation of Vale Royal to the Statute of Carlisle: Edward I and Ecclesiastical Patronage', *TCE IV*, ed. P. R. Coss and S. D. Lloyd (Woodbridge, 1992), pp. 123-37
Ditchfield, P. D. and W. Page (eds), *VCH Berkshire*, 4 vols (London, 1906-24)
Dixon-Smith, S. A., 'Feeding the Poor to Commemorate the Dead: The Pro Anima Almsgiving of Henry III of England 1227-72' (unpublished PhD thesis, University of London, 2003)
——, 'The Image and Reality of Alms-Giving in the Great Halls of Henry III', *Journal of the British Archaeological Association*, 152 (1999), 79-96
Doubleday, H. A. (ed.), *VCH Bedford*, vol. I (London, 1904)
—— and W. Page (eds), *VCH Hampshire and the Isle of Wight*, 5 vols (London, 1900-

1912)

Draper, P., 'King John and St Wulfstan', *JMH*, 10 (1984), 41–50

Duffy, E., 'Religious Belief', *A Social History of Medieval England*, ed. R. Horrox and W. M. Ormrod (Cambridge, 2006), pp. 293–339

Duffy, M., *Royal Tombs of Medieval England* (Stroud, 2003)

Duffy, S., 'John and Ireland: The Origins of England's Irish Problem', *King John: New Interpretations*, ed. S. D. Church (Woodbridge, 1999), pp. 221–45

——, 'King John's Expedition to Ireland, 1210: The Evidence Reconsidered', *Irish Historical Studies*, 30 (1996), 1–24

Duggan, A. J., 'The Cult of St Thomas Becket in the Thirteenth Century', *St Thomas Cantilupe Bishop of Hereford: Essays in his Honour*, ed. M. Jancey (Leominster, 1982), pp. 21–44

——, 'Diplomacy, Status, and Conscience: Henry II's Penance for Becket's Murder', *Forschungen zur Reichs-, Papst- und Landesgeschichte: Peter Herde zum 65. Geburtstag von Freunden, Schülern und Kollegen dargebracht*, ed. K. Borchardt and E. Bünz, 2 vols (Stuttgart, 1998), vol. I, pp. 265–90

——, 'Henry II, the English Church and the Papacy, 1154–76', *Henry II: New Interpretations*, ed. C. Harper-Bill and N. Vincent (Woodbridge, 2007), pp. 154–83

——, *Thomas Becket* (London, 2004)

Duncan, A. A. M., 'John King of England and the Kings of Scots', *King John: New Interpretations*, ed. S. D. Church (Woodbridge, 1999), pp. 248–71

Dunning, R., *Somerset Monasteries* (Stroud, 2001)

Dupont, G., *Histoire du Cotentin et de ses îles*, 4 vols (Caen, 1870–85)

Dutton, K. A., 'Geoffrey, Count of Anjou and Duke of Normandy, 1129–51' (unpublished PhD thesis, University of Glasgow, 2011)

Dyer, C., *Standards of Living in the Later Middle Ages: Social Change in England c. 1200–1520* (Cambridge, 1989)

Eales, R., 'The Political Setting of the Becket Translation of 1220', *Martyrs and Martyrologies*, ed. D. Wood, SCH 30 (1993), pp. 127–39

Empey, C. A., 'Valognes, Hamo de (d. 1202/3)', *ODNB* (Oxford, 2004) [http://www.oxforddnb.com/view/article/50032, accessed 19 August 2014]

Engel, U., 'The Conversion of King John and its Consequences for Worcester Cathedral', *Christianizing Peoples and Converting Individuals*, ed. G. Armstrong and I. N. Wood (Turnhout, 2000), pp. 321–30

—— (trans. H. Heltay), *Worcester Cathedral: An Architectural History* (Chichester, 2007)

Everard, J. A., *Brittany and the Angevins: Province and Empire 1158–1203* (Cambridge, 2000)

—— and J. C. Holt, *Jersey 1204: The Forging of an Island Community* (London, 2004)

Falkiner, C. L., 'The Hospital of St John of Jerusalem in Ireland', *Proceedings of the Royal Irish Academy. Section C: Archaeology, Celtic Studies, History, Linguistics, Literature*, 26 (1906/07), 275–317

Farmer, D. H., *The Oxford Dictionary of Saints*, 4th edn (Oxford, 1997)

Farrer, W., *Feudal Cambridgeshire* (Cambridge, 1920)

—— and J. Brownbill (eds), *VCH Lancaster*, vol. II (London, 1908)

Fawtier, R. (trans. L. Butler and R. J. Adam), *The Capetian Kings of France: Monarchy and Nation (987–1328)* (London, 1964)

Fernie, E., 'The Litigation of an Exempt House, St Augustine's Canterbury, 1182–1237', *Bulletin of the John Rylands Library*, 39 (1957), 390–415

Ferrante, J. M., 'Blanche of Castile, Queen of France', *Epistolae: Medieval Women's Latin Letters* [http://epistolae.ccnmtl.columbia.edu/woman/77.html, accessed 22 August 2014]

Flanagan, M. T., 'Butler, Theobald (d. 1205)', ODNB (Oxford, 2004) [http://www.oxforddnb.com/view/article/4207, accessed 19 December 2013]

Fleming, R., 'Christchurch's Sisters and Brothers: An Edition and Discussion of the Canterbury Obituary Lists', *The Culture of Christendom: Essays in Medieval History in Commemoration of Denis L. T. Bethell*, ed. M. A. Meyer (London and Rio Grande, OH, 1993), pp. 115–53

Flint, V. I. J., 'Honorius Augustodunensis (d. c. 1140)', ODNB (Oxford, 2004) [http://www.oxforddnb.com/view/article/53485, accessed 31 July 2013]

Flori, J. (trans. O. Classe), *Eleanor of Aquitaine: Queen and Rebel* (Edinburgh, 2007)

Franklin, M. J., 'Cornhill, William of (d. 1223)', ODNB (Oxford, 2004) [http://www.oxforddnb.com/view/article/6331, accessed 10 March 2011]

——, 'Nonant, Hugh de (d. 1198)', ODNB (Oxford, 2004) [http://www.oxforddnb.com/view/article/20245, accessed 14 December 2010]

Franklin, R. M., 'Morville, Hugh de (d. 1173/4)', ODNB (Oxford, 2004) [http://www.oxforddnb.com/view/article/19379, accessed 29 October 2013]

Fryde, N., 'King John and the Empire', *King John: New Interpretations*, ed. S. D. Church (Woodbridge, 1999) pp. 334–46

Galbraith, V. H., 'Good Kings and Bad Kings in Medieval English History', *History*, 30 (1945), 119–32

——, *Roger of Wendover and Matthew Paris*, Glasgow University Publications, 61 (Glasgow, 1944, reprinted 1970)

Gelin, M.-P., 'Gervase of Canterbury, Christ Church and the Archbishops', *JEH*, 60 (2009), 449–63

Gerish, D., 'Ancestors and Predecessors: Royal Continuity and Identity in the First Kingdom of Jerusalem', *ANS*, 20 (1998), 127–50

Gervers, M. and N. Hamonic, '*Pro Amore Dei*: Diplomatic Evidence of Social Conflict in the Reign of King John', *Law as Profession and Practice in Medieval Europe: Essays in Honour of James A. Brundage*, ed. K. Pennington and M. H. Eichbauer (Farnham, 2011), pp. 231–59

Gillingham, J., 'At the Deathbeds of the Kings of England, 1066–1216', *Herrscher- und Fürstentestamente im Westeuropäischen Mittelalter*, ed. B. Kasten (Cologne, Weimar, and Vienna, 2008), pp. 509–30

——, 'Historians Without Hindsight: Coggeshall, Diceto and Howden on the Early Years of John's Reign', *King John: New Interpretations*, ed. S. D. Church (Woodbridge, 1999), pp. 1–26

——, 'John (1167–1216)', ODNB (Oxford, 2004, online edn 2010) [http://www.oxforddnb.com/view/article/14841, accessed 1 July 2014]

——, *Richard I* (New Haven, CT, and London, 1999)

Goering, J., 'Montibus, William de (d. 1213)', ODNB (Oxford, 2004) [http://www.oxforddnb.com/view/article/29471, accessed 15 January 2014]

Golding, B., 'Burials and Benefactions: An Aspect of Monastic Patronage in Thirteenth-

Century England', *England in the Thirteenth Century: Proceedings of the 1984 Harlaxton Symposium*, ed. W. M. Ormrod (Grantham, 1985), pp. 64–75

——, *Gilbert of Sempringham and the Gilbertine Order, c. 1130–c. 1300* (Oxford, 1995)

——, 'Gilbert of Sempringham [St Gilbert of Sempringham] (1083–1189)', *ODNB* (Oxford, 2004) [http://www.oxforddnb.com/view/article/10677, accessed 6 April 2011]

——, 'The Hermit and the Hunter', *The Cloister and the World: Essays in Medieval History in Honour of Barbara Harvey*, ed. J. Blair and B. Golding (Oxford, 1996), pp. 95–117

——, 'Robert of Knaresborough (d. 1218?)', *ODNB* (Oxford, 2004) [http://www.oxforddnb.com/view/article/23733, accessed 26 July 2014]

——, 'Wrotham, William of (d. 1217/18)', *ODNB* (Oxford, 2004) [http://www.oxforddnb.com/view/article/30087, accessed 20 December 2013]

Graham, R., 'The Order of St Antoine de Viennois and its English Commandery, St Anthony's, Threadneedle Street', *Archaeological Journal*, 84 (1927), 341–406

——, *S. Gilbert of Sempringham and the Gilbertines: A History of the only English Monastic Order* (London, 1901)

Gransden, A., *Historical Writing in England, c. 550 to c. 1307* (Ithaca, NY, and London, 1974)

——, *A History of the Abbey of Bury St Edmunds 1182–1256: Samson of Tottington to Edmund of Walpole* (Woodbridge, 2007)

——, 'Prologues in the Historiography of Twelfth-Century England', *England in the Twelfth Century: Proceedings of the 1988 Harlaxton Symposium*, ed. D. Williams (Woodbridge, 1990), pp. 55–81

Grant, L, 'Aspects of the Architectural Patronage of the Family of the Counts of Anjou in the Twelfth Century', *Anjou: Medieval Art, Architecture and Archaeology*, ed. J. McNeill and D. Pringent, *British Archaeological Association Conference Transactions*, 26 (2003), pp. 96–110

—— (trans. B. Duchet-Filhol), 'Le patronage architectural de Henri II et de son entourage', *Cahiers de Civilisation Médiévale*, 37 (1994) 73–84

Green, J. A., *Henry I: King of England and Duke of Normandy* (Cambridge, 2009)

——, 'The Piety and Patronage of Henry I', *Haskins Society Journal*, 10 (2001), 1–16

Green, J. R., *A Short History of the English People* (London, 1874, reprinted 1992)

Gwynn, A. and R. N. Hadcock, *Medieval Religious Houses Ireland* (Dublin, 1970)

Haines, R. M., 'Gray, John de (d. 1214)', *ODNB* (Oxford, 2004) [http://www.oxforddnb.com/view/article/11541, accessed 19 August 2013]

Hallam, E. M., 'Aspects of the Monastic Patronage of the English and French Royal Houses, c. 1130–1270' (unpublished PhD thesis, University of London, 1976)

——, 'Henry II as a Founder of Monasteries', *JEH*, 28 (1977), 113–32

——, 'Henry II, Richard I and the Order of Grandmont', *JMH*, 1 (1975), 165–86

——, 'Henry (1155–1183)', *ODNB* (Oxford, 2004, online edn 2006) [http://www.oxforddnb.com/view/article/12957, accessed 22 May 2014]

——, 'Royal Burial and the Cult of Kingship in England and France, 1060–1330', *JMH*, 8 (1982), 359–80

—— and J. Everard, *Capetian France 987–1328*, 2nd edn (Harlow, 2001)

Hardy, T. D., 'Itinerary of King John, &c.', *RLP*, unpaginated

Harper-Bill, C., 'John and the Church of Rome', *King John: New Interpretations*, ed. S. D. Church (Woodbridge, 1999), pp. 289-315
——, 'The Piety of the Anglo-Norman Knightly Class', ANS, 2 (1979), 63-77, 173-6
Harvey, B., *Living and Dying in England 1100-1540: The Monastic Experience* (Oxford, 1993)
Harvey, K., *Episcopal Appointments in England, c. 1214-1344* (Farnham, 2014)
——, 'The Piety of King John' (unpublished MA thesis, King's College London, 2008)
——, 'An Un-Christian King? King John and the Lenten Fast', *Magna Carta Research Project Blog* (12 March 2014) [http://magnacartaresearch.blogspot.co.uk/2014/03/an-un-christian-king-king-john-and.html, accessed 19 June 2014]
Hicks, L. V., *Religious Life in Normandy, 1050-1300: Space, Gender and Social Pressure* (Woodbridge, 2007)
Hicks, M., 'Four Studies in Conventional Piety', *Southern History*, 13 (1991), 1-21
Hockey, F., *Beaulieu: King John's Abbey. A History of Beaulieu Abbey Hampshire 1204-1258* (London, 1976)
Holdsworth, C., 'Forde, John of (c. 1150-1214)', *ODNB* (Oxford, 2004) [http://www.oxforddnb.com/view/article/53109, accessed 16 January 2014]
——, 'John of Forde and the Interdict', *EHR*, 78 (1963), 705-14
——, 'Langton, Stephen (c. 1150-1228)', *ODNB* (Oxford, 2004) [http://www.oxforddnb.com/view/article/16044, accessed 19 August 2013]
——, 'Royal Cistercians: Beaulieu, her Daughters and Rewley', *TCE IV*, ed. P. R. Coss and S. D. Lloyd (Woodbridge, 1992), pp. 139-50
Hollister, C. W., 'King John and the Historians', *Journal of British Studies*, 1 (1961), 1-19
—— and J. W. Baldwin, 'The Rise of Administrative Kingship: Henry I and Philip Augustus', *American Historical Review*, 83 (1978), 867-905
Holt, J. C., 'The End of the Anglo-Norman Realm', *Magna Carta and Medieval Government*, J. C. Holt (London and Ronceverte, WV, 1985), pp. 23-65
——, *King John*, Historical Association Pamphlets, 53 (London, 1963)
——, 'King John and Arthur of Brittany', *Nottingham Medieval Studies*, 44 (2000), 82-103
——, 'King John's Disaster in the Wash', *Nottingham Medieval Studies*, 5 (1961), 75-86
——, *Magna Carta*, 2nd edn (Cambridge, 1992)
——, *The Northerners: A Study in the Reign of King John* (Oxford, 1961)
——, 'What's in a Name? Family Nomenclature and the Norman Conquest', *Colonial England 1066-1215*, J. C. Holt (London and Rio Grande, OH, 1997), pp. 179-96
Horrox, R., 'Purgatory, Prayer, and Plague: 1150-1380', *Death in England: An Illustrated History*, ed. P. C. Jupp and C. Gittings (Manchester, 1999), pp. 90-118
——, 'Richard III (1452-1485)', *ODNB* (Oxford, 2004, online edn 2013) [http://www.oxforddnb.com/view/article/23500, accessed 23 May 2014]
Hoskin, P., 'Coutances, John de (d. 1198)', *ODNB* (Oxford, 2008) [http://www.oxforddnb.com/view/article/95187, accessed 8 March 2011]
——, 'Poor, Richard (d. 1237)', *ODNB* (Oxford, 2004, online edn 2009) [http://www.oxforddnb.com/view/article/22525, accessed 29 July 2014]
Howard-Davis, C. and M. Leah, 'Excavations at St Nicholas Yard, Carlisle, 1996-7', *Transactions of the Cumberland & Westmorland Antiquarian and Archaeological Society*,

99 (1999), 89–115

Howell, M., 'The Children of King Henry III and Eleanor of Provence', *TCE* IV, ed. P. R. Coss and S. D. Lloyd (Woodbridge, 1992), pp. 57–72

——, *Eleanor of Provence: Queenship in Thirteenth-Century England* (Oxford, 1998)

Hubert, J., 'Le miracle de Déols et la trêve conclue en 1187 entre les rois de France et d'Angleterre', *Bibliothèque de l'Ecole des Chartes*, 96 (1935), 285–300

Hudson, J., 'Buckland, Geoffrey of (d. 1225)', *ODNB* (Oxford, 2004) [http://www.oxforddnb.com/view/article/2749, accessed 23 August 2013]

Hume, D., *The History of England from the Invasion of Julius Caesar, to the Revolution of 1688*, 6 vols (Indianapolis, 1983, based on the 8-vol. edn published London, 1778)

Huneycutt, L. L., *Matilda of Scotland: A Study in Medieval Queenship* (Woodbridge, 2003)

Huntington, J., 'Saintly Power as a Model for Royal Authority: The "Royal Touch" and Other Miracles in the Early Vitae of Edward the Confessor', *Aspects of Power and Authority in the Middle Ages*, ed. B. Bolton and C. E. Meek (Turnhout, 2007), pp. 327–43

Jenkins, J. H., 'The King's Beaulieu' (unpublished MA thesis, Cardiff University, 2009)

——, 'King John and the Cistercians in Wales', *Monastic Research Bulletin*, 17 (2011), 16–18

Johnstone, H., 'Poor-Relief in the Royal Households of Thirteenth-Century England', *Speculum*, 4 (1929), 149–67

Jolliffe, J. E. A., 'The Chamber and the Castle Treasuries under John', *Studies in Medieval History Presented to Frederick Maurice Powicke*, ed. R. W. Hunt, W. A. Pantin, and R. W. Southern (Oxford, 1948), pp. 117–42

Jones, M., 'Eleanor, suo jure Duchess of Brittany (1182×4–1241)', *ODNB* (Oxford, 2004, online edn 2008) [http://www.oxforddnb.com/view/article/46702, accessed 21 May 2014]

Jordan, A., 'The St Thomas Becket Windows at Angers and Coutances: Devotion, Subversion, and the Scottish Connection', *The Cult of St Thomas Becket in the Plantagenet World, c. 1170–c. 1250*, ed. P. Webster and M.-P. Gelin (Woodbridge, forthcoming)

Kanter, J. E., 'Peripatetic and Sedentary Kingship: The Itineraries of the Thirteenth-Century English Kings' (unpublished PhD thesis, King's College London, 2010)

Kantorowicz, E. H., *Laudes Regiae: A Study in Liturgical Acclamations and Mediaeval Ruler Worship* (Berkeley and Los Angeles, CA, 1958)

Karn, N., 'Burgh, Geoffrey de (d. 1228)', *ODNB* (Oxford, 2007) [http://www.oxforddnb.com/view/article/95140, accessed 23 August 2013]

Kaufmann, M., 'The Image of St Louis', *Kings and Kingship in Medieval Europe*, ed. A. J. Duggan (London, 1993), pp. 265–86

Kay, R., 'Walter of Coventry and the Barnwell Chronicle', *Traditio*, 54 (1999), 141–67

Kealey, E. J., *Medieval Medicus: A Social History of Anglo-Norman Medicine* (Baltimore, MD, and London, 1981)

Keefe, T. K., 'Cressy, Hugh de (d. 1189)', *ODNB* (Oxford, 2004) [http://www.oxforddnb.com/view/article/57614, accessed 1 November 2013]

——, 'Shrine Time: King Henry II's Visits to Thomas Becket's Tomb', *Haskins Society Journal*, 11 (1998), 115–22

Kellett, A., 'King John in Knaresborough: The First Known Royal Maundy', *Yorkshire*

Archaeological Journal, 62 (1990), 69–90

Kerr, B. M., *Religious Life for Women c. 1100–c. 1350: Fontevraud in England* (Oxford, 1999)

King, E., *King Stephen* (New Haven, CT, and London, 2012)

——, 'Stephen (c. 1092–1154)', *ODNB* (Oxford, 2004, online edn 2010) [http://www.oxforddnb.com/view/article/26365, accessed 27 June 2014]

King, J. N., 'Bale, John (1495–1563)', *ODNB* (Oxford, 2004, online edn 2009) [http://www.oxforddnb.com/view/article/1175, accessed 11 November 2013]

Kingsford, C. L., 'Poor, Herbert (d. 1217)', rev. B. R. Kemp, *ODNB* (Oxford, 2004, online edn 2009) [http://www.oxforddnb.com/view/article/22524, accessed 27 August 2013]

Knowles, M. D., 'The Canterbury Election of 1205–6', *EHR*, 53 (1938), 211–20

——, *The Monastic Order in England: A History of its Development from the Times of St Dunstan to the Fourth Lateran Council, 943–1216* (Cambridge, 1949)

——, C. N. L. Brooke and V. C. M. London (eds), *The Heads of Religious Houses: England and Wales 940–1216* (Cambridge, 1972)

—— and R. N. Hadcock, *Medieval Religious Houses: England and Wales*, 2nd edn (London and New York, 1971)

Kobialka, M., *This Is My Body: Representational Practices in the Early Middle Ages* (Ann Arbor, MI, 1999)

Koziol, G., 'England, France, and the Problem of Sacrality in Twelfth-Century Ritual', *Cultures of Power: Lordship, Status, and Process in Twelfth-Century Europe*, ed. T. Bisson (Philadelphia, PA, 1995), pp. 124–48

Landon, L., *The Itinerary of King Richard I with Studies on Certain Matters of Interest Connected with his Reign*, PRS, 51, ns 13 (London, 1955)

Latimer, P., 'Early Thirteenth-Century Prices', *King John: New Interpretations*, ed. S. D. Church (Woodbridge, 1999), pp. 41–73

Lee, G. A., *Leper Hospitals in Medieval Ireland with a Short Account of the Military and Hospitaller Order of St Lazarus of Jerusalem* (Blackrock Co. Dublin, 1996)

Lewis, A. W., 'The Birth and Childhood of King John: Some Revisions', *Eleanor of Aquitaine: Lord and Lady*, ed. B. Wheeler and J. C. Parsons (New York and Basingstoke, 2002), pp. 159–75

Lewis, K. J., 'Becoming a Virgin King: Richard II and Edward the Confessor', *Gender and Holiness: Men, Women, and Saints in Late Medieval Europe*, ed. S. J. E. Riches and S. Salih (London, 2002), pp. 86–100

Leyser, K. J., 'The Angevin Kings and the Holy Man', *St Hugh of Lincoln: Lectures Delivered at Oxford to Celebrate the Eighth Centenary of St Hugh's Consecration as Bishop of Lincoln*, ed. H. Mayr-Harting (Oxford, 1987), pp. 49–73

——, 'Frederick Barbarossa, Henry II, and the Hand of St James', *EHR*, 90 (1975), 481–506

Licence, T., *Hermits and Recluses in English Society, 950–1200* (Oxford, 2011)

Lloyd, S., 'Chilham, Sir Richard of (d. 1246)', *ODNB* (Oxford, 2004, online edn 2008) [http://www.oxforddnb.com/view/article/46706, accessed 3 July 2013]

——, *English Society and the Crusade 1216–1307* (Oxford, 1988)

——, 'Henry fitz Count (b. in or before 1175, d. 1221)', *ODNB* (Oxford, 2004) [http://www.oxforddnb.com/view/article/47207, accessed 6 August 2013]

———, 'Oliver (d. 1218/19)', *ODNB* (Oxford, 2004) [http://www.oxforddnb.com/view/article/20717, accessed 3 July 2013]

Maddicott, J. R., 'The Oath of Marlborough, 1209: Fear, Government and Popular Allegiance in the Reign of King John', *EHR*, 126 (2011), 281–318

Madeline, F., 'Le don de plomb dans le patronage monastique d'Henri II Plantagenêt: usages et conditions de la production du plomb anglais dans la seconde moitié du XIIe siècle', *Archéologie Médiévale*, 39 (2009), 31–51

Marritt, S., 'Prayers for the King and Royal Titles in Anglo-Norman Charters', *ANS*, 32 (2010), 184–202

Martin, F. X., 'Overlord Becomes Feudal Lord, 1172–85', *A New History of Ireland: II. Medieval Ireland 1169–1185*, ed. A. Cosgrove, second impression (Oxford, 1993)

Martin, G. H., 'Canterbury, Gervase of (b. c. 1145, d. in or after 1210)', *ODNB* (Oxford, 2004) [http://www.oxforddnb.com/view/article/10570, accessed 21 August 2013]

Martindale, J., 'Eleanor, suo jure Duchess of Aquitaine (c. 1122–1204)', *ODNB* (Oxford, 2004, online edn 2006) [http://www.oxforddnb.com/view/article/8618, accessed 10 December 2013]

———, 'The Sword on the Stone: Some Resonances of a Medieval Symbol of Power (The Tomb of King John in Worcester Cathedral)', *ANS*, 15 (1992), 199–241

Mason, E., '*Pro statu et incolumnitate regni mei*: Royal Monastic Patronage 1066–1154', *Religion and National Identity*, ed. S. Mews, SCH, 18 (Oxford, 1982), pp. 99–117

———, '"Rocamadour in Quercy above all other Churches": The Healing of Henry II', *The Church and Healing*, ed. W. J. Shiels, SCH, 19 (Oxford, 1982), pp. 39–54

———, 'St Oswald and St Wulfstan', *St Oswald of Worcester: Life and Influence*, ed. N. Brooks and C. Cubitt (London and New York, 1996), pp. 269–84

———, 'St Wulfstan's Staff: A Legend and its Uses', *Medium Aevum*, 53 (1984), 158–79

———, *St Wulfstan of Worcester c. 1008–1095* (Oxford, 1990)

———, 'The Site of King Making and Consecration: Westminster Abbey and the Crown in the Eleventh and Twelfth Centuries', *The Church and Sovereignty c. 590–1918: Essays in Honour of Michael Wilks*, ed. D. Wood, SCH, Subsidia 9 (Oxford, 1991), pp. 57–76

———, '*Timeo Barones et Donas Ferentes*', *Religious Motivation: Biographical and Sociological Problems for the Church Historian*, ed. D. Baker, SCH, 15 (Oxford, 1978), pp. 61–75

———, 'Westminster Abbey and the Monarchy between the Reigns of William I and John (1066–1216)', *JEH*, 41 (1990), 199–216

———, *Westminster Abbey and its People c. 1050–c. 1216* (Woodbridge, 1996)

———, 'Wulfstan [St Wulfstan] (c. 1008–1095)', *ODNB* (Oxford, 2004), [http://www.oxforddnb.com/view/article/30099, accessed 23 February 2011]

Matthew, D. J. A. 'Brown, Thomas (d. 1180)', *ODNB* (Oxford, 2004) [http://www.oxforddnb.com/view/article/27202, accessed 7 August 2013]

———, *The Norman Monasteries and their English Possessions* (Oxford, 1962)

Matthew, H. C. G., 'Edward VII (1841–1910)', *ODNB* (Oxford, 2004, online edn 2013) [http://www.oxforddnb.com/view/article/32975, accessed 11 June 2014]

Mayr-Harting, H., *Religion, Politics and Society in Britain 1066–1272* (Harlow, 2011)

McGlynn, S., *Blood Cries Afar: The Forgotten Invasion of England 1216* (Stroud, 2011)

McLaughlin, M., *Consorting with Saints: Prayer for the Dead in Early Medieval France*

(Ithaca, NY, and London, 1994)
McNeill, C., 'Rawlinson Manuscripts (Class B)', *Analecta Hibernica*, 1 (1930), 118–78
Meekings, C. A. F. (ed. R. F. Hunnisett), 'The Early Years of Netley Abbey', *Studies in 13th Century Justice and Administration*, C. A. F. Meekings (London, 1981), pp. 1–37
Miller, J. A. K., 'The Building Programme of Archbishop Walter de Gray: Architectural Production and Reform in the Archdiocese of York, 1215–1255' (unpublished PhD thesis, University of Columbia, 2012)
Mitchell, S., 'Richard II: Kingship and the Cult of Saints', *The Regal Image of Richard II and the Wilton Diptych*, ed. D. Gordon, L. Monnas and C. Elam (London, 1997), pp. 115–24
Mollat, M. (trans. A. Goldhammer), *The Poor in the Middle Ages: An Essay in Social History* (New Haven, CT, and London, 1986)
Murphy, M., 'Cumin, John (d. 1212)', *ODNB* (Oxford, 2004) [http://www.oxforddnb.com/view/article/6043, accessed 14 January 2014]
——, 'London, Henry of (d. 1228)', *ODNB* (Oxford, 2004) [http://www.oxforddnb.com/view/article/17036, accessed 27 August 2013]
Le Neve, J., *Fasti Ecclesiae Anglicanae 1066–1300: I. St Paul's, London*, rev. edn by D. E. Greenway (London, 1968)
Nicholson, H. J., *Love, War, and the Grail: Templars, Hospitallers, and Teutonic Knights in Medieval Epic and Romance 1150–1500* (Boston, MA, and Leiden, 2004)
——, 'Margaret de Lacy and the Hospital of St John at Aconbury, Herefordshire', *JEH*, 50 (1999), 629–51
——, 'The Military Orders and the Kings of England in the Twelfth and Thirteenth Centuries', *From Clermont to Jerusalem: The Crusades and Crusader Societies 1095–1500*, ed. A. V. Murray (Turnhout, 1998), pp. 203–18
Nilson, B., *Cathedral Shrines of Medieval England* (Woodbridge, 1998)
Nolan, K., 'The Queen's Choice: Eleanor of Aquitaine and the Tombs at Fontevraud', *Eleanor of Aquitaine: Lord and Lady*, ed. B. Wheeler and J. C. Parsons (New York and Basingstoke, 2002), pp. 377–405
Norgate, K., 'Joan (d. 1237)', rev. A. D. Carr, *ODNB* (Oxford, 2004) [http://www.oxforddnb.com/view/article/14819, accessed 3 July 2013]
——, *John Lackland* (London, 1902)
——, 'Matilda, Duchess of Saxony (1156–1189)', rev. T. Reuter, *ODNB* (Oxford, 2004) [http://www.oxforddnb.com/view/article/18339, accessed 17 December 2013]
O'Neill, A., 'Waterford Diocese, 1096–1363: Part Five. Religious Foundations in the Diocese of Waterford', *Decies. Journal of the Old Waterford Society*, 47 (1993), 42–51
Oram, R. D., 'Quincy, Saer de, Earl of Winchester (d. 1219)', *ODNB* (Oxford, 2004, online edn 2005) [http://www.oxforddnb.com/view/article/22967, accessed 13 May 2014]
Ormrod, W. M., 'The Personal Religion of Edward III', *Speculum*, 64 (1989), 849–77
Owen, D. D. R., *William the Lion: Kingship and Culture* (East Linton, 1997)
Page, W. (ed.), *VCH Derby*, vol. II (London, 1907)
—— (ed.), *VCH Nottingham*, vol. II (London, 1910)
Painter, S., 'Norwich's Three Geoffreys', *Speculum*, 28 (1953), 808–13
——, *The Reign of King John* (Baltimore, MD, 1949)

Palliser, D. M., 'Royal Mausolea in the Long Fourteenth Century (1272-1422)', *Fourteenth Century England* III, ed. W. M. Ormrod (Woodbridge, 2004), pp. 1-16

Parsons, J. C., '"Never was a Body Buried in England with such Solemnity and Honour": The Burials and Posthumous Commemorations of English Queens to 1500', *Queens and Queenship in Medieval Europe*, ed. A. J. Duggan (Woodbridge, 2002), pp. 317-37

———, 'The Year of Eleanor of Castile's Birth and her Children by Edward I', *Mediaeval Studies*, 46 (1984), 245-65

Patterson, R. B., 'Isabella, suo jure Countess of Gloucester (c. 1160-1217)', *ODNB* (Oxford, 2004, online edn 2005) [http://www.oxforddnb.com/view/article/46705, accessed 18 December 2013]

Pavillon, B., *La Vie du Bienheureux Robert d'Arbrissel, patriarche des solitaires de la France et instituteur de l'ordre de Fontevraud* (Saumur and Paris, 1666)

Peltzer, J., *Canon Law, Careers and Conquest: Episcopal Elections in Normandy and Greater Anjou, c. 1140-c. 1230* (Cambridge, 2008)

———, 'The Slow Death of the Angevin Empire', *Historical Research*, 81 (2008), 553-84

Penman, M., 'The Bruce Dynasty, Becket and Scottish Pilgrimage to Canterbury, c. 1178-c. 1404', *JMH*, 32 (2006), 346-70

Phillips, S., *Edward II* (New Haven, CT, and London, 2010)

Poisson, J.-M., 'Altopascio, ordre de San Jacopo d'', *Prier et Combattre: Dictionnaire européen des ordres militaires au Moyen Age*, ed. N. Bériou and P. Josserand (Paris, 2009), pp. 84-5

Poole, A. L., *From Domesday Book to Magna Carta 1087-1216*, 2nd edn (Oxford, 1955)

Power, D., 'Angevin Normandy', *A Companion to the Anglo-Norman World*, ed. C. Harper-Bill and E. van Houts (Woodbridge, 2003), pp. 63-85

———, 'Les Dernières années du régime angevin en Normandie', *Plantagenêts et Capétiens: confrontations et héritages*, ed. M. Aurell and N.-Y. Tonnerre (Turnhout, 2006), pp. 163-92

———, *The Norman Frontier in the Twelfth and Early Thirteenth Centuries* (Cambridge, 2004)

Power, P., 'The Priory, Church and Hospital of St John the Evangelist, Waterford', *Journal of the South East of Ireland Archaeological Society*, 2 (1896), 81-97

Powicke, F. M., 'England: Richard I and John', *The Cambridge Medieval History: Volume VI. Victory of the Papacy*, ed. J. R. Tanner, C. W. Previté-Orton and Z. N. Brooke (Cambridge, 1929), pp. 205-51

———, *The Loss of Normandy 1189-1204: Studies in the History of the Angevin Empire*, 2nd edn (Manchester, 1960, first published 1913, reprinted 1999)

———, 'Master Alexander of St Albans: A Literary Muddle', *Essays in History Presented to Reginald Lane Poole*, ed. H. W. C. Davis (Oxford, 1927), pp. 246-60

———, *Stephen Langton* (Oxford, 1928)

———, *The Thirteenth Century 1216-1307* (Oxford, 1953)

Prestwich, M., *Edward I* (New Haven, CT, and London, 1997)

———, 'The Piety of Edward I', *England in the Thirteenth Century: Proceedings of the 1984 Harlaxton Symposium*, ed. W. M. Ormrod (Grantham, 1985), pp. 120-8

Pugh, R. B. and E. Crittal (eds), *VCH Wiltshire*, vol. III (London, 1956)

Rawcliffe, C., *Leprosy in Medieval England* (Woodbridge, 2006)

Reeve, M. M., 'The Painted Chamber at Westminster, Edward I and the Crusade', *Viator*, 37 (2006), 189-221
Reynolds, K. D., 'John, Prince (1905-1919)', ODNB (Oxford, 2004) [http://www.oxforddnb.com/view/article/76928, accessed 11 June 2014]
Richardson, H. G. and G. O. Sayles, *The Governance of Mediaeval England from the Conquest to Magna Carta* (Edinburgh, 1963)
Ridyard, S. J., '*Condigna Veneratio*: Post-Conquest Attitudes to the Saints of the Anglo-Saxons', ANS, 9 (1987), 179-206
Riley-Smith, J., *The Crusades: A Short History* (London, 1990)
Rubin, M., *Charity and Community in Medieval Cambridge* (Cambridge, 1987)
Russell, J. C., 'The Canonization of Opposition to the King in Angevin England', *Twelfth Century Studies*, J. C. Russell (New York, 1978), pp. 248-60
——, 'The Development of the Legend of Peter of Pontefract', *Medievalia et Humanistica*, 13 (1960), 21-31
Sadourny, A., 'Une famille rouennaise à la fin de la période ducale: les Du Donjon', *La Ville Médiévale en deçà et au-delà de ses murs: Mélanges Jean-Pierre Leguay*, ed. P. Lardin and J.-L. Roch (Rouen, 2000), pp. 183-8
St John Hope, W. H. and H. Brakspear, 'The Cistercian Abbey of Beaulieu, in the County of Southampton', *Archaeological Journal*, 2nd ser. 13, vol. 63 (1906), 129-86
Saul, N., *Richard II* (New Haven, CT, and London, 1997)
——, 'Richard II and Westminster Abbey', *The Cloister and the World: Essays on Medieval History in Honour of Barbara Harvey*, ed. J. Blair and B. Golding (Oxford, 1996), pp. 196-218
Sayers, J., *Innocent III: Leader of Europe 1198-1216* (London and New York, 1994)
——, 'Peter's Throne and Augustine's Chair: Rome and Canterbury from Baldwin (1184-90) to Robert Winchelsey (1297-1313)', *JEH*, 51 (2000), 249-66
Scholz, B. W., 'The Canonisation of Edward the Confessor', *Speculum*, 36 (1961), 38-60
Seabourne, G., 'Eleanor of Brittany and her Treatment by King John and Henry III', *Nottingham Medieval Studies*, 51 (2007), 73-110
Serjeantson, R. M. and W. R. D. Atkins (eds), *VCH Northampton*, vol. II (London, 1906)
Singleton, B., 'The Remodelling of the East End of Worcester Cathedral in the Earlier Part of the Thirteenth Century', *Medieval Art and Architecture at Worcester Cathedral: British Archaeological Association Conference Transactions*, 1 (1978), 105-15
Six, M., 'The Burgesses of Rouen in the Late Twelfth and Early Thirteenth Centuries', *Society and Culture in Medieval Rouen, 911-1300*, ed. L. V. Hicks and E. Brenner (Turnhout, 2013), pp. 247-78
Smith, D. M., 'Wells, Hugh of (d. 1235)', ODNB (Oxford, 2004) [http://www.oxforddnb.com/view/article/14061, accessed 30 September 2013]
Smith, R. J., 'Henry II's Heir: The Acta and Seal of Henry the Young King 1170-83', *EHR*, 116 (2001), 297-326
Snape, M. G., 'Poitou, Philip of (d. 1208)', ODNB (Oxford, 2004) [http://www.oxforddnb.com/view/article/22100, accessed 14 January 2014]
Spiegel, G. M., 'The Cult of St Denis and Capetian Kingship', *JMH*, 1 (1975), 43-69
Stacey, R. C., 'Marsh, Richard (d. 1226)', ODNB (Oxford, 2004) [http://www.

oxforddnb.com/view/article/18061, accessed 6 August 2013]
——, 'Walter, Hubert (d. 1205)', *ODNB* (Oxford, 2004, online edn 2008) [http://www.oxforddnb.com/view/article/28633, accessed 14 December 2010]
Stratford, J., 'John, Duke of Bedford (1389–1435)', *ODNB* (Oxford, 2004, online edn 2011) [http://www.oxforddnb.com/view/article/14844, accessed 23 May 2014]
Strickland, M., *War and Chivalry: The Conduct and Perception of War in England and Normandy, 1066–1217* (Cambridge, 1996)
Strong, R., *Coronation: A History of Kingship and the British Monarchy* (London, 2005)
Summerson, H., 'Bernard (d. 1214)', *ODNB* (Oxford, 2008, online edn 2009) [http://www.oxforddnb.com/view/article/95121, accessed 7 November 2013]
——, 'Cressingham, Hugh of (d. 1297)', *ODNB* (Oxford, 2004, online edn 2008) [http://www.oxforddnb.com/view/article/6671, accessed 29 October 2013]
——, 'Hugh (d. 1223)', *ODNB* (Oxford, 2008) [http://www.oxforddnb.com/view/article/95122, accessed 19 July 2013]
——, 'Thornham, Robert of (d. 1211), *ODNB* (Oxford, 2004) [http://www.oxforddnb.com/view/article/27884, accessed 29 August 2013]
——, 'Vieuxpont, Robert de (d. 1228)', *ODNB* (Oxford, 2004) [http://www.oxforddnb.com/view/article/28276, accessed 16 January 2014]
Sweetinburgh, S., 'Caught in the Cross-Fire: Patronage and Institutional Politics in Late Twelfth-Century Canterbury', *Cathedrals, Communities and Conflict in the Anglo-Norman World*, ed. P. Dalton, C. Insley and L. J. Wilkinson (Woodbridge, 2011), pp. 187–202
Tanner, L. E., 'Lord High Almoners and Sub-Almoners, 1100–1957', *Journal of the British Archaeological Association*, 20–1 (1957–58), 72–83
Tanner, N. and S. Watson, 'Least of the Laity: The Minimum Requirements for a Medieval Christian', *JMH*, 32 (2006), 395–423
Taylor, A. J., 'Edward I and the Shrine of St Thomas of Canterbury', *Journal of the British Archaeological Association*, 132 (1979), 22–8
Taylor, A., 'Robert de Londres, Illegitimate Son of William, King of Scots, c. 1170–1225', *Haskins Society Journal*, 19 (2007), 99–119
Thibodeau, T., 'Western Christendom', *The Oxford History of Christian Worship*, ed. G. Wainwright and K. B. Westerfield Tucker (Oxford, 2006), pp. 216–53
Thomas, H. M., 'Lay Piety in England from 1066 to 1215', *ANS*, 29 (2007), 179–92
Thompson, B., 'From "Alms" to "Spiritual Services": The Function and Status of Monastic Property in Medieval England', *Monastic Studies: The Continuity of Tradition*, 2, ed. J. Loades (Bangor, 1991), pp. 227–61
Thompson, S., *Women Religious: The Founding of English Nunneries after the Norman Conquest* (Oxford, 1991)
Throsby, J. (ed.), *Thoroton's History of Nottinghamshire: Republished with Large Additions*, 3 vols (Nottingham, 1797)
Tierney, B., *Medieval Poor Law: A Sketch of Canonical Theory and its Application in England* (Berkeley and Los Angeles, CA, 1959)
Titow, J. Z., *English Rural Society 1200–1350* (London and New York, 1969)
Todd, H., *Notitia Ecclesiae Cathedralis Carliolensis et Notitia Prioratus de Wedderhal*, Cumberland and Westmorland Antiquarian and Archaeological Society, Tract Series 6 (Kendal, 1892)

Trân-Duc, L., 'Les princes normands et les reliques (X^e-XIe siècles). Contribution du culte des saints à la formation territoriale et identitaire d'une principauté', *Reliques et sainteté dans l'espace médiéval*, ed. J.-L. Deuffic, PECIA, Ressources en médiévistique, vol. 8-11 (Saint-Denis, 2006), pp. 525-61

Truax, J., *Archbishops Ralph d'Escures, William of Corbeil and Theobald of Bec: Heirs of Anselm and Ancestors of Becket* (Farnham, 2012)

Turner, F., 'The Benedictine Priory of Broomhall, Berks: Some New Facts Relating to its History and Suppression', *The Berks, Bucks & Oxon Archaeological Journal*, 27 (1922-23), 90-5, 183-9

Turner, R. V., 'Bastards of King John, Chart' [http://www.academia.edu/3100660/Bastards_of_King_John_Chart, accessed 3 July 2013]

———, 'Briouze, William (III) de (d. 1211)', *ODNB* (Oxford, 2004, online edn 2006) [http://www.oxforddnb.com/view/article/3283, accessed 18 December 2013]

———, *Eleanor of Aquitaine: Queen of France, Queen of England* (New Haven, CT, and London, 2009)

———, *The King and His Courts: The Role of John and Henry III in the Administration of Justice, 1199-1240* (Ithaca, NY, 1968)

———, *King John* (London and New York, 1994)

———, 'Longchamp, William de (d. 1197)', *ODNB* (Oxford, 2004, online edn 2007) [http://www.oxforddnb.com/view/article/16980, accessed 14 December 2010]

———, *Men Raised From the Dust: Administrative Service and Upward Mobility in Angevin England* (Philadelphia, PA, 1988)

——— and R. R. Heiser, *The Reign of Richard Lionheart: Ruler of the Angevin Empire, 1189-99* (London, 2000)

Vale, M., *The Princely Court: Medieval Courts and Culture in North-West Europe 1270-1380* (Oxford, 2001)

van Houts, E. M. C., *Memory and Gender in Medieval Europe, 900-1200* (Basingstoke and London, 1999)

Vauchez, A., 'The Church and the Laity', *The New Cambridge Medieval History: Vol. V. c. 1198-c. 1300*, ed. D. Abulafia (Cambridge, 1999), pp. 182-203

Vaughan, R., *Matthew Paris* (Cambridge, 1958)

Vaughn, S. N., *Archbishop Anselm of Canterbury 1093-1109: Bec Missionary, Canterbury Primate, Patriarch of Another World* (Farnham, 2012)

Venables, E., 'Lucy, Godfrey de (d. 1204)', rev. R. V. Turner, *ODNB* (Oxford, 2004, online edn 2006) [http://www.oxforddnb.com/view/article/17148, accessed 30 March 2011]

Vincent, N., 'Athée, Girard d' (fl. 1198-c. 1210)', *ODNB* (Oxford, 2004, online edn 2008) [http://www.oxforddnb.com/view/article/39497, accessed 6 November 2013]

———, 'Aubigny, Philip d' (d. 1236)', *ODNB* (Oxford, 2004, online edn 2006) [http://www.oxforddnb.com/view/article/47227, accessed 6 November 2013]

———, 'Basset, Thomas (d. 1220)', *ODNB* (Oxford, 2004) [http://www.oxforddnb.com/view/article/47245, accessed 6 August 2013]

———, 'England and the Albigensian Crusade', *England and Europe in the Reign of Henry III (1216-1272)*, ed. B. K. U. Weiler with I. W. Rowlands (Aldershot, 2002), pp. 67-97

——, 'Henry II and the Historians', *Henry II: New Interpretations*, ed. C. Harper-Bill and N. Vincent (Woodbridge, 2007), pp. 1-23

——, *The Holy Blood: King Henry III and the Westminster Blood Relic* (Cambridge, 2001)

——, 'Isabella of Angoulême: John's Jezebel', *King John: New Interpretations*, ed. S. D. Church (Woodbridge, 1999), pp. 165-219

——, 'Jean, comte de Mortain: le futur roi et ses domaines en Normandie. 1183-1199', *1204: La Normandie entre Plantagenêts et Capétiens*, ed. A.-M. Flambard Héricher and V. Gazeau (Caen, 2007), pp. 37-59

——, 'King Henry III and the Blessed Virgin Mary', *The Church and Mary*, ed. R. N. Swanson, SCH, 39 (Woodbridge, 2004), pp. 126-46

——, 'Lacy, John de, Third Earl of Lincoln (c. 1192-1240)', *ODNB* (Oxford, 2004, online edn 2010) [http://www.oxforddnb.com/view/article/15855, accessed 30 August 2013]

——, 'Lusignan, Aymer de (c. 1228-1260)', *ODNB* (Oxford, 2004, online edn 2008) [http://www.oxforddnb.com/view/article/941, accessed 30 July 2013]

——, 'Master Simon Langton, King John and the Court of France', unpublished

——, 'Mauclerk, Walter (d. 1248)', *ODNB* (Oxford, 2004) [http://www.oxforddnb.com/view/article/18355, accessed 23 April 2014]

——, 'The Murderers of Thomas Becket', *Bischofsmord im Mittelalter*, ed. N. Fryde and D. Reitz (Göttingen, 2003), pp. 211-72

——, 'New Charters of King Stephen with Some Reflections upon the Royal Forests During the Anarchy', *EHR*, 114 (1999), 899-928

——, 'Pandulf (d. 1226)', *ODNB* (Oxford, 2004) [http://www.oxforddnb.com/view/article/21230, accessed 30 September 2013]

——, *Peter des Roches: An Alien in English Politics, 1205-1238* (Cambridge, 1996)

——, 'The Pilgrimages of the Angevin Kings of England 1154-1272', *Pilgrimage: The English Experience from Becket to Bunyan*, ed. C. Morris and P. Roberts (Cambridge, 2002), pp. 12-45

——, 'The Politics of Church and State as Reflected in the Winchester Pipe Rolls, 1208-1280', *The Winchester Pipe Rolls and Medieval English Society*, ed. R. Britnell (Woodbridge, 2003), pp. 157-81

——, 'Roches, Peter des (d. 1238)', *ODNB* (Oxford, 2004, online edn 2008) [http://www.oxforddnb.com/view/article/22014, accessed 14 December 2010]

——, 'Simon of Atherfield (d. 1211): A Martyr to his Wife', *Analecta Bollandiana*, 113 (1995), 349-61

——, 'Stephen Langton, Archbishop of Canterbury', *Étienne Langton, Prédicateur, Bibliste, Théologien*, ed. L.-J. Bataillon, N. Bériou, G. Dahan and R. Quinto (Turnhout, 2010), pp. 51-123

——, 'The Strange Case of the Missing Biographies: The Lives of the Plantagenet Kings of England 1154-1272', *Writing Medieval Biography 750-1250: Essays in Honour of Professor Frank Barlow*, ed. D. Bates, J. Crick, and S. Hamilton (Woodbridge, 2006), pp. 237-57

——, 'Why 1199? Bureaucracy and Enrolment under John and his Contemporaries', *English Government in the Thirteenth Century*, ed. A. Jobson (Woodbridge and London, 2004), pp. 17-48

Walker, S., 'John, Duke of Aquitaine and Duke of Lancaster, Styled King of Castile and León (1340-1399)', *ODNB* (Oxford, 2004, online edn 2008) [http://www.oxforddnb.com/view/article/14843, accessed 23 May 2014]

Warren, A. K., *Anchorites and their Patrons in Medieval England* (Berkeley and Los Angeles, CA, and London, 1985)

Warren, W. L., *Henry II* (London, 1973)

——, *King John* (London, 1974, first published 1961)

Watkins, C. S., *History and the Supernatural in Medieval England* (Cambridge, 2007)

——, 'Sin, Penance and Purgatory in the Anglo-Norman Realm: The Evidence of Visions and Ghost Stories', *Past and Present*, 175 (2002), 3–33

Waugh, S., 'Histoire, hagiographie et le souverain idéal à la cour des Plantagenêt', *Plantagenêts et Capétiens: confrontations et héritages*, ed. M. Aurell and N.-Y. Tonnerre (Turnhout, 2006), pp. 429–46

Webb, D., *Pilgrimage in Medieval England* (London and New York, 2000)

Webster, P., 'Crown, Cathedral, and Conflict: King John and Canterbury', *Cathedrals, Communities and Conflict in the Anglo-Norman World*, ed. P. Dalton, C. Insley, and L. J. Wilkinson (Woodbridge, 2011), pp. 203–19

——, 'Crown Versus Church After Becket: King John, St Thomas and the Interdict', *The Cult of St Thomas Becket in the Plantagenet World, c. 1170–c. 1250*, ed. P. Webster and M.-P. Gelin (Woodbridge, forthcoming)

——, 'King John and the Crusades' (in preparation)

——, 'King John and Rouen: Royal Itineration, Kingship, and the Norman "Capital", c. 1199–c. 1204', *Society and Culture in Medieval Rouen, 911–1300*, ed. L. V. Hicks and E. Brenner (Turnhout, 2013), pp. 309–37

——, 'Making Space for King John to Pray: The Evidence of the Royal Itinerary', *Journeying Along Medieval Routes*, ed. A. L. Gascoigne, L. V. Hicks, and M. O'Doherty (Turnhout, forthcoming)

——, 'The Military Orders at the Court of King John', *The Military Orders: Volume V: Politics and Power*, ed. P. W. Edbury (Farnham, 2012), pp. 209–18

Weiler, B., 'Bishops and Kings in England c. 1066–c. 1215', *Religion and Politics in the Middle Ages: Germany and England by Comparison*, ed. L. Körntgen and D. Wassenhoven (Berlin and Boston, MA, 2013), pp. 87–134

West, F. J., 'Geoffrey fitz Peter, Fourth Earl of Essex (d. 1213)', *ODNB* (Oxford, 2004, online edn 2008) [http://www.oxforddnb.com/view/article/9626, accessed 7 December 2010]

——, *The Justiciarship in England 1066–1232* (Cambridge, 1966)

White, S. D., *Custom, Kinship and Gifts to Saints: The Laudatio Parentum in Western France, 1050–1150* (Chapel Hill, NC, and London, 1988)

Wild, B., 'The Empress's New Clothes: A *rotulus pannorum* of Isabella, Sister of King Henry III, Bride of Emperor Frederick II', *Medieval Clothing and Textiles*, VII (2011), 1–31

Williams, D. H., *The Welsh Cistercians* (Leominster, 2001)

Wilson, J. (ed.), *VCH Cumberland*, vol. II (London, 1905)

Wiseman, W. G., 'The Hospital of St Nicholas, Carlisle and its Masters; Part 1 – The Period up to 1333', *Transactions of the Cumberland & Westmorland Antiquarian and Archaeological Society*, 95 (1995), 93–109

——, 'The Hospital of St Nicholas, Carlisle and its Masters; Part 2 – The Period from

1333', *Transactions of the Cumberland & Westmorland Antiquarian and Archaeological Society*, 96 (1996), 51-69

Wood, C. T., 'Fontevraud, Dynasticism, and Eleanor of Aquitaine', *Eleanor of Aquitaine: Lord and Lady*, ed. B. Wheeler and J. C. Parsons (New York and Basingstoke, 2002), pp. 407-22

——, 'La mort et les funérailles d'Henri II', *Cahiers de Civilisation Médiévale*, 37 (1994), 119-23

Wood, S., *English Monasteries and their Patrons in the Thirteenth Century* (Oxford, 1955)

Wormald, P., 'Wulfstan (d. 1023)', *ODNB* (Oxford, 2004) [http://www.oxforddnb.com/view/article/30098, accessed 15 January 2013]

Wright, J. R., 'Reynolds, Walter (d. 1327)', *ODNB* (Oxford, 2004, online edn 2008) [http://www.oxforddnb.com/view/article/23443, accessed 8 March 2011]

Young, C. R., 'King John and England: An Illustration of the Medieval Practice of Charity', *Church History*, 29 (1960), 264-74

Online resources

English Monastic Archives, database 2, [http://www.monasticarchives.org.uk/databrowse/, accessed 18 July 2013]

The 'Lands of the Normans' in England (1204-1244), [http://www.hrionline.ac.uk/normans/index.shtml, accessed 20 December 2012]

Oxford English Dictionary Online [http://www.dictionary.oed.com/, accessed 25 June 2014]

'St Bartholomew's Hospital Newbury', *British Listed Buildings* [http://www.british-listedbuildings.co.uk/en-393611-st-bartholomew-s-hospital-newbury-, accessed 9 November 2013]

Letters, S., *Gazetteer of Markets and Fairs in England and Wales to 1516*, [http://www.history.ac.uk/cmh/gaz/gazweb2.html, accessed 28 October 2013]

Worcester Cathedral, King John [http://www.worcestercathedral.co.uk/King_John.php, accessed 21 May 2014]

Index

Pages with maps and tables are indicated by italics

Names: First names followed by 'of', 'de' or 'fitz' appear under the first name
Otherwise names appear under the surname
Religious houses are, where possible, listed under their place name

Abbé, Herbert, see L'Abbé
Abbey Dore   66 n.29
Abbot, Henry, royal clerk   33
Abroughe, Thomas, pauper   79
Aconbury (Herefordshire) Hospitallers   173, 189
Adam, abbot of Croxton   176
Adam de Wilton   59
Adam of Brill, clerk   101
Adam of Eynsham   14, 20-1, 23, 63, 93, 107, 113, 115-16, 153-4, 199
Adeliza of Louvain, secondnd wife of Henry I of England   91, 100-1
Aelfric   129
Aethelbert, king of England   60
Aethelwold, first bishop of Carlisle   82
Aimery of Saint-Maur, Templar Grand Commander in England   164, 176
Alan of Lille (c.1130-1203)   111
Albigensians   69, 151
Alençon (Normandy)   114
Alexander III, pope   156
Alexander IV, pope   198
Alexander fitz Hugh   185
Alexander John, prince (1871)   192
Alexander of St Albans   157
Alexander of Stainsby, bishop of Coventry and Lichfield   35
Alexander the Mason, '*pseudo theologus*'   157
Alfonso VIII, king of Castile   89
Alice, servant of Joanna, John's sister   89
Alice, sister of Philip II of France   96
Almenêches, nunnery   172
Almoners and almonries   125-8, 161
Alms-giving   10, 13

during the interdict   161
see also John, family, life and death, alms-giving
Alnwick Priory   38, 143
Ambrose, clerk   22, 27
Amesbury Priory   67, 90, 99, 190
Amounderness (Lancs)   106
Anchorites   120, 123-4, 128 n.114
Andelys, see Les Andelys
Anestasius, prior of Beaulieu   67
Angers   135
Angevin kings, historical analysis of   3 n.1
Anglo-Saxon royal saints   48, 59, 179, 197
Anselm, archbishop of Canterbury   136, 172
Aragon   165, 167
Arbroath Abbey   38
Aremburga, first wife of Fulk V, count of Anjou   91
Argentan (Normandy)   33, 86, 94
Armagh, election of archbishop (1206)   136
Armathwaite nunnery   *121*, 121
Armenia, interdict on   137
Arras   155
Arthur of Brittany   83, 95, 108, 135, 190, 196
Aszoni, brother of Beaulieu   67
Augustinians   9, 98-9, 104-5
Austria   167
Auxerre, bishop of   137
Avranches   5, 135
  bishop of, see Tolomeus, William
Aymer de Lusignan, half-brother of Henry III, bishop-elect of Winchester   189

Bakewell (Derbys)   29, 30
Baldwin of Canterbury, archbishop   38, 132, 153
Bale, John, 'Kynge Johan'   191
Balls, William   78
Bangor, bishop of, see Robert, bishop of Bangor
Bapchild (Kent)   34
Barfleur (Cotentin)   99
Barking, abbesses of   97
Barling (Lincs) canons   160

'Barnwell' annalist 140, 169
Bartholomew, chaplain of Bucklebury 54
Bartholomew, finder of John's good luck token 107
Bartholomew, illegitimate son of John 97 and n.67
Basingwerk *182*, 183
Basset family 124 n.82
Basset, Thomas, courtier 119-20
Bath
   bishop of 138, 162; see also Jocelin, bishop of Bath
   priory of St Peter and St Paul 77, 165
Beatrice, servant of Joanna, John's sister 89
Beaulieu Abbey (Beaulieu Regis) 3, 7, 11, 12, 26, 50, 61, 64, 65-8, 70-1, 72, 83, 86, 104, 107, 144, 148, 160, 174-7, *182*, 187-9, 195, 198
   endowments by Henry III 187-8
   foundation charter 65
   see also Hugh, abbot of Beaulieu
Bec Abbey 175
Becket, Thomas, archbishop of Canterbury and saint 5-6, 39, 42, 51, 59, 60, 67, 99, 136, 141, 146, 151, 154, 156, 172
   cult of 9, 10, 11, 15, 32 n.64, 37, 38, 41, 44, 45, 48, 55, 60, 86, 185, 193
   shrine 45, 58, 86, 132, 140, 162
Beckford Priory 146
Bedford *182*
   church of St Peter and St Paul 181
   leper hospital of St Leonard 124
Benedict, hermit 123
Benedict of Sawston, precentor of St Paul's London (bishop of Rochester from 1214) 31
Bellus Locus, see Beaulieu
Bere (Dorset) 24, *25*
Berengaria, wife of Richard I 90, 153
Bernard, bishop of Carlisle 81 n.129, 135, 142
Bernard of Clairvaux 6
Bertrade de Montfort, wife of William IV, count of Anjou 90
Bicchieri, Guala, cardinal priest of San Martino, papal legate 70, 168, 175, 176
Bigod, Roger, earl of Norfolk (1189-1221) 54
Bindon Abbey 62 n.9, 127
   Abbot Henry of 126, 127, 161, 166, 167, 195
Birchwood, see Edwinstowe
Blanche of Castile, John's niece 137, 191
Blanchelande (Normandy), abbey of St Nicholas 31
Les Blanches (or Mortain) nunnery 102-3

Blyth (Notts), collegiate chapel 29 and n.52, 88 and n.12
Le Bois-Halbout (Calvados) 31
Bonport Abbey (Normandy) 71, 99-100
Bordeaux 190
Bourne 34
Bouvines, battle (1214) 167, 169
Boxley, abbot of 35
Brackley (Northants) 94
Bradbury, J. 13
Bradenstoke (Wilts), Priory 104-5, 160
Bradsole (Kent) Priory of St Radegund 100, *182*, 186
Breamore Priory 188
Brewer, William 80, 105-6, 119-20, 184, 187
Brewood nunnery 122
Brian de l'Isle 122, 185
Bridgetown (County Cork) *182*, 185
Bridgnorth (Shropshire) 56-7, 160,
   leper hospital of St James *182*, 183
Bridgwater (Somerset)
   castle chapel *182*, 184, 186
   hospital of St John the Baptist 106
Brill (Bucks) 33
Briouze family, treatment by John 173
   see also Matilda de Briouze, William de Briouze
Bristol 79, *182*
   castle 190
   damage in civil war 181
   hospital of St John the Baptist 78 n.113
   hospital of St Lawrence 71, 72, 78, 83, 195
   Laffard's (or Lawford's) Gate 78
   St Augustine's 96
Broadholme (Notts) canonesses 160
Bromsgrove 178-9
Broomhall (Berks), nunnery of St Margaret 71, 72, 72-3, 84, *121*, 122, 195
Brown, Thomas, almoner and Exchequer official 125
Bruerne *182*, 190
Bucklebury 54
Budleigh (Devon) 73 and n.76
Bulwell (Notts) *182*, 183
Burial, royal 4, 12, 174, 175
Burton (Norfolk) 106 n.127
   Burton annals 155-6, 157
Bury St Edmunds Abbey 21-2, 39-40, 41, 42, 44, 69, 86, 145, 165, 171, *182*, 187, 193
   Abbot Samson 42
   Abbot Hugh of Northwold, election of 42
   dispute over Samson's successor 165-6
Byland Abbey 143
Bynum, C. W. 114, 117

Caen 51, 52
  St Stephen (St Etienne) 9, 52, 98
  La Trinité, 9
Canterbury 38, 40, 41, 42, 44, 45, 58, 86, 154-6, 158-9, 161, 164, 166, *182*, 186, 193, 197-8
  archbishops of, see Anselm; Baldwin; Becket, Thomas; Lanfranc; Langton, Stephen; Reynolds, Walter; Theobald, archbishop of Canterbury; Walter, Hubert
  compensation 161, 166
  John exploits Canterbury estates 140
  monks expelled by John 133, 148
  monks fears 132
  secret election 132
  St Augustine's Canterbury 139, 140
  succession dispute 45, 69, 131-9
  negotiations over the dispute 156
  see also Becket, Thomas; John, Canterbury
Caperon, Roger, knight 106 and n.127
Carlisle *182*
  bishop of 70; see also Bernard; Hatton, John; Mauclerk, Walter
  hospital of St Nicholas 71, 72, 80-2, 84, 195
Carpenter, D. A. 3, 6-7, 162, 167
Cartmel (Lancs) Priory 105, 146, 166
Cat, Adam, chapel servant 159
Cérisy-la-Fôret Abbey (Normandy) 98
Cerne *182*, 183
Channel Islands, lordship of 104
Chantries 20, 28, 29, 36, 159
Chapel
  clerks 24, 27, 33
  royal 11, 27, 33, 35, 159, 195, 198
  servants 159
chaplains 24, 25, 26, 33, 86, 89, 94, 159, 183-4
  royal chaplain H. 186, 193, 195
Charity 8, 10, 13, 15, 16, 28, 110-18, 124-7, 129-30, 161, 196
Charroux (Poitou) 51
Chartres 49
Chateau Gaillard (Normandy) 49, 101
Châteauroux 49
Cheney, C. R. 4, 13, 23 n.24, 115, 143, 145, 146, 147, 151
Cherbourg, Abbey of Notre-Dame-du-Voeu 99
Chertsey Abbey 143
Cheshunt nunnery *121*
Chester
  Abbey 143
  bishop of 57

Chesterfield, hospital of St Leonard 71, 72, 79, 83, 195
Chibnall, M. 8, 9, 107
Chichester *182*
  bishop, dean and canons 96; see also Neville, Ralph; Poor, Richard; Simon of Wells
  Cathedral 34 n.77
Chinon 85
Christus Vincit 22, 27
  see also *Laudes Regiae*
Chroniclers 193, 199, see individual chroniclers
Circumcision, feast of *194*
Cirencester (Gloucs)
  Abbey 98
  abbot of 146
  canons 34
Cistercian Order 35, 61-5, 71, 83, 86, 127, 144, 146, 175, 195
  chroniclers 66
  General Chapter 61, 68, 69, 70, 147, 148
  links with Capetians 71
  taxation (1210) 69, 147
Cîteaux 64, 66, 148, 157
  abbot of 70
Civil War, see John, events during John's reign, civil war
Clairvaux Abbey 66, 71
  abbot of 29, 87
Clarendon, almonry 128
Clarke, P. D. 244
Clay, R. M. 80
Cleeve Prior (Worcs) 47
Clerks, royal 197
Clifford, Roger 175
Clifford, Walter 175
Clipstone (Notts) 24, *25*, 33, 94
  hermit of 123
Cluniacs 9
Cnut, king of England 40
Cockerham (Lancs) 106
Cockersand (Lancs), hospital and Priory 106
Coggeshall
  Abbey 103, 170-1
  see also Ralph of Coggeshall
Colvin, H. M. 28
Comnenus, Isaac, ruler of Cyprus 40
Compostela 40 n.20
Constance, wife of Geoffrey of Brittany 95
Constantinople 55
Cook Hill nunnery *121*, 122
Corfe 34 n.78, 57, 163
Cork, Benedictine cell or hospital 71, 72, 77, 83

236   INDEX

Cornwall   38
Court religious calendar   193, *194*
Coutances
  bishop   135, 136; see also Vivian de l'Etang
  see also Blancheland
Coventry   70
  bishop of, see Lichfield
Crassy, William   160
Crook, J.   175 n.14
Cross, exaltation of, feast   *194*
Crouch, D.   7, 28
Crowland Abbey   171
Croxton
  Abbey   174, *182*, 183
  abbot of   23, 176-7, 184
Croxden (Staffs), Abbey   106
Crusade, Fifth   169, 186
Cumin, John, archbishop of Dublin   153
Curthose, Robert, eldest son of William I   172

Damietta   186
Damme, destruction of the French fleet (1213)   162
David and Goliath   191
Déols (near Châteauroux)   49
Devon   38
Dialogue of the Exchequer   112
Dieulacres   *182*, 190
Dissolution of the Monasteries   75, 184, 186
Dives and Lazarus   112
Dixon-Smith, S.   94, 110, 126 n.95, 128
Dorchester   127
Dorset   38
Dover   119
  Priory   140
  town of River next to   100
Draper, P.   12, 175
Drincourt (Neufchâtel-en-Bray)   53
Dublin
  archbishop of, see Cumin, John; Henry of London
  Priory of St Thomas the Martyr   99
Duffy, M.   175
Dungarvan   77
Dunkeswell (Devon), Abbey   105
Dunstable (Beds)
  annalist   149, 150 n.104, 166
  leper hospital   124, 161
  Priory   98, 166
Dunstan, abbot, archbishop and saint   136
Durand, mason   187
Durand, papal envoy   156
Durford   94
Durham   *182*, 186
  Abbey   143

  bishop   142; see also Marsh, Richard; Philip of Poitou; Poor, Richard
  bishopric during interdict   155
  monks   136

Eadwig, king, drives Dunstan into exile   136
East Anglia   170
East Tilbury (Essex), hospital   104
Edmund, king and martyr   11, 15, 22, 38, 39-40, 42, 43, 44, 48, 55, 59, 60, 86, 145, 193
Edward I, king of England   1, 2, 39, 54-5, 56, 66, 72, 77, 80, 82, 90, 117, 129, 189-92, 198
Edward II, king of England   11, 75, 80, 100, 157, 188, 191-2, 198
Edward III, king of England   1, 2, 11, 73, 81, 117, 188, 192
  public image   12
  religious observance   12
Edward IV, king of England   82
Edward VI, king of England, commissioners for   78
Edward, Prince (youngest son of Elizabeth II)   192 n.110
Edward the Confessor, king of England and saint   6 n.27, 39, 42, 47, 51, 60, 129, 193
  cult of   9, 10, 11, 38, 39, 42-3, 44, 45, 48, 59, 86, 156, 197
  feast   *194*
  shrine of   7, 39
Edward the martyr, king of England   60
Edwinstowe, chapel in hay of Birchwood   33
Edwold, king of England   60
Egerton, chaplain   159-60 and n.12
Egypt, Sultan of   151
Eleanor, daughter of John   96, 178
Eleanor, John's sister, daughter of Eleanor of Aquitaine and Henry II   89, *91*, 95, 196
Eleanor of Aquitaine   29 n.54, 32, 52, 59, 65, 75, 85-90, *91*, 93-4, 98, 102, 107, 186, 190, 195-6
  commemorative masses   30, 32, 59, 93-4
  death   93, 114
Eleanor of Brittany, sister of Arthur of Brittany   190
Eleanor of Castile, wife of Edward I   73, 81, 192
Eleanor of Provence   45, 90, 103, 189, 192
Elena of Papworth   114
Ellerton nunnery   *121*
Ely   40, 165
  bishop of   138, 148, 153, 155, 161, 166; see also Eustace, bishop of Ely; Geoffrey de Burgh; Hugh, bishop of Ely; William de Longchamp

cathedral 172
Engel, U. 12
Epiphany *194*
Ermengarde, wife of William IV, duke of Aquitaine *91*
Ermengarde, wife of William de Folbec 99-100
Essex 170
Eudo (or Ivo), illegitimate son of John 97
Eugenius, archbishop of Armagh 136
Eustace, bishop of Ely 153, 166; see also interdict, executors of
Eustace, clerk of Westminster 22, 27
Eustace du Fauconberg, bishop of London (1221-28) 32, 143, 185
Evesham Abbey 69
Evreux, bishop of, John de la Cour 103
Exchequer, Red Book of 146
Excommunication 13
    see also John, events during John's reign, excommunication
Exeter 68, *182*
    bishop of, see Marshal, Henry; Simon of Apulia
    Church of St Nicholas 184

Falaise
    chaplains 86
    Priory of St. John 32-3
    Treaty of (1174) 38
Famine 114-15, 121
Farewell nunnery (Staffs) 122
Faringdon (Oxon) 64-5, 72, 187-8
Farnham 120
Faversham
    Abbey 103, 140
    Parish church 138
Fécamp Abbey 98
La Ferté-sur-Grosne, abbot of 64
Festivals, main religious 19, 20, 24, 27, 41, 44, 48, 56, 94, 102
    All Saints 52, 56, 160, *194*
    Ascension 16 n.72, 20, 21, 56, 115, *116*, 162, 163, 193
    Ash Wednesday 117, 169 and n.90
    Assumption 48, 50 n.79, 511, 52, 94, 118, 171, *194*
    Christmas 19, 24, 26, 27, 41, 44, 48, 115, 127, 128, 170, 179, *194*
    during the interdict 133
    Easter 19, 24, 27, 29, 40, 41, 55, 76, 111, 115, 117, 118, 119, 120, 145, 159, 193, 196, 198
    Easter Sunday 1199 20, 41, 44, 88, 133

Good Friday 117, 118, 120 n.54, 126, 133, 159, 193
Holy Week 117, 193
Lent 117, 169
    Non-observance of fasts on *116*
Palm Sunday 41, 118, 120, 126, 193
Pentecost (Whitsunday) 193
Trinity Sunday 44 and n.42, 50, 193
see also Maundy Thursday
Finmere (Oxon), hermit 123
Fontevraud Abbey 12, 14, 32, 86, 88-90, 92-3, 96, 108, 175-7, 180, *182*, 186, 190, 196
    chantry chapel of St Lawrence 32, 89
    Fontevraudine houses 93
    martyrologium 90
    royal effigies 180
Forde Abbey 26, 127
    abbot 57, 118, 126, 144, 195
    see also John of Forde
Forests 62, 64, 65, 72, 75, 103, 122, 183, 190
    forest rights 35, 80, 102, 122, 147, 189
    New Forest 65-6, 187-9
    see also Hugh de Neville
Foukeholme nunnery *121*
Fountains Abbey 62, 143
France, Capetian monarchy of 5, 76
    peace with, 1200 62
Frayo of Cuddington 190
Frederick II, Emperor 58
Freemantle 56
Friars 10
Fromond, king of England 60
Fulk IV, le Réchin, abbot of Anjou 90
Fulk V, count of Anjou, king of Jerusalem 90, *91*
Fulk de Cantilupe 34, 139
Furness Abbey (Lancs) 62, 103

Galbraith, V. H. 3
Garter, Order of 11
Gatteville (Cotentin) 99
Gaveston, Piers 11
Geddington (Northants) 24, *25*
Geoffrey V, count of Anjou 9, 75, *91*, 92, 97, 100, 175
Geoffrey de Buckland, archdeacon of Norwich 150
Geoffrey de Burgh, archdeacon of Norwich, bishop of Ely 150
Geoffrey de Mandeville 96, 162
Geoffrey fitz Peter, earl of Essex, justiciar 34, 35, 104, 119-20, 135, 159, 199
Geoffrey fitz Roy, illegitimate son of John 97

Geoffrey, half-brother of John and archbishop of York   76, 85, 87, 138-9
Geoffrey of Brittany   29, 85, 87, 91, 94-5
  burial in Notre-Dame, Paris   95
  lack of provision for the soul of   95, 108, 196
Geoffrey of Coldingham   133
Geoffrey of Henlaw, prior of Llanthony, bishop of St Davids   135
Geoffrey of Norwich, imprisonment and murder   150 and n.104
Gerald of Wales   22, 76, 145
Gervase of Canterbury   133, 139-40, 148, 152, 157
  Mappa Mundi of   78
Gervers, M.   144
Giffard, Hugh   128
Giffard, Osbert, illegitimate son of John   97
Gilbert de Clare   177
Gilbert fitz Reinfrey, sheriff of Lancs   160
Gilbert of Sempringham, see St Gilbert
Gilbertine Order   58-9, 74, 99, 146
Gillingham, J.   4, 174
Girard d'Athée, royal agent, sheriff of Gloucs   79, 98
Glanville, Gilbert, bishop of Rochester, burial   142
  exile in Scotland   142
Gloucester, St Peter's Abbey   146
Godfrey de Lucy, bishop of Winchester (1189-1204)   55 and n.114, 67
Godwin, hermit, 123
Golding, B.   74, 93 n.40
Le Goulet, Treaty (1200)   61, 137
Graham, R.   74
Grandmont   87, 175
  Grandmontines   183
Gransden, A.   40
Gratian, *Decretum*   111
Gregory IX, pope   66, 173, 188
Green, J. [Judith]   2, 9
Green, J. R. [John Richard]   2
Grimsby, Wellow Priory, see Wellow
Grovebury, alien priory   93
Guala, see Bicchieri
Guildford (Surrey)   24, 25, 145
  almonry   128

Hackington, proposed collegiate church   132
Hailes Abbey   67, 109
Hales, see Halesowen
Halesowen (Worcs)   36, 104
Hallam, E. M.   9, 79, 80
Halton, John, bishop of Carlisle   82
Hamo, Brother, of Beaulieu   188

Hamo de Valognes, justiciar of Ireland   153
Hamonic, N.   144
Harold II, king of England   40, 47
Harper-Bill, C.   61
Hartland (Devon)   57
Harvests   114
Harvey, K.   168
Havering, almonry   128
Hawisa, Countess   94
Hereford   119
Henry I, king of England   1, 2, 9, 21 n.10, 22, 31, 49, 52, 53, 54, 66, 73, 75, 86, 91, 92, 98, 100-1, 103, 136, 145, 196
  almoner   125
  annual masses for   103
  White Ship disaster   9
Henry II, king of England   1, 2, 3, 4, 7, 10, 11, 27, 29, 30, 31, 33, 37, 39, 44, 45, 49, 50, 53, 54, 58-9, 62, 65, 67, 71, 74, 75-6, 81, 82, 85-8, 90, 91, 92-5, 98-103, 105-7, 119, 124, 136, 146, 151, 161, 172, 175, 184, 186, 190, 195
  almoners   125
  as founder of monasteries   9
  attitude to the mass   5
  commemorative masses   29, 30, 31, 33, 34, 94 n.45
  Great Rebellion of 1173-74   42, 87
  penance   99, 196
    at Avranches   5
    at Canterbury   5, 37
  re-founds Waltham Holy Cross Priory   57, 67
  seeks to make John king of Ireland   30
  takes cross of a crusader (1188)   40
Henry III, king of England   1, 6, 7, 10, 20, 23 and n.26, 26, 27, 36, 39, 42, 44, 45, 46, 48, 49, 55, 60, 61 n.4, 65, 72, 74, 78, 90, 93, 94, 96, 100, 103, 107, 111-12, 122-3, 146, 156, 163, 171, 177-8, 181, 183-5, 187-92, 197
  almonries   128
  burial   39, 93
  honouring of John's memory   179
  re-coronation (1220)   45
  threatened with interdict   198
  and the poor   110, 114, 117, 129-30
Henry VI, Emperor   149
Henry VIII, king of England   30, 42, 73, 76, 180, 191, 198
Henry the Young King   29, 37, 53, 65, 85-8, 90, 91, 95, 101, 104-5, 175-6, 195
Henry fitz Count   120
Henry of Bindon, see Bindon, Abbot Henry of
Henry of Blois, bishop of Winchester   53
Henry of Cerne, clerk   27

Henry of Cornhill   138 n.44
Henry of Hereford, clerk   27
Henry of London, archbishop of Dublin from
    1212   143, 167, 175
Henry son of Reginald of Winchelsea   170
Henry the Lion, duke of Saxony   58, 97
Henwood nunnery   *121*, 122
Herbert, son of Ralph L'Abbé   135
Hereford   119, *182*
    bishop of   148, 161-2
    church of All Saints   190
Hermits   8, 33, 103, 120, 122, 123-4
Hicks, L. V.   8
Higden, Ranulph, *Polychronicon*   164
Hinchingbrooke nunnery   *121*, 121
Holborn, see London
Hollister, C. W.   4
Holt, Sir J.   117, 137
Holy Innocents, feast of   116, 119, 127, 128,
    194
Holy Land   169-70, 185-6
    masses for   33
    money for   56, 165
    soldiers for   64
Holy relics, feast of   43
Holy Roman Empire   167
Holy Sepulchre, brothers of   190
Honorius III, pope   70, 173-4
Honorius Augustodunensis   112, 129
Hope (Derbys)   30
Horston Castle (Derbys)   24, *25*, 94
Hospitals   9, 78, 128 n.114
    See also Bridgwater, Bristol, Carlisle,
        Chesterfield, Cockersand, Cork, East
        Tilbury, Kingsthorpe (by Northampton),
        Lancaster, Lincoln, London, Newbury,
        Oxford, Portsmouth, Rome, St Mary
        Magdalene, Shrewsbury, Southwark,
        Sutton-at-Hone, Vienne, Waterford
    see also leper hospitals
Hospitallers, see Knights Hospitaller
Howsham (Lincs)   59, 75
Hubert de Burgh   178, 184
Hugh II, abbot of Reading   54
Hugh, abbot of Beaulieu   68-70, 127, 195
    bishop of Carlisle (Hugh of Beaulieu,
        1218-23)   70, 82
    royal envoy to Rome   127, 161
Hugh, bishop of Ely   103
Hugh de Boves, captain of mercenaries   120, 171
Hugh de Cressy, courtier   81
Hugh de Mortemer   175
Hugh de Morville, lord of Burgh-by-Sands   81
    and n.131
Hugh de Neville, chief justice of the forest   117

Hugh de Nonant, bishop of Coventry and
    Lichfield (1188-98)   22, 30, 76
Hugh, earl of Chester   106 n.127
Hugh of Cressingham   81
Hugh of Hereford, clerk   27
Hugh of Lincoln, bishop and saint   10, 14,
    20-1, 21 n.9, 85, 113, 116, 122
    Life of, see Adam of Eynsham
    funeral   52, 63, 71, 193
Hugh of St Victor   157
Hugh of Wells, bishop of Lincoln from
    1209   141, 160, 167
Hugh the Sumpterer, royal servant   56
Hulk of Tykesfleet, the   170
Hume, D.   2
Hunting on feast days   119, 129, 161
Hurley   182, 190

Indulgences   43, 55, 112, 178, 190-1
Ingeborg of Denmark   137
Innocent III   13, 16, 22, 23, 46, 59, 124, 136,
    151, 152, 159, 165-170, 186, 198
    and the disputed Canterbury
        election   131-6, 138, 155-7
    Deeds of Pope Innocent   134, 155
    delays confirmation of Reginald   132
    imposes interdict and
        excommunication   133
    John submits to and does homage   162
Interdict   13, 16, 42, 45, 48, 52, 69, 70, 74, 98,
    118, 121, 130, 166, 198
    compensation for treatment during   161-2,
        166, 169, 172, 198
    executors of   69, 141, 148, 154-6, 197
    other states threatened or placed under
        interdict   137
    religious activity under interdict   159
    threatened on Normandy   135
    see also John, events of the reign, interdict
Invectivum contra regem Johannem   152, 164
Isabella, daughter of John   58, 96, 110
Isabella of Angoulême (second wife of
    John)   22, 26, 27, 30, 39, 41, 62, 69, 90, 96,
    105 n.122, 108, 176 n.20, 184, 191, 196
Isabella of France, wife of Edward II   188
Isabella of Gloucester (first wife of John)   38,
    96, 153, 162, 186
Islip (Oxon)   43
Ivo, companion of Robert of
    Knaresborough   123
Ivo, illegitimate son of John, see Eudo

James of Cirencester, chaplain   24
James of the Temple, clerk   27
Jersey, church of St Lawrence   31

Jerusalem, church   191
Jews   93 n.38
Joan, daughter of John   69, 96
Joan de Neville   117
Joanna, sister of John   70, 88-90, 91, 148, 196
   infancy at Fontevraud   89 n.19
Job (or John) of the Chamber, chapel
   servant   159
Jocelin, bishop of Bath   175
Jocelin of Brakelond   22, 44 n.42
John as a royal name   191-2
John Charles Francis, Prince (1905-19)   192
John de Cella, abbot of St Albans   23
John de Gray, bishop of Norwich, John's
   candidate for Canterbury   132, 138, 142,
   167, 186
   Justiciar of Ireland   142
John de Lacy   163
John de la Cour, bishop of Evreux, see Evreux
John, duke of Bedford   192
John, illegitimate son of Richard III   192
JOHN, lord of Ireland, earl of Gloucester,
   count of Mortain, count of Anjou, duke of
   Normandy, king of England (1199-1216)
   EVENTS DURING JOHN'S REIGN
     Anjou, loss of   197
     arrests partners of clergymen   145
     baronial conspiracy and rebellion   69, 150
     barons, dispute with   170
     Canterbury dispute   13, 131-6, 138-9,
        152, 153-5, 157, 168-70, 197
        accepts Stephen Langton as
           archbishop   164
        Canterbury election   45
        exiling of Canterbury monks   133,
           139-40, 141, 148
        John objects to election of Stephen
           Langton   133
        negotiates settlement of dispute   152,
           154-6, 165
     charter of free elections   167-8, 197
     civil war   12, 26, 43, 66, 70, 80, 102, 124,
        143, 166, 170-2, 173-4, 176-7, 181
     claim to rule England and continental lands
        disputed   108
     coronation   16 n.72, 20, 21, 38, 39, 40-1,
        42, 115, 164, 193
        oath   164
     death and burial   3 and n.9, 12, 23, 42, 45,
        46, 48
     excommunication   7, 13, 23 n.24, 34, 52,
        133, 134, 138, 141, 143, 146, 150, 153-5,
        158-61, 165, 169, 197-8
        absolution from   20, 23, 150, 159, 160,
           164-5, 167-8

        personal immunity   165
     French invasion   12, 26, 70, 161, 163
     Invectivum contra regem Johannem   152, 164
     Ireland   71, 76-8, 78 n.108, 83, 125-6,
        136, 147, 148
        expedition to (1210)   24, 35, 53, 147-8
     Interdict   13-14, 16, 20, 22, 23 and n.24,
        27, 34-5, 39, 42, 45, 48, 52, 68, 98,
        105 n.122, 113, 118, 121, 123, 124, 130,
        133-4, 137, 140-52, 153-5, 159-61, 165,
        169, 175-7, 197-8
        John exiles observers of the
           interdict   141, 142, 148, 149
        lifting of sanctions   159, 161, 165, 166
        John's reaction to   141-2
        John submits to the Pope   150, 151
        John threatened with local
           interdict   153
     levies carucage (1200)   61
     Magna Carta   16, 26, 43, 57, 78, 79 n.115,
        143, 166, 167-8, 170, 172, 197-8
     military campaigns
        1214   16, 32, 51-2, 143
        against the Scots (1209)   148
        Bouvines, allies defeated at (1214)   167,
           169
        Ireland (1210)   24, 35, 53, 147-8
        La-Roche-aux-Moines, setback
           (1214)   167
        Rochester castle siege   43 n.39, 50 n.79,
           172
        sacrilegious actions of troops   170-1
        Welsh campaign (of 1212)   56-7
     murder of children   149-50
     negotiates for settlement of dispute with
        church   141, 143
     Normandy, loss of   33, 42, 45-6, 49, 51,
        60, 73-4, 83, 87 n.10, 93, 96, 107, 135,
        146, 197
        consequent seizure of Norman lands in
           England   103
     oaths of homage and fealty   146-7
     opponents   163
     opposition to   163, 176
     rebellion against   106, 161
     reform of the realm, demands for   124
     regnal years of John   16 n.72
     supporters   157, 171-2
     surrender of England and Ireland to
        papacy   158, 162-3, 168, 170, 198
     treatise against John   152, 164
     Treaty of Le Goulet (1200)   61
     Wash, disaster in   26-7, 56, 173
   FAMILY, LIFE AND DEATH
     abstinence   8, 16

failure to abstain   118-20, 196
  see also fasting
absolution of John   7
adultery of   7
almonry and almoners of   118, 125, 126, 127, 128, 161, 195
alms-giving   7, 16, 80, 94, 159, 161, 184, 195-6, 198 see also charity
apostasy, alleged consideration of   150-1
baptism   7, 193
birth   37
body of John   174, 176-80, 186
burial   3 and n.9, 12, 17, 61, 63, 71, 174-5, 175 n.15, 176-8, 180-1, 186, 199
character of   4, 14
children of   26, 58, 67 and n.35, 69, 90, 95-7, 108, 110, 128, 146, 177-8, 188-9
  illegitimate children   186
  names of John's children   96-7
  see also Bartholomew; Eleanor; Eudo (Ivo); Giffard, Osbert; Henry (III); Isabella; Joan; Matilda; Oliver; Philip, Richard
coif of unction   121, 174-5
communion, failure to take   20, 21
confesses sins   7, 22, 64, 71, 193
death and last rites   7, 17, 66, 75, 80, 96, 106, 157, 167, 172, 173, 175, 177, 180, 184, 187, 190, 192, 193, 195
  deathbed   173-4, 176, 189, 191, 193
  final absolution of sins   173
decision to be buried at Worcester   174, 175-7
entrails buried at Croxton   176, 183
family   76; see also under individual names
fasting   8, 20, 115, 116, 117, 121
  failure to fast   115, *116*, 117, 118, 119, 120, 126, 129, 161, 196
  failure to fast on Fridays   115, *116*, 117, 120 n.54
  failure to respect Wednesday as a day of abstinence   118-19, 120
funeral   174-5, 178
gambling debts, payment of   52
heart burial   176, 183
hunting
  lodges   71
  on feast days   119, 127, 129, 161, 196
last illness   173
marriages   7
  to Isabella of Gloucester   38, 154, 162
  see Isabella of Angoulême
naming of John   90 n.26
proposal to transfer John's body to Beaulieu (1228)   174, 177

regalia   180
said to have been poisoned   191
skull   180
testament, final   142, 172, 174, 176, 181, 185
tomb   175, 177, 178-81
  coffin/sarcophagus   178, 180
  tomb effigy   179-81
  tomb cleaning and restoration   180-1
  translation to a new tomb (1232)   178, 180, 186
wears good luck token   107
HOUSEHOLD AND RELIGIOUS MATTERS
chapels of   1, 16, 24-5, 28, 32-3, 159, 173
  right not to be placed under interdict   165
  travelling royal chapel   26-7
chaplains of   1, 24, 25, 26, 33, 86, 159, 186
chantries   28-33, 36, 195
charity   13, 15, 16, 110, 113, 129, 130, 161, 196 see also alms-giving
Cistercians, relations with   61-5, 71, 83, 195
  John *confrater* of the order   63, 65
  taxation of Cistercians (1210)   69, 147
courtiers of   117, 119, 120, 128, 184-5, 196, 199
election of heads of religious houses   16, 143
  Johns attitude   155-8, 168
episcopal elections and appointments   134-6, 143, 167, 197-8
excommunication   7, 13, 68, 69, 118
  absolved from   164, 198
famine, responds to   115, 121
fines religious communities for the return of their property   146
Fontevraud   12
  see also Fontevraud Abbey
  childhood at   90
gifts to laymen   16
heresy, suppression ordered   151
heretical ideas, alleged   151
and holy days   8, 16
hospital foundations   76-82, 191
  see also Carlisle, Chesterfield, Kingsthorpe, Newbury, Waterford, St Katherine's, Lancaster St Leonards
household of   16, 19, 52, 57, 113, 119, 122, 125, 160, 169, 195-6
household knights   120, 140
itinerary of   24, 26, 38 n.9, 41, 50 n.79, 57, 68, 105, 113, 128, 160, 189
lepers, patronage of   101

242 INDEX

Mass 1, 7, 116, 159, 164
   attendance at Mass 19-28, 36, 164, 193
   commissions masses 19, 20, 28-33, 86, 88, 93, 94, 129, 195
   masses, services and prayers commissioned by others 33-6, 86
   receives the Eucharist 174
Maundy Thursday observance 7, 13, 196
   see also Maundy Thursday
monastic foundations 195
   proposed 62-4
   See Beaulieu, Faringdon, Newstead-on-Ancholme, Kingsthorpe, Otterton
monastic orders, dealings with 15, 16
oaths on relics or gospels 21, 85, 162
offering made by 20, 23, 42, 49, 56, 159, 160, 164, 193
patron of lepers 100-1
penance 7, 61, 64
pilgrimages of 38, 39-45
the poor 1, 16, 32, 94, 113-20, 126, 127, 129, 130, 191, 195-6, 198
   feeds the poor 114, 115, 118, 119, 120, 126, 128-9, 130, 187, 189, 196-7
   possibly washes feet of the poor 117-18
relics 27, 53-7
   held by 1, 56, 60, 160, 173, 195
   religious calendar of the court 193
religious foundations 1, 129
religious observance during sanctions 154, 159-61
religious rituals, attitude to 193
remission of sins 64
restores church property 98, 141, 145, 146, 154-5, 159, 164-5
and saints and their shrines 1, 108-9, 115, 118, 129; see also individual saints
sanctified kingship 43-5
seizes church property 16, 76, 98, 141, 144-5, 146, 148, 149, 197
sermons 20
and the sick 113
taxation of the English church (1210) 146-7, 157-8, 197
JOHN PRIOR TO HIS ACCESSION AS KING
Actions as earl of Gloucester, lord of Ireland, count of Mortain, 22, 30, 38, 49-50, 53, 57, 62 nn.8 and 9, 63 n.15, 74-80, 83, 85, 88, 96-7, 98, 99, 100, 102-3, 105, 106, 108, 123, 132, 153, 172, 196
ambulatory interdict on 153
attempted seizure of the throne (1194) 85, 106, 153

possible coronation as Lord of Ireland 30
POSTHUMOUS EVENTS AND REPUTATION
anniversary masses for 29-32, 34, 178-9, 184-7, 190
historical reputation 1-4, 13-14, 61, 74, 83, 110, 117 n.43, 121, 131, 148, 149, 152, 164-6, 169, 172, 177-8, 191, 193, 195, 197, 199
portrayal as a tyrant 148-9
indulgence for the forgiveness of John's sins 190-1
posthumous provision 17, 199
   alms for John's soul 181, 184-7
   anniversary masses 178-9, 184-7, 190
   commemoration of John's soul 177-81, *182*, 183-8, 190
posthumous reparation for John's sins 181, 183, 190
regarded as impious/irreligious 2-3 and n.8, 13-14, 148, 151, 172
John of Anagni, papal legate 38
John of Coutances, bishop of Worcester (1196-98) 46
John of Forde, abbot of Forde and chronicler 26, 126, 127 n.103, 144, 149, 158
John of Gaunt 192
John of Monmouth 175
John of Salisbury 151
Johnstone, H. 13, 110
Jordan du Hommet, archdeacon and bishop of Lisieux, see Lisieux
Joshua 191

Keldholme nunnery *121*, 122
Kellett, A. 13, 118, 120 n.54
Kempton 128
Kenelm, king of England 60
Kent 170
   men of 155
Kerry 34
Kimbolton (Cambs) 114
King, E. 2
Kingshaugh (Notts) 24, *25*
Kingsthorpe (by Northampton), hospital of St David or Holy Trinity 72, 79, *182*, 187, 195
Knaresborough 13, 118, 122, 123
Knights Hospitaller 120, 144, 146, 173, 183
Knights Templar 5, 76, 94, 125-7, 144, 190, 195
   chaplain 183

L'Abbé, Herbert, son of Ralph 135
Lambley nunnery *121*, 122

INDEX   243

Lancaster
  hospital of St Leonard   71, 72, 80, 83, 191
  Priory   143
  sheriff of   106
Lanfranc
  archbishop of Canterbury   47
  Monastic Constitutions   111, 118, 128
Langley Priory (Norfolk)   106
Langton, Simon, brother and procurator of Stephen Langton   155
Langton, Stephen, archbishop of Canterbury   23, 38, 44 n.42, 45, 69, 112, 138-9, 142, 149, 152, 154, 157, 164-5, 177, 185, 196
  compensation   161-2
  elected archbishop   132
  John accepts as archbishop   161, 164
  John meets   164
  John refuses to accept   133
  letters on eve of interdict   140
  Magna Carta re-issue of 1225   167
Last Judgement   8, 14 and n.65, 111, 129
Lateran Council, Second (1139)   111
  Fourth (1215)   19, 24, 69
Laudes Regiae   27, 86, 159, 193
  see also *Christus Vincit*
Laurence du Donjon, Rouen merchant   114
Lawrence, chaplain of Shrewsbury   183
Laxton (Notts)   119
La Nöe Abbey (in the Evrecin)   99
La Roche-aux-Moines (1214)   167
La Trinité (Caen), see Caen
Leicester   143
  Augustinian canons   106
Lenton (Notts) Priory   100
Leland, John   180
Leominster   55
Léon, interdict on   137
Leper hospitals, see Les Andelys, Bedford, Bridgnorth, Dunstable, Lincoln, London, Northampton, Oxford, Preston, Rouen, Shrewsbury, Westminster, Wilton, Windsor
Lepers   100-1, 196
Les Andelys, (Normandy), lepers   101
Leyser, K. J.   10, 122
Liber Regalis   21
Lichfield   182, 187
  bishop of, see Alexander of Stainsby; Hugh de Nonant; Muschamp, Geoffrey; William de Cornhill
  bishopric   167
  cathedral   29-31, 50, 52, 86, 95, 161, 183
Le Liget (Touraine) Carthusian Priory   99
Lilley (Herts)   41 n.28
Lincoln   62-3, 65, 136, 166

  bishop   162; see also Hugh of Lincoln; Hugh of Wells
  bridge chapel   28, 94
  Cathedral   50, 52, 160; see also William de Montibus
  leper hospital of the Holy Innocents   101
Lindridge   47
Lisieux, archdeacon and bishop of, Jordan du Hommet   134
Lismore   77
Little Bampton (Cumbria)   81 n.129
Llanthony Priory   146
Lombard, Peter   157
London   41 n.28, 43, 127, 128 n.4
  annals   149
  bishop of   138, 148, 155, 162; see also Eustace de Fauconberg; Richard fitz Nigel; William de Ste-Mère-Église
  Holy Trinity, Aldgate   43 n.40
  hospital   43 n.40
  leper hospital of St Giles, Holborn   102
  St Martin's   43 n.40
  St Mary Graces   11
  St Paul's Cathedral   31-2, 43, 52, 86, 94, 169, 182, 185
  Temple or New Temple   43 n.40, 175, *182*, 183
  Tower of   118, 192
Louis VII, king of France   37, 44, 85, *91*
Louis of France (Louis VIII, king of France 1223-26)   70, 171-2, 176, 191
  occupies London 1216   43
Louis IX, king of France (St Louis)   5-6, 7, 20, 117, 191
Ludgershall (Hants)   24, *25*, 26

Magna Carta, see John, main events of the reign
Maldon (Essex)   31
Malmesbury   *182*, 184
Le Mans   175
Margam Abbey   69, 144, 148
  annalist   144
Margaret de Lacy   173
Margaret of France, widow of Henry the Young King   29, 87
Marlborough (Wilts)   126
  almonry   128
  castle   190
  Gilbertine Priory of St Margaret   71, 72, 74, 83, 195
  Oath of (1209)   146-7, 197
  recluse of   124
Marmont Priory   59, 93
Marritt, S.   14, 107
Marsh, Richard, chancery clerk and bishop of Durham   119-20, 127, 157, 167

INDEX

Marshal, Henry, bishop of Exeter (d.1206)   68
Marshal, Isabella, first wife of Richard of Cornwall   177
Marshal, Richard, second son of William Marshal   120
Marshal, William   70, 105, 146, 166, 174-5, 187
    testament   57
Martel, Alan, Templar, preceptor of New Temple   69 n.53, 126
Martin, G. H.   140
Martindale, J.   175
Mary, the Blessed Virgin, see Virgin Mary
Mary de Vernon, heiress of the Isle of Wight   104-5 n.118
Mason, E.   9, 12, 48, 92, 175-6
Matilda de Briouze   34 n.78, 173
Matilda de Hauvill   59, 93
Matilda, Empress   9, 53, 71, *91*, 92, 96, 99-101, 103, 175, 195-6
Matilda, illegitimate daughter of Henry II   97
Matilda, illegitimate daughter of John   96
Matilda, niece of Geoffrey V, count of Anjou   92
Matilda of Flanders   92, 96
Matilda of Newburgh   127
Matilda of Scotland, first wife of Henry I of England   *91*, 96, 100-1, 118
Matilda, sister of Geoffrey V, count of Anjou, wife of William, son of Henry I   92 and n.30
Matilda, sister of John   58, *91*, 95 and n.54, 96, 196
Matthew of Rievaulx   133
Matthew of Westminster   172
Mauclerk, Walter, bishop of Carlisle   185
Mauger, bishop of Worcester (1200-12)   46, 155
    death at Pontigny   155
    see also interdict, executors of
Maundy Thursday   7, 11, 13, 111, 117, 118, 127, 159, 193, 196
Mayr-Harting, H.   64
Meiler fitz Henry, justiciar of Ireland   34
Meaux Abbey   143, 144
    chronicle   144, 146
Melisende, second wife of Fulk V, count of Anjou   *91*
Melksham (Wilts)   31
Merlin, prophesies of   175
Misterton (Notts)   76
Mohammad-al-Nasir, embassy to   150-1
Mollat, M.   130
Montacute   *182*, 187
Mont-aux-Malades, see Rouen
Mont-St-Michel Abbey   73 and n.76, 74
Morroco   151
Mortain nunnery, see Les Blanches
Morville (Shropshire)   183
Moses   191
Mottisfont (Hants), Priory   105, *182*, 185
Moxby nunnery   *121*, 122
Muschamp, Geoffrey, bishop of Coventry and Lichfield (1198-1208)   29, 86, 95, 115

Navarre, interdict on   137
Neithan, king of England   60
Netley (Hants)   67, 109
Neufchâtel-en-Bray, see Drincourt
Neville, Ralph, bishop of Chichester   184
Newbury (Berks)   41 n.28
Newbury, hospital of St Bartholomew   72, 78, 83, 195
Newcastle, nunnery   *121*, 122
Newenham   67
New Forest, see Forests
Newnham, anchorite   123
Newstead Augustinian Priory (Notts)   11, 71, 72, 75-6, 83, 87, *182*, 195
Newstead-on-Ancholme Gilbertine Priory (Lincs)   58-9, 71, 72, 74-6, 83, 87, 99, *182*, 187, 195
Newstead Priory (Lincs), see Newstead-on-Ancholme
Nicholas, chaplain at Winchester   24
Nicholas (de Romanis) of Tusculum, Cardinal bishop, papal legate   43, 161, 162, 167-8
Nicholas, prior of Otterton   73-4
Norham, Treaty of   148
Nöe, see La Nöe
Normandy   4, 6, 38, 41, 45, 50, 51, 62, 71, 87, 88, 93 n.38, 96, 98, 104, 108, 115, 135, 137, 196
    see also John, events during John's reign, Normandy, loss of
Northampton   41, 124, *182*
    hospital of St John the Baptist and St John the Evangelist   184
    leper hospital of St Leonard   102, 124, 195
    negotiations of 1211   156
    Priory of St Andrew   79, 161
    see also Kingsthorpe
Norwich, bishop of, see John de Gray; Pandulf
Nostell Priory   143
Nottingham
    almonry   128
    castle   24, *25*, 26
Nun Cotham nunnery   *121*, 122
Nunneries   120-2, *121*,
    See also, Almenêches; Armathwaite;

INDEX 245

Les Blanches; Brewood, Broomhall, Cheshunt, Cook Hill, Ellerton, Farewell, Foukeholme, Henwood, Hinchingbrooke, Keldholme, Lambley, Moxby, Newcastle, Nun Cotham, Oldbury, Pinley, Polesworth, St Mary de Pré, Sewardsley, Wallingwells, Wroxall

Oath of 1209, see Marlborough
Odiham (Hants) 56
Odo of Paris 137
Oldbury nunnery *121*
Old Testament kings and queens 179
Oliver, illegitimate son of John 97, 186
Ongar (Essex) 41 n.28
Orderic Vitalis 4
Oriel 24
Origen 157
Ormrod, W. M. 11
Osbert of Clare 39, 47
Osney Priory 100
Oswin, king of England 60
Otterton (Devon) 71, 72, 73-4, 83, 191, 195
Otto IV, emperor 97, 137 and n.31
Outlawry of churchmen 161
Owton (County Durham) 59
Oxford *25*
    Carmelite house 11
    church of St Mary 94
    leper hospital of St Bartholomew 101
Oxton (Notts) 75

Painter, S. 3, 9 n.42, 37, 61, 121, 150
Pandulf, papal envoy 156, 161
    bishop of Norwich 167
Papal envoys, negotiations with 156
Papal legates, see Bicchieri, Guala; John of Anagni; Nicholas of Tusculum; Pandulf
Paris 95, 132, 138, 142
Paris, Matthew 2, 14, 150-2, 158, 174, 185, 197, 199
Peltzer, J. 155
Perche 97
Peter of Blois, dean of Wolverhampton college 35
Peter the Chanter 112, 129
Peter de Préaux 104
Peter, prior of Beaulieu 70
Peter des Roches, bishop of Winchester 16, 30, 34, 35, 36, 60, 67 and n.35, 70, 104, 112, 114, 136, 141-2, 143, 145, 155, 167, 176, 178, 199
Peter of Ludgershall 34
Peter of Wakefield (or Pontefract) 123, 162-3, 198

Peterborough 58
Philip I, count of Flanders 37, 40
Philip II, Augustus, king of France 5, 21, 42, 43, 46, 49, 50, 61, 85, 95, 138, 163, 169
    under interdict (1200) 137
Philip d'Aubigny, constable of Bristol 79
Philip, illegitimate son of John 97
Philippa of Hainault, wife of Edward III 73, 192
Philip of Poitou, bishop of Durham 142, 155
Philippa of Toulouse 90, *91*
Pilgrimage 5, 8, 9, 11, 12, 38-45, 53, 54, 86, 133, 160, 175, 186, 193
Le Pin (near Poitiers) 71
    abbot and almoner of Richard I 126
Pinley nunnery *121*, 122
Pliny 157
Poitou 95
Polesworth nunnery *121*,
Pontefract, Peter of, see Peter of Wakefield
Pontigny 66, 155
Poole, A. L. 3
Poor, feeding of 10, 11, 114-15, 118, 119, 126, 128-30, 161, 197
Poor, Herbert, bishop of Salisbury 114
    exile in Scotland 142
Poor, Richard, bishop of Chichester (1215), Salisbury (1217), Durham (1228) 31 n.62, 142, 176, 184
Portsmouth, hospital of the Trinity, the Blessed Virgin Mary, the Holy Cross and St Nicholas 104
Portugal, interdict on 137
Portswood, see Southampton
Powicke, Sir F. M. 2, 3, 158
Premonstratensians 144
Preston (Lancs), leper hospital of St Mary Magdalene 101
Prestwich, M. 2, 10
Prisoners, release of 93
Psalm, fiftieth 164
Purgatory 8, 20, 28 and n.48-9, 185

Radmore (Staffs) 103
Ragusa (Dubrovnik), archbishop 135, and see also Bernard, bishop of Carlisle
Ralph of Coggeshall 62, 63, 66, 115, 147, 148, 166, 170-1
Ralph de Hauvill 59, 93
Ralph, priest of Les Blanches 102
Ralph de Merle 135
Ralph, prior of Worcester 47
Ramsey Abbey (Hants) 186
Ranulph, earl of Chester 175
Raymond VI, count of Toulouse 69, 148, 151

Raymond VII, count of Toulouse 69
Raymond, archdeacon of Leicester 143
Reading Abbey 9, 22, 49, 51, 52-6, 66, 73 n.76, 86, 157-8, 160, 181, *182*, 186
   abbot of, see Hugh II
   hand of St James 9, 53-4
   head of St Philip 55-7
   holding letters of John 181
   John borrows books from 157-8
   relic collection 52, 55, 86
Regalia 21, 39, 120, 180
Regency Council 181, 184
Reginald, count of Boulogne 162
Reginald of Cornhill, sheriff of Kent 138, 155
Reginald, sub-prior of Canterbury 132, 138
Regularis Concordia 47
Relics 1, 21, 39, 43, 44, 51, 55, 56-7, 60, 145, 160, 173, 195
   True Cross 55, 58
   see also Becket Thomas; Reading Abbey; St Ouen; St Petroc; St Wulfstan
Religious practice, relationship with kingship 7
Reynolds, Walter, bishop of Worcester and archbishop of Canterbury 157
Rheims, archbishop of, see William of Blois, archbishop of Rheims
Richard I, king of England 3, 4, 5, 6 and n.32, 10, 20, 27, 29, 30, 32 n.64, 38, 39, 40, 41, 42, 43, 44, 45, 49, 50, 53, 57, 62, 65, 71, 74, 75, 81, 83, 85-7, 88, 89-90, 91, 92, 94-5, 98-100, 101, 106, 108, 114 n.27, 126, 131, 153, 161, 176, 184, 186 and n.72, 187, 190, 195
   absence on crusade 22, 85
   almoner 126
   burial 89 n.17
   commemorative masses 29, 30, 34, 94
   confrater of Cistercians 71
   coronation of 21, 39
   crown wearing 165 and n.67
   crusade 57
   denudes the Reading hand of St James 54
   and episcopal elections 135-6
   funds Fontevraud cloister 89
   return from Holy Land 5
Richard II, king of England 1, 2, 3, 12
Richard III, king of England 192
Richard, anchorite of St Sepulchre 123
Richard de Morins, prior of Dunstable 166
Richard, duke of Gloucester (youngest grandchild of George V) 192 n.110
Richard, earl of Cornwall 67 and n.35, 69, 90, 96, 109, 123, 177, 188-9
Richard fitz Nigel, bishop of London 1189-98 32 n.64

Richard, illegitimate son of John 97, 186
Richard of St Christopher, royal clerk 33
Ridel, Stephen, archdeacon of Ely 172
Rievaulx Abbey 143
   abbot of, see William of Rievaulx
Ringwood 188
Ripon, church of St Peter and St Wilfrid 172
River, see Dover
Robert I, duke of Normandy 98
Robert II, duke of Normandy 98
Robert, bishop of Bangor 142
Robert de Courcy 43
Robert de Lexington 185
Robert de Quincy, son of Saer de Quincy, earl of Winchester 183
Robert fitz Ralph, clerk of John 82
Robert fitz Roger 106
Robert of Gloucester, bishop of Worcester (1163-79) 46
Robert, hermit of St Werburg 33
Robert of Knaresborough 122-3
Robert of London 150
Robert of Saintes, clerk 27-8
Robert of Thornham, royal servant 160
Robert de Vieuxpont 155
Rocamadour 49
Roche-aux-Moines, see La Roche-aux-Moines
Rochester 43 n.39, 118, 140
   bishop of 138; see also Benedict of Sawston; Glanville, Gilbert
   castle siege 43 n.39, 50 n.79, 172
   cathedral 142, 172 and n.102
Roger, abbot of Reading 54
Roger de Kyvilly, citizen of Bristol 65 and n.26
Roger le Gros 93 n.40
Roger of Newburgh 127
Roger of Howden 21, 39
Roger of Wendover 14, 23, 41, 139, 149-50, 152, 154, 157, 161, 164, 169, 171, 173, 197, 199
Roger, Templar brother, almoner 125-6
Rollo, duke of Normandy 87
Rome 13, 30, 69, 132
   hospital of St Mary in Sassia 124, 161, 182, 186
Romsey (Hants) Abbey 160
Rouen 51, 88, 176
   archbishop of, see Walter of Coutances
   cathedral 29, 50-1, 87-8, 175
   church land 145
   fire of 1200 88
   leper hospital of Mont-aux-Malades 99, 101
   Notre-Dame du Parc 88
   St Katherine-du-Mont 101

St Ouen Abbey 51
Rubin, M. 130
Ruffus, Robert of Kimbolton 114
Russell J. C. 45
Rutland 103

St Alban 40-1,
St Albans (Herts) 150, 185
    Abbey 2, 40-1, 172, 179 n.14
    abbot 128, 159, 177; see also John de
        Cella; William of Trumpington
    chronicler, see Roger of Wendover, Matthew
        Paris
    see also St Mary de Pré
St Andrew 116, 194
St Andrews, bishopric 137
St Anthony, order of 124
St Audoenus, anchorite 123
    See also St Ouen
St Augustine 157
St Augustine's, Canterbury, see Canterbury
St Bartholomew 116, 194
    See also Newbury
St Benedict, Rule 111
St Benet Holme
    Abbot Ralph 143
    Abbot Reginald 143
St Bertin, abbey, see St Omer
St David's Cathedral, disputed election 22,
    145
St David, see Kingsthorpe
St Denis 32 n.64
St Denys Priory, see Southampton
St Edmund, king and martyr, see Edmund
St Edward the Confessor, see Edward the
    Confessor
St Edwin 33
St Etheldreda 40
St Etienne (Caen), see Caen
St George 11
St Gilbert of Sempringham 58-9, 75, 86, 193
St Hugh of Lincoln, see Hugh of Lincoln
St James the Great 53-5, 60, 116, 193, 194
St James the Less 55
St Jean d'Angely 52
St John the Baptist 34, 120, 179, 193
    Feast of 194
St John the Evangelist 90 n.26, 179
    See also Cork and Waterford
St John's priory, Falaise, see Falaise
St Katherine 24, 34; see also Waterford
St Keverne church (Cornwall) 188
St Lawrence 116, 194
    See also Bristol
St Leonard 119

Feast 194
    See also Chesterfield and Lancaster
St Louis, see Louis IX
St Lucy 116, 194
St Luke, feast 194
St Mark the Evangelist 116
St Margaret, see Broomhall and Marlborough
St Margaret, queen of Scotland 118
St Margaret the Virgin 116, 194
St Martin 119
    Feast 194
St Mary Graces, see London
St Mary Magdalene 119
    hospital 104
    feast 194
St Mary de Pré nunnery (by St Albans) 102,
    121, 122
St Matthew 111-12
St Michael, feast 194
St Nectan 57-8
St Nicholas 40, 41, 119
    feast 194
    see also Carlisle, Exeter
St Omer, abbey of St Bertin 133
St Oswald, bishop of Worcester (961-92),
    archbishop of York (971-92) 48, 58, 175,
    177, 179-80
St Oswald, king of Northumbria and
    martyr 58, 60
St Osyth Abbey (Essex) 52
St Ouen 50-1
St Paul 52, 116, 193
    feast of conversion 194
St Peter 43, 48, 58, 60, 116, 193
    St Peter *in Cathedra*, feast 194
    St Peter in Chains, feast 194
    Sts Peter and Paul, feast 194
St Petroc 40 n.20, 53 n.99
St Philip 55-7, 60, 116, 193
'St' Robert of Knaresborough, see Robert of
    Knaresborough
St Sepulchre 123
St Stephen, see Caen, Waterford and
    Westminster
St Thomas of Acre, Order of 184
St Thomas, the Apostle 116, 194
St Thomas Aquinas 111
St Thomas Becket, see Becket, Thomas
St Werburg 33
    hermit of 123
St Wulfstan, bishop of Worcester (1062-
    95) 12, 45-9, 58, 59, 156, 171, 177, 178,
    193
    cult 174-6, 179-80
    Wulfstan's staff legend 46, 156-7, 176, 198

INDEX

Sainte-Chapelle 7
Saint-Maixent Abbey 32
Saint-Sauveur Abbey, Charroux 51
Saints
   All Saints, feast *194*
   cult of 108-9, 156, 160, 193, 198
   See also under the names of individual saints
Salisbury 27
   bishop of, see Poor, Herbert; Poor, Richard
   Cathedral 31, 86, 94
Sallay Abbey 143
Samson, Abbot of Bury, see Bury St Edmunds
Sancho I, king of Portugal 137
Sancho VII, king of Navarre, treaty with 151
Sanctified kingship 43-5
Saul, N. 2
Saumur 89
   Abbey of Saint-Florent 97
Savary de Mauléon, mercenary leader 170
Savigny (Normandy) Abbey 103
Scarborough 190
Schoolmen 19, 112 and n.17, 132-3
Scotland, bishops in exile in 142
Sées (Normandy), episcopal election (1201-03) 135, 136
   see also Silvester, archdeacon and bishop
Seven corporal works of mercy 111
Sewardsley nunnery *121*, 122
Shaftesbury Abbey 55
Shakespeare, William 164, 191
Shoreditch 31
Shrewsbury *182*, 183
   burial of Robert bishop of Bangor in marketplace 142
   hospital of St Giles 101
   market 101
Sicily 167, 198
Sidmouth (Devon) 73
Silverstone *25*, 25
Silvester, archdeacon and bishop of Sées 135
Silvester, bishop of Worcester 175, 176-7, 185
Simon de Montfort 172
Simon of Apulia, bishop of Exeter (from 1214) 68
Simon of Tallington 127
Simon of Wells, bishop-elect of Chichester 34
Somerset 38
Southampton
   custodians of the kings wine at 26
   port bailiffs 187
   Priory of St Denys, Portswood (by Southampton) 98-9
Southwark, hospital of St Thomas 112
Southwell Minster, chapel of St Thomas Becket *182*, 185

Spigurnell', Godfrey, chancery officer 159
Stanley, abbot of 70
   annalist 44 n.42, 66, 147, 163 and n.56, 169
Stephen, king of England 2, 62, 92, 136, 145, 196
   as count of Mortain 102-3
   crown wearing 165
Stoke Prior 47
Stoneleigh (Warks) Abbey 103
Stow 141
Strata Florida Abbey 62
Stubbs, Bishop W. 3 and n.8, 61
Suger, abbot of St Denis 5
Summa Theologiae 111
Sutton-at-Hone (Kent), hospital 104

Tanner, N. 117
Tanner, T. 74
Te deum laudamus 23, 164
Templars, see Knights Templar
Temple Ewell (near Dover) 155
Tewkesbury Abbey 146, 177
   chronicle 144, 152, 178
Theobald V, count of Blois 37
Theobald, archbishop of Canterbury 136
Theobald, count of Champagne 130
Thomas, archbishop of York 48
Thomas, Brother, almoner 125-6, 127
Thomas de Samford, courtier 120
Thomas of St Valéry 34 and n.78
Thorney Abbey (Cambs) 166
Thurgarton Priory 75
Tickhill hermits 123
Tideswell (Derbys) 30
Tilty, raid (1215) 170
Titchfield (Hants) 178, *182*
Tithes 7, 80-1 n.129, 114
Tolomeus, William, bishop of Avranches 135
Torre (Devon), Priory 105-6
Toulouse 89
Trinité (Caen), see Caen
Troarn (Calvados), abbey of St Martin 98
Turner, R. V. 4, 184

Ulster 24

Val, Nôtre-Dame du (Calvados) 31
Vale, M. 125
Vale Royal Abbey 10, 66
Valor Ecclesiasticus 76, 79
Venice, excommunicated (1202) 137
Vienne, province of, hospital of St Anthony 124, 189
Vincent, N. 5, 6, 9, 15 nn. 66 and 67, 35 n.80, 52, 96 n.57, 117, 170

Visions of John 185
Virgin Mary
  Annunciation, feast of *194*
  Assumption, feast of *194*
  Conception of, feast *194*
  cult of 10, 14, 48, 49–52, 55, 60, 86, 88, 109, 160, 176, 193, 196
  letters purportedly from 152
  Nativity, feast *194*
  Presentation feast of 50 n.79
  Purification, feast of *194*
  relics of 49, 51, 55
  Visitation, feast of *194*
Viterbo, abbot of St Martin Cimino 161
Vivian de l'Etang, bishop of Coutances 135

Wakefield, see Peter of Pontefract
Wales 56, 66
Wallingwells nunnery *121*
Walter de Gray, royal chancellor, archbishop of York 167, 175
Walter de Lacy 173, 175
Walter, Hubert, archbishop of Canterbury 17, 22, 30, 33, 35, 41, 45, 61, 62, 65, 68, 69, 71, 83, 104, 114–15, 131, 136, 145, 147, 154, 199
  confirms testament of John 181
  death (1205) 35, 65, 68, 69, 131, 134, 136, 148
  excommunicates John 153
Walter of Coutances, archbishop of Rouen 21, 29, 88, 131, 135
Walter, Theobald, brother of Hubert Walter 106
Waltham Holy Cross Priory 57, 67, 99, *182*, 190
Wareham 163
Warren, A. K 123
Warren, W. L. 2, 4
Waterford
  Priory of St John the Evangelist 195
  Priory of St Katherine, hospital and alms houses 71, 72, 77–8, 83, 191, 195
  hospital of St Stephen 71, 72, 77, 82
Watson, S. 117
Watton (Yorks) 59
Waverley Abbey 114
Wendover, see Roger of Wendover
Wellow Priory, Lincs (by Grimsby) 99
West Bromwich 184
West Dereham (Norfolk) Priory 104
Westminster 41, 66, 135
  Abbey 7, 10, 12, 20, 21, 22, 24, 38–9, 41, 42–3, 44, 45, 47, 51, 62, 86, 156, 175, 182, 190, 193, 197

forged charters 43 n.37
almonry 128
chapels 24, *25*
leper nuns of St James 102
Wight, Isle of 104–5 n.118
William I (the Conqueror), king of England 6, 8, 35, 46, 47, 51, 73, 92, 93, 98, 102, 124, 156
William I, (the Lion), king of Scots 38, 97, 137, 148
William II (Rufus), king of England 6, 40, 80, 82, 93, 136, 172
William II, king of Sicily 89
William IV, earl of Warenne 42, 162
William IX, duke of Aquitaine *91*
William X, duke of Aquitaine 52, 90, *91*
William, almoner of Henry I 125
William, Brother, almoner of John 126, 127
William, brother of Henry II 87 n.10, 102
William, chaplain at Oxford 24
William, chaplain at Winchester 24
William, count of Mortain (second son of King Stephen) 102, 176
William, crossbowman 74
William de Beauchamp, earl of Warwick 175 n.14
William de Beaumont, bishop of Angers, see Angers
William de Briouze 66, 105, 173
William de Cornhill, bishop of Coventry and Lichfield 120, 167, 184
William de Folbec 100
William de Longchamp, Chancellor, bishop of Ely 22, 30
William de Ste-Mère-Église, bishop of London 31, 51, 52, 169
  see also interdict, executors of
William of St Ouen, Hospitaller 69 n.53
William de Stuteville, royal sheriff
William de Montibus, chancellor of Lincoln Cathedral 142
William de Wrotham, keeper of the king's ships 104, 106
William, earl Ferrars 162, 175
William, earl of Salisbury (half-brother of John) 150 n.104, 162
William, hermit of Finmere 123
William Longsword, duke of Normandy 87
William of Blois, archbishop of Rheims 37
William of Blois, bishop of Worcester 178–9
William of Malmesbury 9
William of Rievaulx, abbot 64
William of Trumpington, abbot of St Albans (1214–35) 128, 177
William, son of Henry I 92

William, son of Henry II 53, *91*
Wilton Diptych 12
Wilton (Wilts), leper hospital of St Giles 101
Winchcombe Abbey 146
Winchester 24, *25*, 25, 26, 34, 35, 56-7, 60, 160, 164-5, 176, 189
   almonry 128
   annalist 133
   bishop of 138; see also Aymer de Lusignan; Henry of Blois; Godfrey de Lucy; Peter des Roches
   castle 24
   Cathedral 23, 34-5, 145, 159, 164
      altar of St Katherine 34
      chapels of St Stephen and St John 24
Windsor 72, 122, 128, *182*
   almonry 128
   leper hospital 190
Wiseman, W. G. 81 n.129
Wistan, king of England 60
Wolverhampton, secular college 35, 66, 104
Wolverley 47
Woodstock (Oxon) 24, *25*, 26
Worcester *182*, 184-5
   annalist 147, 148, 152, 171
   bishop 148, 155; see also John of Coutances; Mauger; Reynolds, Walter; Robert of Gloucester; St Oswald; St Wulfstan; Silvester; William of Blois, bishop of Worcester; Wulfstan, archbishop of York
   castle 175
   cathedral 12, 17, 35, 46-7, 48, 49, 50, 51, 69, 157, 171, 174-80, 184, 199
   infirmary 179
Writtle (Essex) 124
Wroxall nunnery *121*, 122
Wulfstan, bishop of Worcester and saint, see St Wulfstan
Wulfstan, archbishop of York and bishop of Worcester 47
Wykes, Thomas, chronicle 164
Wymondley *182*, 190

York 61, 138, 171
   archbishop of, see Geoffrey, half-brother of John; St Oswald; Thomas, archbishop of York; Walter de Gray; Wulfstan, archbishop of York
Young, C. 13, 110
Young, John, pauper 79

Other volumes in
Studies in the History of Medieval Religion

Details of volumes I–XXIX can be found on our website.

XXX: The Culture of Medieval English Monasticism
Edited by James G. Clark

XXXI: A History of the Abbey of Bury St Edmunds, 1182–1256:
Samson of Tottington to Edmund of Walpole
Antonia Gransden

XXXII: Monastic Hospitality:
The Benedictines in England, c.1070–c.1250
Julie Kerr

XXXIII: Religious Life in Normandy, 1050–1300:
Space, Gender and Social Pressure
Leonie V. Hicks

XXXIV: The Medieval Chantry Chapel: An Archaeology
Simon Roffey

XXXV: Monasteries and Society in the British Isles
in the Later Middle Ages
Edited by Janet Burton and Karen Stöber

XXXVI: Jocelin of Wells: Bishop, Builder, Courtier
Edited by Robert Dunning

XXXVII: War and the Making of Medieval Monastic Culture
Katherine Allen Smith

XXXVIII: Cathedrals, Communities and Conflict in the Anglo-Norman World
Edited by Paul Dalton, Charles Insley and Louise J. Wilkinson

XXXIX: English Nuns and the Law in the Middle Ages:
Cloistered Nuns and Their Lawyers, 1293–1540
Elizabeth Makowski

XL: The Nobility and Ecclesiastical Patronage in Thirteenth-Century England
Elizabeth Gemmill

XLI: Pope Gregory X and the Crusades
Philip B. Baldwin

XLII: A History of the Abbey of Bury St Edmunds, 1257–1301:
Simon of Luton and John of Northwold
Antonia Gransden

XLIII: King John and Religion
Paul Webster

XLIV: The Church and Vale of Evesham, 700–1215:
Lordship, Landscape and Prayer
David Cox

XLV: Medieval Anchorites in their Communities
Edited by Cate Gunn and Liz Herbert McAvoy

XLVI: The Friaries of Medieval London: From Foundation to Dissolution
Nick Holder

XLVII: 'The Right Ordering of Souls':
The Parish of All Saints' Bristol on the Eve of the Reformation
Clive Burgess

XLVIII: The Lateran Church in Rome and the Ark of the Covenant:
Housing the Holy Relics of Jerusalem, with an edition and translation of the
Descriptio Lateranensis Ecclesiae (BAV Reg. Lat. 712)
Eivor Andersen Oftestad

XLIX: Apostate Nuns in the Later Middle Ages
Elizabeth Makowski

L: St Stephen's College, Westminster:
A Royal Chapel and English Kingship, 1348–1548
Elizabeth Biggs

www.ingramcontent.com/pod-product-compliance
Lightning Source LLC
Chambersburg PA
CBHW051607230426
43668CB00013B/2020